D0553738

JOHN STOTT

THE CONTEMPORARY CHRISTIAN

APPLYING GOD'S WORD TO TODAY'S WORLD

INTERVARSITY PRESS
DOWNERS GROVE, ILLINOIS 60515

InterVarsity Press® is the book-publishing division of InterVarsity Christian Fellowship®, a student movement active on campus at hundreds of universities, colleges and schools of nursing in the United States of America, and a member movement of the International Fellowship of Evangelical Students. For information about local and regional activities, write Public Relations Dept., InterVarsity Christian Fellowship, 6400 Schroeder Rd., P.O. Box 7895, Madison, WI 53707-7895.

ISBN 0-8308-1316-0

Printed in the United States of America ♾

Library of Congress Cataloging-in-Publication Data

Stott, John R. W.
The contemporary Christian: applying God's word to today's world / John Stott.
p. cm.
Includes bibliographical references.
ISBN 0-8308-1316-0
1. Christian life—1960- 2. Theology. 3. Time—Religious aspects—Christianity. I. Title.
BV4501.2.S786 1992
230—dc20 *92-9541*
CIP

---

17 16 15 14 13 12 11 10 9 8 7 6 5 4 3 2 1
05 04 03 02 01 00 99 98 97 96 95 94 93 92

Chief Abbreviations

AV	The Authorized (King James') Version of the Bible (1611).
ET	English translation.
GNB	The Good News Bible (NT 1966, 4th edition 1976; OT 1976).
LXX	The Old Testament in Greek according to the Septuagint, third century BC.
NEB	The New English Bible (NT 1961, 2nd edition 1970; OT 1970).
NIV	The New International Version of the Bible (1973, 1978, 1984).
REB	The Revised English Bible (1989).
RSV	The Revised Standard Version of the Bible (NT 1946, 2nd edition 1971; OT 1952).
RV	The English Revised Version of the Bible (1881–85).
TDNT	*Theological Dictionary of the New Testament*, ed. G. Kittel and G. Friedrich, translated by G. W. Bromiley, 10 vols. (Eerdmans, 1964–76).

Preface

To be 'contemporary' is to live in the present, and to move with the times, without necessarily concerning ourselves with either the past or the future. To be a 'contemporary Christian', however, is to ensure that our present is enriched to the fullest possible extent both by our knowledge of the past and by our expectation of the future. Our Christian faith demands this. For the God we trust and worship is 'the Alpha and the Omega, . . . who is, and who was, and who is to come, the Almighty',[1] while the Jesus Christ to whom we are committed is 'the same yesterday and today and for ever'.[2]

So this book is an essay in the Christian handling of time, in how we are meant to bring the past, the present and the future together in our thinking and living. Two main problems confront us. The first is the tension between the 'then' (past) and the 'now' (present), and the second the tension between the 'now' (present) and the 'not yet' (future).

The Introduction opens up the first problem. I ask whether it is possible for us truly to honour the past and live in the present simultaneously. Can we preserve Christianity's historic identity intact, without thereby cutting ourselves adrift from our contemporaries? And can we communicate the gospel in exciting, modern terms, without thereby distorting and even destroying it? Can we be authentic and fresh at the same time, or do we have to choose?

The Conclusion opens up the second problem, namely the tension between the 'now' and the 'not yet'. I ask how far we can explore and experience now everything God has said and done through Christ, without unwarrantably trespassing into the area of what has not yet been revealed or given. Alternatively, how can we develop a proper

[1] Rev. 1:8. [2] Heb. 13:8.

humility before the unrealized future, without becoming complacent about our present degree of attainment?

In between these enquiries into the influence upon us of the past and the future come twenty-one chapters about our present Christian responsibilities.

I think of *The Contemporary Christian* as a companion volume to *Issues Facing Christians Today*, in that the latter explores questions of social ethics, while this book relates to questions of doctrine and discipleship under the five headings 'The Gospel', 'The Disciple', 'The Bible', 'The Church' and 'The World'. I make no attempt to be systematic, let alone exhaustive. Instead, I have selected a number of issues which are either in the forefront of current debate or of importance in my own thinking. And, although the book is emphatically not a random collection of essays and sermons, much of the material presented here has been used in lectures and addresses in different parts of the world.

In addition to the topic of time, and the relations between past, present and future, there is a second theme which runs through this book. It concerns the need to talk less and listen more. Christians certainly have a reputation for being garrulous. Many of my readers will remember E. M. Forster's description in *A Passage to India* of the elderly Mrs Moore's experience in one of the famous Marabar Caves, especially its monotonous but terrifying echo 'boum'. While inside, she had almost fainted. Now outside she was trying to write a letter. But a strange feeling of despair began to creep over her, when 'suddenly, at the edge of her mind, Religion appeared, *poor little talkative Christianity*, and she knew that all its divine words from "Let there be light" to "It is finished" only amounted to "boum"'.[1]

Needless to say, the words of God are much more substantial than 'boum' echoes in a cave, for they are words of truth and of life, which Mrs Moore did not acknowledge. Nevertheless, the crucial thing is to listen to them with reverent attention and not drown them by our own premature talkativeness.

[1] E. M. Forster, *A Passage to India* (1924; Penguin, 1985), p. 144.

In particular, as indicated in this book's sub-title, I believe we are called to the difficult and even painful task of 'double listening'. That is, we are to listen carefully (although of course with differing degrees of respect) both to the ancient Word and to the modern world, in order to relate the one to the other with a combination of fidelity and sensitivity. Every chapter is, in fact, an attempt at double listening, although I am sure that some are much less successful than others. It is, however, my firm conviction that, only if we can develop our capacity for double listening, will we avoid the opposite pitfalls of unfaithfulness and irrelevance, and be able to speak God's Word to God's world with effectiveness today.

I express my special gratitude to Todd Shy, my current student assistant, who has worked laboriously through the whole book in draft and made some helpful suggestions; to Steve Andrews, one of my former study assistants, for his meticulous labours in compiling the indexes; to David Stone for his skill in composing the study guide; and to Frances Whitehead, my omnicompetent secretary, for producing yet one more immaculate typescript.

Christmas, 1991 JOHN STOTT

INTRODUCTION

THE THEN AND THE NOW

The very expressions 'the contemporary Christian' and 'contemporary Christianity' (as, for example, in 'the Institute for Contemporary Christianity') strike many people as a contradiction in terms. How can Christianity be called 'contemporary'? Is it not an ancient faith? Did not its Founder live and die nearly two millennia ago? Is not Christianity a period piece, a museum exhibit, an antique relic from the remote past, irrelevant to modern men and women? My purpose in this book is to try to answer these questions, and to demonstrate that there is such a thing as 'contemporary Christianity'. It is not a new version of Christianity which we are busy inventing, but original, historic, orthodox, biblical Christianity sensitively related to the modern world.

Christianity both historical and contemporary

The way to begin is to reaffirm without apology that Christianity is a historical religion. Of course every religion can claim to be to some degree 'historical', because each arose in a particular historical context and looks back to its founder (*e.g.* the Buddha, Confucius or Muhammad), and/or to a succession of formative teachers. Christianity, however, makes an even stronger claim to be historical because it does not rest only on a historical person, Jesus of Nazareth, but on certain historical events which involved him, especially his birth, death and resurrection. It is also events rather than persons which make Judaism historical. The Old Testament presents Yahweh not only as 'the God of Abraham, Isaac and Jacob' but as the God of the covenant which he made with Abraham, and renewed with

Isaac and Jacob; not only as the God of Moses, but as the Redeemer responsible for the exodus, who went on to renew the covenant yet again at Mount Sinai. Christian people, then, are for ever tethered in heart and mind to these decisive, historical events of the past. We are constantly exhorted in Scripture to look back to them with thankfulness. Indeed God deliberately made provision for his people's regular recall of his saving actions. What the Passover was to the exodus, as an annual festival celebrating God's salvation, the Lord's Supper is to the atoning death of Christ, enabling us to call it regularly to mind and to feast on its great benefits. It is thus, through word and sacrament, that the past becomes present again.

The historical origins of Christianity are a great blessing. They give us a solid foundation. Our faith is not built on legends, fairy tales or even myths, but on actual events. These also constitute a problem, however, because they took place such a long time ago. The wide gap between then and now, the past and the present, the historical and the contemporary, is something of an embarrassment. The younger generation tell us they are not interested in history. It provokes from them only a long, rude, noisy yawn. They are concerned with the now, they say, not the then. They resemble Huckleberry Finn, when the widow Douglas first told him the story of Moses and the bulrushes:

> I was in a sweat to find out all about him; but by and by she let it out that Moses had been dead a considerable long time; so then I didn't care no more about him; because I don't take no stock in dead people.[1]

For more than twenty years I have been haunted by a conversation I had on this topic with two brothers, which I have related in full in *I Believe in Preaching*.[2] They were university students, who told me they had repudiated the faith of their parents, in which they had been brought up. One was now an

[1] Mark Twain, *The Adventures of Huckleberry Finn* (1884; Pan, 1968), p. 202.
[2] John Stott, *I Believe in Preaching* (Hodder and Stoughton, 1982), pp. 138–139.

agnostic, the other an atheist. I enquired why. Did they no longer believe in the truth of Christianity? No, that was not their problem, they replied. Their dilemma was not whether Christianity was true, but whether it was relevant. How could it be? Christianity, they went on, was a primitive, Palestinian religion. It had arisen in a primitive, Palestinian culture. So what on earth did it have to offer them, who lived in the exciting, modern world of space travel, transplant surgery and genetic engineering? It was irrelevant!

This feeling of the remoteness, obsolescence and irrelevance of Christianity is widespread. The world has changed dramatically since Jesus' day, and goes on changing with ever more bewildering speed. People reject the gospel, not necessarily because they think it false, but because it no longer resonates with them. Can the church survive the challenge of modernity? Or will it suffer the ignominious fate of the dinosaur, equally unable to adapt to a changing environment, and become extinct?

In response to this common feeling that Christianity is hopelessly out of date, we need to re-state our fundamental Christian conviction that God continues to speak through what he has spoken. His Word is not a prehistoric fossil, to be exhibited under glass, but a living message for the contemporary world. It belongs to the market place, not the museum. Through his ancient Word God addresses the modern world, for, as Dr J. I. Packer has said, 'the Bible is God preaching'. Even granted the historical particularities of the Bible, and the immense complexities of the modern world, there is still a fundamental correspondence between them, and God's Word remains a lamp to our feet and a light for our path.[1]

At the same time, our dilemma remains. Can the gospel really be 'modernized'? Is it feasible to expect the church to apply the historic faith to the contemporary scene, the Word to the world, without either betraying the former or alienating the latter? Can Christianity retain its authentic identity and demonstrate its

[1] Ps. 119:105; *cf.* 2 Pet. 1:19.

relevance at the same time, or must one of these be sacrificed to the other? Are we obliged to choose between retreating into the past and making a fetish of the present, between reciting old truths which are stale and inventing new notions which are spurious? Perhaps the greater of these two dangers is that the church will attempt to recast the faith in such a way as to undermine its integrity and render it unrecognizable to its original heralds. I propose to focus on this problem now; the rest of the book is addressed in different ways to the complementary problem of relevance.

In 1937 the Harvard scholar Henry J. Cadbury's book *The Peril of Modernizing Jesus* was published. He conceded that the laudable purpose of the 'modernizers' of Jesus was to 'interpret him in terms that will seem real, that is, modern and congenial to the modern mind'.[1] But the result was often to falsify him, and in particular to lose sight of his first-century 'Jewishness'. Like the soldiers who mocked Jesus, 'stripped him and put on him a scarlet military cloak', and then after the mockery 'took the cloak off him and put on him his own raiment', so we put on Jesus our 'own kind of clothes', investing him with 'our own thoughts'.[2]

Yet the desire to present Jesus in a way that appeals to our own generation is obviously right. This was Bonhoeffer's preoccupation in prison: 'What is bothering me incessantly', he wrote to his friend Eberhard Bethge in 1944, 'is the question . . . who Christ really is for us today?'[3] It is without doubt a bothersome question. Yet in answering it, the church has tended in every generation to develop images of Christ which deviate from the portrait painted by the New Testament authors.

Helmut Thielicke was outspoken about this. 'Over and over, the figure of Jesus has been horribly amputated', he wrote, to suit each age's taste.

[1] Henry J. Cadbury, *The Peril of Modernizing Jesus* (Macmillan, 1937; SPCK, 1962), p. 28.
[2] *Ibid.*, p. 42.
[3] Dietrich Bonhoeffer, *Letters and Papers from Prison* (SCM, enlarged edition, 1971), p. 279.

> Throughout the whole history of the church Jesus Christ has suffered a process of repeated crucifixion. He has been scourged and bruised and locked in the prison of countless systems and philosophies. Treated as a body of thought, he has literally been lowered into conceptual graves and covered with stone slabs so that he might not arise and trouble us any more ... But this is the miracle, that from this succession of conceptual graves Jesus Christ has risen again and again![1]

Attempts to modernize Jesus

Here is a sample of the church's many attempts to present a contemporary picture of Christ. It will be seen that some have been more successful than others in remaining loyal to the original.

I think first of *Jesus the ascetic*, who inspired generations of monks and hermits. He was not markedly different from John the Baptist, for he too was clad in a camel's hair cloak, wore sandals or went barefoot, and munched locusts with evident relish, while otherwise renouncing the delights of the table and the joys of God's creation. It would be hard to reconcile this portrait with his contemporaries' criticism that he 'came eating and drinking'.[2]

Then there was *Jesus the pale Galilean*. It was the apostate emperor Julian, who tried to reinstate Rome's pagan gods after Constantine had replaced them with the worship of Christ, who is reported as having said on his deathbed in AD 363, 'You have conquered, O Galilean'. His words were popularized by the nineteenth-century poet Swinburne in his lines:

> Thou hast conquered, O pale Galilean;
> The world has grown grey from thy breath.

[1] Helmut Thielicke, *How Modern Should Theology Be?* (1967; ET Fortress, 1969 and Collins, 1970), pp. 18–19. See also his *Modern Faith and Thought* (1983; ET Eerdmans, 1990), p. 78.
[2] Mt. 11:19.

This image of Jesus was perpetuated in medieval art and stained glass, with a heavenly halo and a colourless complexion, his eyes lifted to the sky and his feet never quite touching the ground.

In contrast to the presentations of Jesus as weak, suffering and defeated, was *Jesus the cosmic Christ*, who was much loved by the Byzantine church leaders. Over against the advancing barbarians they depicted him as the King of kings and Lord of lords, the *pantokrator*, creator and ruler of the universe. Yet, exalted high above all things, glorified and reigning, he seemed aloof from the real world and even from his own humanity as revealed in the incarnation and the cross.

At the opposite end of the theological spectrum, the seventeenth- and eighteenth-century deists of the Enlightenment constructed in their own image *Jesus the teacher of common sense*,[1] all human and not divine. The most dramatic example is the work of that versatile genius Thomas Jefferson, President of the United States 1801–9. Rejecting the supernatural as incompatible with reason, he twice produced his own edition of the Gospels, calling the first *The Philosophy of Jesus of Nazareth* (1804) and the second *The Life and Morals of Jesus of Nazareth* (1820). From both books all miracles and mysteries were systematically eliminated. What is left is the plain man's guide to a merely human moral teacher.

Coming into the twentieth century, we are presented with a large variety of options. Two of the best known owe their popularity to musicals. There is *Jesus the clown* of *Godspell*, who spends his time singing and dancing, and thus captures something of the gaiety of Jesus, but hardly takes his mission seriously. Somewhat similar is *Jesus Christ Superstar*, the disillusioned celebrity, who once thought he knew who he was, but in Gethsemane was no longer sure:

> Then I was inspired;
> Now I'm sad and tired.

[1] See Jaroslav Pelikan, *Jesus Through the Centuries* (Yale University Press, 1985), pp. 182–193.

Next is that extraordinary invention, *Jesus the founder of modern business.* I am referring to a book entitled *The Man Nobody Knows* (1925), which for two years topped the best-seller list in the United States. Its author, Bruce Barton, was an American advertising man, who was rebelling against the anaemic, 'sissified' Jesus of his boyhood Sunday School. He depicted Jesus not only as a bronzed, muscular 'outdoor man', friendly, sociable and convivial, but as a leader of blazing conviction, whose whole life was a story of achievement, and who emphasized in his teaching the secrets of business success. Chapter 6 is headed 'The Founder of Modern Business'. Why, Bruce Barton writes, at the age of only twelve Jesus actually described himself as needing to be 'about his Father's *business*'!

Economics expertise as well as business success has been attributed to Jesus. Surprisingly enough, it is George Bernard Shaw who, doubtless with tongue in cheek, introduces us to *Jesus the economist.* 'Decidedly', he wrote, 'whether you think Jesus was God or not, you must admit that he was a first-rate political economist', who among other things recommended equal distribution.[1] But writers have completely disagreed with one another about the nature of his economics. On the one hand there is the vision of *Jesus the capitalist*, the promoter of free enterprise, investment and conservation, so that T. N. Carver could claim in his *The Economic Factor in the Messiahship of Jesus* (1922) that 'every essential feature of the modern economic system is explicitly set forth in the teachings of this young Jew'.[2]

On the other hand there is *Jesus the socialist.* I cite as my example Arthur Scargill, who was elected President of the National Union of Mineworkers in 1981. During a press interview at the time he said he was a Christian, and that he loved the old Moody and Sankey hymns, his favourite being 'What a friend we have in Jesus'. Pressed as to whether he believed the Creed, he first hedged and then declared: 'I do believe in

[1] Preface to *Androcles and the Lion* (1912; Constable, 1916), p. lxx.
[2] Quoted by H. J. Cadbury, *The Peril of Modernizing Jesus*, pp. 12–14.

Christianity in this sense: I believe that Jesus Christ was in fact a socialist.'[1]

Fidel Castro of Cuba has frequently referred to Jesus as 'a great revolutionary', and there have been many attempts to portray him as *Jesus the freedom fighter*, the urban guerrilla, the first-century Che Guevara, with black beard and flashing eyes, as in Pasolini's *Gospel according to Matthew*, whose most characteristic gesture was to overthrow the tables of the money-changers and to drive them out of the temple with a whip.

Perhaps the most sustained effort to depict Jesus in revolutionary terms is Upton Sinclair's novel *They Call Me Carpenter*.[2] Over the altar in St Bartholomew's Church, New York, there was a stained-glass figure of Christ, who one day came alive, stepped down and began a public ministry in the city. 'Who are you?' people asked. 'They call me Carpenter', he replied. So 'Mr Carpenter' he became, and later 'Prophet Carpenter', as his words and actions in New York paralleled those of Jesus in Palestine. He too was tempted (he was offered a $1,500-a-week contract as a movie star); he raised a dead child who had been knocked down by a car, and gathered other children round him; he healed the sick and handicapped; he rescued 'Mary Magna' from her life of prostitution; and he stood on the tail end of a truck in order to harangue the crowd about love and justice. But when he quoted Amos' denunciations of the idle rich, identified with strikers in a mass protest rally, inveighed against employers for alienating the workers from their product, and during a service in St Bartholomew's Church uttered a tirade against theologians and doctors of divinity ('Woe unto you Episcopalians, hypocrites!'), the local *Times* accused him of being a Bolshevik anarchist and of 'disguising the doctrine of Lenin and Trotsky in the robes of Christian revelation'.[3] He spent his last night in an upper room at the Socialist headquarters. And finally the mob, enraged by this

[1] Interview with Terry Coleman, which appeared in the *Guardian Weekly* on 20 December 1981.
[2] Upton Sinclair, *They Call Me Carpenter* (Werner Laurie, 1922).
[3] *Ibid.*, pp. 127–128.

'Ranting Red Prophet', captured him, poured gallons of red paint over his head, stood him on top of a wagon, and hauled him through the streets shouting, 'Hi! Hi! the Bolsheviki Prophet!' Thrown out of a theatre window, he was unharmed, he returned running to St Bartholomew's Church, he leapt back into the window, . . . and behold, it had all been a dream.

Lest one should conclude that such reconstructions of Jesus have been attempted only by imaginative writers of fiction, I give as my final example a serious scholarly study entitled *Jesus the Magician*. I think it may justly be seen as another attempt to portray Jesus in ancient-modern dress, in that it is a convenient and contemporary way of getting rid of the miracles. It is surely significant that the book's most recent publisher is the Aquarian Press. Professor Morton Smith's thesis is that, although in the Gospels the followers of Jesus depict him as the mythical Son of God, yet his most ancient opponents saw him as a magician. Third-century documents, which Professor Smith claims were suppressed and destroyed by Christians, show (he declares) that Jesus went to Egypt as a young man, 'where he became expert in magic and was tattooed with magical symbols or spells'; that he returned to Galilee and 'made himself famous by his magical feats';[1] and that he finally united his followers to himself by the meal he instituted, 'an unmistakeably magic rite'.[2] The evidence, Morton Smith concludes, gives 'a coherent picture of a magician's life and work'.[3]

This selection of thirteen different portraits of Jesus illustrates the perennial tendency to fashion a Christ with a modern appeal. It began already in the apostolic age, as Paul needed to warn people of false teachers who were preaching 'a Jesus other than the Jesus we (apostles) preached'.[4] And one is amazed by the ingenuity with which people have developed the representations of Jesus which we have considered. Yet all of them were anachronisms. Each generation read back into him its own

[1] Morton Smith, *Jesus the Magician* (1978; Aquarian Press, 1985), p. 67.
[2] *Ibid.*, p. 146. [3] *Ibid.*, p. 152.
[4] 2 Cor. 11:4.

ideas and aspirations, and created him in its own image. Their motive was right (to paint a contemporary portrait of Jesus), but the result was to some extent wrong (the portrait was unauthentic). The challenge before us is to present Jesus to our generation in a way that is both historical and contemporary, both authentic and appealing, new in the sense of 'fresh' (*neos*), not new in the sense of being a novelty (*kainos*).

The call for double listening

The main reason for every betrayal of the authentic Jesus is that we listen with exaggerated deference to contemporary fashion, instead of listening to God's Word. The demand for relevance becomes so imperious that we feel we have to capitulate to it, at whatever cost. We are familiar with this kind of pressure in the business world, in which it is the marketing people who determine the firm's product by discovering what will sell, what the public will buy. It sometimes seems as if market forces rule in the church as well. We become obsequious to the modern mood, slaves to the latest fad, even idolaters who are prepared to sacrifice truth on the altar of modernity. Then the quest for relevance has degenerated into a lust for popularity.

For the opposite extreme to irrelevance is accommodation, which is a feeble-minded, unprincipled surrender to the *Zeitgeist*, the spirit of the time. Thielicke was haunted by this danger, because he could not forget how the so-called 'German Christians' during Hitler's Third Reich accepted and even defended the racial myths of the Nazis. He insisted, therefore, that true theology 'always involves a debate between the *kerygma* and the self-understanding of an age, . . . between eternity and time'. Moreover, in this debate 'faith believes *against* as well as *in*'; it is born in a conscious reaction to current ideas.[1] Thus Thielicke writes of theology's 'polar structure', one pole being 'a superior, eternal basis derived from revelation' and the other being 'specific constellations of the spirit of the age'.[2]

[1] H. Thielicke, *Modern Faith and Thought*, p. 5. [2] *Ibid.*, p. 7.

'Faith', he insists, 'will always be a venture; . . . it will involve not a Because but a Nevertheless in face of the reality of the human.'[1]

Peter Berger also, as a Christian sociologist, has some pertinent things to say about the need to tread delicately between irrelevance and accommodation:

> I would like to make it clear once more that I am *not* saying that Christians ought not to listen to others' ideas, or to take seriously what happens in their cultural milieu, or to participate in the political struggles of the times. What troubles me is not the stance of listening as such, but that of listening with uncritical adulation if not idolatrous intent – of listening, if you will, with wide-eyed and open-mouthed wonder.[2]

'It seems to me', Peter Berger goes on, 'that quite simply, it is time to say "Enough!" to the dance around the golden calves of modernity.'[3] More important than the question 'What does modern man have to say to the church?' is the question 'What does the church have to say to modern man?'[4]

The people of God live in a world which is often unfriendly and sometimes actively hostile. We are constantly exposed to the pressure to conform. Yet throughout Scripture the summons is given to a vigorous nonconformity, and warnings are sounded to those who give in to worldliness. In the Old Testament the Lord said to his people after the exodus: 'You must not do as they do in Egypt, where you used to live, and you must not do as they do in the land of Canaan, where I am bringing you. Do not follow their practices. You must obey my laws . . .'.[5] Yet the people said to Samuel: 'Now appoint a king to lead us, such as all the other nations have.'[6] And later Ezekiel had to rebuke them for their idolatry: 'You say, "We want to be like the nations, like the peoples of the world, who serve wood

[1] *Ibid.*, p. 563.
[2] Peter L. Berger, *Facing Up to Modernity* (1977; Penguin, 1979), p. 232.
[3] *Ibid.*, p. 233. [4] *Ibid.*, p. 233. [5] Lv. 18:3–4a. [6] 1 Sa. 8:5.

and stone.'"[1] It was similar in New Testament days. In spite of the clear commands of Jesus, 'Do not be like them',[2] and of Paul, 'Do not conform . . . to the pattern of this world',[3] the constant tendency of God's people was, and still is, to behave 'like the heathen',[4] until nothing much seems to distinguish the church from the world, the Christian from the non-Christian, in convictions, values or standards.[5]

Thank God, however, that there have always been some noble souls who have stood firm, sometimes alone, and refused to compromise. I think of Jeremiah in the sixth century BC, and Paul in his day ('everyone . . . has deserted me'),[6] Athanasius in the fourth century and Luther in the sixteenth. C. S. Lewis wrote his tribute to Athanasius, who maintained the deity of Jesus and the doctrine of the Trinity, when the whole church was determined to follow the heretic Arius: 'It is his glory that he did *not* move with the times; it is his reward that he now remains when those times, as all times do, have moved away.'[7]

So today, we are resolved to struggle to present the gospel in such a way as to speak to modern dilemmas, fears and frustrations, but we are equally determined not to compromise the biblical gospel in order to do so. Some stumbling-blocks are intrinsic to the original gospel and cannot be eliminated, or even soft-pedalled, in order to render it more palatable to contemporary taste. The gospel contains some features so alien to modern thought that it will always appear 'folly' to intellectuals, however hard we strive (and rightly) to show that it is 'true and reasonable'.[8] The cross will always constitute an assault on human self-righteousness and a challenge to human self-indulgence. Its 'scandal' (stumbling-block) simply cannot

[1] Ezk. 20:32. [2] Mt. 6:8. [3] Rom. 12:2.
[4] 1 Thes. 4:5; *cf.* 1 Cor. 5:1; Eph. 4:17.
[5] For brave Christian challenges to the church to stand firm against the cultural and moral trends of today see, for example, *Christianity Confronts Modernity*, ed. Peter Williamson and Kevin Perrotta (Servant, 1981) and *The Gravedigger File: Papers on the Subversion of the Modern Church*, by Os Guinness (IVP USA, 1983).
[6] 2 Tim. 1:15; *cf.* 4:11, 16.
[7] From C. S. Lewis' Introduction to *St Athanasius on the Incarnation* (Mowbray, 1953), p. 9.
[8] Acts 26:25.

be removed. Indeed, the church speaks most authentically to the world not when it makes its shameful little prudential compromises, but when it refuses to do so; not when it has become indistinguishable from the world, but when its distinctive light shines most brightly.

Thus Christian people, who live under the authority of God's revelation, however anxious they are to communicate it to others, manifest a sturdy independence of mind and spirit. This is not obstinacy, for we are willing to listen to everybody. But we are determined to be faithful, and if necessary to suffer for it. God's word to Ezekiel is an encouragement to us: 'Do not be afraid of them ... You must speak my words to them, whether they listen or fail to listen, for they are rebellious.'[1] So we have to apply the Word, but not manipulate it. We must do our utmost to ensure that it speaks to our time, but not bowdlerize it in order to secure a fake relevance. Our calling is to be faithful and relevant, not merely trendy.

How, then, can we be both conservative and radical simultaneously, conservative in guarding God's revelation and radical in our thoroughgoing application of it? How can we develop a Christian mind which is both shaped by the truths of historic, biblical Christianity, and acquainted with the realities of the contemporary world? How can we relate the Word to the world, understanding the world in the light of the Word, and even understanding the Word in the light of the world? We have to begin with a double refusal. We refuse to become either so absorbed in the Word, that we *escape* into it and fail to let it confront the world, or so absorbed in the world, that we *conform* to it and fail to subject it to the judgment of the Word. Escapism and conformity are opposite mistakes, but neither is a Christian option.

In place of this double refusal we are called to double listening, listening both to the Word and to the world. It is a truism to say that we have to listen to the Word of God, except perhaps that we need to listen to him more expectantly and

[1] Ezk. 2:6–7.

humbly, ready for him to confront us with a disturbing, uninvited word. It is less welcome to be told that we must also listen to the world. For the voices of our contemporaries may take the form of shrill and strident protest. They are now querulous, now appealing, now aggressive in tone. There are also the anguished cries of those who are suffering, and the pain, doubt, anger, alienation and even despair of those who are estranged from God. I am not suggesting that we should listen to God and to our fellow human beings in the same way or with the same degree of deference. We listen to the Word with humble reverence, anxious to understand it, and resolved to believe and obey what we come to understand. We listen to the world with critical alertness, anxious to understand it too, and resolved not necessarily to believe and obey it, but to sympathize with it and to seek grace to discover how the gospel relates to it.

Everybody finds listening difficult. But are Christians for some reason (perhaps because we believe ourselves called to speak what God has spoken) worse listeners than others? Our symbol is rather the tongue than the ear. Yet we should have learned a lesson from Job's garrulous comforters. They began well. For when they heard about Job's troubles, they left their homes and visited him. And when they arrived, and could hardly recognize him because of his disfiguring sores, they wept, tore their robes, sprinkled dust on their heads, and then sat beside him on the ground for seven days. During that whole week they said nothing to him, because they saw how great his sufferings were. Indeed, nobody said anything, because there was simply nothing to say. One only wishes that they had continued as they began, and kept their mouths shut. Instead, they trotted out their conventional orthodoxy, that every sinner suffers for his own sins, in the most unfeeling, insensitive way. They did not really listen to what Job had to say. They merely repeated their own thoughtless and heartless claptrap, until in the end God rebuked them for not having spoken about him what was right.

We are familiar with the concept of 'double-think', an expression coined by George Orwell in his famous book *Nineteen*

Eighty-Four. It denotes the ability to hold simultaneously in the mind two conflicting views or beliefs. Double-think is the speciality of unscrupulous propagandists. 'Double-speak' is even more disreputable. It is the ability to say one thing to one person and something entirely different to somebody else, and even to speak mutually contradictory things to the same person. Double-speak is the stock-in-trade of hypocrites, of consummate liars. 'Double listening', however, contains no element of self-contradiction. It is the faculty of listening to two voices at the same time, the voice of God through Scripture and the voices of men and women around us. These voices will often contradict one another, but our purpose in listening to them both is to discover how they relate to each other. Double listening is indispensable to Christian discipleship and Christian mission.

It is only through the discipline of double listening that it is possible to become a 'contemporary Christian'. For then we see that the adjectives 'historical' and 'contemporary' are not incompatible, we learn to apply the Word to the world, and we proclaim good news which is both true and new. In sum, we live in the 'now' in the light of the 'then'.

PART ONE

THE GOSPEL

Christianity presents itself not as a religion, let alone as one religion among many, but as God's good news for the world. This implies that the gospel has both a divine origin (it comes from God) and a human relevance (it speaks to our condition). In consequence, before we are ready to ask the question 'What is the gospel?', we must obtain a satisfactory answer to the logically prior question, 'What is a human being?'

Chapter 1 ('The Human Paradox') is an attempt to do justice to what the Bible teaches and our own experience endorses, namely the glory and the shame of our humanness, both our dignity as creatures made in God's image and our depravity as sinners under his judgment. Chapter 2 then presents what is traditionally called 'salvation' in terms of 'Authentic Freedom'.

Chapters 3 and 4 handle the central themes of the death and resurrection of Jesus, which secured our freedom. I try to face first the five main objections to the gospel of Christ crucified and then the current denials of his bodily resurrection. I argue that the New Testament significance of the resurrection of Jesus depends on the church's traditional belief that it was an event which involved the raising and transforming of his body.

In chapter 5 ('Jesus Christ is Lord') we review the far-reaching implications, for both faith and life, of this seemingly innocent affirmation. Radical indeed is the discipleship which takes Christ's lordship seriously.

CHAPTER ONE
THE HUMAN PARADOX

Twice the question 'What is man?' (that is, 'What does it mean to be human?') is asked and answered in the Old Testament. And on both occasions the question expresses surprise, even incredulity, that God should pay so much attention to his human creation. For we are insignificant in comparison to the vastness of the universe, and impure in contrast to the brightness of the stars, even just 'a maggot' and 'a worm'.[1]

There are at least three major reasons for the importance of this question.

Personally speaking, to ask 'What is man?' is another way of asking 'Who am I?'. Only so can we respond both to the ancient Greek adage *gnōthi seauton*, 'know yourself', and to the modern western preoccupation with the discovery of our true selves. There is no more important field for search or research than our own personal identity. For until we have found ourselves, we can neither fully discover anything else, nor grow into personal maturity. The universal cry is 'Who am I?' and 'Do I have any significance?'

The story is told that Arthur Schopenhauer, the philosopher of pessimism, was sitting one day in the Tiergarten at Frankfurt, looking somewhat shabby and dishevelled, when the park-keeper mistook him for a tramp and asked him gruffly, 'Who are you?' To this enquiry the philosopher replied bitterly, 'I wish to God I knew.'

Professionally, whatever our work may be, we are inevitably involved in serving people. Doctors and nurses have patients,

[1] Jb. 7:17; 25:4–6; Ps. 8:3–4.

teachers pupils, lawyers and social workers clients, members of parliament constituents, and business people customers. How we treat people in our work depends almost entirely on how we view them.

Politically, it is arguable that the nature of human beings has been one of the chief points at issue between the rival visions of Jesus and Marx. Have human beings an absolute value because of which they must be respected, or is their value only relative to the state, because of which they may be exploited? More simply, are the people the servants of the institution, or is the institution the servant of the people? As John S. Whale has written, 'ideologies . . . are really anthropologies'; they are different doctrines of man.[1]

The Christian critique of contemporary answers to the question 'What is man?' is that they tend to be either too naive in their optimism or too negative in their pessimism about the human condition. Secular humanists are generally optimistic. Although they believe that *homo sapiens* is nothing but the product of a random evolutionary process, they nevertheless believe that human beings are continuing to evolve, have limitless potential, and will one day take control of their own development. But such optimists do not take seriously enough the human streak of moral perversity and self-centredness which has constantly retarded progress and so led to disillusion in social reformers.

Existentialists, on the other hand, tend to be extremely pessimistic. Because there is no God, they say, there are no values, ideals or standards any more, which is at least logical. And although we need somehow to find the courage to be, our existence has neither meaning nor purpose. Everything is ultimately absurd. But such pessimists overlook the love, joy, beauty, truth, hope, heroism and self-sacrifice which have enriched the human story.

What we need, therefore, to quote J. S. Whale again, is

[1] J. S. Whale, *Christian Doctrine* (1941; Fontana, 1957), p. 33.

'neither the easy optimism of the humanist, nor the dark pessimism of the cynic, but the radical realism of the Bible'.[1]

Our human dignity

The intrinsic value of human beings by creation is affirmed from the first chapter of the Bible onwards.

> Then God said, 'Let us make man in our image, in our likeness, and let them rule over the fish of the sea and the birds of the air, over the livestock, over all the earth, and over all the creatures that move along the ground.'
>
> So God created man
> in his own image.
> In the image of God
> he created him;
> male and female
> he created them.
>
> God blessed them and said to them, 'Be fruitful and increase in number; fill the earth and subdue it. Rule over the fish of the sea and the birds of the air and over every living creature that moves on the ground.'[2]

There has been a long-standing debate about the meaning of the divine 'image' or 'likeness' in human beings, and where their superiority lies. Keith Thomas collected a number of quaint suggestions in his book *Man and the Natural World*.[3] He points out that a human being was described by Aristotle as a political animal, by Thomas Willis as a laughing animal, by Benjamin Franklin as a tool-making animal, by Edmund Burke as a religious animal, and by James Boswell the gourmet as a

[1] *Ibid.*, p. 41. [2] Gn. 1:26–28.
[3] Keith Thomas, *Man and the Natural World: Changing Attitudes in England 1500–1806* (1983; Penguin, 1984).

cooking animal.[1] Other writers have focused on some physical feature of the human body. Plato made much of our erect posture, so that animals look down, and only human beings look up to heaven, while Aristotle added the peculiarity that only human beings are unable to wiggle their ears.[2] A Stuart doctor was greatly impressed by our intestines, by their 'anfractuous circumlocutions, windings and turnings', whereas in the late eighteenth century Uvedale Price drew attention to our nose: 'Man is, I believe, the only animal that has a marked projection in the middle of the face.'[3]

Scholars who are familiar with ancient Egypt and Assyria, however, emphasize that in those cultures the king or emperor was regarded as the 'image' of God, representing him on earth, and that kings had images of themselves erected in their provinces to symbolize the extent of their authority. Against that background God the Creator entrusted a kind of royal (or at least vice-regal) responsibility to all human beings, appointing them to 'rule' over the earth and its creatures, and 'crowning' them with 'glory and honour' to do so.[4]

In the unfolding narrative of Genesis 1 it is clear that the divine image or likeness is what distinguishes humans (the climax of creation) from animals (whose creation is recorded earlier). A continuity between humans and animals is implied. For example, they share 'the breath of life'[5] and the responsibility to reproduce.[6] But there was also a radical discontinuity between them, in that only human beings are said to be 'like God'. This emphasis on the unique distinction between humans and animals keeps recurring throughout Scripture. The argument takes two forms. We should be ashamed both when human beings behave like animals, descending to their level, and when animals behave like human beings, doing better by instinct than we do by choice. As an example of the former, men and women are not to be 'senseless and ignorant' and behave like 'a brute beast', or 'like the horse or the mule, which have no

[1] *Ibid.*, p. 31. [2] *Ibid.*, p. 31.
[3] *Ibid.*, p. 32. See also pp. 37–39, 43, 166 and 177.
[4] Gn. 1:26, 28; Ps. 8:5–8. [5] Gn. 2:7; 7:22. [6] Gn. 1:22, 28.

understanding'.[1] As an example of the latter, we are rebuked that oxen and donkeys are better at recognizing their master than we are,[2] that migratory birds are better at returning home after going away,[3] and that ants are more industrious and more provident.[4]

Returning to the early chapters of Genesis, all God's dealings with Adam and Eve presuppose their uniqueness among his creatures. He addresses them in such a way as to assume their understanding; he tells them which fruit they may eat and not eat, taking it for granted that they can discern between a permission and a prohibition, and choose between them. He planted the garden, and then put Adam in it 'to work it and take care of it',[5] thus initiating a conscious, responsible partnership between them in cultivating the soil. He created them male and female, pronounced solitude 'not good', instituted marriage for the fulfilment of their love, and blessed their union. He also 'walked in the garden in the cool of the day', desiring their companionship, and missed them when they hid from him. It is not surprising, therefore, that this cluster of five privileges (understanding, moral choice, creativity, love and fellowship with God) are all regularly mentioned in Scripture, and continue to be recognized in the contemporary world, as constituting the unique distinction of our 'humanness'.

To begin with, there is *our self-conscious rationality*. It is not only that we are able to think and to reason. For so, it may be said, can computers. They can perform the most fantastic calculations, and do so much faster than we can. They also have a form of memory (they can store information) and a form of speech (they can communicate their findings). But there is still one thing (thank God!) they cannot do. They cannot originate new thoughts; they can only 'think' what is fed into them. Human beings, however, are original thinkers. More than that. We can do what we (author and reader) are doing at this very moment: we can stand outside ourselves, look at ourselves, and evaluate ourselves, asking ourselves who and what we are. We

[1] Ps. 73:22; 32:9. [2] Is. 1:3. [3] Je. 8:7. [4] Pr. 6:6–8. [5] Gn. 2:8, 15.

are self-conscious and can be self-critical. We are also restlessly inquisitive about the universe. True, as one scientist said to another, 'astronomically speaking, man is infinitesimally small'. 'That is so,' responded his colleague, 'but then, astronomically speaking, man is the astronomer.'

Next, there is *our ability to make moral choices*. Human beings are moral beings. Although our conscience reflects our upbringing and culture, and is therefore fallible, nevertheless it remains on guard within us, like a sentinel, warning us that there is a difference between right and wrong. It is also more than an inner voice. It represents a moral order outside and above us, to which we sense an obligation, so that we have a strong urge to do what we perceive to be right, and feelings of guilt when we do what we believe to be wrong. Our whole moral vocabulary (commands and prohibitions, values and choices, obligation, conscience, freedom and will, right and wrong, guilt and shame) is meaningless to animals. True, we can train our dog to know what it is allowed and forbidden. And when it disobeys, and cringes from us by a reflex action, we can describe it as looking 'guilty'. But it has no sense of guilt; it knows only that it is going to be walloped.

Thirdly, there are *our powers of artistic creativity*. It is not only that God calls us into a responsible stewardship of the natural environment, and into partnership with himself in subduing and developing it for the common good, but that he has given us innovative skills through science and art to do so. We are 'creative creatures'. That is, as creatures we depend upon our Creator. But, having been created in our Creator's likeness, he has given us the desire and the ability to be creators too. So we draw and we paint, we build and we sculpt, we dream and we dance, we write poetry and we make music. We are able to appreciate what is beautiful to the eye, the ear and the touch.

In the next place, there is *our capacity for relationships of love*. God said, 'Let us make man in our image . . . So God created man in his own image . . .; male and female he created them.'

Although we must be careful not to deduce from this text

more than it actually says, it is surely legitimate to say that the plurality within the Creator ('Let us make man') was expressed in the plurality of his creatures ('male and female he created them'). It became even clearer when Jesus prayed for his own people 'that all of them may be one, Father, just as you are in me and I am in you'.[1] And this unity of love is unique to human beings. Of course all animals mate, many form strong pair bonds, most care for their young, and some are gregarious. But the love which binds human beings together is more than an instinct, more than a disturbance in the endocrine glands. It has inspired the greatest art, the noblest heroism, the finest devotion. God himself is love, and our experiences of loving are an essential reflection of our likeness to him.

Fifthly, there is *our insatiable thirst for God.* All human beings are aware of an ultimate personal reality, whom we seek, and in relation to whom alone we know we will find our human fulfilment. Even when we are running away from God, instinctively we know that we have no other resting-place, no other home. Without him we are lost, like waifs and strays. Our greatest claim to nobility is our created capacity to know God, to be in personal relationship with him, to love him and to worship him. Indeed, we are most truly human when we are on our knees before our Creator.

It is in these things, then, that our distinctive humanness lies, in our God-given capacities to think, to choose, to create, to love and to worship. 'In the animal,' by contrast, wrote Emil Brunner, 'we do not see even the smallest beginning of a tendency to seek truth for truth's sake, to shape beauty for the sake of beauty, to promote righteousness for the sake of righteousness, to reverence the Holy for the sake of its holiness . . . The animal knows nothing "above" its immediate sphere of existence, nothing by which it measures or tests its existence . . . The difference between man and beast amounts to a whole dimension of existence.'[2]

No wonder Shakespeare made Hamlet break out into his

[1] Jn. 17:21.
[2] Emil Brunner, *Man in Revolt* (1937; ET Lutterworth, 1939), pp. 419–420.

eulogy: 'What a piece of work is a man! how noble in reason! how infinite in faculty! in action how like an angel! in apprehension how like a god! the beauty of the world! the paragon of animals!'[1]

How I wish I could stop there and we could live the rest of our lives glowing with unadulterated self-esteem! But alas! There is another and darker side to our human being, of which we are only too well aware, and to which Jesus himself drew our attention.

Our human depravity

Here are some words of Jesus:

> Again Jesus called the crowd to him and said, 'Listen to me, everyone, and understand this. Nothing outside a man can make him "unclean" by going into him. Rather, it is what comes out of a man that makes him "unclean". . . . For from within, out of men's hearts, come evil thoughts, sexual immorality, theft, murder, adultery, greed, malice, deceit, lewdness, envy, slander, arrogance and folly. All these evils come from inside and make a man "unclean".'[2]

Jesus did not teach the fundamental goodness of human nature. He undoubtedly believed the Old Testament truth that humankind, male and female, were made in the image of God, but he also believed that this image had been marred. He taught the worth of human beings, not least by devoting himself to their service, but he also taught our unworthiness. He did not deny that we can give 'good things' to others, but he added that even while doing good we do not escape the designation 'evil'.[3] And in the verses quoted above he made important assertions about the extent, nature, origin and effect of evil in human beings.

First, he taught *the universal extent of human evil.* He was

[1] Act II, Scene 2. [2] Mk. 7:14–15, 21–23. [3] Mt. 7:11.

not portraying the criminal segment of society or some particularly degraded individual or group. On the contrary, he was in conversation with refined, righteous and religious Pharisees, and generalized about 'a man' and 'men'. Indeed, it is often the most upright people who are the most keenly aware of their own degradation. As an example, take Dag Hammarskjöld, Secretary-General of the United Nations from 1953 to 1961. He was a deeply committed public servant, whom W. H. Auden described as 'a great, good and lovable man'. Yet his view of himself was very different. In his collection of autobiographical pieces entitled *Markings*, he wrote of 'that dark counter-centre of evil in our nature', so that we even make our service of others 'the foundation for our own life-preserving self-esteem'.[1]

Secondly, Jesus taught *the self-centred nature of human evil.* In Mark 7 he listed thirteen examples. What is common to them all is that each is an assertion of the self either against our neighbour (murder, adultery, theft, false witness and covetousness – breaches of the second half of the Ten Commandments – are all included) or against God ('pride and folly' being well defined in the Old Testament as denials of God's sovereignty and even of his existence). Jesus summarized the Ten Commandments in terms of love for God and neighbour, and every sin is a form of selfish revolt against God's authority or our neighbour's welfare.

Thirdly, Jesus taught *the inward origin of human evil.* Its source has to be traced neither to a bad environment nor to a faulty education (although both these can have a powerful conditioning influence on impressionable young people), but rather to our 'heart', our inherited and twisted nature. One might almost say that Jesus introduced us to Freudianism before Freud. At least what he called the 'heart' is roughly equivalent to what Freud called the 'unconscious'. It resembles a very deep well. The thick deposit of mud at the bottom is usually unseen, and even unsuspected. But when the waters of the well are stirred by the winds of violent emotion, the most evil-looking,

[1] Dag Hammarskjöld, *Markings*, translated by Leif Sjöberg and W. H. Auden (Faber, 1964), pp. 128–129.

evil-smelling filth bubbles up from the depths and breaks the surface – rage, hate, lust, cruelty, jealousy and revenge. In our most sensitive moments we are appalled by our potentiality for evil. Superficial remedies will not do.

Fourthly, Jesus spoke of *the defiling effect of human evil*. 'All these evils come from inside', he said, 'and make a human being "unclean".'[1] The Pharisees considered defilement to be largely external and ceremonial; they were preoccupied with clean foods, clean hands and clean vessels. But Jesus insisted that defilement is internal and moral. What renders us unclean in God's sight is not the food which goes into us (into our stomach) but the evil which comes out of us (out of our heart).

All those who have caught even a momentary glimpse of the holiness of God have been unable to bear the sight, so shocked have they been by their own contrasting uncleanness. Moses hid his face, afraid to look at God. Isaiah cried out in horror over his own pollution and lostness. Ezekiel was dazzled, almost blinded, by the sight of God's glory, and fell face down on the ground.[2] As for us, even if we have never like these men glimpsed the splendour of Almighty God, we know we are unfit to enter his presence in time or in eternity.

In saying this, we have not forgotten our human dignity with which this chapter began. Yet we must do justice to Jesus' own evaluation of evil in our human condition. It is universal (in every human being without exception), self-centred (a revolt against God and neighbour), inward (issuing from our heart, our fallen nature) and defiling (making us unclean and therefore unfit for God). We who were made by God like God are disqualified from living with God.

The resulting paradox

Here, then, is the paradox of our humanness: our dignity and our depravity. We are capable both of the loftiest nobility and of the basest cruelty. One moment we can behave like God, in

[1] Mk. 7:23. [2] Ex. 3:1–6; Is. 6:1–5; Ezk. 1, especially verse 28.

whose image we were made, and the next like the beasts, from whom we were meant to be completely distinct. Human beings are the inventors of hospitals for the care of the sick, universities for the acquisition of wisdom, parliaments for the just rule of the people, and churches for the worship of God. But they are also the inventors of torture chambers, concentration camps and nuclear arsenals. Strange, bewildering paradox! – noble and ignoble, rational and irrational, moral and immoral, God-like and bestial! As C. S. Lewis put it through Aslan, 'You come of the Lord Adam and the Lady Eve. And that is both honour enough to erect the head of the poorest beggar, and shame enough to bow the shoulders of the greatest emperor on earth.'[1]

I do not know any more eloquent description of the human paradox than one which was given by Richard Holloway, now Bishop of Edinburgh, at the Catholic Renewal Conference at Loughborough in April 1978:

> 'This is my dilemma . . .', he said, 'I am dust and ashes, frail and wayward, a set of predetermined behavioural responses, . . . riddled with fears, beset with needs . . ., the quintessence of dust and unto dust I shall return . . . *But* there is something else in me . . . Dust I may be, but troubled dust, dust that dreams, dust that has strange premonitions of transfiguration, of a glory in store, a destiny prepared, an inheritance that will one day be my own . . . So my life is stretched out in a painful dialectic between ashes and glory, between weakness and transfiguration. I am a riddle to myself, an exasperating enigma . . . this strange duality of dust and glory.'

Faced with the horror of their own dichotomy, some people are foolish enough to imagine that they can sort themselves out, banishing the evil and liberating the good within them. The classic expression both of our human ambivalence and of our hopes of self-salvation was given by Robert Louis Stevenson in his famous tale *The Strange Case of Dr Jekyll and Mr Hyde*

[1] C. S. Lewis, *Prince Caspian* (Geoffrey Bles, 1951), p. 185.

(1886). Henry Jekyll was a wealthy and respectable doctor, inclined to religion and philanthropy. But he was conscious that his personality had another and darker side, so that he was 'committed to a profound duplicity of life'. He discovered that 'man is not truly one, but truly two'. He then began to dream that he could solve the problem of his duality if only both sides of him could be 'housed in separate identities', the unjust going one way, and the just the other. So he developed a drug by which he could assume the deformed body and evil personality of Mr Hyde, his *alter ego*, through whom he gave vent to his passions – hatred, violence, blasphemy and even murder.

At first Dr Jekyll was in control of his transformations, and boasted that the moment he chose he could be rid of Mr Hyde for ever. But gradually Hyde gained ascendancy over Jekyll, until he began to become Hyde involuntarily, and only by great effort could resume his existence as Jekyll. 'I was slowly losing hold of my original and better self, and becoming slowly incorporated with my second and worse.' Finally, a few moments before his exposure and arrest, he committed suicide.

The truth is that every Jekyll has his Hyde, whom he cannot control and who threatens to take him over. In fact, the continuing paradox of our humanness throws much light on both our private and our public lives. Let me give an example of each.

I begin with *personal redemption*. Because evil is so deeply entrenched within us, self-salvation is impossible. So our most urgent need is redemption, that is to say, a new beginning in life which offers us both a cleansing from the pollution of sin and a new heart, even a new creation, with new perspectives, new ambitions and new powers. And because we were made in God's image, such redemption is possible. No human being is irredeemable. For God came after us in Jesus Christ, and pursued us even to the desolate agony of the cross, where he took our place, bore our sin and died our death, in order that we might be forgiven. Then he rose, ascended and sent the Holy Spirit, who is able to enter our personality and change us from within. If there is any better news for the human race than this, I for one have never heard it.

My second example of our paradoxical human situation relates to *social progress*. The fact that men and women – even very degraded people – retain vestiges of the divine image in which they were created is evident. This is why, on the whole, all human beings prefer justice to injustice, freedom to oppression, love to hatred, and peace to violence. This fact of everyday observation raises our hopes for social change. Most people cherish visions of a better world. The complementary fact, however, is that human beings are 'twisted with self-centredness' (as Archbishop Michael Ramsey used to define original sin), and this places limits on our expectations. The followers of Jesus are realists, not Utopians. It is possible to improve society (and the historical record of Christian social influence has been notable), but the perfect society, which will be 'the home of righteousness' alone,[1] awaits the return of Jesus Christ.

[1] 2 Pet. 3:13.

CHAPTER TWO

AUTHENTIC FREEDOM

One of the best ways of sharing the gospel with modern men and women is to present it in terms of freedom. At least three arguments may be used for this approach.

First, freedom is an extremely appealing topic. The world-wide revolt against authority, which began in the 1960s, is seen as synonymous with a world-wide quest for freedom. Many people are obsessed with it, and are spending their lives in pursuit of it. For some it is still *national* freedom, emancipation from a colonial or neo-colonial yoke. For others it is *civil* rights, as they protest against racial, religious or ethnic discrimination and demand the protection of minority opinions. Yet others are preoccupied with the search for *economic* freedom, freedom from hunger, poverty and unemployment. At the same time, all of us are concerned for our *personal* freedom. Even those who campaign most vigorously for the other freedoms I have mentioned (national, civil and economic) often know that they are not liberated people themselves. They cannot always put a name to the tyrannies which oppress them. Yet they feel frustrated, unfulfilled and unfree.

In an interview with the widely acclaimed novelist John Fowles, published under the title 'A Sort of Exile in Lyme Regis', Daniel Halpern asked him: 'Is there a particular picture of the world that you would like to develop in your writing? Something that has remained important to you?' 'Freedom, yes,' John Fowles replied, 'how you achieve freedom. That obsesses me. All my books are about that.'[1]

Secondly, freedom is a great Christian word. Jesus Christ is

[1] *London Magazine*, March 1971.

portrayed in the New Testament as the world's supreme liberator. 'The Spirit of the Lord is on me,' he claimed, applying an Old Testament prophecy to himself, 'because he has anointed me to preach good news to the poor. He has sent me to proclaim freedom for the prisoners and recovery of sight for the blind, to release the oppressed, to proclaim the year of the Lord's favour.'[1] Whether Jesus intended the poor, the prisoners, the blind and the oppressed to be understood as material or spiritual categories or both (the question continues to be hotly debated), the good news he proclaimed to them was certainly 'freedom' or 'release'. Later in his public ministry he added the promise: 'If the Son sets you free, you will be free indeed.'[2] Then the apostle Paul became the champion of Christian liberty and wrote: 'It is for freedom that Christ has set us free. Stand firm, then, and do not let yourselves be burdened again by a yoke of slavery.'[3] For those who find 'salvation' a bit of meaningless religious jargon, and even an embarrassment, 'freedom' is an excellent substitute. To be saved by Jesus Christ is to be set free.

Thirdly, freedom is much misunderstood. Even those who talk loudest and longest about freedom have not always paused first to define what they are talking about. A notable example is the Marxist orator who was waxing eloquent on the street corner about the freedom we would all enjoy after the revolution. 'When we get freedom', he cried, 'you'll all be able to smoke cigars like that,' pointing at an opulent gentleman walking by.

'I prefer my fag,' shouted a heckler.

'When we get freedom,' the Marxist continued, ignoring the interruption and warming to his theme, 'you'll all be able to drive in cars like that,' pointing to a sumptuous Mercedes which was driving by.

'I prefer my bike,' shouted the heckler.

And so the dialogue continued until the Marxist could bear his tormentor no longer. Turning on him, he said: 'When we get freedom, you'll do what you're told.'

[1] Lk. 4:18–19, quoting Is. 61:1–2. [2] Jn. 8:36. [3] Gal. 5:1.

The negative: freedom *from*

So what is freedom? A true definition is bound to begin negatively. We have to identify the forces which tyrannize us and so inhibit our freedom. Only then can we grasp how Christ is able to liberate us.

First, Jesus Christ offers us *freedom from guilt.* We should be thankful for the current reaction against Freud's insistence that guilt feelings are pathological, symptoms of mental sickness. Some doubtless are, especially in certain kinds of depressive illness, but not all guilt is false guilt. On the contrary, an increasing number of contemporary psychologists and psychotherapists, even if they make no Christian profession, are telling us that we must take our responsibilities seriously. The late Dr Hobart Mowrer of the University of Illinois, for example, understood human life in contractual terms and saw 'sin' as a breach of contract for which restitution must be made. Certainly the Bible has always emphasized both our obligations as human beings and our failure to meet them. In particular, we have asserted ourselves against the love and authority of God and against the welfare of our neighbours. To use straightforward Christian language, we are not only sinners but guilty sinners, and our conscience tells us so. According to one of Mark Twain's witticisms, 'Man is the only animal that blushes – or needs to.'[1]

Now no-one is free who is unforgiven. If I were not sure of God's mercy and forgiveness, I could not look you in the face, or (more important) God. I would want to run away and hide, as Adam and Eve did in the Garden of Eden. For it was in Eden, not at Watergate, that the device called 'cover-up' was first invented. I would certainly not be free. Not long before she died in 1988, in a moment of surprising candour on television, Marghanita Laski, one of our best-known secular humanists and novelists, said: 'What I envy most about you Christians is your forgiveness; I have nobody to forgive me.'

'But', as Christians want to shout from the housetops, echoing the penitential psalmist, 'there is forgiveness with

[1] *Following the Equator* (1897), Vol. 1, ch. 27.

God.'[1] For in his love for sinners like us, God entered our world in the person of his Son. Having lived a life of perfect righteousness, he identified himself in his death with our unrighteousness. He bore our sin, our guilt, our death in our place, in order that we might be forgiven.

So freedom begins with forgiveness. I remember a student at a university in the north of England, who had been brought up in spiritism but was taken by a fellow student to a Christian meeting, where he heard the gospel. The following weekend the battle for his soul began in earnest, until (as he wrote later) he cried in despair to Jesus Christ to save him. Then, he went on, 'he really came to me. I felt actual, real love, I can't describe it. It was just pure beauty and serenity. And despite the fact that I knew nothing about salvation and sin, and did not even know what they meant, I just *knew* I was forgiven ... I was unbelievably happy.'

Secondly, Jesus Christ offers us *freedom from self*. Talking once with some Jewish believers, he is recorded as having said to them: 'If you hold to my teaching, you are really my disciples. Then you will know the truth, and the truth will set you free.'

They were immediately indignant. How dared he say that they needed in some way to be liberated? 'We are Abraham's descendants', they expostulated, 'and have never been slaves of anyone. How can you say that we shall be set free?'

Jesus replied, 'I tell you the truth, everyone who sins is a slave to sin.'[2]

So if guilt is the first slavery from which we need to be freed, sin is the second. And what does that mean? Like 'salvation', 'sin' is a word which belongs to the traditional Christian vocabulary. 'I am not a sinner', people often say, because they seem to be associating sin with specific and rather sensational misdeeds like murder, adultery and theft. But 'sin' has a much wider connotation than that. I can myself remember what a revelation it was to me to learn, especially through the teaching of Archbishop William Temple, that what the Bible means by

[1] *Cf.* Ps. 130:4. [2] Jn. 8:31–34.

'sin' is primarily self-centredness. For God's two great commandments are first that we love him with all our being and secondly that we love our neighbour as we love ourselves. Sin, then, is the reversal of this order. It is to put ourselves first, virtually proclaiming our own autonomy, our neighbour next when it suits our convenience, and God somewhere in the background.

That self-centredness is a world-wide phenomenon of human experience is evident from the rich variety of words in our language which are compounded with 'self'. There are more than fifty which have a pejorative meaning – words like self-applause, self-absorption, self-assertion, self-advertisement, self-indulgence, self-gratification, self-glorification, self-pity, self-importance, self-interest and self-will.

Moreover, our self-centredness is a terrible tyranny. Malcolm Muggeridge used often to speak and write of 'the dark little dungeon of my own ego'. And what a dark dungeon it is! To be engrossed in our own selfish concerns and ambitions, without regard either for the glory of God or for the good of others, is to be confined in the most cramped and unhealthy of prisons.

Yet Jesus Christ, who rose from the dead and is alive, can liberate us. It is possible for us to know 'the power of his resurrection'.[1] Or, to put the same truth in different words, the living Jesus can enter our personality by his Spirit and turn us inside out. Not of course that we claim to be perfect, but that by the power of his indwelling Spirit we have at least begun to experience a transformation from self to unself. Our previously closed personality is starting to unfold to Christ, like a flower to the rising sun.

Thirdly, Jesus Christ offers us *freedom from fear.* The ancient world into which he came lived in apprehension of the powers which, it was believed, inhabited the stars. Still today the traditional religion of primitive tribespeople is haunted by malevolent spirits who need to be placated. The lives of modern men and women are also overshadowed by fear. There are the

[1] Phil. 3:10.

common fears which have always plagued human beings – the fear of sickness, bereavement, old age and death, together with the fear of the unknown, the occult and of nuclear extinction. Most of us have also sometimes suffered from irrational fears, and it is extraordinary how many educated people entertain superstitious fears. They touch wood, cross their fingers, carry charms and refuse to sit down thirteen to a meal because it is an unlucky number. For this reason many highrise hotels in the United States have no thirteenth floor. As you go up in the elevator and watch the illuminated panel, the numbers jump from 10, 11 and 12 to 14. For people are too superstitious to sleep on the thirteenth floor and do not seem to realize that it is still the thirteenth even if you call it the fourteenth! As for us in Britain, according to a recent opinion poll, although nine tenths of the population still believe in a God of some kind, twice as many adults read their horoscope each week as their Bible.

All fear brings a measure of paralysis. Nobody who is afraid is free. Moreover, fear is like fungus: it grows most rapidly in the dark. It is essential, therefore, to bring our fears out into the light and look at them, especially in the light of the victory and supremacy of Jesus Christ. For he who died and rose has also been exalted to his Father's right hand, and everything has been put 'under his feet'.[1] So where are the things of which we were previously afraid? They are under the feet of the triumphant Christ. It is when we see them there that their power to terrify is broken.

That fear and freedom are mutually incompatible was well illustrated for me once by a young African lecturer. We had been discussing the need for Christians to take a greater interest in natural history as God's creation. 'Before I became a Christian,' he responded, 'I was afraid of many things, especially snakes. But now I find it hard to kill one because I enjoy watching them. I thank God that now I am really free.'

[1] Eph. 1:22.

The positive: freedom *for*

So far we have related the tyrannies which impede our freedom to the three major events in the experience of Jesus Christ, his death, resurrection and exaltation. There is freedom from guilt because he died for us, freedom from self because we may live in the power of his resurrection, and freedom from fear because he reigns, with all things under his feet.

It is a serious error, however, to define freedom in entirely negative terms, even if dictionaries make this mistake. According to one, freedom is 'the absence of hindrance, restraint, confinement, repression', while according to another to be free is to be 'not enslaved, not imprisoned, unrestricted, unrestrained, unhampered'. Every negative, however, has its positive counterpart. The true cry for freedom is not only for rescue from some tyranny, but also for liberty to live a full and meaningful life. Once a country has been delivered from a colonial regime, it is free to discover and develop its own national identity. Once the press is delivered from governmental control and censorship, it is free to publish the truth. Once a racial minority is delivered from discrimination, it is free to enjoy self-respect and dignity. For it is nationhood which is denied when a country is not free, truth when the press is not free, and self-respect when a minority is not free.

What, then, is the positive freedom of human beings? In 1970 Archbishop Michael Ramsey preached a series of four Cambridge University sermons, which were subsequently published under the title *Freedom, Faith and the Future*. In the first he posed the question: 'We know what we want to free men *from*. Do we know what we want to free men *for*?' He went on to answer his own question. Our striving for those freedoms 'which most palpably stir our feelings' (*e.g.* freedom from persecution, arbitrary imprisonment, crippling hunger and poverty) should always be 'in the context of the more radical and revolutionary issue of the freeing of man from self and for the glory of God'.[1]

[1] Michael Ramsey, *Freedom, Faith and the Future* (SPCK, 1970), p. 12.

It is this question of what we are set free for by Christ which we need to pursue. The principle is this: *True freedom is freedom to be our true selves, as God made us and meant us to be.* How can this principle be applied?

We must begin with God himself. Have you ever considered that God is the only being who enjoys perfect freedom? You could argue that he is not free. For his freedom is certainly not absolute in the sense that he can do absolutely anything whatsoever. Scripture itself tells us that he cannot lie, tempt or be tempted, or tolerate evil.[1] Nevertheless, God's freedom is perfect in the sense that he is free to do absolutely anything which he wills to do. God's freedom is freedom to be always entirely himself. There is nothing arbitrary, moody, capricious or unpredictable about him. He is constant, steadfast, unchanging. In fact the chief thing Scripture says he 'cannot' do (cannot because he will not) is to contradict himself. 'He cannot deny himself.'[2] To do this would not be freedom, but self-destruction. God finds his freedom in being himself, his true self.

What is true of God the Creator is also true of all created things and beings. Absolute freedom, freedom unlimited, is an illusion. If it is impossible for God (which it is), it is most certainly impossible for God's creation. God's freedom is freedom to be himself; our freedom is freedom to be ourselves. The freedom of every creature is limited by the nature which God has given it.

Take fish. God created fish to live and thrive in water. Their gills are adapted to absorb oxygen from water. Water is the only element in which a fish can find its fishiness, its identity as a fish, its fulfilment, its freedom. True, it is limited to water, but in that limitation is liberty. Supposing you keep a tropical fish at home. It lives not in a modern, rectangular, aerated tank, but in one of those old-fashioned, Victorian, spherical goldfish bowls. And supposing your fish swims round and round its blessed bowl until it finds its frustration unbearable, decides to make a

[1] *E.g.* Heb. 6:18; Jas. 1:13; Hab. 1:13. [2] 2 Tim. 2:13 (RSV).

bid for freedom and leaps out of its confinement. If somehow it manages to leap into a pond in your garden, it will increase its freedom. It is still in water, but there is more water to swim in. If instead it lands on the carpet, or on a concrete path, then of course its attempt to escape spells not freedom but death.

What, then, about human beings? If fish were made for water, what are human beings made for? I think we have to answer that, if water is the element in which fish find their fishiness, then the element in which humans find their humanness is love, the relationships of love. Morris West gives a striking example of this in his book *Children of the Sun*, which tells the story of the *scugnizzi*, the abandoned street children of Naples, and of Father Mario Borelli's love for them. 'There is one thing about us (that is Neapolitans)', Mario said to Morris, 'that never changes. *We have need of love as a fish has need of water*, as a bird has need of air.'[1] He went on to explain that every single one of the *scugnizzi* he knew 'had left home because there was no longer any love for him'.

But it is not the world's street children only who need to love and to be loved, and who discover that life spells love. It is all of us. It is in love that we find and fulfil ourselves. Moreover, the reason for this is not far to seek. It is that God is love in his essential being, so that when he made us in his own image, he gave us a capacity to love as he loves. It is not a random thing, therefore, that God's two great commandments are to love him and each other, for this is our destiny. A truly human existence is impossible without love. Living is loving, and without love we wither and die. As Robert Southwell, the sixteenth-century Roman Catholic poet, expressed it: 'Not when I breathe, but when I love, I live.' He was probably echoing Augustine's remark that the soul lives where it loves, not where it exists.

True love, however, places constraints on the lover, for love is essentially self-giving. And this brings us to a startling Christian paradox. True freedom is freedom to be my true self, as God made me and meant me to be. And God made me for loving.

[1] Morris West, *Children of the Sun* (1957; Pan, 1958), pp. 94–95.

But loving is giving, self-giving. Therefore, in order to be myself, I have to deny myself and give myself. In order to be free, I have to serve. In order to live, I have to die to my own self-centredness. In order to find myself, I have to lose myself in loving.

True freedom is, then, the exact opposite of what many people think. It is not freedom from all responsibility to God and others, in order to live for myself. That is bondage to my own self-centredness. Instead, true freedom is freedom from my silly little self, in order to live responsibly in love for God and others.

Yet the secular mind cannot come to terms with this Christian paradox of freedom through love. For example, Françoise Sagan, the French novelist, was interviewed shortly before her fiftieth birthday in 1985. She said she was perfectly satisfied with her life and had no regrets.

'You have had the freedom you wanted?'

'Yes.' Then she qualified her statement. 'I was obviously less free when I was in love with someone . . . But one's not in love all the time. Apart from that . . ., I'm free.'

The implication was clear: love inhibits liberty. The more you love, the less free you are, and *vice versa*. Presumably, therefore, the way to be completely free is to avoid all the entanglements of love, indeed to give up loving altogether.[1]

But Jesus taught the opposite in one of his favourite epigrams, which he seems to have quoted in different forms and contexts. In the formerly familiar language of the King James' Version, he said: 'Whoever would save his life will lose it; and whoever loses his life for my sake and the gospel's will save it.'[2] I used to imagine that Jesus was referring to martyrs who lay down their life for him. And the principle he is enunciating certainly includes them. But the 'life' he is talking about, which can be either saved or lost, is not our physical existence (*zōē*) but our soul or self (*psychē*), which is not infrequently used in place of

[1] The interview appeared in *Le Monde*, and in an English translation in the *Guardian Weekly* on 23 June 1985.
[2] Mk. 8:35.

the reflexive 'himself' or 'herself'. One could, then, perhaps paraphrase Jesus' epigram in these terms: 'If you insist on holding on to yourself, and on living for yourself, and refuse to let yourself go, you will lose yourself. But if you are willing to give yourself away in love, then, at the moment of complete abandon, when you imagine that everything is lost, the miracle takes place and you find yourself and your freedom.' It is only sacrificial service, the giving of the self in love to God and others, which is perfect freedom.

Authentic freedom, then, combines the negative (freedom from) with the positive (freedom for). Or, to put it another way, it brings together freedom from tyranny and freedom under authority. Jesus illustrated this in one of his best-known invitations:

> Come to me, all you who are weary and burdened, and I will give you rest. Take my yoke upon you and learn from me, for I am gentle and humble in heart, and you will find rest for your souls. For my yoke is easy and my burden is light.[1]

Here are actually two invitations, to which is attached a single promise. The promise is 'rest', which seems to include the notion of freedom. 'I will give you rest', Jesus says (verse 28). Again, 'you will find rest for your souls' (verse 29). But to whom does he promise rest? He gives it first to those who come to him 'weary and burdened', for he lifts their burdens and sets them free. He gives it secondly to those who take his yoke upon them and learn from him. Thus, true rest is found in Jesus Christ our Saviour, who frees us from the tyranny of guilt, self and fear, and in Jesus Christ our Lord, when we submit to his teaching authority. For his yoke is easy, his burden is light, and he himself is 'gentle and humble in heart'.

[1] Mt. 11:28–30.

CHAPTER THREE

CHRIST AND HIS CROSS

The gospel is good news of freedom. That was my theme in the last chapter. Yet this on its own is a one-sided emphasis. For what the gospel announces, according to the New Testament, is not just what Christ offers people today, but what he once did to make this offer possible. The apostolic gospel brings together the past and the present, the once and the now, historical event and contemporary experience. It declares not only that Jesus saves, but that he died for our sins, and was raised from death, in order to be able to do so. The gospel is not preached if the saving power is proclaimed and the saving events omitted, especially the cross.

In this chapter we will reflect on one of Paul's greatest statements about the origin, content and power of the gospel, and in particular about the centrality of Christ's cross.

> When I came to you, brothers, I did not come with eloquence or superior wisdom as I proclaimed to you the testimony about God. For I resolved to know nothing while I was with you except Jesus Christ and him crucified. I came to you in weakness and fear, and with much trembling. My message and my preaching were not with wise and persuasive words, but with a demonstration of the Spirit's power, so that your faith might not rest on men's wisdom, but on God's power.[1]

From this essentially trinitarian text three major lessons about evangelism stand out. They concern the Word of God, the cross of Christ and the power of the Spirit.

[1] 1 Cor. 2:1–5.

The Word of God

The gospel is truth from God. What Paul proclaimed to the Corinthians, he said, was not 'superior wisdom', that is, human wisdom or the wisdom of the world,[1] but the word of God or the wisdom of God, which he here calls either God's 'testimony' (*martyrion*) or God's 'mystery' (*mystērion*). The Greek words are similar and the manuscript evidence between them is fairly evenly balanced. Further, both occur within the first two chapters of this letter: *martyrion* may look back to 1:6, while *mystērion* may look forward to 2:7. Whichever is the correct reading, the sense is the same, namely that Paul's message came from God. If 'testimony' is right, then it is 'God's attested truth' (NEB). If 'mystery' is right, then it is 'God's secret truth' (GNB). In either case the apostle's gospel is God's truth.

This is where all true evangelism must begin. We have not invented our message. We do not come to people with our own human speculations. We are rather bearers of God's word, trustees of God's gospel, stewards of God's revealed secrets.

Moreover, Paul's delivery was compatible with his message. He came to the Corinthians neither with 'eloquence' nor with 'superior wisdom' (verse 1). As to content, he renounced proud human wisdom, humbly submitting instead to the word of God about Christ (verse 2). As to delivery, he renounced proud human rhetoric, humbly relying instead on the Holy Spirit's power (verses 3–5). As C. H. Hodge put it in his commentary, he came 'neither as a rhetorician nor as a philosopher'.[2]

Please do not misinterpret this. There is no possible justification here either for a gospel without content or for a style without form. What Paul was renouncing was neither doctrinal substance, nor rational argument, but only the wisdom and the rhetoric of the world. We know this because Luke tells us in Acts 18 what Paul's evangelistic ministry in Corinth had been like. First, 'he reasoned in the synagogue' every sabbath, 'trying

[1] 1 Cor. 1:20–21.
[2] C. H. Hodge, *The First Epistle to the Corinthians* (1857; Banner of Truth, 1959), p. 29.

to persuade Jews and Greeks' (verse 4). Then he stayed on for eighteen months 'teaching them the word of God' (verse 11). In consequence, he could sum up his preaching in Corinth in terms of 'trying to persuade people'.[1] He both taught the truth and convinced people of the truth.

We have no liberty, then, to invite people to come to Christ by closing, stifling or suspending their minds. No. Since God has made them rational beings, he expects them to use their minds. To be sure, they will never believe apart from the illumination of the Spirit. Without this all our arguments will be fruitless. 'But', wrote Gresham Machen, 'because argument is insufficient, it does not follow that it is unnecessary. What the Holy Spirit does in the new birth is not to make a person a Christian regardless of the evidence, but on the contrary to clear away the mists from his eyes and enable him to attend to the evidence.'[2]

So then, the gospel is truth from God, which has been committed to our trust. Our responsibility is to present it as clearly, coherently and cogently as we can, and like the apostles to argue it as persuasively as we can. And all the time, as we do this, we will be trusting the Holy Spirit of truth to dispel people's ignorance, overcome their prejudices and convince them about Christ.

The cross of Christ

We come now to verse 2: 'I resolved to know nothing while I was with you except Jesus Christ and him crucified.' Some people misread this as if Paul had written 'except Jesus Christ crucified' and conclude that his sole topic was the cross. What Paul actually wrote, however (and what is consistent with Luke's description in the Acts of his evangelistic labours), was that he determined to know nothing 'except Jesus Christ' (his message focused on him) 'and (especially though not exclusively) him crucified'. What about Christ's resurrection, then? It certainly loomed large in the

[1] 2 Cor. 5:11; *cf.* Acts 18:13.
[2] J. Gresham Machen, *The Christian Faith in the Modern World* (1936; Eerdmans, 1947), p. 63.

preaching of the apostles. Yet they understood and proclaimed it not as an isolated or independent event, but in relation to the cross. For the resurrection was not only the sequel to the death of Jesus; it was the reversal of the human verdict passed on him and the public vindication of the divine purpose in his death.

We now note that, before Paul arrived in Corinth, he made a decision to concentrate in his preaching on Christ, and especially on the cross. 'I decided' (RSV), he wrote, 'I determined' (AV), 'I resolved' (NEB, NIV) to do so. It is this decision which we have to investigate; why did he need to make it?

The popular reconstruction of the situation is well known. Paul arrived in Corinth from Athens. His sermon to the Athenian philosophers (so the theory goes) had been a flop. Not only had it been too intellectual, but Paul had not preached the gospel. He had focused on the creation instead of the cross. As a result, there had been no conversions. So, on his way from Athens to Corinth, Paul repented of the distorted gospel he had preached in Athens and resolved in Corinth to limit his message to the cross.

I confess that when I first heard this theory propounded, many years ago now, I swallowed it hook, line and sinker. Since then, however, I have had to reject it, for it does not stand up to examination. First, Paul's Athens mission had not been a failure. On the contrary, 'some men joined him and believed, among them Dionysius the Areopagite and a woman named Damaris and others with them'.[1] Secondly, Luke in his Acts narrative gives no hint that he thinks Paul's Athenian sermon a mistake; on the contrary he records it as a model of the apostle's preaching to Gentile intellectuals. Thirdly, Paul almost certainly did preach the cross in Athens, since he proclaimed 'Jesus and the resurrection',[2] and you cannot preach the resurrection without the death which preceded it. To be sure, because of his Gentile audience Paul began situationally with idolatry and creation, rather than with Old Testament Scripture, but he did not stop there. The sermon Luke records would have taken only

[1] Acts 17:34 (RSV). [2] Acts 17:18.

two minutes to preach; Paul must have elaborated this outline considerably. Fourthly, Paul did not in fact change his tactics in Corinth. As in Athens, so in Corinth, Luke portrays him continuing to argue, to teach and to persuade.[1]

What was Paul's decision, then? Behind every resolute decision there lies some previous indecision, a situation in which various options present themselves and we are obliged to choose, deciding for one of them over against the others. Evidently, then, behind Paul's decision to preach only Christ, and especially the cross, there lay an alternative, indeed a temptation, either to preach Christ without the cross, or not to preach Christ at all but rather the wisdom of the world. So why was this a temptation to Paul as he travelled from Athens to Corinth? It was not surely his imagined failure in Athens, but rather his fear of the reception awaiting him in Corinth. So who were these Corinthians that Paul should have been so intimidated by them and so apprehensive as he approached them ('in weakness and fear, and with much trembling', verse 3), and that he should have found it necessary to make a firm decision in relation to them?

As we ask and answer these questions, we shall also uncover the chief contemporary objections to the message of Christ and his cross. Indeed, we shall see why we ourselves need to make the same resolute decision today.

(a) *The intellectual objection*, or the foolishness of the cross. Paul had already encountered intellectual scorn in Athens. The philosophers had insulted him by calling him a *spermologos* or 'seed-picker'. The word was applied literally to scavenging birds, and so to vagrants who lived on scraps they could find in the gutter. Metaphorically it denoted teachers who trade only in second-hand ideas. The Athenians worshipped at the shrine of originality;[2] they despised the old-fashioned and the obsolete.

The philosophers scoffed when the resurrection was men-

[1] For a fuller refutation of the popular reconstruction, see my *The Message of Acts* in the Bible Speaks Today series (IVP, 1990), pp. 289–290.
[2] Acts 17:18, 21.

tioned.[1] 'They made fun of him' (GNB). I think that means they burst out laughing. How they reacted when Paul preached the cross Luke does not say. But Paul knew that it was 'a stumbling block to Jews and foolishness to Gentiles'.[2] To the unbelieving Jew it was inconceivable that the Messiah should die 'on a tree', that is, under the curse of God.[3] To the unbelieving Gentile it was ludicrous to suppose that a god, one of the immortals, should die. Celsus, the second-century cynic, was scathing in criticizing Christians for this. He imagined, wrote Origen, that '"in worshipping him who", as *he* says, "was taken prisoner and put to death, we are acting like"' others who actually worshipped dead people.[4]

Corinth had not escaped the intellectual arrogance of Athens. These cities were only about fifty miles apart as the crow flies. Paul's first letter to the Corinthians provides plenty of evidence that pride of intellect was one of the chief sins of the Corinthian church. This was the background against which Paul made his decision to renounce the wisdom of the world in favour of 'the foolishness of the cross'. Sneers and jeers awaited him. But he knew that 'the foolishness of God is wiser than man's wisdom'.[5]

Still today the message of the cross is deeply despised. The biblical, evangelical doctrine of the atonement (that Christ died instead of us, as our substitute, the death we deserved to die) is opposed and even mocked. It is said to be 'primitive', 'forensic', 'unjust', 'immoral' and 'barbaric'. A. J. Ayer called the allied Christian doctrines of sin and atonement 'intellectually contemptible and morally outrageous'.[6] And a contemporary liberal theologian has described aspects of my own presentation in *The Cross of Christ* as 'untenable', 'unintelligible', 'not only inexplicable but also incomprehensible', and so 'incommunicable'. How are we to respond to this battery of negative epithets? We do not deny that some evangelical formulations have been unbalanced and unbiblical. Whenever we have cast Jesus Christ in the role of a third party, who intervened to rescue us from an angry God, we

[1] Acts 17:32. [2] 1 Cor. 1:23. [3] Gal. 3:13.
[4] Origen, *Against Celsus*, III. 34.
[5] 1 Cor. 1:25.
[6] The *Guardian Weekly*, 30 August 1979.

have been guilty of a travesty which stands condemned, since it is God who loved the world and God who took the initiative to send his Son to die for us. Yet the initiative he took led to Christ being 'made sin' and 'made a curse' for us,[1] and such language often arouses an extraordinarily emotional hostility. Hence the temptation to trim the gospel of Christ crucified, to eliminate its more objectionable features, and to try to make it more palatable to sensitive modern palates. No wonder the apostle sounds almost fierce in expressing his decision to know only Jesus Christ and especially his cross. It was a choice between faithfulness and popularity.

(b) *The religious objection*, or the exclusiveness of the gospel. If Paul found Athens 'full of idols',[2] he is not likely to have found Corinth less idolatrous. It is known to have had at least two dozen temples, each dedicated to a different deity. Even today, surviving from the ancient temple of Apollo, seven massive pillars are still standing among the ruins of Corinth. And behind the city the rocky Acrocorinth rises nearly 2,000 feet above it, on which the temple of Aphrodite once stood. So the Corinthians, like the Athenians, were 'very religious'.[3] They honoured many gods, who tolerated one another in amicable co-existence.

The Corinthians would not have raised any objection if the Christian evangelists were content to add Jesus to their already well stocked pantheon. But the apostle Paul had a very different object in view when he visited the city. He wanted Corinth, with all its inhabitants and all its gods, to bow down and worship Jesus. He came to Corinth with the firm intention of knowing nothing 'except Jesus Christ and him crucified'. He knew very well, as he wrote to them later, that there were 'many "gods" and many "lords"' who were competing for their allegiance. But, as far as he was concerned, 'there is but one God, the Father, from whom all things came and for whom we live; and there is but one Lord, Jesus Christ, through whom all things came and through whom we live',[4] and he was not prepared to compromise. He thought of his visit as having effected their

[1] 2 Cor. 5:21; Gal. 3:13. [2] Acts 17:16. [3] Acts 17:22. [4] 1 Cor. 8:5–6.

betrothal to Christ, and he felt a godly jealousy for them. 'I promised you to one husband, to Christ, so that I might present you as a pure virgin to him,' he wrote. 'But I am afraid that just as Eve was deceived by the serpent's cunning, your minds may somehow be led astray from your sincere and pure devotion to Christ.'[1] For Jesus Christ would not share his glory with Apollo or Aphrodite or anybody else.

The world's religious situation has not greatly changed. True, the old gods of Greece and Rome have long since been discredited and discarded. But new gods have arisen in their place, and other ancient faiths have experienced a resurgence. As a result of modern communication media and ease of travel, many countries are increasingly pluralistic. What people want is an easygoing syncretism, a truce in inter-religious competition, a mishmash of the best from all religions. But we Christians cannot surrender either the finality or the uniqueness of Jesus Christ. There is simply nobody else like him; his incarnation, atonement and resurrection have no parallels. In consequence, he is the one and only mediator between God and the human race.[2] This exclusive affirmation is strongly, even bitterly, resented. It is regarded by many as intolerably intolerant. Yet the claims of truth compel us to maintain it, however much offence it may cause. I elaborate this topic in chapter 18.

(c) *The personal objection*, or the humbling of human pride. Common to all religions except Christianity is the flattering notion (expressed in different ways) that we are capable, if not of achieving our salvation, at least of contributing substantially to it. This doctrine of self-salvation is exceedingly conducive to our self-esteem. It appeals to our proud ego; it saves us from the ultimate embarrassment of being humbled before the cross.

The Corinthians were no exception; they were a proud people. They were proud of their city, which had been beautifully rebuilt by Julius Caesar in 46 BC, following its destruction for rebellion a century previously; proud that Augustus had promoted Corinth over Athens to be the capital of the new

[1] 2 Cor. 11:2–3. [2] 1 Tim. 2:5.

province of Achaia; proud of their trade, their affluence, their culture, their Isthmian games, and their religious zeal.

Then along came this brash Christian missionary, this whippersnapper, this ugly little fellow with a bald pate, bandy legs and beetle brows, who appeared to have no respect for their distinguished city. He presumed to tell them that neither their wisdom, nor their wealth, nor their religion could save them; that they could not in fact save themselves from the judgment of God – or even help towards their salvation – by anything they could do; that this was why Jesus Christ had died for them; and that apart from him they would perish. Who did he think he was to insult them in this way? It was a stunning humiliation to a proud people. The message of the cross was a stumbling-block to proud Jews and proud Gentiles alike. No wonder the main response to the gospel in Corinth came from the lower echelons of society: 'Not many of you were wise by human standards; not many were influential; not many were of noble birth.' Instead, it was the foolish, the weak, the lowly, and the despised, who knew they had nothing to offer, whom God chose and called.[1]

Still today nothing keeps people out of the kingdom of God more than pride. As Emil Brunner put it, in all other religions 'man is spared the final humiliation of knowing that the Mediator (*sc.* Jesus Christ) must bear the punishment instead of him . . . He is not stripped absolutely naked'.[2] But the gospel strips us naked (we have no clothing in which to appear before God), and declares us bankrupt (we have no currency with which to buy the favour of heaven).

(d) *The moral objection*, or the call to repentance and holiness. Corinth was a flourishing commercial centre, which commanded the trade routes both north–south by land and east–west by sea. So the city was full of merchants, travellers and sailors. Being strangers in a strange city, they exercised little moral restraint. Besides, Aphrodite, known to the Romans as Venus, the goddess of love, held court in her temple above the

[1] 1 Cor. 1:26–29.
[2] Emil Brunner, *The Mediator* (1927; Westminster, 1947), p. 474.

city, encouraged sexual promiscuity among her devotees, and provided a thousand prostitutes to roam the city's streets by night. Corinth was the Vanity Fair of the ancient world. The Greek verb *korinthiazomai* meant 'to practise immorality'.

A brazenly immoral city like Corinth could hardly be expected to welcome the gospel, with its summons to repentance, its warnings that the sexually dissolute will not inherit God's kingdom,[1] and its insistence that after justification comes sanctification (growth in holiness) and after sanctification glorification (when evil will be abolished).

The modern world is no more friendly to the gospel's call to self-control than was the ancient world. It likes to say that there are no such things as moral absolutes any longer, that sexual morality is only a matter of sexual mores, that restraint is bad and permissiveness good, and that Christianity with its prohibitions is the enemy of freedom.

(e) *The political objection*, or the lordship of Jesus Christ. There was a lot of political fervour – even fanaticism – in the Roman Empire. Loyal Roman procurators tended to encourage it, and acted ruthlessly to put down any attempt at rebellion. We need to remember that Jesus himself was condemned in a Roman court for the political offence of sedition, for claiming to be a king in rivalry to Caesar. Similarly, Paul and Silas were accused in Philippi of 'advocating customs unlawful for us Romans to accept or practise',[2] while in Thessalonica they were said to be 'defying Caesar's decrees, saying that there is another king, one called Jesus'.[3]

Were these charges true or untrue? They were both. Of course neither Jesus nor the apostles ever stirred up armed rebellion against Rome. They were not zealots. But they did proclaim that Jesus had ushered in God's kingdom, that his kingdom took precedence over all lesser loyalties, that it would spread throughout the world, and that the king was coming back to take his power and reign. It sounded positively seditious. Indeed, it *was* seditious if 'sedition' means denying

[1] 1 Cor. 6:9–10. [2] Acts 16:21. [3] Acts 17:7.

undisputed authority to the state by according it to God's Christ.

Still today the one thing a totalitarian regime cannot endure is to be refused the total allegiance which it covets. Christians submit conscientiously to the state, in so far as its God-given authority is used to promote good and punish evil, but we will not worship it. It is Christ we worship, to whom all authority in heaven and on earth has been given. For he died and rose in order to be Lord of all.

Here then are five objections which are levelled against the gospel of Christ and his cross, and which Paul expected to encounter in Corinth. He knew that his message of Christ crucified would be regarded as intellectually foolish (incompatible with wisdom), religiously exclusive (incompatible with tolerance), personally humiliating (incompatible with self-esteem), morally demanding (incompatible with freedom) and politically subversive (incompatible with patriotism).

No wonder Paul felt 'weak . . ., nervous and shaking with fear',[1] and recognized that he had to make a decision. It was on the one hand a negative decision to renounce the wisdom of the world, namely every system which is offered as an alternative to the gospel, and on the other hand a positive decision to proclaim nothing but Jesus Christ, and especially his cross. The same alternative faces us today. It is the choice between the wisdom of the world, which is foolishness to God, and the foolishness of the cross, which is the wisdom of God.

The power of the Spirit

Some contemporary Christians, hearing Paul's confession of weakness, fear and trembling, would doubtless have rebuked him. 'Paul,' they might have said, 'you've no business to feel nervous or afraid. Pull yourself together! Don't you know what it is to be filled with the Spirit? You ought to be strong, confident and bold.'

[1] 1 Cor. 2:3 (NEB).

But Paul was not afraid to admit that he was afraid. To be sure, he had a mighty intellect and a strong personality, and these powers he had dedicated to Christ. But he was also physically weak and emotionally vulnerable. According to tradition his appearance was unprepossessing. His critics said that 'in person he is unimpressive and his speaking amounts to nothing'.[1] So he was nothing much to look at or to listen to. In addition, disease of some kind (his so-called 'thorn in the flesh'[2]) seems to have affected his eyesight and even disfigured him.[3] And he knew the unpopularity of his gospel, the opposition it would arouse in Corinth, and so the cost of being faithful to it.

In what, then, did he put his trust? He tells us in 1 Corinthians 2:4–5. His confidence was not in 'wise and persuasive words' (NIV) or 'plausible words of wisdom' (RSV). That is, he relied neither on the wisdom nor on the eloquence of the world. Instead of the world's wisdom he preached Christ and his cross (verses 1–2), and instead of the world's rhetoric he trusted in the powerful demonstration which the Holy Spirit gives to the word. For only the Holy Spirit can convince people of their sin and need, open their eyes to see the truth of Christ crucified, bend their proud wills to submit to him, set them free to believe in him, and bring them to new birth. This is the powerful 'demonstration' which the Holy Spirit gives to words spoken in human weakness.

This theme of 'power through weakness' is a vital element in Paul's Corinthian correspondence. In both extant letters the apostle emphasizes that it is through human weakness that divine power operates best. He hints that God deliberately makes and keeps his people weak in order to show that the power is his.[4] Paul even adds that the principle applies to God as well as to us, for it is through his own weakness in the cross that he puts forth his power to save.

In 1 Corinthians 1 and 2 the same theme of power through weakness is repeated in three variations. First, we have a weak

[1] 2 Cor. 10:10. [2] 2 Cor. 12:7. [3] *E.g.* Gal. 4:13–14.
[4] See *hina* ('in order that') in 2 Cor. 4:7 and 12:9–10.

and foolish message (Christ and the cross). Secondly, it is proclaimed by weak and foolish preachers. Thirdly, it is welcomed by weak and foolish people. Thus God chose a weak instrument (Paul) to bring a weak message (the cross) to weak people (the Corinthian working class). Why? It was 'so that no-one may boast before him' and so that he who does boast will 'boast in the Lord' alone.[1]

The first five verses of 1 Corinthians 2 are perhaps the noblest and richest statement on evangelism in the New Testament. They tell us that the gospel is truth from God about Christ and his cross in the power of the Spirit. Thus the gospel is not human speculation but divine revelation; not popular wisdom but Christ and his despised cross; not by the pressures of advertisement or personality, but by the Holy Spirit. The gospel comes from God, focuses on Christ and him crucified, and is authenticated by the Holy Spirit. This is the trinitarian evangelism of the New Testament.

[1] 1 Cor. 1:29–31.

CHAPTER FOUR

THE RELEVANCE OF THE RESURRECTION

The most fantastic of all Christian claims is that Jesus Christ rose from the dead. It strains our credulity to the limit. Human beings have tried with all possible ingenuity both to defy and to deny death. But only Christ has claimed to conquer it, that is, to defeat it in his own experience, and to deprive it of its power over others. 'I am the resurrection and the life,' he declared. 'He who believes in me will live, even though he dies; and whoever lives and believes in me will never die.'[1] Again, 'I am the Living One; I was dead, and behold I am alive for ever and ever! And I hold the keys of (*i.e.* have authority over) death and Hades.'[2]

Moreover, the very first Christians already enjoyed this confidence. This is clear both from their brave and even joyful readiness to die for Christ, and from the earliest preaching of the apostles. Soon after Pentecost, Luke tells us, the Jewish authorities in Jerusalem 'were greatly disturbed because the apostles were . . . proclaiming in Jesus the resurrection of the dead'.[3] The heart of their sermons follows the same pattern: 'you killed him, God raised him, and we are witnesses'.[4] And Paul did not deviate from this,[5] so that the Athenian philosophers, listening to him in the market-place, concluded that he was advocating two foreign deities, because they heard his repeated references to *Iēsous* and *Anastasis* (resurrection).[6] Then, when he came later to pass on to the Corinthians an

[1] Jn. 11:25–26. [2] Rev. 1:18. [3] Acts 4:2.
[4] *E.g.* Acts 2:23–24, 32; 3:13–15; 5:30–32.
[5] *E.g.* Acts 13:28–31. [6] Acts 17:18.

outline of the original gospel he had himself received, he concentrated 'as of first importance' on the death, burial, resurrection and appearances of Jesus.[1] Those earliest followers of Jesus seem to have been both clear and confident about his resurrection.

Three major questions are raised by the claim that Jesus rose (or was raised) from the dead. First, what does it mean (a question of semantics)? Secondly, did it really happen (a question of history)? Thirdly, is it important (a question of relevance)?

What does the resurrection mean?

The semantic question was forced into the public mind in the 1980s by some provocative remarks of David Jenkins, Bishop of Durham. These were interpreted, at least by the popular press, as a rather shocking denial of the resurrection of Jesus Christ.

It is important to be fair to Dr Jenkins, however. He describes himself as a 'believing', not a 'doubting', bishop. He insists that he responded to the questions put to him when he was consecrated a bishop 'unhesitatingly', 'affirmatively' and 'in complete good faith'. Certainly in his earlier books he clearly affirmed the doctrines of the divine–human person of Jesus and of the Trinity. Thus, in his 1966 Bampton Lectures entitled *The Glory of Man* he wrote: 'God and man are distinct realities, who, in and as Jesus Christ, are in perfect union.'[2] And in his 1974 Edward Cadbury Lectures in Birmingham University, which were entitled *The Contradiction of Christianity* and explored what it means to be human, he spoke of the Trinity as 'the necessary legitimate interpretation of the experienced and perceived story of God, Jesus and the Spirit'.[3]

Dr Jenkins also declares that he believes in the resurrection of Jesus Christ. He made the following statement to his Diocesan Synod in early November 1984: 'I do believe in the resurrection of Jesus Christ from the dead. . . . Anyone who says that I do

[1] 1 Cor. 15:3–8. [2] (SCM, new edition, 1971), p. 99. [3] (SCM, 1976), p. 154.

not believe in the resurrection . . . is a liar. This I must say fiercely and categorically.' He will not convince people, however, merely by the use of strong and rather intemperate language. We still have to press the semantic question: what does he mean? In what sense does he believe in the resurrection?

During the service in York Minster in which he was made a bishop, he was asked: 'Do you accept the doctrine of the Christian faith as the Church of England has received it?' Those last eight words are an important qualification. They imply a distinction between two possible ways of 'accepting' Christian doctrine. One might be called 'traditional', namely the acceptance of doctrine in the same way as the Church of England has itself received and understood it from the Scriptures and the Creeds. The other might be called 'idiosyncratic', namely the acceptance of doctrine in the way in which the individual person questioned feels able to receive it, which may deviate widely from biblical teaching and traditional understanding. Dr Jenkins must have answered 'yes' to the question in the latter sense, since he does not believe that the resurrection involved the transformation of the body of Jesus, which is what the Church of England has always believed and taught. Indeed, he caricatured this view in 1988 as 'a conjuring trick with bones', and at Easter 1989 declared that the risen Lord was 'neither a corpse nor a ghost', as if we were shut up to that alternative.

What light can be thrown on the semantic question? What is meant in the Creed by the resurrection of Jesus Christ? How should we think of the risen Lord? It may be helpful if we clarify what we do not believe, before coming on to affirm what we do.

First, the risen Lord is not just *a surviving influence*. On the one hand, we are not to think of him as having merely survived death, like a ghost. 'Look at my hands and my feet,' he said. 'It is I myself! Touch me and see; a ghost does not have flesh and bones, as you see I have.'[1] On the other hand, 'resurrection' does not mean the mere survival of an influence. Many leaders, who during their lifetime have held sway over their contem-

[1] Lk. 24:39.

poraries' hearts and minds, live on after death in the sense that the memory of their example is a continuing inspiration.

This was certainly true of Che Guevara. He had an extraordinary following. Sartre once described him as 'the most complete man of his age'. In his thirty-nine years (before he was killed in the jungle) he had been a doctor, author, economist, banker, political theorist and guerrilla fighter. He became a legend during his lifetime, a folk hero. In every Cuban classroom the children would chant, 'We will be like Che.' And after his death his influence became greater still. He provided Marxists with the image of a secular saint and martyr. For years the walls of Latin American student buildings were chalked with the words 'Che lives!' [1]

It was similar when Archbishop Makarios of Cyprus died in August 1977. His followers paint-sprayed public buildings with the words 'Makarios lives!'

Is this all Christians mean when they say that 'Jesus lives'? Some seem to be saying little more than this, namely that he exerts his power and spreads his love in the world. Others are affirming some kind of continuing, personal existence for Jesus, so that 'he walks with me and talks with me along life's narrow way'. Yet the grand affirmation of the New Testament is not 'he lives', but 'he is risen'. The resurrection becomes an experience for us only because it was first an event which actually inaugurated a new order of reality.

Secondly, the risen Lord is not *a resuscitated corpse.* Resurrection is not a synonym for resuscitation in either of this word's two uses. To 'resuscitate' can mean either to revive a patient who has gone into a coma or to bring someone back to life who has been pronounced clinically dead. In this second sense Jesus is recorded as having performed three resuscitations during his public ministry. He 'raised from death' (*i.e.* restored to this life) the daughter of Jairus, the son of the widow of Nain, and Lazarus. Each of these three was dead, but was brought back to this life by Jesus. One understands the sympathy which

[1] See Andrew Sinclair, *Guevara* (Fontana, 1970), especially pp. 70 and 88.

C. S. Lewis expressed for Lazarus: 'To be brought back and have all one's dying to do again was rather hard.'[1]

But Jesus' own resurrection was not a resuscitation in either sense. On the one hand, he was not revived from a swoon or coma, for he had been dead for about thirty-six hours. On the other hand, he was not brought back to this life, with the need to die again. Yet it is popularly supposed that this is what Christians believe about 'resurrection', namely that the body is miraculously reconstituted out of the identical particles of which it is at present composed, and that it then resumes this vulnerable and mortal life. But on the contrary, Jesus was raised to a new plane of existence, in which he was now no longer mortal but 'alive for ever and ever'.[2]

In these first two negatives we agree with the Bishop of Durham. The resurrection was not 'a conjuring trick with bones', and the risen Lord is 'neither a corpse nor a ghost'. The tragedy is that, in using this rather sensational language, the bishop gave the impression that traditional Christian believers are committed to one or other of these options. But, whatever popular notions some people may have entertained, the faith of the church has never been to regard the risen Lord either as a rather ethereal ghostly influence or as a resuscitated corpse.

Thirdly, the risen Lord is not *a revived faith* in the experience of his disciples. This was Rudolf Bultmann's 'demythologized' reconstruction. He began by declaring that the resurrection of Jesus was 'obviously . . . not an event of past history'. Why was this so obvious to him? Because 'an historical fact which involves a resurrection from the dead is utterly inconceivable'. But since the church in every age seems to have had very little difficulty in conceiving what Bultmann pronounced inconceivable, what was his problem? It lay in the 'incredibility of a mythical event like the resuscitation of a corpse – for that is what the resurrection means'. What is truly incredible, however, is not the resurrection of Jesus, but the misunderstanding of Bultmann who confused it with a resuscitation. How then

[1] *Letters of C. S. Lewis*, ed. W. H. Lewis (Geoffrey Bles, 1966), p. 307.
[2] Rev. 1:18.

did he interpret the 'myth' of Jesus' resurrection? In this way: 'if the event of Easter Day is in any sense an historical event additional to the event of the cross, it is nothing else than the rise of faith in the risen Lord . . . All that historical criticism can establish is the fact that the first disciples came to believe in the resurrection.' In other words, Easter was not an event, but an experience; not the objective, historical resurrection of Jesus from the dead, but a subjective, personal recovery of faith in the hearts and minds of his followers.[1]

Fourthly, the risen Lord is not just *an expanded personality*. Yet this seems to express what David Jenkins believes. In 1969 he wrote: 'The resurrection means that God acted to establish Jesus in his person, in his achievements and in his continuing effect.'[2] In a later statement he declared his conviction that Jesus 'rose from the dead', and went on to explain this by affirming that 'the very life and power and purpose and personality which was in him was actually continuing . . . in the sphere of history, so that he was a risen and living presence and possibility'.[3] Elsewhere, he has spoken of the resurrection as an 'explosion' of the personality of Jesus. In fact, he constantly refers to Jesus' 'personality', and thinks of the resurrection as its 'establishment' or 'liberation' or 'explosion'. So the resurrection was a kind of event, even though it did not involve his body. Dr Jenkins believes in the 'risenness' and 'livingness' of Jesus, though his personality is not now embodied (except in the church).

Fifthly, the risen Lord is not merely *a living experience of the Spirit*. Probably the most comprehensive treatment of the resurrection theme in recent years is *The Structure of Resurrection Belief* by Dr Peter Carnley, Anglican Archbishop of Perth, Western Australia. Like Dr Jenkins he emphasizes that we should think of the resurrection as a present experience rather than a past event, especially as an experience of the Spirit. In his

[1] Rudolf Bultmann, *Kerygma and Myth* (1941; ET SPCK, 1953), pp. 38–42.
[2] David Jenkins, *Living with Questions* (SCM, 1969), pp. 138–139. See also the critique by J. Murray Harris entitled *Easter in Durham* (Paternoster, 1985).
[3] From the television programme *Credo* in April 1984.

opening chapter he makes plain his sceptical stance. He asserts that Paul nowhere alludes to the empty tomb, even in 1 Corinthians 15:3–8, and that the so-called appearances were not objective. He argues that *ōphthē* ('he appeared') means not so much perception through sight (a visible appearance) as the reception of a new revelation (an intellectual apprehension), or at most a mixture of the two, with the emphasis on the second.[1]

Next come three long chapters in which Archbishop Carnley urges that there was, in fact, no post-mortem event; the real Easter event was the disciples' coming to faith.[2] Consequently, from chapter 5 onwards he refers no longer to 'the resurrection' (an event) but to 'the raised Christ' (an experience). For the Easter faith 'involves a post-mortem experience of encounter with the raised Christ', who is known as the Spirit.[3] And the way we come to recognize the true Spirit of Jesus is that he continues to manifest today in the Christian fellowship the same self-giving love which he displayed on the cross.[4] But, ingenious as this attempted reconstruction is, it cannot be said to do justice to the data of the New Testament, as I hope soon to show.

Sixthly, and in contrast to the previous five proposals, the risen Lord is *a transformed person*. The evidence adduced by the Gospels is that, before and after the resurrection, Jesus is the same person with the same identity ('It is I myself'),[5] but that the resurrection gave him a transformed, transfigured, glorified body. The resurrection was a dramatic act of God by which he arrested the natural process of decay and decomposition ('you will not . . . let your Holy One see decay'[6]), rescued Jesus out of the realm of death, and changed his body into a new vehicle for his personality, endowed with new powers and possessing immortality.

'I believe in the resurrection', Dr Jenkins has said, 'in exactly the same sense as St Paul believed in the resurrection.'[7] But how

[1] Peter Carnley, *The Structure of Resurrection Belief* (Clarendon Press, 1987), pp. 17ff.
[2] *Ibid.*, p. 164. [3] *Ibid.*, pp. 200, 266. [4] *Ibid.*, p. 368. [5] Lk. 24:39.
[6] Acts 2:27.
[7] Although I cannot trace this exact quotation, Bishop Jenkins has written similarly: 'I share the faith of the Apostles and I follow St Paul's account of the Resurrection' (*Free to Believe* by David Jenkins and his daughter Rebecca, BBC Enterprises, 1991, p. 44).

can he say this when he does not believe in a bodily resurrection? It is because of 1 Corinthians 15. This great chapter is in two parts, the first relating to the *fact* (verses 1–34), and the second to the *nature* (verses 35–38), of the resurrection. In the first part the resurrection appearances of Jesus appear to be physical; but in the second part the body is said to be 'sown a natural (RSV 'physical') body, . . . raised a spiritual body' (verse 44). How, then, are we to harmonize the two halves of 1 Corinthians 15 with each other? Some scholars seize on the expression 'a spiritual body' and insist that the resurrection appearances of verses 5–8 must be understood in the light of it.

According to the New Testament as a whole, however, the assimilation process should be the other way round, and the nature of the 'spiritual body' must be interpreted in such a way as not to contradict the evidence that the resurrected Jesus had a physical body. This evidence is not to be found only in the Gospel narratives of the empty tomb (which liberal scholars tend to dismiss as being in their view too late to be trustworthy), but in the first sermons of Peter and in the early verses of 1 Corinthians 15. I will focus on the latter. In Paul's statement of the gospel, which he claims to be both the *original* gospel, which he had himself 'received' (verse 3), and the *universal* gospel, which they and he all believed (verse 11), he made four affirmations, namely that 'Christ died . . ., that he was buried, that he was raised on the third day . . ., and that he appeared . . .'. Two aspects of the resurrection of Jesus are clear from this.

First, it was *an objective, historical event*. Indeed, it was datable; it happened 'on the third day'. David Jenkins has called it 'not an event, but a series of experiences'. But no, it became a series of experiences only because it was first an event. And in God's providence the words 'on the third day' witness to the historicity of Jesus' resurrection, much as the words 'under Pontius Pilate' in the Apostles' Creed witness to the historicity of his sufferings and death.

Secondly, the resurrection was *a physical event*; it involved his body. The argument now is that the four verbs (died, was buried, was raised, appeared) all have the same subject, namely 'Christ' as a historical, physical person. This is beyond question in the case of the first two. It was his body which died and his body which was buried. The natural presumption, then, is that the very same historical, physical Christ is the subject of the third and fourth verbs, namely that he was raised and then appeared. It would take a high degree of mental gymnastics to claim that without warning the subject changes in the middle of the sentence, that although his body died and was buried, only his personality was raised and seen, and that in fact he was raised while still remaining buried. No, since it was his body which was buried, it must have been his body which was raised. This probably explains the mention of his burial in some of the early apostolic sermons.[1] It is entirely gratuitous, in the light of this, to maintain that the apostle Paul was ignorant of the empty tomb.

It is true that, when the dead and buried body of Jesus was 'raised', it was changed in the process. We are envisaging neither a resuscitation (in which he was raised bodily but not changed), nor a survival (in which he was changed into a ghost, but not raised bodily at all), but a resurrection (in which he was both raised and changed simultaneously).

Did the resurrection really happen?

Let us grant that the apostles, including Paul, did believe in a literal, datable, physical resurrection and transformation of Jesus; were they correct? Can we, who live in the sophisticated, contemporary world of astrophysics, microbiology and computer science, also believe in the resurrection? Yes, we can and we should. Many millions do.

Several books have been written to marshal the evidence for the resurrection.[2] This is an important part of Christian apolo-

[1] *E.g.* Acts 2:23–32; 13:28–31, 37.

[2] See for example Frank Morison, *Who Moved the Stone?* (Faber, 1930); J. N. D. Anderson, *The Evidence for the Resurrection* (IVP, 1950); Stuart Jackman, *The Davidson File* (Lutterworth, 1982); E. M. B. Green, *The Day Death Died* (IVP, 1982); J. W. Wenham, *Easter Enigma* (Paternoster, 1984).

getics. All I can attempt here is a straightforward summary of the main lines of evidence.

First, there is *the disappearance of the body*. Everybody agrees that Joseph's tomb was empty, even those who deny the Gospel writers' stories; the rumours of resurrection could never have gained credence if people could have visited the tomb and found the body still in position. So the body had gone. The question has always been, 'What became of it?' No satisfactory explanation has been given of its disappearance, except for the resurrection.

We cannot accept that Jesus only fainted on the cross, then revived in the tomb, and subsequently came out of it by himself. For one thing, first the centurion and later Pilate assured themselves that Jesus was dead. For another, when he did emerge, he gave people the impression that he had conquered death, not that he had almost been conquered by it and was now a seriously sick man in need of hospital treatment.

So did the authorities (Roman or Jewish) deliberately remove the body, in order to prevent the disciples from spreading the rumour that he had risen? It is hard to believe this, since, when the apostles began to proclaim 'Jesus and the resurrection',[1] the authorities could have immediately scotched the new movement by producing the body, instead of which they resorted to violence.

In this case, did the disciples steal the body as part of a hoax, in order to deceive people into thinking that he had risen? That is an impossible theory, for they were prepared to suffer and die for the gospel, and people are not willing to become martyrs for a lie which they have themselves perpetrated.

No explanation of the empty tomb holds water except that God had raised him from the dead.

Secondly, there is *the reappearance of the Lord*. For if Jesus' body had disappeared from the tomb where it had been laid to rest, Jesus himself kept reappearing during a period of nearly six weeks. He is said to have showed himself to certain individuals

[1] Acts 4:2.

(*e.g.* Mary Magdalene, Peter and James), to the Twelve, both with and without Thomas, and on one occasion 'to more than five hundred of the brothers at the same time', most of whom were still alive when Paul wrote this in about AD 54,[1] and could therefore have been cross-examined.

These resurrection appearances cannot be dismissed as inventions, since it is plain beyond doubt that the apostles really believed that Jesus had risen. The stories had not been made up. But nor were they hallucinations. Tough fishermen like Peter, James and John are not the kind of personalities who might be susceptible to such symptoms of mental disorder. Further, the great variety of time, place, mood and people in regard to the appearances, together with people's initial reaction of unbelief, make the theory of wishful thinking untenable. The only alternative to inventions and hallucinations is valid, objective appearances.

Thirdly, there is *the emergence of the church*. Something happened to change the apostles and to send them out on their mission to the world. When Jesus died, they were heartbroken, confused and frightened. But within less than two months they came out of hiding, full of joy, confidence and courage. What can account for this dramatic transformation? Only the resurrection, together with Pentecost which followed soon afterwards. From that bunch of disillusioned nobodies has grown a universal community numbering one third of the population of the world. It would take a lot of credulity, even of cynicism, to believe that the whole Christian edifice had been built on a lie, since Jesus Christ never rose from the dead.

The disappearance of the body, the reappearance of the Lord and the emergence of the church together constitute a solid foundation for believing in the resurrection.

Why is the resurrection important?

What we have to ask about the resurrection is not only whether

[1] 1 Cor. 15:6.

it happened, but whether it really matters whether it happened. For if it happened, it happened nearly 2,000 years ago. How can an event of such remote antiquity have any great importance for us today? Why on earth do Christians make such a song and dance about it? Is it not irrelevant? No; my argument now is that the resurrection resonates with our human condition. It speaks to our needs as no other distant event does or could. It is the mainstay of our Christian assurance.

First, the resurrection of Jesus assures us of *God's forgiveness*. We have already noted that forgiveness is one of our most basic needs and one of God's best gifts. The head of a large English mental hospital has been quoted as saying, 'I could dismiss half my patients tomorrow if they could be assured of forgiveness.'[1] For we all have a skeleton or two in some dark cupboard, memories of things we have thought, said or done, of which in our better moments we are thoroughly ashamed. Our conscience nags, condemns, torments us.

Several times during his public ministry Jesus spoke words of forgiveness and of peace, and in the upper room he referred to the communion cup as his 'blood of the covenant ... poured out for many for the forgiveness of sins'.[2] Thus he linked our forgiveness with his death. And since throughout Scripture death is always welded to sin as its just desert ('the wages of sin is death'),[3] he can have meant only that he was going to die in our place the death which we deserved to die, in order that we might be spared and forgiven.

That is what he said. But how can we know that he was right, that he achieved by his death what he said he would achieve, and that God accepted his death in our place as 'a full, perfect, and sufficient sacrifice, oblation, and satisfaction, for the sins of the whole world'? The answer is that, if he had remained dead, if he had not been visibly and publicly raised from death, we would never have known. Rather, without the resurrection we would have to conclude that his death was a failure. The apostle Paul saw this logic clearly: 'If Christ has not been raised, our

[1] Jack C. Winslow, *Confession and Absolution* (Hodder and Stoughton, 1960), p. 22.
[2] Mt. 26:28. [3] Rom. 6:23.

preaching is useless and so is your faith.' Again, 'if Christ has not been raised, your faith is futile; you are still in your sins. Then those also who have fallen asleep in Christ are lost.'[1] The terrible consequences of no resurrection would be that the apostles are false witnesses, believers are unforgiven, and the Christian dead have perished. But in fact, Paul continued, Christ was raised from the dead, and by raising him God has assured us that he approves of his sin-bearing death, that he had not died in vain, and that those who trust in him receive a full and free forgiveness. The resurrection validates the cross.

Secondly, the resurrection of Jesus assures us of *God's power*. For we need God's power in the present as well as his forgiveness of the past. Is God really able to change human nature, which appears to be so intractable, to make cruel people kind, selfish people unselfish, immoral people self-controlled, and sour people sweet? Is he able to take people who are dead to spiritual reality, and make them alive in Christ? Yes, he really is! He is able to give life to the spiritually dead, and to transform us into the likeness of Christ.

But these are great claims. Can they be substantiated? Only because of the resurrection. Paul prays that the eyes of our heart may be enlightened, so that we may know 'his incomparably great power for us who believe'. And to help us grasp the measure of this power, not only does God give us an inward illumination by his Spirit, but he has given us an outward, public, objective demonstration of it in the resurrection. For the power available for us today is the very power 'which he exerted in Christ when he raised him from the dead . . .'.[2] The resurrection is thus portrayed as the supreme evidence in history of the creative power of God.

We are always in danger of trivializing the gospel, of minimizing what God is able to do for us and in us. We speak of becoming a Christian as if it were no more than turning over a new leaf, making a few superficial adjustments to our usual patterns of behaviour, and becoming a bit more religious. Then

[1] 1 Cor. 15:14, 17–18. [2] Eph. 1:18–20.

scratch the surface, crack the veneer, and behold! underneath we are still the same old pagan, unredeemed and unchanged. But no, becoming and being a Christian according to the New Testament is something much more radical than this. It is a decisive act of God. It is nothing less than a resurrection from the death of alienation and self-centredness, and the beginning of a new and liberated life. In a word, the same God of supernatural power, who raised Jesus from physical death, can raise us from spiritual death. And we know he can raise *us* because we know he raised *him*.

Thirdly, the resurrection of Jesus assures us of *God's ultimate triumph*. One of the major differences between the religions and ideologies of the world concerns their vision of the future. Some offer no hope, but sink into existential despair. Bertrand Russell, when still a young man of only thirty, expressed his conviction that

> no fire, no heroism, no intensity of thought and feeling, can preserve an individual life beyond the grave; that all the labours of the ages, all the devotion, all the inspiration, all the noonday brightness of human genius, are destined to extinction in the vast death of the solar system, and that the whole temple of man's achievement must inevitably be buried beneath the debris of a universe in ruins.[1]

Others think of history more in circular than in linear terms, as an endless cycle of reincarnations, with no release but the non-existence of *nirvana*. Marxists continue to promise Utopia on earth, but the vision has lost credibility. Secular humanists dream of taking control of their own evolution, but, in so far as this would involve genetic manipulation, the dream degenerates into a nightmare.

Christians, on the other hand, are confident about the future, and our Christian 'hope' (which is a sure expectation) is both individual and cosmic. Individually, apart from Christ, the fear

[1] Bertrand Russell, *A Free Man's Worship* (1902; Unwin Paperbacks, 1976), pp. 10–17.

of personal death and dissolution is almost universal. For us in the West Woody Allen typifies this terror. It has become an obsession with him. True, he can still joke about it. 'It's not that I'm afraid to die,' he quips; 'I just don't want to be there when it happens.'[1] But mostly he is filled with dread. In a 1977 article in *Esquire* he said: 'The fundamental thing behind *all* motivation and *all* activity is the constant struggle against annihilation and against death. It's absolutely stupefying in its terror, and it renders anyone's accomplishments meaningless.'

Jesus Christ, however, rescues his disciples from this horror. We will not only survive death, but be raised from it. We are to be given new bodies like his resurrection body,[2] with new and undreamed-of powers.[3] For he is called both the 'firstfruits' of the harvest[4] and 'the firstborn from the dead'.[5] Both metaphors give the same assurance. He was the first to rise; all his people will follow. We will have a body like his. 'Just as we have borne the likeness of the earthly man (Adam) so shall we bear the likeness of the man from heaven (Christ).'[6]

Our hope for the future, however, is also cosmic. We believe that Jesus Christ is going to return in spectacular magnificence, in order to bring history to its fulfilment in eternity. He will not only raise the dead, but regenerate the universe;[7] he will make all things new.[8] We are persuaded that the whole creation is going to be set free from its present bondage to decay and death; that the groans of nature are the labour pains which promise the birth of a new world;[9] and that there is going to be a new heaven and a new earth, which will be the home of righteousness.[10]

So then, the living hope of the New Testament is an impressively 'material' expectation for both the individual and the cosmos. The individual believer is promised not survival merely, not even immortality, but a resurrected, transformed body. And

[1] Graham McCann, *Woody Allen, New Yorker* (Polity Press, 1990), pp. 43 and 83.
[2] *E.g.* Phil. 3:21. [3] 1 Cor. 15:42–44. [4] 1 Cor. 15:20, 23.
[5] Rom. 8:29; Col. 1:18; Rev. 1:5.
[6] 1 Cor. 15:49. [7] Mt. 19:28. [8] Rev. 21:5. [9] Rom. 8:20–23.
[10] 2 Pet. 3:13; Rev. 21:1.

the destiny of the cosmos is not an ethereal 'heaven', but a re-created universe.

Is there any evidence, however, for this amazing assertion that both we and our world are to be totally renewed? Yes, the resurrection of Jesus is the ground of both expectations. It provides solid, visible, tangible, public evidence of God's purpose to complete what he has begun, to redeem nature, to give us new bodies in a new world. As Peter expressed it, God 'has given us new birth into a living hope through the resurrection of Jesus Christ from the dead'.[1] For the resurrection of Jesus was the beginning of the new creation of God. It is not enough to believe that the personality, presence and power of Jesus live on. We need to know that his body was raised. For the resurrection body of Jesus was the first bit of the material order to be redeemed and transfigured. It is the divine pledge that the rest will be redeemed and transfigured one day.[2]

Thus the resurrection of Jesus assures us of God's forgiveness, power and ultimate triumph. It enables us to face our past (however much reason we have to be ashamed of it), confident of God's forgiveness through him who died for our sins and was raised; to face our present (however strong our temptations and heavy our responsibilities), confident of the sufficiency of God's power; and to face our future (however uncertain it may be), confident of God's final triumph, of which the resurrection is the pledge. The resurrection, precisely because it was a decisive, public, visible act of God, within the material order, brings us firm assurance in an otherwise insecure world.

[1] 1 Pet. 1:3.

[2] Professor Oliver O'Donovan goes much further than this in his formative book *Resurrection and Moral Order: An Outline for Evangelical Ethics* (IVP and Eerdmans, 1986). He argues that the resurrection of Jesus is the foundation on which Christian ethics rests, because it proclaims that the created world order has been vindicated and reaffirmed by God; indeed, redeemed, renewed and transformed. 'From the resurrection we look not only back to the created order which is vindicated, but forwards to our eschatological participation in that order' (p. 22), not only 'back to what is reaffirmed there, the order of creation', but also 'forward to what is anticipated there, the kingdom of God' (p. 26).

CHAPTER FIVE

JESUS CHRIST IS LORD

The apostolic gospel went beyond the fact and significance of the cross and resurrection to their purpose: 'For to this end Christ died and lived again, that he might be Lord both of the dead and of the living.'[1]

Indeed, it is well known that the earliest, shortest, simplest of all Christian creeds was the affirmation 'Jesus is Lord'. Those who acknowledged his lordship were baptized and received into the Christian community. For it was recognized, as Paul wrote, on the one hand that 'if you confess with your mouth, "Jesus is Lord," and believe in your heart that God raised him from the dead, you will be saved',[2] and on the other that 'no-one can say, "Jesus is Lord," except by the Holy Spirit'.[3]

It may at first sight seem extraordinary that two Greek words, *Kyrios Iēsous* or 'Lord Jesus' (for there is no connecting verb in either of the two verses quoted in the previous paragraph), could possibly be a satisfactory basis for identifying and welcoming somebody as a genuine Christian. Are they not hopelessly inadequate? Is this not theological reductionism at its worst?

The answer to these questions is 'No'. For the two words concerned, which sound like a minimal Christian confession, are pregnant with meaning. They have enormous implications for both Christian faith and Christian life. In particular, they express first a profound theological conviction about the historic Jesus and secondly a radical personal commitment to him in consequence. It is this conviction and this commitment which I propose to explore in this chapter.

[1] Rom. 14:9 (RSV). [2] Rom. 10:9. [3] 1 Cor. 12:3.

Theological conviction

Perhaps the best way to investigate the doctrinal overtones of calling Jesus 'Lord' is to take a fresh look at Philippians 2:9–11. These verses form the climax of what is sometimes called *carmen Christi*, 'the song of Christ'. For Paul is probably quoting an early Christian hymn about Christ. In doing so, he gives it his apostolic imprimatur. He affirms that Christ, although he shared God's nature and enjoyed equality with him, yet both emptied himself of his glory and humbled himself to serve, becoming obedient even to death on a cross (verses 6–8). He continues:

> Therefore God exalted him to the highest place
> and gave him the name that is above every name,
> that at the name of Jesus every knee should bow,
> in heaven and on earth and under the earth,
> and every tongue confess that Jesus Christ is Lord,
> to the glory of God the Father (verses 9–11).

As a Christian hymn, used by the church and endorsed by the apostle, it indicates how the early Christians thought of Jesus. Three points stand out.

First, *Paul gave Jesus a God-title*. That is, he referred to him as 'Lord'. It is true, of course, that *kyrios* was used with different meanings in different contexts. Sometimes it meant no more than 'sir', as when Mary Magdalene thought the risen Jesus was the gardener[1] and when the priests asked Pilate to have the tomb made secure.[2] But when used by Jesus' disciples in relation to him, *kyrios* was more than a polite form of address; it was a title, as when they called him 'the Lord Jesus' or 'the Lord Jesus Christ'. This becomes clear against the background of the Old Testament.

When the Old Testament came to be translated into Greek in Alexandria about 200 BC, the devout Jewish scholars did not

[1] Jn. 20:15. [2] Mt. 27:62–63.

know how to handle the sacred name Yahweh or Jehovah. They were too reticent to pronounce it; they did not feel free to translate or even to transliterate it. So they put the paraphrase *ho kyrios* ('the Lord') instead, which is why 'Yahweh' still appears in most English versions as 'the LORD'. Lovers of biblical numerology may like to know that it occurs 6,156 times in this Greek version, the Septuagint. Or so I have read somewhere; I have not had the inclination or the patience to check it.

What is truly amazing is that the followers of Jesus, knowing that at least in Jewish circles *ho kyrios* was the traditional title for Yahweh, Creator of the universe and covenant God of Israel, did not scruple to apply the same title to Jesus, or see any anomaly in doing so. It was tantamount to saying that 'Jesus is God'.

Secondly, *Paul transferred to Jesus a God-text.* In Isaiah 45:23 Yahweh had soliloquized:

> By myself I have sworn,
> my mouth has uttered in all integrity
> a word that will not be revoked:
> Before me every knee will bow;
> by me every tongue will swear.

Now Paul, or the hymn-writer he is quoting, has the audacity to lift this text out of Isaiah and reapply it to Jesus. The implication is unavoidable. The homage which the prophet said was due to Yahweh, the apostle says is due to Christ; it was also to be universal, involving 'every knee' and 'every tongue'.

A similar example is the New Testament use of Joel 2:32. The prophet had written that 'everyone who calls on the name of the LORD (*sc.* God) will be saved'. On the Day of Pentecost, however, Peter reapplied this promise to Jesus, urging his hearers to believe in Jesus and be baptized in his name.[1] Similarly, Paul wrote later that the Lord Jesus 'is Lord of all and richly blesses all who call on him, for, "Everyone who calls on the name of

[1] Acts 2:21, 38.

the Lord will be saved.'"[1] Thus the saving power of Yahweh to Israel has become the saving power of Jesus to Jewish and Gentile believers alike.

Thirdly, *Paul demanded for Jesus God-worship.* However we may interpret the confession of the tongue that he is Lord, the bowing of the knee to him is certainly worship. Indeed, prayer is regularly addressed to Jesus in the New Testament, especially when Paul links 'God our Father' and 'our Lord Jesus Christ' as being together the source of grace and the object of petition.[2] One is reminded too of Hebrews 1:6: 'Let all God's angels worship him.' It is assumed in the New Testament documents that grace flows from Christ, and that prayer and worship are due to him. Indeed, Christolatry (the worship of Christ) preceded Christology (the developed doctrine of Christ). But Christolatry is idolatry if Christ is not God, as Athanasius saw clearly in the fourth century when arguing against the Arian heresy that Christ was a created being.

Here, then, are three important data contained in the Christian hymn Paul was quoting. The early Christians gave Jesus a God-title ('Lord'), transferred to him God-texts (regarding the salvation he bestows and the homage he deserves) and offered him God-worship (the bowed knee). These facts are incontrovertible, and they are all the more impressive for being uncontrived and almost casual.

It is noteworthy, moreover, that the New Testament writers did not argue the rightness of making the daring identification that Jesus is God, for there was no need for them to do so. Paul defended the gospel of justification by grace through faith, and that fiercely, because it was being challenged. But he did not debate the divine lordship of Jesus (the truth that 'there is but one Lord, Jesus Christ'),[3] which must mean that it was not being disputed. So already within a few years of the death and resurrection of Jesus his deity was part of the universal faith of the church.

The confession that 'Jesus is Lord' has a second theological

[1] Rom. 10:12–13. [2] *E.g.* 1 Thes. 1:1; 3:11; 2 Thes. 1:2, 12; 2:16.
[3] 1 Cor. 8:6.

inference, namely that he is Saviour as well as God. The tradition in some evangelical circles is to distinguish sharply between Jesus the Saviour and Jesus the Lord, and even to suggest that conversion involves trusting him as Saviour, without necessarily surrendering to him as Lord. The motive behind this teaching is good, namely to safeguard the truth of justification by faith alone and not introduce works-righteousness (obeying Christ as Lord) by the back door. Nevertheless this position is biblically indefensible. Not only is Jesus 'our Lord and Saviour', one and indivisible, but his lordship implies his salvation and actually announces it. That is, his title 'Lord' is a symbol of his victory over all the forces of evil, which have been put under his feet. The very possibility of our salvation is due to this victory. It is precisely because he is Lord that he is able also to be Saviour.[1] There can be no salvation without lordship. The two affirmations 'Jesus is Lord' and 'Jesus saves' are virtually synonymous.

Radical commitment

The word *kyrios* could be used, as we have seen, as no more than a respectful designation. But it was most commonly employed of owners, whether of land, property or slaves. Possession carried with it full control and the right of disposal. It is with this understanding that Paul, Peter and James began their letters by designating themselves 'slave of Jesus Christ'. They knew that he had bought them at the cost of his lifeblood, and that in consequence they belonged to him and were entirely at his service.

This personal ownership by Christ, and commitment to Christ, is to penetrate every part of his disciples' lives. It has at least six dimensions.

First, it has *an intellectual dimension*. I begin with our mind because it is the central citadel of our personality and effectively rules our lives. Yet it is often the last stronghold to capitulate to

[1] *Cf.* Acts 2:33–39.

the lordship of Jesus. The truth is that we rather like to think our own thoughts and ventilate our own opinions, and if they conflict with the teaching of Jesus, so much the worse for him!

But Jesus Christ claims authority over our minds. 'Take my yoke upon you and learn from me,' he said.[1] His Jewish hearers will immediately have understood him. For they commonly spoke of 'the yoke of Torah' (the law), to whose authority they submitted. Now Jesus spoke of *his* teaching as a yoke. His followers were to become his pupils, his disciples, to subject themselves to his instruction, and to learn from him. Nor need they be afraid of this. For on the one hand he was himself 'gentle and humble in heart', and on the other his yoke was 'easy' and under its light discipline they would find 'rest' for their souls. In other words, true 'rest' is found under Christ's yoke (not in resisting it), and true freedom under his authority (not in discarding it). The apostle Paul was later to write something similar, when he expressed his resolve to 'take captive every thought to make it obedient to Christ'.[2]

The contemporary Christian, who is anxious to respond sensitively to the challenges of the modern world, nevertheless may not jettison the authority of Jesus Christ in order to do so. Disciples have no liberty to disagree with their divine teacher. What we believe about God, about man, male and female, made in his image, about life and death, duty and destiny, Scripture and tradition, salvation and judgment, and much else besides, we have learned from him. There is an urgent need in our day, in which wild and weird speculations abound, to resume our rightful position at his feet. 'Only the person who follows the command of Jesus without reserve', wrote Dietrich Bonhoeffer, 'and submits unresistingly to his yoke, finds his burden easy, and under its gentle pressure receives the power to persevere in the right way. The command of Jesus is hard, unutterably hard, for those who try to resist it. But for those who willingly submit, the yoke is easy and the burden is light.'[3]

Secondly, radical commitment to Jesus Christ has a *moral*

[1] Mt. 11:29. [2] 2 Cor. 10:5.
[3] Dietrich Bonhoeffer, *The Cost of Discipleship* (1937; ET SCM, 1948), p. 31.

dimension. All round us today moral standards are slipping. People are confused whether there are any moral absolutes left. Relativism has permeated the world and is seeping into the church.

Even some evangelical believers misrepresent Scripture on the subject of the law. They quote the apostle Paul's well-known statements that 'Christ is the end of the law'[1] and 'you are not under law',[2] turn a blind eye to their context, and misinterpret them as meaning that the category of law has now been abolished, that we are no longer under obligation to obey it, but are free to disobey it. But Paul meant something quite different. He was referring to the way of salvation, not the way of holiness. He was insisting that for our acceptance with God we are 'not under law but under grace', since we are justified by faith alone, not by works of the law. But we are still under the moral law for our sanctification. As Luther kept saying, the law drives us to Christ to be justified, but Christ sends us back to the law to be sanctified.

The apostle is quite clear about the place of the law in the Christian life. He insists that both the atoning work of Christ and the indwelling presence of the Spirit are with a view to our obeying the law. Why did God send his Son to die for our sins? Answer: 'in order that the righteous requirements of the law might be fully met in us, who . . . live . . . according to the Spirit.'[3] And why has God put his Spirit in our hearts? Answer: in order to write his law there.[4] Consequently, God's Old Testament promise of the new covenant could be expressed equally as 'I will put my law in their minds and write it on their hearts'[5] and as 'I will put my Spirit in you and move you . . . to keep my laws'.[6]

So Jesus Christ calls us to obedience. 'Whoever has my commands and obeys them, he is the one who loves me. He who loves me will be loved by my Father, and I too will love him and show myself to him.'[7] The way to prove our love for Christ is

[1] Rom. 10:4. [2] Rom. 6:14. [3] Rom. 8:3–4. [4] 2 Cor. 3:3, 6.
[5] Je. 31:33. [6] Ezk. 36:27. [7] Jn. 14:21.

neither by loud protestations of loyalty like Peter, nor by singing sentimental ditties in church, but by obeying his commandments. The test of love is obedience, he said, and the reward of love is a self-revelation of Christ.

Thirdly, Christian commitment has a *vocational dimension*. That is to say, it includes our life work. To say 'Jesus is Lord' commits us to a lifetime of service. We should not hesitate to say that every single Christian is called to ministry, indeed to give his or her life in ministry. If this strikes you as an extraordinary statement, it is probably because you are thinking of 'ministry' as synonymous with the ordained pastoral ministry. But the pastoral ministry is only one of many ministries. My point is that we are all called to ministry or service (*diakonia*) of some kind. The reason it is possible to say this is that we are followers of one who assumed 'the very nature of a servant',[1] insisted that he had 'not come to be served but to serve'[2] and added 'I am among you as one who serves'.[3] If we claim to follow Jesus, therefore, it is inconceivable that we should spend our lives in any other way than in service. And this means that we must be able to see our job or profession in terms of service. Our daily work is meant to be a major sphere in which Jesus exercises his lordship over us. Beyond and behind our earthly employer we should be able to discern our heavenly Lord. Then we can be 'working for the Lord, not for men', since 'it is the Lord Christ (we) are serving'.[4]

In November 1940 the city of Coventry was devastated by aerial bombardment, including its fourteenth-century cathedral. After the war the ruins of the old cathedral were preserved, while a new cathedral was built beside it. From medieval times the old cathedral had, situated round its walls, a series of guild chapels (*e.g.* for the smiths, the drapers, the mercers and the dyers), symbolizing the close link between the church and the crafts. These chapels were destroyed, but in their place 'hallowing places' have been set round the ruined walls, expressing the implications of the prayer 'Hallowed be your name':

[1] Phil. 2:7. [2] Mk. 10:45. [3] Lk. 22:27. [4] Col. 3:23–24.

In industry, God be in my hands and in my making.
In the arts, God be in my senses and in my creating.
In the home, God be in my heart and in my loving.
In commerce, God be at my desk and in my trading.
In healing, God be in my skill and in my touching.
In government, God be in my plans and in my deciding.
In education, God be in my mind and in my growing.
In recreation, God be in my limbs and in my leisure.

Fourthly, the lordship of Christ has *a social dimension*. This means partly that the followers of Jesus have social as well as individual responsibilities, for example, to family, firm, neighbourhood, country and world. But it means more than this.

There is a sense in which to confess 'Jesus is Lord' is to acknowledge him as Lord of society, even of those societies or segments of society which do not explicitly acknowledge his lordship. Consider this dilemma which the New Testament sets before us. On the one hand, we are told that Jesus is Lord. He has dethroned and disarmed the principalities and powers, triumphing over them in the cross.[1] God has exalted him to his right hand and put everything under his feet.[2] In consequence, he can claim that all authority has been given to him.[3] On the other hand, we continue to struggle against the principalities and powers of darkness. They may have been defeated, even deprived of power; but they are still active, influential and unscrupulous.[4] The apostle John even goes so far as to declare that 'the whole world is under the control of the evil one'.[5] In fact, this dilemma is well summed up in Psalm 110:1, which was quoted by Jesus and several New Testament writers: 'The LORD says to my Lord: "Sit at my right hand until I make your enemies a footstool for your feet."' Within the compass of this one verse the Messiah is depicted both as *reigning* at God's right hand and as *waiting* for the overthrow of his enemies.

How can we reconcile these two perspectives? Is Jesus Lord, or is Satan? Is Christ reigning over his enemies, or waiting for

[1] Col. 2:15. [2] Eph. 1:20–22. [3] Mt. 28:18. [4] Eph. 6:11–18.
[5] 1 Jn. 5:19.

them to surrender? The only possible answer to these questions is 'both'. We have to distinguish between what is *de jure* (by right) and what is *de facto* (in fact or reality). *De jure* Jesus is Lord, for God has exalted him to the highest place. *De facto*, however, Satan rules, for he has not yet conceded defeat or been destroyed.

How does this tension affect our discipleship? Because Jesus is Lord by right, that is, by divine appointment, we cannot acquiesce in any situation which denies it. We long that he who is Lord should be acknowledged as Lord; this is our evangelistic task. But even in a society which does not specifically acknowledge his lordship, we are still concerned that his values will prevail, that human rights and human dignity be accorded to people of all races and religions, that honour be given to women and children, that justice be secured for the oppressed, that society become more just, compassionate, peaceful and free. Why? Why do we care about these things? Because Jesus is Lord of society by right, and because he cares about them. This is not to resurrect the old 'social gospel' of theological liberalism, which made the mistake of identifying a caring society with the kingdom of God. It is rather to take seriously the truth that Jesus is Lord of society and therefore to seek to make it more pleasing to him.

It was during his inaugural address at the opening of the Free University of Amsterdam in 1880 that Abraham Kuyper, who was later to become Prime Minister of the Netherlands, said: 'There is not one inch in the entire area of human life about which Christ, who is Sovereign of all, does not cry out "Mine!"' Similarly, Dr David Gill of New College, Berkeley, has written: 'Jesus is Lord not just of the inner life, after life, family life and church life, but of intellectual life, political life – all domains.'[1]

Fifthly, a radical commitment to Christ has *a political dimension.* We need to remember that Jesus was condemned for both a political and a religious offence. In the Jewish court he was found guilty of blasphemy, because he called himself the Son of

[1] David W. Gill, *The Opening of the Christian Mind* (IVP USA, 1989), p. 131.

God, while in the Roman court he was condemned for sedition because he called himself a king, and Rome recognized no king but Caesar. Thus the claims of Jesus had inescapable political implications. His statement that we are to 'give to Caesar what is Caesar's and to God what is God's'[1] may have been deliberately enigmatic. But it certainly implied that there are areas over which God is Lord, into which Caesar may not intrude.

The early Christians faced a continuing conflict between Christ and Caesar. During the first century the emperors manifested an ever-increasing megalomania. They had temples erected in their honour, and demanded divine homage from their subjects. These claims came into direct collision with the lordship of Christ, whom Christians honoured as king,[2] indeed as 'the ruler of the kings of the earth'.[3] Pliny, the early-second-century governor of Bithynia, described in a letter to the Emperor Trajan how he brought before him in court those Christians he suspected of disloyalty, and how he discharged only those who 'offered invocation with wine and frankincense to your (*sc.* the Emperor's) image'.[4] But how could believers say 'Caesar is Lord' when they had confessed that 'Jesus is Lord'? They went to prison and death rather than deny the lordship of Christ.

The deification of the state did not end with the Roman Empire. Still today there are totalitarian regimes which demand from their citizens an unconditional allegiance which Christians cannot possibly give. The disciples of Jesus are to respect the state, and within limits submit to it, but they will neither worship it, nor give it the uncritical support it covets. Consequently, discipleship sometimes calls for disobedience. Indeed, civil disobedience is a biblical doctrine, for there are four or five notable examples of it in Scripture.[5] It arises naturally from the affirmation that Jesus is Lord. The principle is clear, even though its application may involve believers in agonies of conscience. It is this. We are to submit to the state, because its

[1] Mk. 12:17. [2] Acts 17:7. [3] Rev. 1:5. [4] *Epistles*, 10:96.
[5] *E.g.* Ex. 1:15–17; Dn. 3 and 6; Acts 4:19; 5:29.

authority is derived from God and its officials are God's ministers,[1] right up to the point where obedience to the state would involve us in disobedience to God. At that point our Christian duty is to disobey the state in order to obey God. For if the state misuses its God-given authority, and presumes either to command what God forbids or to forbid what God commands, we have to say 'no' to the state in order to say 'yes' to Christ. As Peter put it, 'we must obey God rather than men!'[2] Or in Calvin's words, 'obedience to man must not become disobedience to God'.[3]

Let me give a fairly recent example from South Africa. In 1957 Hendrik Verwoerd, then Minister of Native Affairs, announced the 'Native Laws Amendment Bill', whose 'church clause' would have prevented any racial association in 'church, school, hospital, club or any other institution or place of entertainment'. The Archbishop of Cape Town at the time was a gentle scholar called Geoffrey Clayton. He decided with his bishops, albeit with reluctance and apprehension, to disobey. He wrote to the Prime Minister to say that if the Bill were to become law, he would be 'unable to obey it or to counsel our clergy and people to do so'. The following morning he died, perhaps under the pain and strain of threatened civil disobedience. The Bill was amended, but in a mischievous way which would have penalized the black worshippers rather than the church leaders. After it became law, a letter was read out in all Anglican churches calling on the clergy and people to disobey it.

Sixthly, commitment to Christ has *a global dimension.* To affirm 'Jesus is Lord' is to acknowledge his universal lordship. For God has 'super-exalted' Jesus,[4] as we might render *hyperypsoō* – a word that occurs nowhere else in the New Testament, and may even have been coined by Paul. It means that God has raised him 'to the loftiest heights'.[5] And God's purpose in doing

[1] Rom. 13:1–7. [2] Acts 5:29. [3] *Institutes*, IV.xx.32. [4] Phil. 2:9.
[5] Walter Bauer, *A Greek-English Lexicon of the New Testament and Other Early Christian Literature*, translated and adapted by W. F. Arndt and F. W. Gingrich (University of Chicago Press, second edition, 1979).

so was that every knee should bow to him and every tongue confess him Lord. We have no liberty to place any limitation on the repeated word 'every'. Therefore, if it is God's desire that everybody acknowledge Jesus, it must be our desire as well. Hindus speak of 'the Lord Krishna' and Buddhists of 'the Lord Buddha', but we cannot accept these claims. Only Jesus is Lord. He has no rivals.

There is no greater incentive to world mission than the lordship of Jesus Christ. Mission is neither an impertinent interference in other people's private lives, nor a dispensable option which may be rejected, but an unavoidable deduction from the universal lordship of Jesus Christ.

The two-word affirmation *Kyrios Iēsous* sounded pretty harmless at first hearing. But we have seen that it has far-reaching ramifications. Not only does it express our conviction that he is God and Saviour, but it also indicates our radical commitment to him. The dimensions of this commitment are intellectual (bringing our minds under Christ's yoke), moral (accepting his standards and obeying his commands), vocational (spending our lives in his liberating service), social (seeking to penetrate society with his values), political (refusing to idolize any human institution) and global (being jealous for the honour and glory of his name).

PART TWO

THE DISCIPLE

We turn now from 'the gospel' to 'the disciple'. For if Christ crucified and risen is our Lord, we are his servants; if he is our teacher, we are his pupils.

Christian discipleship (that is, following Christ) is a many-faceted responsibility. My choice of four aspects of it could be described as random, except that all of them tend to be underrated and even overlooked.

I begin with 'The Listening Ear'. For, although all our bodily organs are to be consecrated and presented to God (including our eyes and lips, our hands and feet), a good case can be made for regarding our ears as the most important. Every true disciple is a listener.

Chapter 7 ('Mind and Emotions') not only recalls that our Creator has made us both rational and emotional persons, but explores some of the more significant relations between these two components of the human personality.

In chapter 8, under the title 'Guidance, Vocation and Ministry', we reflect that discipleship implies service, and consider how we can discern the will of God and the call of God in our lives.

For the final chapter of Part II I have reserved a discussion of the first fruit of the Spirit, which is love. Its primacy in Christian disciples is well expressed in *The Book of Common Prayer*, which describes it as 'that most excellent gift of charity, the very bond of peace and of all virtues, without which whosoever liveth is counted dead before God'.

CHAPTER SIX
THE LISTENING EAR

One of the most important – and much neglected – ingredients of Christian discipleship is the cultivation of a listening ear. Bad listeners do not make good disciples. The apostle James was clear about this. His strictures on the tongue as 'a restless evil, full of deadly poison'[1] are well known, but he has no comparable criticism of the ear. He urges us not to talk too much, but seems to suggest that we can never listen too much. Here is his exhortation:

> My dear brothers, take note of this: Everyone should be quick to listen, slow to speak and slow to become angry, for man's anger does not bring about the righteous life that God desires.[2]

What a remarkable organ God has created in the human ear! In comparison with it, the most sophisticated computer (it has been said) is 'as crude as a concrete mixer'. Of course what we usually call the ear is only the *outer ear*, that fleshy excrescence on the side of the head which comes in a variety of shapes and sizes. From it a one-inch canal leads to the ear drum, behind which is the *middle ear*, where the body's three tiniest bones (popularly known as the anvil, the hammer and the stirrup) amplify sound twenty-two times and pass it on to the *inner ear*, where the real hearing takes place. Its main component is the snail-shaped tube named the cochlea. It contains thousands of microscopic, hairlike cells, each of which is tuned to one particular vibration. The vibrations are now converted into electric

[1] Jas. 3:8. [2] Jas. 1:19–20.

impulses which convey sound to the brain for decoding along 30,000 circuits of the auditory nerve, enough for a sizeable city's telephone service. The human ear has rightly been celebrated as 'a triumph of miniaturization'.[1]

When you think how versatile and sensitive this organ is, which God has made, it is a thousand pities that we do not put it to better use and develop our capacity for listening. I am not thinking only of music, bird song and animal calls, but also of the value of conversation for our relationships. Involuntary deafness is a grievous handicap; deliberate deafness is both a sin and a folly.

This is one of the main themes of Alan Parker's film *Birdy*, which is based on William Wharton's novel. Its key statement seems to be the throwaway line near the end that 'nobody listens to anybody any longer'. The film depicts the friendship of two adolescent boys in Philadelphia, Al and Birdy, which blossoms in spite of Birdy's weird obsession with bird flight. Drafted to Vietnam, they are both blown up. Al has to have surgery on his disfigured face, while Birdy is damaged psychologically, retreats into impenetrable silence, and is committed to a mental hospital. He cowers in his cell like a caged bird, and constantly looks up at the barred window, dreaming of escape. The two men urgently need each other's support in the cruel aftermath of war, but they cannot communicate. At last, however, the breakthrough takes place, and their friendship is restored. But the background to it is a hostile world in which people are out of touch with each other – an unsympathetic mother, an uncomprehending girlfriend, a bloody and senseless war, and a psychotherapist who lacks both insight and compassion. Al and Birdy are now listening to each other again, but they seem to be the exceptions in a world in which 'nobody listens to anybody any longer'.

James's appeal to us to be 'quick to listen' is not one we find easy to heed. Many of us are compulsive talkers, especially

[1] See Alan E. Nourse, *The Body* (Time Life, 1968); also two books by Paul Brand and Philip Yancey entitled *In His Image* (Hodder and Stoughton, 1984) and *Fearfully and Wonderfully Made* (Hodder and Stoughton, 1981).

preachers! We prefer to talk than to listen, to volunteer information than to confess our ignorance, to criticize than to receive criticism. But who am I to be saying these things? I have myself been as great an offender in this area as anybody. Let me share with you an experience of about twenty-five years ago, which proved to be formative. It was Monday morning in London, the All Souls church staff team had gathered for our weekly meeting, and I was in the chair. The others were carrying on about something which did not particularly interest me (I now forget what it was), and I am ashamed to say that I had switched off. Suddenly Ted Schroder, who might not unfairly be described at that time as 'a brash young colonial from New Zealand', and who is now a close and valued friend, blurted out: 'John, you're not listening!' I blushed. For he was quite right, and it is intolerably rude not to listen when somebody is speaking. Moreover, the tensions which were surfacing in our staff team relationships at that time were largely due to my failure to listen. So I repented, and have many times since prayed for grace to be a better listener.

To whom, then, shall we listen? First and foremost to God.

Listening to God

One of the distinctive truths about the God of the biblical revelation is that he is a speaking God. Unlike heathen idols which, being dead, are dumb, the living God has spoken and continues to speak. They have mouths but do not speak; he has no mouth (because he is spirit), yet speaks. And since God speaks, we must listen. This is a constant theme of the Old Testament in all three of its main sections. Take the Law: '... love the Lord your God, listen to his voice.'[1] And the wisdom literature in the Writings: 'To-day, Oh that ye would hear his voice!'[2] There are also many examples in the Prophets. For instance, Israel's 'stubbornness' of heart, of which God kept complaining to Jeremiah, was precisely that they 'refuse to

[1] Dt. 30:20. [2] Ps. 95:7 (RV).

listen to my words'.[1] The tragedy inherent in this situation is that what constituted Israel a special, a distinct, people was precisely that God had spoken to her and called her. Yet she neither listened nor responded. The result was judgment: 'When I called, they did not listen; so when they called, I would not listen.'[2] One might almost say that the epitaph engraved on the nation's tombstone was: 'The Lord God spoke to his people, but they refused to listen.' So then God sent his Son, saying, 'They will listen to my Son,' but they killed him instead.

Still today God speaks, although there is some disagreement in the church as to how he does so. I do not myself believe that he speaks to us nowadays directly and audibly, as he did for example to Abraham,[3] to the boy Samuel[4] or to Saul of Tarsus outside Damascus.[5] Nor should we claim that he addresses us 'face to face, as a man speaks with his friend',[6] since this intimate relationship which God had with Moses is specifically said to have been unique.[7] To be sure, Christ's sheep know the Good Shepherd's voice and follow him,[8] for this is essential to our discipleship, but we are not promised that his voice will be audible.

What, then, about indirect utterances of God through prophets? We should certainly reject any claim that there are prophets today comparable to the biblical prophets. For they were the 'mouth' of God, special organs of revelation, whose teaching belongs to the foundation on which the church is built.[9] There may well, however, be a prophetic gift of a secondary kind, as when God gives some people special insight into his Word and his will. But we should not ascribe infallibility to such communications. Instead, we should evaluate both the character and the message of those who claim to speak from God.[10]

The principal way in which God speaks to us today is through Scripture, as the church in every generation has recognized. The words which God spoke through the biblical

[1] Je. 13:10; *cf.* Is. 30:9. [2] Zc. 7:13; *cf.* Je. 21:10–11. [3] Gn. 22:1.
[4] 1 Sa. 3:4, 6, 8, 10. [5] Acts 9:3–7. [6] Ex. 33:11.
[7] Dt. 34:10. [8] Jn. 10:3–5. [9] Eph. 2:20.
[10] Mt. 7:16; 1 Thes. 5:20–22.

authors, which he caused in his providence to be written and preserved, are not a dead letter. One of the special ministries of the Holy Spirit is to make God's written Word 'living and active' and 'sharper than any double-edged sword'.[1] So we must never separate the Word from the Spirit or the Spirit from the Word, for the simple reason that the Word of God is 'the sword of the Spirit',[2] the chief weapon he uses to accomplish his purpose in his people's lives. It is this confidence which enables us to think of Scripture equally as written text and as living message. Thus, Jesus could ask, 'What is written?'[3] and, 'Have you never read?',[4] while Paul could ask, 'What does the Scripture say?',[5] almost personifying it. In other words, Scripture (which means the written Word) can be either read or listened to, and what it says is what he (God) says through it. Through his ancient Word God addresses the modern world. He speaks through what he has spoken.

And God calls us to listen to what through Scripture 'the Spirit says to the churches'.[6] The tragedy is that still today, as in Old Testament days, people often do not, cannot or will not listen to God. The non-communication between God and us is not because God is either dead or silent, but because we are not listening. If we are cut off during a telephone conversation, we do not jump to the conclusion that the person at the other end has died. No, it is the line which has gone dead.

The same state of being cut off from God is often true of us Christians. Is this not the main cause of the spiritual stagnation we sometimes experience? We have stopped listening to God. Perhaps we no longer have a daily quiet time of Bible reading and prayer. Or if we continue to do so, perhaps it is more a routine than a reality, because we are no longer expecting God to speak. We need, then, to adopt the attitude of Samuel and say, 'Speak, Lord, for your servant is listening.'[7] Like the servant of the Lord we should be able to say: 'He wakens me morning by morning, wakens my ear to listen like one being

[1] Heb. 4:12. [2] Eph. 6:17. [3] *E.g.* Lk. 10:26. [4] *E.g.* Mt. 19:4; 21:42.
[5] *E.g.* Rom. 4:3; Gal. 4:30.
[6] *E.g.* Rev. 2:7. [7] 1 Sa. 3:9–10.

taught.'[1] We should imitate Mary of Bethany who 'sat at the Lord's feet listening to what he said'.[2] Of course we have to be active as well as contemplative, to work as well as pray, to be Marthas as well as Marys. But have we allowed the Martha in us to crowd out the Mary? Have we neglected what Jesus called the 'better' option?[3]

Listening to one another

In this second sphere of listening, the principle is clear: community depends on communication. It is only when we speak and listen to one another that our relationships develop and mature, whereas when we stop listening to each other, they fall apart. There is a heavy emphasis in the book of Proverbs on the necessity and value of mutual listening. For example, 'the way of a fool seems right to him, but a wise man listens to advice'.[4] Similarly, 'he who listens to a life-giving rebuke will be at home among the wise'.[5] Again, 'the heart of the discerning acquires knowledge; the ears of the wise seek it out'.[6] Here, then, are exhortations to listen to advice, to rebuke and to instruction, together with the statement that those who do so are wise. Moreover, this need to listen applies in every sphere of life, including the home, the workplace, the state and the church.

First, it applies to *the home*. Although I almost feel the need to apologize for saying something so traditional, children and young people need to listen to their parents. 'Listen, my son, to your father's instruction, and do not forsake your mother's teaching.'[7] For the fact is that parents have more experience, and therefore usually more wisdom, than their offspring tend to give them credit for. Mark Twain had the candour to admit this. 'When I was a boy of fourteen,' he said, 'my father was so ignorant I could hardly stand to have the old man around. But when I got to be twenty-one, I was astonished at how much he had learned in seven years!'[8]

[1] Is. 50:4. [2] Lk. 10:39. [3] Lk. 10:42.
[4] Pr. 12:15; *cf.* 13:10; 15:12, 22; 20:18.
[5] Pr. 15:31; *cf.* 9:8; 17:10; 25:12; 27:5. [6] Pr. 18:15. [7] Pr. 1:8.
[8] *Reader's Digest*, September 1937.

But if children need to listen to their parents, parents need to be humble enough to listen to their children, or they will never understand their problems. For the world in which their children are growing up is vastly different from the world of their own youth. Only patient, mutual listening can bridge the generation gap.

Next, husband and wife need to listen to one another. Marriage breakdown is nearly always preceded by communication breakdown. For whatever reason (neglect, fatigue, self-centredness or pressure of business), husband and wife are no longer taking time to listen to each other. So they drift apart, and misunderstandings, suspicions, grievances and resentments increase, until it is too late – although in fact it is never too late to start listening again.

Secondly, listening is essential in *the workplace*. This seems to be widely recognized, as the art of listening is now included in books and seminars on business management. For example, there is *The Language of Effective Listening* by Arthur Robertson, founder and president of Effective Communication and Development Inc.[1] It is an American self-help book, based on the conviction that 'effective listening is the number one communication skill requisite to success in your professional and personal life'.[2]

Listening is specially important in conflict situations. Whenever there is an industrial dispute, it is almost certain that both sides have a reasonable case. Neither side is totally selfish or totally crazy. The essence of conciliation, therefore, is to persuade each side to listen to the other. There have been several painful examples of this in Britain in recent years. Management and labour (sometimes with the Government involved as well) have been at loggerheads, with strikes and picketing on one side, sackings on the other, and bitter recriminations all round. It has been a case of almost total mutual deafness and non-comprehension. People prefer to shout at one another than to

[1] Arthur Robertson, *The Language of Effective Listening* (Scott Foresman Professional Books, 1991).
[2] *Ibid.*, p. xv.

listen to one another. Yet only when both sides are willing to sit down together, put aside their prejudiced positions and listen, does any possibility of reconciliation emerge.

Thirdly, the same principle is applicable to *the state*. If democracy is government with the consent of the governed, then the governed have to be listened to. Otherwise, they cannot be deemed to have given their consent. In 1864, shortly before the end of the American Civil War and before Congress's adoption of the Thirteenth Amendment abolishing slavery, Harriet Beecher Stowe interviewed Abraham Lincoln and wrote: 'Surrounded by all sorts of conflicting claims, by traitors, by half-hearted timid men, by Border States men and Free States men, by radical Abolitionists and Conservatives, Lincoln has listened to all, weighed the words of all . . .'.[1] I guess that the willingness to listen to all shades of opinion is a *sine qua non* of statesmanship.

Fourthly, it is true in *the church*. Church history has been a long and somewhat dismal record of controversy. Usually, important theological issues have been at stake. But, as often as not, they have been exacerbated by an unwillingness or inability to listen. I have myself tried to observe the rule never to engage in theological debate without first listening to the other person, or reading what he or she has written, or preferably both. Some evangelical friends joined me in meeting Bishop John Robinson after the publication of *Honest to God*, five contributors to *The Myth of God Incarnate* after its publication, and Bishop David Jenkins after his provocative remarks about the resurrection. I do not of course claim that disagreement is overcome by such dialogue, but at least our misunderstanding is diminished and our integrity preserved.

This is even more so in the case of domestic evangelical debate. When we stay apart, and our only contact is to lob hand grenades at one another across a demilitarized zone, a caricature of one's 'opponent' develops in one's mind, complete with horns, hooves and tail! But when we meet, and sit

[1] Stephen B. Oates, *Abraham Lincoln: The Man Behind the Myths* (New American Library, 1984), pp. 125–126.

together, and begin to listen, not only does it become evident that our opponents are not after all demons, but actually normal human beings, and even sisters and brothers in Christ, the possibility of mutual understanding and respect grows. More than this: when we listen not only to what others are saying, but to what lies behind what they are saying, and in particular to what it is that they are so anxious to safeguard, we often find that we want to safeguard the same thing ourselves.[1]

I am not claiming that this discipline is easy. Far from it. Listening with patient integrity to both sides of an argument can cause acute mental pain. For it involves the interiorizing of the debate until one not only grasps but feels the strength of both positions. Yet this is another aspect of the 'double listening' for which I am pleading in this book.

It is perhaps specially to pastors that God has committed the ministry of listening. Bonhoeffer wrote of it with his customary insight:

> The first service that one owes to others in the fellowship consists in listening to them. Just as love to God begins with listening to his Word, so the beginning of love for the brethren is learning to listen to them. It is God's love for us that he not only gives us his Word but also lends us his ear. So it is his work that we do for our brother when we learn to listen to him. Christians, especially ministers, so often think they must always contribute something when they are in the company of others, that this is the one service they have to render. They forget that listening can be a greater service than speaking . . .
>
> Brotherly pastoral care is essentially distinguished from preaching by the fact that, added to the task of speaking the Word, there is the obligation of listening. There is a kind of listening with half an ear that presumes already to know what the other person has to say. It is an impatient, inattentive listening, that despises the brother, and is only waiting for a

[1] See, for example, *Evangelism and Social Responsibility: An Evangelical Commitment*, known as 'The Grand Rapids Report' (Paternoster, 1982), especially pp. 5–7.

chance to speak and thus get rid of the other person. This is no fulfilment of our obligation . . .

Christians have forgotten that the ministry of listening has been committed to them by him who is himself the great listener and whose work they should share. We should listen with the ears of God that we may speak the Word of God.[1]

Listening to the world

The contemporary world is positively reverberating with cries of anger, frustration and pain. Too often, however, we turn a deaf ear to these anguished voices.

First, there is the pain of those who have never heard the name of Jesus or, having heard of him, have not yet come to him, and in their alienation and lostness are hurting dreadfully. Our evangelical habit with such is to rush in with the gospel, to climb on to our soapbox, and to declaim our message with little regard for the cultural situation or felt needs of the people concerned. In consequence, more often than we care to admit, we put people off, and even increase their alienation, because the way we present Christ is insensitive, clumsy and even irrelevant. Truly, 'he who answers before listening – that is his folly and his shame'.[2]

The better way is to listen before we speak, to seek to enter into the other person's world of thought and feeling, to struggle to grasp what their objections to the gospel may be, and to share with them the good news of Jesus Christ in a way which speaks to their need. This humble, searching, challenging activity is rightly called 'contextualization'. But it is essential to add that to contextualize the gospel is not in any way to manipulate it. Authentic evangelism necessitates 'double listening'. For Christian witnesses stand between the Word and the world, with the consequent obligation to listen to both. We listen to the Word in order to discover ever more of the riches of Christ. And we listen to the world in order to discern which of

[1] Dietrich Bonhoeffer, *Life Together* (Harper and Brothers, 1954), pp. 97–99.
[2] Pr. 18:13.

Christ's riches are needed most and how to present them in their best light.

This shows the nature and purpose of inter-faith dialogue. Dialogue is neither a synonym nor a substitute for evangelism. Dialogue is a serious conversation in which we are prepared to listen and learn as well as to speak and teach. It is therefore an exercise in integrity. 'It is an activity in its own right,' Max Warren wrote. 'It is in its very essence an attempt at mutual "listening", listening in order to understand. Understanding is its reward.'[1] Besides, Max Warren knew what he was talking about, as he tells us in his autobiography:

> My earliest memory is of dancing firelight, and of my mother reading to me. I am looking into the flames and listening. I must have been three or four years old . . . Long before I could read I was learning to listen, perhaps the most valuable lesson I ever learnt . . . What is more, reading has always been for me a form of listening. Books have always been 'persons' to me, not just the person of the author so much as the book itself talking, while I listened.[2]

Secondly, there is the pain of the poor and the hungry, the dispossessed and the oppressed. Many of us are only now waking up to the obligation which Scripture has always laid on the people of God to care about social justice. We should be listening more attentively to the cries and sighs of those who are suffering. Let me share with you a Bible verse which we have neglected, and which on that account we should perhaps underline. It contains a solemn word from God to those of his people who lack a social conscience. It is Proverbs 21:13: 'If a man shuts his ears to the cry of the poor, he too will cry out and not be answered.'

To turn a deaf ear to somebody is a signal mark of disrespect. If we refuse to listen to someone, we are saying that we do not

[1] From a paper entitled *Presence and Proclamation* read at a European Consultation on Mission Studies in April, 1968.
[2] M. A. C. Warren, *Crowded Canvas* (Hodder and Stoughton, 1974), pp. 16, 18.

consider that person worth listening to. But there is only one person we should refuse to listen to, on the ground that he is not worth listening to, and that is the devil, together with his emissaries. It is the essence of wisdom to be a discerning, discriminating listener and to choose carefully whom to listen to. Failure to do this was the folly of our first parents in the Garden of Eden. Instead of listening to the truth of God, they gave credence to the lies of Satan. And we are often crazy enough to copy them!

But we should not listen to the devil's talk, whether it be lies or propaganda, slander or gossip, filth or insults. 'A prudent man overlooks an insult.'[1] The same applies to anonymous letters. It is possible to be very upset by them, since they are usually rude. But why should we take seriously the criticisms of a correspondent who lacks the courage to disclose his or her identity? A good story illustrating this is told of Joseph Parker, who was minister of the City Temple in London at the end of the last century. As he climbed into his tall pulpit one Sunday morning, a lady in the gallery threw a piece of paper at him. Picking it up, he found that it contained the single word 'Fool!' Dr Parker commented: 'I have received many anonymous letters in my life. Previously they have been a text without a signature. Today for the first time I have received a signature without a text!'

If we steadfastly refuse to listen to anything that is untrue, unfair, unkind or impure, we should at the same time listen carefully to instruction and advice, criticism, reproof and correction, together with other people's views, concerns, problems and troubles. For, as has been well said, 'God has given us two ears, but only one mouth, so that he evidently intends us to listen twice as much as we talk.'

To take time to listen to God and to our fellow human beings begins as a mark of courtesy and respect, continues as the means to mutual understanding and deepening relationships,

[1] Pr. 12:16.

and above all is an authentic token of Christian humility and love. So, dear sisters and brothers, 'everyone should be quick to listen, slow to speak and slow to become angry'.

CHAPTER SEVEN

MIND AND EMOTIONS

Christian discipleship involves the whole of our human personality. We are to love the Lord our God with all our heart, soul, mind and strength.[1] Our mind is to be renewed,[2] our emotions purified,[3] our conscience kept clear[4] and our will surrendered to God's will.[5] Discipleship entails all that we know of ourselves being committed to all that we know of God. Yet, of the various constituent elements which go to make up our human being, it is our mind and our emotions which the biblical writers treat most fully. So we will consider each separately, and then the two in relation to each other.

The mind

The story is told of two women who were having a chat in their local supermarket. One said to the other: 'What's the matter with you? You look so worried.'

'I am,' responded her friend; 'I keep thinking about the world situation.'

'Well,' said the first lady, 'you want to take things more philosophically, and stop thinking!'

It is a rather delicious idea that the way to become more philosophical is to do less thinking. Yet those two ladies were reflecting the modern anti-intellectual mood, which has given birth to the ugly twins called mindlessness and meaninglessness.

Over against this trend we need to set the instruction of the apostle Paul: 'Brothers, stop thinking like children. In regard to

[1] Mk. 12:30. [2] Rom. 12:2; Eph. 4:23. [3] *E.g.* Eph. 4:26; 1 Pet. 1:22.
[4] Acts 24:16. [5] *E.g.* Mk. 14:36; Mt. 6:10; Col. 4:12.

evil be infants, but in your thinking be adults.'[1] It is noteworthy that he begins with the very words used by one of the ladies in the supermarket, 'Stop thinking'; but he continues, 'like children'. True, Jesus told us to become like children, but he did not mean that we are to copy children in everything. Similarly, Paul urges us to be children, indeed 'infants' or 'babies', in evil (the less sophisticated we are in relation to evil, the better); but in our thinking, he adds, we are to grow up, to become mature. The whole biblical revelation lies behind Paul's appeal.

First, a responsible use of our minds *glorifies our Creator*. For he is (among other things) a rational God, who made us in his own image rational beings, has given us in nature and in Scripture a double, rational revelation, and expects us to use our minds to explore what he has revealed. All scientific research is based on the convictions that the universe is an intelligible, even meaningful, system; that there is a fundamental correspondence between the mind of the investigator and the data being investigated; and that this correspondence is rationality. In consequence, 'a scientist faced with an apparent irrationality does not accept it as final ... He goes on struggling to find some rational way in which the facts can be related to each other ... Without that passionate faith in the ultimate rationality of the world, science would falter, stagnate and die ...'.[2] It is therefore no accident that the pioneers of the scientific revolution were Christians. They believed that the rational God had stamped his rationality both upon the world and upon them. In this way all scientists, whether they know it or not, are 'thinking God's thoughts after him', as the seventeenth-century German astronomer Johannes Kepler put it.

Conscientious Bible students are also 'thinking God's thoughts after him'. For God has given us in Scripture an even clearer and fuller revelation of himself. He has 'spoken', communicating his thoughts in words. In particular, he has disclosed his love for sinners like us and his plan to save us through Jesus Christ.

Has God, then, made us rational persons, and shall we deny

[1] 1 Cor. 14:20. [2] Lesslie Newbigin, *Foolishness to the Greeks* (SPCK, 1986), p. 70.

this essential feature of our creation? Has he taken the trouble to reveal himself, and shall we neglect his revelation? No, the proper use of our minds is neither to abdicate our responsibility and go to sleep, nor to proclaim the autonomy of human reason (as the leaders of the Enlightenment did) and so stand in judgment on the data of divine revelation, but to sit in humility under them, to study, interpret, synthesize and apply them. Only so can we glorify our Creator.

Secondly, a responsible use of our minds *enriches our Christian life*. I am not now thinking of education, culture and art, which enhance the quality of human life, but of our discipleship in particular, no part of which is possible if we stifle our minds. 'Looking back over my experience as a pastor for some thirty-four years,' wrote Martyn Lloyd-Jones, 'I can testify without the slightest hesitation that the people I have found most frequently in trouble in their spiritual experience have been those who have lacked understanding. You cannot divorce these things. You will go wrong in the realms of practical living and experience if you have not a true understanding.'[1]

Let me illustrate this in relation to faith. It is amazing how many people suppose that faith and reason are incompatible. But they are never set over against each other in Scripture. Faith and sight are contrasted,[2] but not faith and reason. For faith according to Scripture is neither credulity, nor superstition, nor 'an illogical belief in the occurrence of the improbable',[3] but a quiet, thoughtful trust in the God who is known to be trustworthy. Consider Isaiah 26:3–4:

> You will keep in perfect peace
>   him whose mind is steadfast,
>   because he trusts in you.
> Trust in the LORD for ever,
>   for the LORD, the LORD, is the Rock eternal.

[1] D. Martyn Lloyd-Jones, *The Christian Warfare* (Banner of Truth, 1976), p. 114.
[2] 2 Cor. 5:7.
[3] H. L. Mencken, who wrote for the *Baltimore Sun* and was sometimes called 'the sage of Baltimore'.

In these verses to trust in God and to set the mind steadfastly upon him are synonyms, the reasonableness of trusting him is that he is an immovable rock, and the reward of faith is peace. It is only by reflecting on the changelessness of God that our faith grows. And the more we perceive his steadfastness, the more steadfast does our faith become.

Or take our need of divine guidance. Too many people regard it as an alternative to human thought, even a convenient device for saving them the bother of thinking. They expect God to flash on to their inner screen answers to their questions and solutions to their problems, in such a way as to bypass their minds. And of course God is free to do this; perhaps occasionally he does. But Scripture gives us the warrant to insist that God's normal way of guiding us is rational, not irrational, namely through the very thought processes which he has created in us.

Psalm 32 makes this clear. Verse 8 contains a marvellous threefold promise of divine guidance, in which God says, 'I will instruct you and teach you in the way you should go; I will counsel you and watch over you' (RSV 'counsel you with my eye upon you'). But *how* will God fulfil his promise? Verse 9 continues: 'Do not be like the horse or the mule, which have no understanding, but must be controlled by bit and bridle or they will not come to you.' If we put together the promise and the prohibition, what God is saying to us is this: 'I promise that I will guide you, and show you the way to go. But do not expect me to guide you as you guide horses and mules (namely by force, not intelligence), for the simple reason that you are neither a horse nor a mule. They lack "understanding", but you don't. Indeed, I myself have given you the precious gift of understanding. Use it! Then I will guide you *through* your minds.'

Thirdly, a responsible use of our minds *strengthens our evangelistic witness*. So much modern evangelism is an assault on the emotions and the will, without any comparable recognition of the mind. But our evangelistic appeal should never ask people to close or suspend their minds. The gospel requires us to humble our minds, indeed, but also to open them to God's truth.

That this is God's way is clear from the practice of the apostles. We saw in chapter 3 that Paul in Corinth renounced the wisdom of the world and the rhetoric of the Greeks,[1] but that he did not renounce either doctrinal content in his preaching or the deployment of arguments. In Corinth itself Luke describes him as 'reasoning' with people and trying to 'persuade' them,[2] while in Ephesus he lectured and debated daily in a secular lecture hall for two years.[3] To be sure, his confidence was in the Holy Spirit. But, being the Spirit of truth, the Holy Spirit brings people to faith in Christ because of the evidence, and not in spite of it. There is an urgent need in our day to include apologetics in our evangelism, that is, to defend the gospel as well as to proclaim it. In all our evangelism we need to be able to declare, as Paul did to Festus: 'What I am saying is true and reasonable.'[4] In addition, God is surely calling some men and women in our generation, as he has done in the past, to dedicate their God-given intellect to the task of 'defending and confirming the gospel'.[5]

So then, we need to repent of the cult of mindlessness, and of any residual anti-intellectualism or intellectual laziness of which we may be guilty. These things are negative, cramping and destructive. They insult God, impoverish us and weaken our testimony. A responsible use of our minds, on the other hand, glorifies God, enriches us and strengthens our witness in the world.

Two qualifications seem to be needed, however, since there are two 'isms' which, if we are not on our guard, might result from this emphasis on the mind, namely elitism and intellectualism. Elitism in this context would limit Christian thinking to a small minority of university-educated people. It would give the impression that only a select, even exclusive, bunch of eggheads are capable of using their minds. We must set ourselves fiercely against this bizarre notion, however. True, Christians have been the pioneers of education, and want everybody

[1] 1 Cor. 2:1–5. [2] Acts 18:4. [3] Acts 19:9–10. [4] Acts 26:25. [5] Phil. 1:7.

to have the best possible education to develop their maximum potential. But formal education is not indispensable to the development of Christian thinking. For *all* human beings are created rational in God's image and are able to learn how to think. A few years ago I was addressing a group of clergy in Liverpool and said something about the need to use our God-given minds. As soon as I had finished, somebody stood up and objected that I was limiting Christianity to intellectuals and excluding the working classes, among whom he worked. I did not need to reply. For immediately several inner-city workers were on their feet, flushed with anger. 'You're insulting the working classes,' they said to the first speaker. 'They may not have had as much formal education as you, but they're just as intelligent and just as able to think.' Our task, then, is to encourage all God's people to think, and not to develop an intellectual elite.

The second danger is intellectualism, the encouragement of a Christianity which is too cerebral, and not visceral enough. That is, it is all brain, with no gut. But in order to urge people to use their minds, it is not necessary to urge them to suppress their feelings. I often say to our students at the Institute for Contemporary Christianity in London that we are not in the business of 'breeding tadpoles'. A tadpole is a little creature with a huge head and nothing much else besides. Certainly there are some Christian tadpoles around. Their heads are bulging with sound theology, but that is all there is to them. No, we are concerned to help people to develop not only a Christian mind, but also a Christian heart, a Christian spirit, a Christian conscience and a Christian will, in fact to become whole Christian persons, thoroughly integrated under the lordship of Christ. This will include our emotions.

Chaim Potok's book *The Chosen*[1] and the film based on it illustrate this well. He tells the story of two Jewish youths who were brought up in Brooklyn, New York, during and after the Second World War. Danny Saunders' father was a strict Hasidic

[1] Chaim Potok, *The Chosen* (1967; Penguin, 1970).

rabbi, while Ruevan Malter's father was a writer in the liberal Jewish tradition. In the boys' friendship these two traditions came into conflict. Throughout most of the book Rabbi Saunders astonishes us because, although he is a very human person, he never talks to Danny except when he is teaching him out of the Talmud. Instead, he maintains between them a 'weird silence'.[1] Not until near the end is the mystery explained. Rabbi Saunders says that God had blessed him with a brilliant son, 'a boy with a mind like a jewel'. When Danny was only four years old, his father saw him reading a book and was frightened because he 'swallowed' it. The book described the sufferings of a poor Jew, yet Danny had enjoyed it! 'There was no soul in my four-year-old Daniel, there was only his mind. He was a mind in a body without a soul.'[2] So the rabbi cried to God: 'What have you done to me? A mind like this I need for a son? A *heart* I need for a son, a *soul* I need for a son, compassion . . ., righteousness, mercy, strength to suffer and carry pain. *That* I want from my son, not a mind without a soul!'[3] So Rabbi Saunders followed an ancient Hasidic tradition and brought the boy up in silence, for then 'in the silence between us he began to hear the world crying'.[4] In the final scene of reconciliation between father and son, the rabbi says that Danny had to learn 'through the wisdom and the pain of silence that a mind without a heart is nothing'.

The emotions

My readers will probably not suspect me of being an emotional person. For I am one of those cold fish called an Englishman, descended from hard Norsemen and blunt Anglo-Saxons, with no spark of Celtic or Latin fire in my blood. With that ancestry, I am supposed to be shy, reserved and even buttoned up. Moreover, I was brought up in an English public school on the philosophy of the 'stiff upper lip'. That is, since a trembling of the upper lip is the first visible sign of emotion, the tradition was

[1] *Ibid.*, p. 200. [2] *Ibid.*, p. 273. [3] *Ibid.*, p. 274. [4] *Ibid.*, p. 277.

to stiffen it. I was taught the manly virtues of courage, fortitude and self-discipline, and warned that, if I should ever feel any emotion, I was on no account to show it. Weeping was strictly for women and children only, not for men.

But then I was introduced to Jesus Christ. I learned to my astonishment that God, whose 'impassibility' I thought meant that he was incapable of emotion, speaks (though in human terms) of his burning anger and vulnerable love.[1] I discovered too that Jesus of Nazareth, the perfect human being, was no tight-lipped, unemotional ascetic. On the contrary, I read that he turned on hypocrites with anger, looked on a rich young ruler and loved him, could both rejoice in spirit and sweat drops of blood in spiritual agony, was constantly moved with compassion, and even burst into tears twice in public.

From all this evidence it is plain that our emotions are not to be suppressed, since they have an essential place in our humanness and therefore in our Christian discipleship.

First, there is a place for emotion in *spiritual experience*. The Holy Spirit is the Spirit of truth, as we have noted. But his ministry is not limited to illuminating our minds and teaching us about Christ. He also pours God's love into our hearts.[2] Similarly, he bears witness with our spirit that we are God's children, for he causes us to say '*Abba*, Father'[3] and to exclaim with gratitude 'how great is the love the Father has lavished on us, that we should be called children of God!'[4] In addition, although we have not yet seen Christ, nevertheless already we love him and trust him, and so 'are filled with an inexpressible and glorious joy'.[5]

There are, of course, many varieties of spiritual experience, and we must not try to stereotype them, insisting that everybody has exactly the same experience. Nevertheless, all Christian people, at least from time to time, have feelings both of profound sorrow and of profound joy. On the one hand, we 'groan inwardly', in solidarity with the fallen creation, burdened with our own fallenness and longing for our final

[1] *E.g.* Ho. 11:8–9. [2] Rom. 5:5. [3] Rom. 8:15–16. [4] 1 Jn. 3:1.
[5] 1 Pet. 1:8.

redemption.[1] On the other, we rejoice in the Lord, overwhelmed with gratitude for the great love with which he has loved us.

Secondly, there is a place for emotion in *public worship*. We are told in Hebrews 12:22–24 that when we assemble for worship, we do not just 'come to church', that is, to a building. For already we 'have come to Mount Zion, to the heavenly Jerusalem, the city of the living God'. We 'have come to thousands upon thousands of angels in joyful assembly, to the church of the firstborn, whose names are written in heaven'. We 'have come to God, the judge of all men, to the spirits of righteous men made perfect, to Jesus the mediator of a new covenant, and to the sprinkled blood that speaks a better word than the blood of Abel'. The recognition of this cosmic dimension transforms worship. On some particular Sunday perhaps only a handful of God's people have gathered, and a heterogeneous handful at that. But then we remember, as the 1928 Prayer Book put it, that we have come together 'in the presence of Almighty God and of the whole company of heaven'. And in the communion service we expressly join 'with angels and archangels, and with all the company of heaven' in praising God's glorious name. That is, we are transported beyond ourselves into eternal, unseen reality. We are deeply moved by the glories of which we speak and sing, and we bow down before God in humble and joyful worship.

Thirdly, there is a place for emotion in *gospel preaching*. The apostle Paul used his mind, as we have seen. He believed in the truth of his message. He took time and trouble to defend, explain, argue and proclaim it in its fulness. But his unfolding of the whole plan of God was never cold or arid. On the contrary, he wrote that God 'has committed to us the message of reconciliation. We are therefore Christ's ambassadors, as though God were making his appeal through us. We implore you on Christ's behalf: Be reconciled to God.'[2] Paul was not satisfied with a statement of the gospel; he went on to beg people to respond to

[1] Rom. 8:22–25; 2 Cor. 5:2–4. [2] 2 Cor. 5:19–20.

it. To his systematic exposition he added an urgent personal appeal. And often, he added, his proclamation was accompanied by tears.[1]

Some preachers are impeccable in both doctrine and diction, but would never lean over the pulpit with tears in their eyes, imploring people to be reconciled to God. Others whip themselves up into a frenzy of excitement, begging for a decision, but never make a careful, cogent statement of the gospel. Why must we polarize? It is the combination of truth and tears, of mind and emotion, of reason and passion, of exposition and appeal, which makes the authentic preacher. For 'What is preaching?' asked Dr Lloyd-Jones, and went on to answer his own question. 'Logic on fire! Eloquent reason! Are these contradictions? Of course they are not. Reason concerning this Truth ought to be mightily eloquent . . . Preaching is theology coming through a man who is on fire.'[2]

Fourthly, there is a place for emotion in *social and pastoral ministry*. In this, as in all things, Jesus himself is our perfect model. Let us visualize him at the graveside of Lazarus, face to face with the reality of death. According to Scripture death is an alien intrusion into God's good world, and is no part of either his original or his ultimate purpose. The Bible calls death an 'enemy', in fact 'the last enemy to be destroyed'.[3] How, then, will Jesus react when confronted by this arch-enemy of God and of the human race? He reacted, surprisingly, with two violent emotions.

First, he was moved with anger, or indignation. In John 11:33 and 38 we are told that he 'groaned' (AV), 'sighed' (NEB), or 'was deeply moved' (RSV, NIV). The Greek verb *enebrimēsato* (verse 33) means that he 'snorted'; the word is used literally of horses and metaphorically of indignation.[4] C. K. Barrett in his commentary on John 11 writes: 'It is beyond question that *embrimasthai* implies anger.' B. B. Warfield went even further:

[1] *E.g.* Acts 20:19, 31; Phil. 3:18.

[2] D. Martyn Lloyd-Jones, *Preaching and Preachers* (Hodder and Stoughton, 1971), p. 97.

[3] 1 Cor. 15:26. [4] *Cf.* Mk. 14:5.

'What John tells us ... is that Jesus approached the grave of Lazarus in a state not of uncontrollable grief but of irrepressible anger.' Why? Because he saw 'the evil of death, its unnaturalness, its "violent tyranny" as Calvin phrases it.' He 'burns with rage against the oppressor of men ... Fury seizes upon him; his whole being is discomposed and perturbed ... It is death that is the object of his wrath, and behind death him who has the power of death, and whom he has come into the world to destroy.'[1]

Then we are told of a second emotional response of Jesus, namely sorrow and compassion. On seven separate occasions in the Gospels Jesus was 'moved with compassion', for example towards the hungry and leaderless crowds, the widow of Nain, leprosy sufferers and a blind beggar. And in John 11 we read that 'Jesus wept' (verse 35) – not now tears of anger in the face of death but tears of sympathy for the bereaved sisters. Is it not beautiful to see Jesus, when confronted by death and bereavement, so deeply moved? He felt indignation in the face of death, and compassion towards its victims. First, he 'snorted' (verse 33) and then he 'wept' (verse 35).

Speaking personally, I long to see more Christian anger towards evil in the world, and more Christian compassion for its victims. Think of social injustice and political tyranny, of the callous killing of human foetuses in the womb as if they were no more than pieces of tissue, or the cynical wickedness of drug-pushers and pornographers who make their fortunes out of other people's weaknesses and at the cost of their ruin. Since these and many other evils are hateful to God, should his people not react against them in anger? And what about the victims of evil – the poor, the hungry and the homeless, street kids abandoned by their parents, unborn children at risk in a selfish society, tortured prisoners of conscience, and the alienated and lost who have never heard the gospel? Where is our sense of outrage? Where is the compassion of Jesus, which will express itself in practical action for those who suffer?

[1] B. B. Warfield, *The Person and Work of Christ* (Presbyterian and Reformed, 1950), pp. 115–117.

I do not know how much Christian profession Bob Geldof makes, but his social conscience and drive put many of us Christians to shame. What happened, then, to transform the 'scruffy Irish pop singer' into 'St Bob', the cult hero who alerted the world to the famine holocaust in Africa? Watching the televised news report on famine in Ethiopia towards the end of 1984, he experienced what one might call a 'secular conversion'. The people he saw on his TV screen were 'so shrunken by starvation that they looked like beings from another planet'.[1] 'I felt disgusted, enraged and outraged', he has said, 'but more than all those, I felt deep shame.'[2] Out of this experience came Band Aid and Live Aid and other initiatives, which raised many millions of pounds. What drove him? It was a combination of 'pity and disgust'.[3]

Mind and emotions

So far we have looked at our intellect and our emotions separately, and we have seen that both have an indispensable place in our Christian discipleship. We are to be neither such emotional Christians that we never think, nor such intellectual Christians that we never feel. No, God has made us human beings, and human beings are by creation both rational and emotional.

But how are our mind and our emotions to be related to one another? There are two particular relationships on which Scripture lays emphasis, and in which the mind exercises the primary role. They are also complementary, in that the first is negative, and the second positive.

First and negatively, *the mind controls the emotions*, or should do so. There have always been some who campaign for the unfettered expression of human emotions. Bacchus, for example, whom the Greeks identified with Dionysus, was worshipped in orgies of wine, dance and sex. In our day popular Freudianism, which has not entirely grasped what Freud meant by 'repression', has taught the peril of suppressing our

[1] Bob Geldof with Paul Vallely, *Is That It?* (Penguin, 1986), p. 269.
[2] *Ibid.*, p. 271. [3] *Ibid.*, p. 386.

emotions. And some forms of existentialism have added impetus to these ideas by urging us to find our authenticity in being and expressing ourselves.

But Christians cannot possibly follow this teaching and give free rein to our emotions. For our whole human being has been tainted and twisted by inherited sin, and that includes our emotions. They are ambiguous because we are ambiguous. Some are good, but others evil, and we have to learn to discriminate between them.

Take anger. The instruction 'In your anger do not sin'[1] recognizes that there are two different kinds of anger. There is righteous anger, such as God himself feels towards evil, and there is unrighteous anger (contaminated by pride, envy, malice, spite and revenge) which is one of the 'acts of the sinful nature'.[2] Consequently, when feelings of anger arise within us, it would be very foolish to give vent to them uncritically. Instead, we should say to ourselves: 'Wait a minute! What is this anger which is beginning to burn inside me? Is it righteous anger or unrighteous? Is it anger against evil, or merely injured vanity?'

Or take love. What should we say to a married man who confesses that he has fallen in love with another woman, that he cannot help himself, that this is 'the real thing', and that he must divorce his wife? I think we would have to say: 'Wait a minute! You are not the helpless victim of your emotions. You have accepted a life-long commitment to your wife. You should (and can) put this other woman out of your mind.'

In these two examples, the one of anger and the other of love, there is a recognition that both emotions can be tainted with self-centredness, and that we should never give in to either without first asking ourselves some searching questions. In both cases, the mind is meant to stand censor over the emotions.

Secondly and positively, the *mind stimulates the emotions*. It is when we reflect on the truth that our heart catches fire. Think of the Emmaus disciples on the afternoon of Easter Day. The risen Lord joined them on their walk and explained to them out

[1] Eph. 4:26. [2] Gal. 5:19–21.

of the Scriptures how the Messiah had to suffer before entering his glory. Later, after he had left them, they said to each other: 'Were not our hearts burning within us while he talked with us on the road and opened the Scriptures to us?'[1] This inner burning of the heart is a profound emotional experience, but it was Jesus' biblical teaching which prompted it. Nothing sets the heart ablaze like fresh vistas of truth. As F. W. Faber put it, 'deep theology is the best fuel of devotion; it readily catches fire, and once kindled it burns long.'[2]

Or consider Paul's well-known statement that 'Christ's love compels us'.[3] Literally, it 'hems us in' or 'leaves us no choice' (NEB), so that we must live our lives for him. But how does the love of Christ constrain or move us? Is it that we are overwhelmed emotionally at the foot of the cross? Yes and no! Yes, in that we cannot contemplate the cross and not be moved by it. But no, if we suppose that our mind plays no part in the process. For what Paul writes is that 'Christ's love compels us, because we are convinced that . . .'. It is through certain convictions that Christ's love tightens its grip upon us. In brief, it is because we have received our life from Christ crucified and risen, that we realize we must live it for him. It is as we reflect upon this logic that the fires of love within us are fanned into flame.

One more example may be mentioned. In the area of social responsibility it is essential that we both think clearly and feel deeply. A cool analysis of injustice is necessary, so long as it leads to hot anger and action.

It is important, then, to keep our mind and our emotions together, allowing our mind both to control and to stimulate our emotions. I think it was Bishop Handley Moule at the end of the last century who gave this good advice: 'Beware equally of an undevotional theology (*i.e.* mind without heart) and of an untheological devotion (*i.e.* heart without mind).'

[1] Lk. 24:32.
[2] Quoted by Ralph G. Turnbull in *A Minister's Obstacles* (1946; Baker, 1972), p. 97.
[3] 2 Cor. 5:14.

CHAPTER EIGHT

GUIDANCE, VOCATION AND MINISTRY

If God has a purpose for the lives of his people, and if his purpose is discoverable, then nothing could be more important than for us to discern and do it. The apostle Paul certainly indicated that this was his expectation. 'We are God's workmanship,' he affirmed, 'created in Christ Jesus to do good works, which God prepared in advance for us to do.'[1] If, therefore, there are good works which God has planned and designed for us, presumably from before we were born, we surely must find out what they are. No wonder Paul wrote later in the same letter: 'Do not be foolish, but understand what the Lord's will is.'[2]

In the companion letter to the Colossians Paul also prayed that God would 'fill (them) with the knowledge of his will through all spiritual wisdom and understanding',[3] and mentioned how Epaphras was 'always wrestling in prayer' for them, that they might 'stand firm in all the will of God, mature and fully assured'.[4]

Whenever we talk about discovering God's will for our lives, three words are almost bound to crop up in the conversation; they are 'guidance', 'vocation' and 'ministry'. Each has a distinctive meaning. 'Guidance' implies that God is willing to direct us, 'vocation' that he calls us, and 'ministry' that he wants us to give our lives in service. At the same time, what is common to the three concepts is that the initiative in each is God's, and that each has both a general aspect (which applies equally to all

[1] Eph. 2:10. [2] Eph. 5:17. [3] Col. 1:9. [4] Col. 4:12.

of us) and a particular (which is different for each of us). This will become clearer as we go on.

Guidance

We sometimes say with a sigh, 'If only I had ten lives . . .'. There is a myth that cats have nine, but we human beings have only one, and we cannot duplicate or replicate ourselves. Hence the urgency that we should discover God's will for the one and only life he has given us.

But before we are in a position to discover God's will, it is essential to draw a distinction between his 'general' will and his 'particular' will. God's general will is so called because it is his will for the generality of his people; it is the same for all of us in all places and at all times. God's particular will is so called, however, because it is his will for particular people at particular places and times. His general will is that we should 'be conformed to the likeness of his Son'.[1] Christlikeness is God's will for all of us; it does not vary from disciple to disciple. His particular will, on the other hand, concerns such questions as the choice of a life work and of a life partner, and how we should spend our energies, time, money and holidays. These will be different for each of us. Only when we have made this essential distinction between the 'general' and the 'particular' are we in a position to repeat our earlier question how we can discover God's will. His general will has been revealed in Scripture. Not that Scripture contains slick solutions to complex twentieth-century ethical problems, but that it contains principles which can be applied to them. Generally speaking, it is correct to say that the will of God for the people of God is in the Word of God.

The particular will of God will not be found in Scripture, however. I cannot deny that occasionally God seems to have guided individuals through a specific verse wrenched out of its context. But I must add that he has done it only in condescension to our weakness. For Scripture is not an anthology of unrelated

[1] Rom. 8:29.

texts, but a cumulative, historical revelation. We have no liberty to ignore its original meaning in order to oblige it to speak to us. What the Bible does contain, however, is principles which are relevant to particular questions. Take marriage as an example. Scripture gives us general guidance and settles some issues in advance. It tells us that marriage is God's good purpose for human beings and that singleness is the exception, not the rule; that one of his primary purposes in instituting marriage is companionship, so that this is an important quality to look for in a spouse; that a Christian is at liberty to marry only a fellow-Christian; and that marriage (as a lifelong, loving, monogamous and heterosexual commitment) is the only God-ordained context for sexual intercourse. These general guidelines are clearly laid down in the Bible. But the Bible will not tell any individuals whether God is calling them to marriage or to remain single, or (if they should marry) who their spouse should be.

How, then, are we meant to discover God's particular will, if he does not disclose it through Scripture? Since God is sovereign and free, I do not think we have the liberty to stereotype our answer. But I have found that the following five monosyllables are safe guides. First, *yield*. The word is a familiar road sign in the United States, telling traffic to give way to other vehicles. Just so, we are to give in to, or give way to, God's purpose. An unsurrendered will is the most serious of all obstacles to the discovery of God's will. If God does not reveal his truth to those who are not willing to believe it, neither does he reveal his will to those unwilling to do it. No, 'he guides the humble in what is right and teaches them his way'.[1]

Secondly, *pray*. A vague surrender is not enough; sustained, expectant prayer is also necessary. 'Ask and it will be given to you,' Jesus taught, and 'You do not have, because you do not ask God,' James added.[2] Our heavenly Father does not spoil his children. He does not disclose his will to us unless we really want to know it and express our desire in our prayers.

[1] Ps. 25:9. [2] Mt. 7:7; Jas. 4:2.

Thirdly, *talk*. Although one of the strengths of Protestant Christianity is its insistence on 'the right of private judgment', we must not imagine that this means we should make all our decisions alone. On the contrary, God has given us to each other in his family. So we need to be humble enough to talk to others, including our parents, in order to seek their counsel, for 'wisdom is found in those who take advice'.[1] Let our decisions be group decisions, taken responsibly in the rich fellowship in which God has put us.

Fourthly, *think*. Although we must yield, pray and ask advice, ultimately we have to make up our own minds. As we saw in the last chapter, God balances his promises of guidance with his prohibition of behaviour like horses and mules which lack understanding.[2] We must not expect him to fulfil his promises to guide us either by using 'bit and bridle' (*i.e.* force) or by giving us irrational hunches, but rather through the minds he has given us, as in every situation we carefully weigh up the pros and cons.

Fifthly, *wait*. It is a mistake to be in a hurry or grow impatient with God. It took him about 2,000 years to fulfil his promise to Abraham in the birth of Christ. It took him eighty years to prepare Moses for his life work. It takes him about twenty-five years to make a mature human being. So then, if we *have* to make a decision by a certain deadline, we must make it. But if not, and the way forward is still uncertain, it is wiser to wait. I think God says to us what he said to Joseph and Mary when sending them into Egypt with the child Jesus: 'Stay there until I tell you.'[3] In my experience, more mistakes are made by precipitate action than by procrastination.

Vocation

'Vocation' is one of many biblical words which over the years has changed its meaning and become devalued. In popular usage it refers to our work or career. 'What's your vocation?' is

[1] Pr. 13:10. [2] Ps. 32:8–9. [3] Mt. 2:13.

a rather grandiose way of asking somebody what his job is, and 'vocational training' means training for a particular trade. In biblical usage, however, 'vocation' has a much broader and nobler connotation. Its emphasis is not on the human (what *we* do) but on the divine (what *God* has called us to do). For 'vocation' is a Latin word, whose Anglo-Saxon equivalent is 'calling'.

In the New Testament the Greek verb to 'call' occurs about 150 times, and in most cases of God calling human beings. In the Old Testament God called Moses, Samuel and the prophets; in the New Testament Jesus called the Twelve and later Saul of Tarsus. Today, although we are neither prophets nor apostles, he still calls us into his service. It is a wonderful fact that God cares about us enough to call us personally and individually. In consequence, God is 'he who called you';[1] and we are the 'called according to his purpose'.[2]

The question before us is this: what, according to Scripture, does God call us to? What is our divine vocation? In answer to this question about 'vocation', we have to make a similar distinction to the one we made with regard to 'guidance', namely between our 'general' calling and our particular 'callings'. Our general calling is that of all God's people, and is therefore the same. Our particular calling is that of each of us, and is therefore different. We all share in the same general call of God; we have each received a different particular call from God.

God's *general call* to us is not so much to do something (a job) as to be something (a person). Although he does call us to different tasks, as we shall shortly see, he first calls us to something even more significant, namely to be a disciple of Jesus Christ, to live a new life in his new society and in the world. So if somebody asks us, 'What is your calling?', our first and correct answer should be: 'I am called to belong to Jesus Christ.'[3] In fact, we are called to embrace and enjoy all the blessings which God has locked up in Jesus Christ: 'to this you were called so that you may inherit a blessing'.[4] What, then, is

[1] *E.g.* Gal. 5:8; 1 Pet. 1:15. [2] *E.g.* Rom. 8:28; Heb. 9:15. [3] Rom. 1:6.
[4] 1 Pet. 3:9.

this blessing? It has many facets.

First, we are called to *fellowship with Jesus Christ*. This is basic. His invitation is still 'Come to me' and 'Follow me'. For 'God . . . has called you into fellowship with his Son Jesus Christ our Lord'.[1] Just as Christ called the Twelve to be 'with him',[2] so he calls us to know him and to enjoy his fellowship. Eternal life is to know God and his Christ,[3] and nothing can take the place of this fundamental relationship with him.

Secondly, we are called to *freedom*. 'You, my brothers,' Paul wrote to the Galatians, 'were called to be free.'[4] The kind of freedom to which the apostle was alluding here is freedom from the condemnation of the law through God's forgiveness and acceptance of us in Christ. It is freedom from guilt and from a guilty conscience, the freedom of access to God as his adopted sons and daughters. It is not, however, freedom to sin or freedom from social responsibilities. On the contrary, Paul goes on: 'But do not use your freedom to indulge the sinful nature; rather serve one another (literally, 'be slaves to one another') in love.' It is the paradox we have already noted that it is only through serving that we become free.

Thirdly, we are called to *peace*. 'Let the peace of Christ rule in your hearts, since as members of one body you were called to peace.'[5] The reference to the 'one body' gives us the clue to Paul's meaning. He is not here referring to peace of mind, heart or conscience, but to the peace (*shalom*) of reconciliation with each other in the kingdom community of Christ. Our calling is to belong not only to Christ, but also to the people of Christ.

Fourthly, we are called to *holiness*,[6] or 'called to be saints'.[7] Since God himself is holy, he calls us to be holy too.[8] Unfortunately, 'holiness' suggests to many people the false image of pious folk with an anaemic look and a vacant stare, who seem to have contracted out of life. But true holiness is a Christlikeness which is lived out in the real world.

Fifthly, we are called to *witness*. 'But you are . . . a people

[1] 1 Cor. 1:9. [2] Mk. 3:14. [3] Jn. 17:3.
[4] Gal. 5:13. [5] Col. 3:15. [6] 1 Cor. 1:2.
[7] Rom. 1:7. [8] *E.g.* 1 Pet. 1:15; 1 Thes. 4:7; 2 Tim. 1:9.

belonging to God, that you may declare the praises of him who called you out of darkness into his wonderful light.'[1] Peter is contrasting what we once were with what we now are. We were in darkness, but now we are in light. We were not a people, but now we are God's people. We had not received mercy, but now we have. The logical deduction is that we cannot possibly keep these blessings to ourselves. Having been called into God's light, we are inevitably called to let our light shine.

Sixthly, we are called to *suffering*. 'If you suffer for doing good and you endure it, this is commendable before God. To this you were called.'[2] Peter was writing when Nero's hostility to Christians was growing and the storm clouds of persecution were gathering ominously on the horizon. At any moment the storm might break. How then should Christians react if they suffered unjustly? Peter's answer was straightforward. They were called to follow Christ's example of non-retaliation. It comes as a shock to many people that unjust suffering is an unavoidable part of the Christian calling. But Jesus himself warned us of it. 'If the world hates you, keep in mind that it hated me first. . . . If they persecuted me, they will persecute you also.'[3]

Seventhly, we are called to *glory*. The Christian calling is a 'heavenly calling'.[4] 'The God of all grace, who called you to his eternal glory in Christ, after you have suffered a little while, will himself . . . make you strong, firm and steadfast.'[5] Suffering and glory are constantly bracketed in the New Testament. It was through suffering that Jesus entered his glory, and it will be the same for us. If we share in Christ's suffering, we will also share in his glory.[6] Thus, the call of God is not for this life only; it is also to spend eternity with him in the new universe.

Here, then, is God's sevenfold, general calling. He calls all of us to Christ, freedom, peace, holiness, witness, suffering and glory. More simply, it is a call to belong to Christ in time and eternity, to love one another in the peace of his new community,

[1] 1 Pet. 2:9. [2] 1 Pet. 2:20–21. [3] Jn. 15:18, 20. [4] Heb. 3:1; *cf.* Phil. 3:14.
[5] 1 Pet. 5:10. [6] Rom. 8:17.

and to serve, witness and suffer in the world. This is the fundamental meaning of 'Christian vocation'. It is the same for all of us, and we are exhorted to live a life that is worthy of it.[1]

If our general call (which is the same for us all) is to be free and holy and Christlike, our *particular calling* (which is different for each of us) relates to the highly individual details of our lives. Consider the teaching of Paul: 'Each one should remain in the situation (literally, 'the calling') which he was in when God called him.'[2] We note at once the two senses in which the apostle uses the notion of 'calling'. The words 'when God called him' refer to a person's conversion when God's general call is heard and obeyed. 'The situation' ('calling') which he was 'in', on the other hand, is a reference to his particular calling at the time of his conversion. This situation is regarded as something God has 'called' us to and something God has 'assigned' to us.[3] And the general principle the apostle lays down, repeating it three times,[4] is that we should 'remain' in it. He gives three examples – our domestic situation (married or single), cultural situation (Jewish or Gentile) and social situation (slaves or free). In order to understand Paul's teaching, we need to grasp the background and context. It appears that the Corinthian converts found life in Christ so new ('a new creation')[5] and exciting, and so radically different from their unregenerate state, that they imagined that nothing belonging to the old life could be retained; everything had to be repudiated.

Take the example of marriage. Now that they belonged to Christ, they seem to have been asking, how could a pre-conversion contractual obligation still be valid post-conversion? Would not such a relationship be 'unclean'?[6] Paul answers, 'No.' Why not? Because God's providence embraced both their pre- and their post-conversion lives. Their marriage, though entered into before they became Christians, was a part of the 'calling' they were in when God called them. They had no

[1] Eph. 4:1. [2] 1 Cor. 7:20. [3] 1 Cor. 7:20, 17. [4] 1 Cor. 7:17, 20, 24.
[5] 2 Cor. 5:17. [6] 1 Cor. 7:14.

liberty therefore to repudiate it. Transform it by God's grace – yes; reject it – no.

We have to be very cautious in applying this teaching to ourselves. Paul is laying down a general rule, not an absolute one. For example, he himself had not remained a Pharisee when called to be an apostle of Christ. Similarly, the Twelve had given up their fishing and their tax-collecting when called to become apostles. And Paul says here that if a slave can gain his freedom he should do so.[1] We too need to be open to the possibility that God is calling us to something different. What Paul was opposing was thoughtless and reckless actions, change for change's sake, and especially the notion that nothing before conversion and nothing outside religion has any value to God.

From Scripture we turn to history, and to the teaching of the Reformers and the Puritans in this area. The Reformers insisted that every Christian man and woman has a divine 'calling'. They were reacting against the teaching of medieval Catholicism that bishops, priests, monks and nuns had a superior, because a 'religious', calling. The Reformers rejected this as both 'clericalism', separating clergy from laity, and 'dualism', separating 'sacred' activities like prayer from 'secular' ones like running a home or earning a living. They affirmed that God is interested in the whole of life, and that to be a farmer, craftsman, magistrate or housewife was just as much a divine calling as to be a 'priest' or 'pastor'. Luther insisted much on this:

> Those who are now called 'spiritual', that is, priests, bishops or popes, are neither different from other Christians nor superior to them, except that they are charged with the administration of the word of God and the sacraments, which is their work and office.

But 'tailors, cobblers, stonemasons, carpenters, cooks, innkeepers, farmers and all the temporal craftsmen' have also

[1] 1 Cor. 7:21.

been 'consecrated' like priests, each to 'the work and office of his trade'.

> Further, everyone must benefit and serve every other by means of his own work or office, so that in this way many kinds of work may be done for the bodily and spiritual welfare of the community, just as all the members of the body serve one another (1 Cor. 12:14–26).[1]

Again, 'serving God is not tied to one or two works, nor is it confined to one or two callings, but it is distributed over all works and all callings'.[2] 'But what I want to do is to keep a distinction between the callings and offices, so that everyone can see to what God has called him and fulfil the duties of his office faithfully and sincerely in the service of God.'[3]

Calvin's teaching was similar:

> The Lord bids each one of us in all life's actions to look to his calling . . . Therefore, lest through our stupidity and rashness everything be turned topsy-turvy, he has appointed duties for every man in his particular way of life. And that no one may thoughtlessly transgress his limits, he has named these various kinds of living 'callings'. Therefore each individual has his own kind of living assigned to him by the Lord as a sort of sentry post so that he may not heedlessly wander about throughout life . . . From this will arise also a singular consolation: that no task will be so sordid and base, provided you obey your calling in it, that it will not shine and be reckoned very precious in God's sight.[4]

The Puritans developed this theme further. William Perkins, for example, who had a very influential ministry in Cambridge, wrote *A Treatise of the Vocations or Callings of Men* (published in 1603). Here is a sample of his thesis:

[1] Luther *Weimarer Ausgabe* (1883—), vol. 44, pp. 130–131.
[2] Luther W. A., vol. 52, p. 124. [3] Luther W. A., vol. 46, p. 166.
[4] Calvin, *Institutes*, III.x.6.

> The action of a shepherd in keeping sheep ... is as good a work before God as is the action of a judge in giving sentence, or of a magistrate in ruling, or a minister in preaching. Thus then we see there is good reason why we would search how every man is rightly to use his particular calling.[1]

A century later, and on the other side of the Atlantic, Cotton Mather, the Harvard Puritan, wrote *A Christian at his Calling* (1701). In it he taught that every Christian has two callings – 'a general calling' ('to serve the Lord Jesus Christ ...') and 'a personal calling' ('a particular employment by which his usefulness in his neighbourhood is distinguished').[2]

Moreover, the two callings should be pursued in balance. For 'a Christian at his two callings is a man in a boat rowing for heaven ... If he mind but one of his callings, be it which it will, he pulls the oar but on one side of the boat, and will make but a poor dispatch to the shore of eternal blessedness.'[3]

It would be easy to criticize this kind of teaching. The Reformers and the Puritans were people of their age and culture, as we are of ours. They held a static, medieval view of society. In their reaction against the revolutionary overtones of some Anabaptist teaching, they tended to be too resistant to change. Sometimes they got close to the embarrassing verse in the hymn 'All Things Bright and Beautiful':

> The rich man in his castle,
> The poor man at his gate,
> God made them, high or lowly,
> And ordered their estate.

We certainly should not use the biblical teaching about 'callings' to resist social change.

Paul in the first century, the Reformers in the sixteenth, and

[1] William Perkins, *A Treatise of the Vocations or Callings of Men* in *The Work of William Perkins*, The Courtenay Library of Reformation Classics, ed. Ian Breward (Sutton Courtenay Press, 1970), p. 458.

[2] Cotton Mather, *A Christian at his Calling* (1701), p. 37.

[3] *Ibid.*, pp. 37–38.

the Puritans in the seventeenth all seem rather remote from us. So what is the underlying principle, which Paul taught and the Reformers and Puritans recovered, which we need to hold on to today? I think it is this. The whole of our life belongs to God and is part of his calling, both before conversion and outside religion. We must not imagine that God first became interested in us when we were converted, or that now he is interested only in the religious bit of our lives.

Consider our life before conversion. What was our calling in which we were when God called us? If at the time of our conversion we were looking after elderly relatives, we should not abandon them now. If we were students, we have no liberty to give up our studies and drop out of college or university. If we had entered into a contract with somebody, we have no right to break it. If we were musical, artistic, athletic, or intelligent when God called us, we must not now disown these good things which a good Creator gave us. For these things were not accidental aspects of our life. They were part of God's providence to which he had called us and which he had assigned to us. God's sovereignty extends over both halves of our life. He did not begin to work in and for us at our conversion, but at our birth, even before our birth in our genetic inheritance, as later in our temperament, personality, education and skills. And what God made us and gave us before we became Christians, he redeems, sanctifies and transforms afterwards. There is a vital continuity between our pre- and post-conversion life. For although we are a new person in Christ, we are still the same person we were by creation, whom Christ has made new.

Now consider our life outside religion. The God many of us worship is altogether too religious. We seem to imagine that he is interested only in religious books and buildings and services. But no, he is interested in *us*, in our home, family and friends, in our work and hobbies, in our citizenship and community. So God's sovereignty extends over *both* halves and over *all* sections of our life. We must not marginalize God, or try to squeeze him out of the non-religious section of our life. We must remember that our vocation (*i.e.* God's calling) includes these things. It is in these that we are to serve and glorify God.

Ministry

If we are concerned to discover where God is leading us (guidance) and to what he is calling us (vocation), we may be sure that this will relate to how best we may serve him (ministry). Moreover, as with the words 'guidance' and 'vocation', so with the word 'ministry', we need to distinguish between a broader and a narrower meaning, between a general and a particular application.

Here are three affirmations about ministry.

First, *all Christians without exception are called to ministry*, indeed to spend their lives in ministry. Ministry is not the privilege of a small elite, but of all the disciples of Jesus. You will have noticed that I did not say that all Christians are called to *the* ministry, but to ministry, *diakonia*, service. We do a great disservice to the Christian cause whenever we refer to the pastorate as 'the ministry'. For by our use of the definite article we give the impression that the pastorate is the only ministry there is, much as medieval churchmen regarded the priesthood as the only (or at least the most 'spiritual') vocation there is. I repented of this view, and therefore of this language, about twenty-five years ago, and now invite my readers, if necessary, to join me in penitence. Nowadays, whenever somebody says in my presence that 'So-and-so is going into the ministry', I always ask innocently, 'Oh really? Which ministry do you mean?' And when my interlocutor probably replies, 'The pastoral ministry', I come back with the gentle complaint, 'Then why didn't you say so?!' The fact is that the word 'ministry' is a generic term; it lacks specificity until we add an adjective.

I come back to my first proposition that all Christians without exception are called to ministry. How can I make such a dogmatic statement? Because of Jesus Christ. His lordship over us has a vocational dimension, as we saw in chapter 5. Since he is 'the servant' *par excellence*, who gave himself without reserve to the service of God and human beings, it would be impossible to be his disciple without seeking to follow his example of service. He preached the kingdom, healed the sick, fed the hungry, befriended the friendless, championed the oppressed, comforted the bereaved, sought the lost and washed his apostles' feet. No task was too demanding, and no ministry too mean, for him to undertake. He lived his life and died his death in utterly self-forgetful service. Shall we not imitate him? The world measures greatness by success; Jesus measures it by service.

Secondly, *there is a wide variety of Christian ministries*. This is because 'ministry' means 'service', and there are many different ways in which we can serve God and people. Acts 6:1–4 provides a firm biblical base for this conviction. An ethnic or cultural squabble was tearing the Jerusalem church apart. The 'Grecian Jews' were complaining against the 'Hebraic Jews' that their widows were being discriminated against in the daily distribution of food. Moreover, the apostles had become embroiled in this quarrel; it was occupying a great deal of their time, and threatening to distract them from the preaching and teaching role to which Jesus had commissioned them. So they wisely called a church meeting and said: 'It would not be right for us to neglect the ministry of the word of God in order to wait on (*diakonein*) tables.' The church was then asked to choose seven men for that responsibility, while, the apostles added, 'We . . . will give our attention to prayer and the ministry (*diakonia*) of the word.'

It is essential to note that both distributing food and teaching the word were referred to as ministry (*diakonia*). Indeed, both were Christian ministry, could be full-time Christian ministry, and required Spirit-filled people to perform them. The only difference between them was that one was pastoral ministry, and the other social. It was not that one was 'ministry' and the other not; nor that one was spiritual and the other secular; nor that one was superior and the other inferior. It was simply that Christ had called the Twelve to the ministry of the word and the Seven to the ministry of tables.

I was myself brought up as a young Christian to think of different vocations or ministries as forming a hierarchy or pyramid. Perched precariously at the top of the pyramid was the cross-cultural missionary. He was our hero, she our heroine. I was taught that if I was really out and out for Christ I would undoubtedly join their ranks overseas. If I was not as keen as that, I would stay at home and be a pastor. If I did not aspire even to that, I would probably become a doctor or a teacher, whereas, if I were to go into business, politics or the media, I would not be far from backsliding! Please do not misunderstand me. It is a wonderful privilege to be a missionary or a pastor, *if God calls us to it*. But it is equally wonderful to be a Christian lawyer, industrialist, politician, manager, social worker, television script-writer, journalist, or home-maker, *if God calls us to it*. According to Romans 13:4 an official of the state (whether legislator, magistrate, policeman or policewoman) is just as much a 'minister of God' (*diakonos theou*) as a pastor. It is the hierarchy we have to reject, the pyramid we have to demolish.

There is still, of course, an urgent need for missionaries of the right kind, men and women who are characterized above all by humility – for example, the humility to repent of cultural imperialism and identify with another culture, the humility to work under national church leadership, the humility to serve people's felt needs (social as well as evangelistic), and the humility to rely on the Holy Spirit as the chief communicator.[1] World evangelization remains at the top of the church's agenda, and the fifth section of this book is devoted to it. Pastors also are greatly needed to teach the word of God. Chapters 13 and 17 take up this ministry.

At the same time, there is a crying need for Christian men and women who see their daily work as their primary Christian ministry and who determine to penetrate their secular environment for Christ.

Christian people in business and industry are needed to

[1] See *The Willowbank Report: Gospel and Culture*, especially chapter 6: 'Wanted: Humble Messengers of the Gospel' (Lausanne Committee for World Evangelization, 1978).

specify 'service to the public' as the first goal on their 'mission' statement, to make bold experiments in labour relations, worker participation and profit-sharing, and to accept their responsibility to produce an annual 'social audit' alongside their annual financial audit.

Christian politicians are needed to identify the major injustices in their society, refuse to come to terms with them, and determine to secure legislative change, however long it takes. And Christian economists are needed to find a way of controlling inflation and reducing unemployment simultaneously.

Christian film-makers are needed to produce not only overtly Christian or evangelistic films, but wholesome films which indirectly commend Christian personal and family values, and so honour and glorify Christ.

More Christian doctors are needed who, in cooperation with moral theologians, face the contemporary challenges of medical ethics and develop ways of maintaining the uniquely Christian vision of the human person and the human family.

Dedicated Christian teachers are needed, in both Christian and secular schools, who count it a privilege to serve their students in such a way as to help them develop their full God-given potential.

And more Christian social workers are needed who, in their concern for the handicapped in mind or body, abused children, drug-abusers, Aids victims and others, combine the latest medical treatment and social care with Christian love, believing prayer and church support.

Thirdly, *the particular ministry to which Christ calls us is likely to be determined by our gifts*. That is, the major factor in deciding on our life work will probably be what kind of person we are by God's creation and redemption. God is not a random creator; he has not given us natural gifts in order that they may be wasted. Nor is he a random redeemer, who has given us spiritual gifts to be wasted. Instead, he wants his gifts to us to be discerned, cultivated and exercised. He surely does not want us to be frustrated (because our gifts are lying idle), but rather fulfilled (because our gifts are being used).

It seems to me fully compatible with our Christian doctrines of creation and redemption that we should talk to ourselves somewhat as follows: 'I am a unique person. (That is not conceit. It is a fact. If every snowflake and every blade of grass is unique, how much more is every human being?) My uniqueness is due to my genetic endowment, my inherited personality and temperament, my parentage, upbringing and education, my talents, inclinations and interests, my new birth and spiritual gifts. By the grace of God I am who I am. How then can I, as the unique person God has made me, be *stretched* in the service of Christ and of people, so that nothing he has given me is wasted, and everything he has given me is used?'

There may be exceptions to this principle, but it appears to me to be the right question to ask oneself. And in trying thus to evaluate ourselves honestly, with neither pride nor false modesty, our parents and friends who know us best are likely to help us most.

The three words we have been considering (guidance, vocation and ministry) all relate to God's will for our lives and how to discover it. As I conclude, let me anticipate two fears which my readers may be feeling, and try to relieve them.

First, there is no need to fear God's will on the assumption that it is bound to be difficult. Some Christians seem to imagine that the more disagreeable some prospect is, the more likely it is to be God's will! But God is not an ogre, bent on spoiling our lives; he is our Father, committed to our welfare and determined to give us only what is for our good. 'If you . . ., though you are evil, know how to give good gifts to your children,' Jesus said, 'how much more will your Father in heaven give good gifts to those who ask him!'[1] We can be assured that God's will is 'good, pleasing and perfect'.[2]

Secondly, there is no need to fear that we shall never discover God's will. We have no cause to fret or worry, to work ourselves into a state of nervous tension, or spend sleepless nights

[1] Mt. 7:11. [2] Rom. 12:2.

of anxiety. Strangely enough, one of my earliest childhood memories, when I cannot have been more than six or seven, was of my mother coming into my bedroom daily to say goodnight. I plagued her with the constantly repeated, anguished question: 'Mummy, what am I going to be when I grow up?' She replied to the effect that I need not worry, since it would be shown me in due time. And now, more than sixty years later, with the benefit of hindsight, I know that she was right, and that all those childish apprehensions were unnecessary. We have every reason to be confident that our Father's will is discoverable as well as good. He has ways and means of showing us what he wants us to do. The main condition is that we ourselves really want to discern his will, in order to do it.

CHAPTER NINE

THE FIRST FRUIT OF THE SPIRIT

I invite you in this chapter to reflect on a biblical text which has come to mean much to me. Every day for perhaps twenty years I have quoted it to myself in my morning devotions, and prayed for its fulfilment in my life. When I am asked what my favourite text is, I usually give this one. It seems to me to contain truths which are of enormous importance to all the people of God. Here it is:

> But the fruit of the Spirit is love, joy, peace, patience, kindness, goodness, faithfulness, gentleness and self-control. Against such things there is no law.[1]

From these two verses I think we may legitimately derive five affirmations about love.

Love, joy and peace

The first truth is that *love is the preeminent Christian grace*: 'the fruit of the Spirit is love'. True, Paul lists a cluster of nine qualities, which together he calls the Spirit's 'fruit', but love has pride of place. We hear much about the Holy Spirit nowadays (he is no longer the 'neglected' person of the Trinity), and many people are claiming spectacular manifestations of his power, but the first fruit of his indwelling presence is not power, but love.

[1] Gal. 5:22–23.

It is salutary to ask ourselves this question: What is the chief distinguishing mark of a Christian? What is the hallmark which authenticates people as the children of God? Different answers are given by different people.

Some reply that what distinguishes the genuine Christian is *truth*, orthodoxy, correct belief, loyalty to the doctrines of Scripture, the Catholic Creeds and the Reformation Confessions. Right! Truth is sacred. Sound doctrine is vital to the health of the church. We are summoned to 'fight the good fight of the faith',[1] to 'guard the deposit' of revealed religion,[2] to 'stand firm and hold to the teachings' of the apostles,[3] and to 'contend for the faith that was once for all entrusted to the saints'.[4] We must never forget these solemn exhortations. Nevertheless, 'if I ... can fathom all mysteries and all knowledge, ... but have not love, I am nothing'.[5] Besides, 'knowledge puffs up, but love builds up'.[6] So love is greater than knowledge.

Others insist that the hallmark of genuine disciples is *faith*. 'For we maintain that a man is justified by faith apart from observing the law.'[7] As Luther wrote, justification by faith is 'the principal article of all Christian doctrine' which 'maketh true Christians indeed'.[8] And Cranmer added the negative counterpart: 'This (*sc.* doctrine) whosoever denieth is not to be counted for a true Christian man.'[9] Or to quote from a modern evangelical statement, justification by faith is 'the heart and hub, the paradigm and essence, of the whole economy of God's saving grace'.[10] I agree. *Sola fide*, 'by faith alone', which was the watchword of the Reformation, must be our watchword too. Nevertheless, 'if I have a faith that can move mountains, but have not love, I am nothing'.[11] The great apostle of faith is clear that love is greater than faith.

[1] 1 Tim. 6:12. [2] 1 Tim. 6:20, literally; *cf.* 2 Tim. 1:14.
[3] 2 Thes. 2:15. [4] Jude 3.
[5] 1 Cor. 13:2. [6] 1 Cor. 8:1. [7] Rom. 3:28.
[8] Luther's *Commentary on the Epistle to the Galatians* (1531; James Clarke, 1953), pp. 101, 143.
[9] From the 'Sermon on Salvation' in the *First Book of Homilies* (1547).
[10] R. T. Beckwith, G. E. Duffield and J. I. Packer, *Across the Divide* (Lyttleton Press, 1977), p. 58.
[11] 1 Cor. 13:2.

A third group emphasizes *religious experience* as the hallmark of the Christian, often of a particular and vivid kind, which they believe must be reproduced in everybody. And this group also is to some extent correct. A first-hand personal relationship with God through Christ is essential. The internal witness of the Spirit is real. There is such a thing as 'unutterable and exalted joy',[1] and 'compared to the surpassing greatness of knowing Christ Jesus my Lord' everything else is indeed a loss.[2] Nevertheless, 'if I speak in the tongues of men and of angels' and 'if I have the gift of prophecy' (claiming a direct communication from God), 'but have not love, I am nothing'.[3] So love is greater than experience.

A fourth and final category of people, being of a practical bent, emphasize *service* as the distinguishing mark of the people of God, especially the service of the poor. Right again! Without good works faith is dead. Since Jesus was himself a champion of the poor, his disciples must be also. If we see people in need, and have the wherewithal to meet it, but do not take pity on them, how can we claim to have God's love in us?[4] Thank God for the renewed emphasis on his 'preferential option' or priority concern for the poor. Nevertheless, 'if I give all I possess to the poor and surrender my body to the flames' (perhaps in a heroic gesture of sacrifice), 'but have not love, I gain nothing'.[5] So love is greater than service.

To sum up, knowledge is vital, faith indispensable, religious experience necessary, and service essential, but Paul gives precedence to love. Love is the greatest thing in the world. For 'God is love'[6] in his innermost being. Father, Son and Spirit are eternally united to each other in self-giving love. So he who is love, and has set his love upon us, calls us to love him and others in return. 'We love because he first loved us.'[7] Love is the principal, the paramount, the preeminent, the distinguishing characteristic of the people of God. Nothing can dislodge or replace it. Love is supreme.

[1] 1 Pet. 1:8 (RSV). [2] Phil. 3:8. [3] 1 Cor. 13:1–2. [4] 1 Jn. 3:17. [5] 1 Cor. 13:3. [6] 1 Jn. 4:8, 16. [7] 1 Jn. 4:19.

Secondly, *love brings joy and peace*. For 'the fruit of the Spirit is love, joy, peace'. The sequence is surely significant.

Human beings have always pursued joy and peace, though they have usually employed the more secular word 'happiness'. Thomas Jefferson, before becoming the third President of the United States, was so convinced that 'the pursuit of happiness' was an inalienable human right that he wrote it into the Declaration of Independence and called it a 'self-evident truth'.

But Christians feel obliged to add that those who pursue happiness never find it. Joy and peace are extremely elusive blessings. Happiness is a will-o'-the-wisp, a phantom. Even as we reach out a hand to grasp it, it vanishes into thin air. For joy and peace are not suitable goals to pursue; they are by-products of love. God gives them to us, not when we pursue *them*, but when we pursue *him* and *others* in love.

It is urgent that we bear witness to this truth in the contemporary world, in which 'self-realization' is the rage and the 'human potential movement' continues to gather momentum. In his perceptive book *Psychology as Religion*,[1] sub-titled *The Cult of Self-Worship*, Dr Paul Vitz of New York University began by analysing the four principal 'self-theorists' of that decade – Erich Fromm (who argued that vice is indifference to one's self and virtue self-affirmation), Carl Rogers (whose 'client-centred' therapy aimed at helping the client become an integrated, autonomous person through 'unconditional self-regard'), Abraham Maslow (who emphasized creative 'self-actualization') and Rollo May (who, influenced by existentialism, stressed decision and commitment as the means to becoming oneself). These four writers, who reached their peak in the 1970s, were all self-confessed secular humanists. They believed in human beings, not in God. They have had many popularizers, and their basic emphasis on self-esteem and self-actualization seems to have seeped into almost every segment of society. Dr David Wells comments that 'in the mid-1980s a full 87.5% of what was

[1] Eerdmans, 1977.

published in the USA was catering to the interests and appetites of the self-movement'.[1]

To be sure, there is a right and healthy kind of self-affirmation, which balances the self-denial to which Jesus called his disciples. It is not, however, the humanist's uncritical, unqualified affirmation of the self, for it is heavily qualified by the acknowledgment of our own sinfulness. Christian believers are able to affirm only those aspects of the self which derive from our creation in God's image (*e.g.* our rationality, moral responsibility and capacity for love), while at the same time denying (that is, disowning and repudiating) all those aspects of the self which derive from the fall and from our own personal fallenness (*e.g.* our selfishness, covetousness, malice, hypocrisy and pride). These Christian forms of self-affirmation and self-denial are very far from being expressions of a preoccupation, let alone an infatuation, with ourselves. For, on the contrary, they are directed not towards self but towards God. They are part and parcel of our worship of God as our Creator and our Judge.

Yet some Christian writers have tried to argue that Christianity itself is about self-esteem, that we must give up concentrating on sin, guilt, judgment and atonement, that we must present salvation instead as the discovery of the self, and that this is what Jesus meant when he endorsed the second commandment, thereby implicitly telling us to love ourselves as well as our neighbour. But this is really not so. Self-love in Scripture is a synonym for sin, not the path to freedom. Besides, *agapē*-love means the sacrifice of oneself in the service of others. By its very nature it cannot be self-directed. How can we sacrifice ourselves to serve ourselves? It is impossible. The very idea is a nonsense. The way of Jesus is the opposite, as we saw in chapter 2 on 'Authentic Freedom'. He taught the great paradox that only when we lose ourselves do we find ourselves, only when we die to ourselves do we learn to live, and only through serving others are we ourselves free. Or, to return to Paul in Galatians, only when we love, do joy and peace follow. The self-conscious

[1] David Wells, *No Place for Truth* (to be published by Eerdmans in 1993).

pursuit of happiness will always end in failure. But when we forget ourselves in the self-giving service of love, then joy and peace come flooding into our lives as incidental, unlooked-for blessings.

Love in action

Thirdly, *love issues in action*. For if love is the first fruit of the Spirit, with joy and peace following in its wake, next come 'patience, kindness, goodness'. Love is not just romance, let alone eroticism. It is not even pure sentiment or emotion. It sounds abstract, but it leads to positive attitudes and concrete actions, namely 'patience', 'kindness' and 'goodness'. And, as I believe Dostoyevsky wrote, 'love in action is much more terrible than love in dreams'. For love is always seeking the true welfare of others, at whatever personal cost.

'Patience' (*makrothymia*) is a negative quality. It is often translated 'longsuffering', for it denotes patience with people rather than with circumstances. It includes forbearance towards those who are demanding or aggravating. It never forgets the 'unlimited patience' of Christ towards us.[1]

'Kindness' (*chrēstotēs*) and 'goodness' (*agathōsynē*) are both positive qualities. The former is benevolence, generosity of thought, *wishing* good to other people, while the latter is beneficence, generosity of deed, actually *doing* for them the good we wish them.

It seems right, then, to discern a progression in these three Christian graces. Patience endures the malice of others and refuses to retaliate. Kindness turns toleration into kindliness, not wishing people ill, but wishing them well. And goodness converts the wish into the deed, taking the initiative to serve people in action.

All three qualities are characteristics and outworkings of love. For, as the apostle writes elsewhere, 'love is patient (*makrothymei*), love is kind (*chrēsteuetai*)',[2] and we are to 'serve one

[1] 1 Tim. 1:16. [2] 1 Cor. 13:4.

another in love'.[1] It is of little value that we make noble protestations of love for the human race; we have to get involved with real people in real situations. It is then that love's 'patience, kindness, goodness' will be put to the test.

Fourthly, *love is balanced by self-control*. For 'the fruit of the Spirit is . . . faithfulness, gentleness and self-control'. These three qualities seem to be different nuances of the mastery of ourselves. 'Faithfulness' is reliability or trustworthiness in such areas as keeping our promises and fulfilling our undertakings. 'Gentleness' translates *prautēs*, which is often rendered 'meekness'. But it is not a compliant, spineless, unprincipled kind of meekness. It certainly means being gentle, humble and considerate towards other people, but to this end it will often necessitate the taming of our strengths and the harnessing of our energies. The third word 'self-control' is *egkrateia*, 'which expresses the power or lordship which one has either over oneself or over something'.[2] It includes disciplining our instincts, restraining our temper and our tongue, and curbing our passions.

But why have I written above that love is 'balanced' by self-control? Because love is self-giving, and self-giving and self-control complement one another. For how can we give ourselves until we have first learned to control ourselves? Our self has to be mastered before it can be offered in the service of others. It is surely significant, therefore, that the ninefold fruit of the Spirit begins with self-giving and ends with self-control.

Love is the fruit of the Spirit

The fifth truth which emerges from this great text is that the *love* we have been thinking about (preeminent, bringing joy and peace, issuing in action, and balanced by self-control) *is the fruit of the Spirit*, that is, the natural consequence of the supernatural work of the Holy Spirit within us.

In the context Paul is drawing a contrast between 'the flesh'

[1] Gal. 5:13. [2] From the article on *egkrateia* by Walter Grundmann in *TDNT*.

and 'the Spirit', between 'the works of the flesh' and 'the fruit of the Spirit'. We need to pause for some definitions. By 'flesh' he means neither the soft tissue of skin and muscle which covers our bony skeleton, nor the human body (a mistake people make when they talk of greed and sexual immorality as 'the sins of the flesh'), but rather our inherited, fallen, twisted nature with its bias towards evil, its corrupt desires and its selfish demands. It has been well said that if we erase the last letter of the word 'flesh' and read it backwards, we discover exactly what it is.

By 'Spirit' Paul means neither the breath which animates our body, nor the spiritual side of human beings in contrast to the material, but the Holy Spirit himself, who enters our personality when we repent and trust in Jesus, and whose indwelling presence is the mark of Christian identity[1] and the secret of Christian holiness.

Here, then, are the two protagonists in the struggle which Paul describes. On the one hand, there is 'the flesh', our self-centred fallen nature, and on the other 'the Spirit', the personal indwelling Spirit of God. Paul tells us three truths about the conflict between these forces.

First, the desires of the flesh and of the Spirit are *active* desires. 'For the sinful nature (*i.e.* 'the flesh') desires what is contrary to the Spirit, and the Spirit what is contrary to the sinful nature. They are in conflict with each other.'[2] Thus both the flesh and the Spirit have desires, which are alive, active, energetic and strong. The reason for stressing this is that throughout church history perfectionist groups have taught that after the new birth our fallen nature is inert and inactive, even dead. But Scripture is not on their side. The command that we should 'not gratify the desires of the sinful nature'[3] and the statement that 'the sinful nature desires what is contrary to the Spirit'[4] would both be nonsensical if our fallen nature no longer had any desires. No, the Christian life is one of unremitting conflict with the world, the flesh and the devil.

Secondly, the desires of the flesh and of the Spirit are *opposite*

[1] Rom. 8:9. [2] Gal. 5:17. [3] Gal. 5:16. [4] Gal. 5:17.

desires. A fierce antagonism exists between them. 'The desires of the flesh are against the Spirit, and the desires of the Spirit are against the flesh; for these are opposed to each other.'[1] As Bishop J. B. Lightfoot put it in his commentary on Galatians, 'between the Spirit and the flesh there is not only no alliance; there is an interminable deadly feud'.[2]

Moreover, the opposite desires of the flesh and the Spirit are made plain in the contrast between 'the works of the flesh'[3] and 'the fruit of the Spirit'.[4] The former are very unpleasant. Paul lists fifteen of them. They seem to fall into four categories – sexual sins (immorality and licentiousness), religious sins (idolatry and sorcery, the latter being the secret attempt to steal divine or demonic power by magic), social sins (eight of them including malice, jealousy, temper, quarrelling and selfish ambition) and personal sins (drunkenness and orgies). It is an ugly catalogue of activities in which people assert themselves against God and others.

The ninefold fruit of the Spirit,[5] which we have already considered, presents a beautiful contrast. Indeed, it would be hard to imagine a greater contrast. For here is godliness instead of godlessness, authentic joy and peace in place of the pursuit of sinful pleasure, kindness and goodness over against malice and envy, and self-control rather than self-indulgence.

Thirdly, Paul insists that the desires of the flesh and of the Spirit are *controllable* desires. It is possible, he writes, for the Spirit to gain ascendancy over the flesh and subdue it, for love to triumph over selfishness, and for goodness to be victorious over evil. How? The secret lies in our adopting the right attitude to both the flesh and the Spirit.

Our attitude to our fallen nature should be one of ruthless repudiation. For 'those who belong to Christ Jesus have crucified the sinful nature with its passions and desires'.[6] That is, we have taken this evil, slimy, slippery thing called 'the flesh' and nailed it to the cross. This was our initial repentance.

[1] Gal. 5:17 (RSV). [2] J. B. Lightfoot, *Galatians* (1865), p. 209. [3] Gal. 5:19–21. [4] Gal. 5:22–23. [5] Gal. 5:22–23. [6] Gal. 5:24.

Crucifixion is dramatic imagery for our uncompromising rejection of all known evil. Crucifixion does not lead to a quick or easy death; it is an execution of lingering pain. Yet it is decisive; there is no possibility of escaping from it.

Our attitude to the Holy Spirit, on the other hand, is to be one of unconditional surrender. Paul uses several expressions for this. We are to 'live by the Spirit', to be 'led by the Spirit' and to 'keep in step with the Spirit'.[1] That is, we are to allow him his rightful sovereignty over us, and follow his righteous promptings.

Thus both our repudiation of the flesh and our surrender to the Spirit need to be repeated daily, however decisive our original repudiation and surrender may have been. In Jesus' words, we are to 'take up (our) cross daily' and follow him.[2] We are also to go on being filled with the Spirit,[3] as we open our personality to him daily. Both our repudiation and our surrender are also to be worked out in disciplined habits of life. It is those who 'sow to the Spirit'[4] who reap the fruit of the Spirit. And to 'sow to the Spirit' means to cultivate the things of the Spirit, for example, by our wise use of the Lord's Day, the discipline of our daily prayer and Bible reading, our regular worship and attendance at the Lord's Supper, our Christian friendships and our involvement in Christian service. An inflexible principle of all God's dealings, both in the material and in the moral realm, is that we reap what we sow. The rule is invariable. It cannot be changed, for 'God cannot be mocked'.[5] We must not therefore be surprised if we do not reap the fruit of the Spirit when all the time we are sowing to the flesh. Did we think we could cheat or fool God?

To change the metaphor, I remember reading years ago of a visitor to the mountains of southern California. He met an old mountaineer, whose two dogs were continuously fighting. The visitor asked him which dog usually won. The mountaineer chewed his tobacco for a while in silence, and then replied: 'The one I feeds the most.' Just so, our new nature will gain the

[1] Gal. 5:16, 18, 25. [2] Lk. 9:23. [3] Eph. 5:18.
[4] Gal. 6:8 (RSV). [5] Gal. 6:7.

victory over the old only in so far as we feed the new and starve the old.

There is only one person, in the long history of the world, in whom the fruit of the Spirit has ever ripened to perfection. That person is Jesus of Nazareth. Indeed, Paul's ninefold fruit may be seen as a portrait of Jesus Christ. For he loved as no-one else has ever loved, in laying down his life for his enemies. He spoke both of 'my joy' and of 'my peace'.[1] He was wonderfully patient with his dim-witted apostles. He was invariably kind and full of good works. He was also steadfastly reliable and always gentle, in fact 'gentle and humble in heart'.[2] And he had perfect self-control so that, 'when they hurled insults at him, he did not retaliate'.[3]

Dr Kenneth Moynagh, who worked for many years as a medical missionary at Matana in Burundi, once summarized the fruit of the Spirit, with its emphasis on love, in this way:

> Joy is love exulting, and peace is love at rest;
> Patience, love enduring in every trial and test.
> Gentleness, love yielding to all that is not sin,
> Goodness, love in actions that flow from Christ within.
> Faith is love's eyes opened the living Christ to see;
> Meekness, love not fighting, but bowed at Calvary.
> Temperance, love in harness and under Christ's control,
> For Christ is love in person, and love, Christ in the soul.

Moreover, if the fruit of the Spirit is Christlikeness, Christlikeness is God's personal purpose for all his people. It is his *eternal* purpose, 'for those whom God foreknew he also predestined to be conformed to the likeness of his Son'.[4] Next, it is his *historical* purpose, as 'we . . . are being transformed into his likeness with ever-increasing glory'.[5] And thirdly, it is his *eschatological* purpose. For, although 'what we will be has not

[1] *E.g.* Jn. 15:11; 14:27. [2] Mt. 11:29. [3] 1 Pet. 2:23.
[4] Rom. 8:29. [5] 2 Cor. 3:18.

yet been made known', nevertheless 'we know that when he appears, we shall be like him, for we shall see him as he is'.[1]

The only way to understand the disappointments and frustrations of life, the loneliness, the suffering and the pain, is to see them as part of our loving Father's discipline in his determination to make us like Christ.[2]

I am sometimes asked, perhaps in a newspaper, radio or television interview, whether at my age I have any ambitions left. I always now reply: 'Yes, my overriding ambition is (and, I trust, will be until I die) that I may become a little bit more like Christ.'

[1] 1 Jn. 3:2. [2] *E.g.* Heb. 12:4–11.

PART THREE

THE BIBLE

'We present you with this Book, the most valuable thing that this world affords. Here is wisdom; this is the royal law; these are the lively oracles of God.' With these words in the coronation service the Moderator of the General Assembly of the Church of Scotland handed to the newly crowned Queen Elizabeth a copy of the Bible.

It might be tempting to dismiss such claims for the Bible as idle rhetoric, were it not that successive generations of Christian people have found them to be true. Scripture has brought us light in darkness, strength in weakness, comfort in sadness. It is not difficult for us to endorse the psalmist's experience that the words of God 'are more precious than gold, than much pure gold; they are sweeter than honey, than honey from the comb'.[1]

This being so, it has been distressing in recent decades in the West to watch the Bible being dislodged from its position of acknowledged authority, not only in the nation but also in the church. There is

[1] Ps. 19:10.

little hope for thoroughgoing national reform or church renewal unless the Word of God is once more widely respected and read, and its teaching heeded.

Part III of this book is my small contribution to this goal, as I write about the urgent need to continue in, respond to, interpret and expound God's Word.

CHAPTER TEN

CONTINUING IN THE WORD

It is a regular theme of the New Testament authors that the people of God must be steadfast. On the one hand, we must resist the intellectual and moral pressures of our contemporary world, and refuse to conform to the fashions of the day. We are not to allow ourselves to slip, slither and slide in the mud of relativity or be torn from our moorings and carried away by the flood. On the other hand, and positively, we are summoned to persevere in the truth we have received, to cling to it as a secure handhold in the storm, and to stand firm on this foundation.

Here are some examples of this kind of exhortation by three of the major contributors to the New Testament.

Paul: 'So then, brothers, stand firm and hold to the teachings we passed on to you.'[1]

Hebrews: 'We must pay more careful attention, therefore, to what we have heard, so that we do not drift away.'[2]

John: 'See that what you have heard from the beginning remains in you.'[3] 'Anyone who runs ahead and does not continue in the teaching of Christ does not have God; whoever continues in the teaching has both the Father and the Son.'[4]

Common to these quotations is the recognition that certain truths had been 'taught' or 'passed on' by the apostles, and had consequently been 'heard' or 'received' by the church. This body of doctrine was now a sacred deposit to be guarded.[5] It had a normative quality. The church must remain in it and hold to it, neither going back from it, nor going on beyond it in such a way as to contradict it.

[1] 2 Thes. 2:15. [2] Heb. 2:1. [3] 1 Jn. 2:24. [4] 2 Jn. 9.
[5] *E.g.* 1 Tim. 6:20; 2 Tim. 1:14.

Part of Paul's final charge to Timothy elaborates this theme. In order to grasp its implications, we need to have the text before us. It is 2 Timothy 3:1 – 4:8.

> 3 [1]But mark this: There will be terrible times in the last days.
> [2]People will be lovers of themselves, lovers of money,
> boastful, proud, abusive, disobedient to their parents,
> ungrateful, unholy, [3]without love, unforgiving, slanderous,
> without self-control, brutal, not lovers of the good, [4]treacher-
> ous, rash, conceited, lovers of pleasure rather than lovers of
> God – [5]having a form of godliness but denying its power.
> Have nothing to do with them.
>
> [6]They are the kind who worm their way into homes and
> gain control over weak-willed women, who are loaded down
> with sins and are swayed by all kinds of evil desires, [7]always
> learning but never able to acknowledge the truth. [8]Just as
> Jannes and Jambres opposed Moses, so also these men
> oppose the truth – men of depraved minds, who, as far as the
> faith is concerned, are rejected. [9]But they will not get very far
> because, as in the case of those men, their folly will be clear to
> everyone.
>
> [10]You, however, know all about my teaching, my way of
> life, my purpose, faith, patience, love, endurance, [11]persec-
> utions, sufferings – what kinds of things happened to me in
> Antioch, Iconium and Lystra, the persecutions I endured. Yet
> the Lord rescued me from all of them. [12]In fact, everyone who
> wants to live a godly life in Christ Jesus will be persecuted,
> [13]while evil men and impostors will go from bad to worse,
> deceiving and being deceived. [14]But as for you, continue in
> what you have learned and have become convinced of,
> because you know those from whom you learned it, [15]and
> how from infancy you have known the holy Scriptures, which
> are able to make you wise for salvation through faith in
> Christ Jesus. [16]All Scripture is God-breathed and is useful for
> teaching, rebuking, correcting and training in righteousness,
> [17]so that the man of God may be thoroughly equipped for
> every good work.

4 [1]In the presence of God and of Christ Jesus, who will judge the living and the dead, and in view of his appearing and his kingdom, I give you this charge: [2]Preach the Word; be prepared in season and out of season; correct, rebuke and encourage – with great patience and careful instruction. [3]For the time will come when men will not put up with sound doctrine. Instead, to suit their own desires, they will gather around them a great number of teachers to say what their itching ears want to hear. [4]They will turn their ears away from the truth and turn aside to myths. [5]But you, keep your head in all situations, endure hardship, do the work of an evangelist, discharge all the duties of your ministry.

[6]For I am already being poured out like a drink offering, and the time has come for my departure. [7]I have fought the good fight, I have finished the race, I have kept the faith. [8]Now there is in store for me the crown of righteousness, which the Lord, the righteous Judge, will award to me on that day – and not only to me, but also to all who have longed for his appearing.

Standing in the Word

Paul's exhortation to Timothy was given against the background of the kind of society he was living in (3:1–13). It was not at all friendly to the gospel. Nor could the gospel possibly be reshaped in order to accommodate to its ideas and standards. On the contrary, Paul was aware of a radical incompatibility between the Word and the world. 'Mark this,' he wrote: 'There will be terrible times in the last days.'

It is important to realize that by 'the last days' the apostle was not alluding to a future epoch which would immediately precede the return of Christ. For in verse 5 he tells Timothy to 'have nothing to do' with the people he has been describing. How could Timothy avoid them if they had not even been born? No, 'the last days' from the perspective of the New Testament began with Jesus Christ. He ushered them in.[1] The last days are therefore

[1] *Cf.* Mk. 1:15; 1 Cor. 10:11.

these days, the days in which Timothy lived and in which we also live, that is, the whole era which stretches between the first and second comings of Christ. What are the characteristics of the last days? Three seem to stand out from Paul's description.

The first is *misdirected love*. Of the nineteen distinguishing marks which the apostle lists (verses 2–4), it is striking that six have to do with love. 'People will be lovers of themselves, lovers of money, . . . without love, . . . not lovers of the good, . . . lovers of pleasure rather than lovers of God.' The expression 'without love' must be understood as meaning 'without true love'. For the people in view are not altogether devoid of love; they love themselves, they love money and they love pleasure. But these are examples of misdirected love. Self, money and pleasure are inappropriate objects of human love. They even become idolatrous when they displace God from his rightful place as the One to be loved with all our being. Yet we see misdirected love everywhere today. Self-absorption, covetousness and hedonism are rife, while the first and second commandments, to love God and our neighbour, are neglected. Moreover, when people's love is directed to the wrong objects, all their relationships go wrong. They become 'boastful, proud, abusive, disobedient, . . . ungrateful, . . . unforgiving, slanderous' (verses 2–3).

The second characteristic of our age may be called *empty religion*. Our contemporaries are described as 'having a form of godliness but denying its power' (verse 5). It may seem extraordinary that people characterized by self-love could also be religious. But it is so. Indeed, it is possible for religion, which is intended to express the worship of God, to become perverted into a means of ego-inflation. The proper name for this sick distortion is hypocrisy, and Jesus inveighed against it.[1] Such religion is 'form' without 'power', outward show without inward reality. It is also an enemy of the gospel, because nominal Christianity hardens people against real Christianity.

Thirdly, the last days are distinguished by *the cult of an open mind*. Paul writes here of people who are 'always learning but

[1] *E.g.* Mt. 6:1–18.

never able to acknowledge the truth' (verse 7). They sit on the fence and refuse to come down on either side of it. Tolerance is their watchword. Determined to avoid the pain of reaching definite conclusions, they make a fetish of keeping their mind open. They cannot endure what C. S. Lewis called 'the tyrannous noon of revelation';[1] they greatly prefer the twilight of free thought. They have overlooked the distinction which Allan Bloom has recently pointed out between two kinds of 'openness' – 'the openness of indifference . . . and the openness that invites us to the quest for knowledge and certitude'.[2] The latter is an aspect of the Christian virtue of humility, acknowledging that our understanding is provisional and incomplete, and always seeking to increase it. The former, on the other hand, is not only insulting to truth but personally perilous. It exposes us to the danger, as a bishop of the American Episcopal Church has put it, of having our minds so open that our brains fall out!

Here, then, are three characteristics of our time, which Scripture trenchantly criticizes and tells us to avoid. We are to love God and our neighbour, and not misdirect our love to self, money or pleasure. We are to value the reality and power of religion above its outward forms. And we are to submit humbly to God's revelation and not cultivate a wishy-washy, undemanding agnosticism.

Thus Paul calls Timothy to be different from the world around him. After his portrayal of these ungodly trends, Paul twice writes *su de*, meaning 'You, however', or 'But as for you' (verses 10 and 14). These words introduce the apostle's two exhortations to Timothy to resist the mood of the world, and to stand firm against it. The first exhortation focuses on what Timothy has already come to know about Paul (verses 10–13) – his 'teaching', his 'way of life', his 'purpose', together with his 'faith, patience, love, endurance, persecutions, sufferings'. Timothy had seen Paul's ministry with his own eyes, including the opposition and persecution which he had had to endure in

[1] C. S. Lewis, *Surprised by Joy* (Geoffrey Bles, 1955), p. 63.
[2] Allan Bloom, *The Closing of the American Mind* (Simon and Schuster, 1987), p. 41.

Antioch, Iconium and Lystra (verse 11). For the fact is that 'everyone who wants to live a godly life in Christ Jesus will be persecuted' (verse 12), since 'evil men and impostors', who reject the gospel, 'will go from bad to worse' (verse 13).

Thus the apostle sets over against each other the low standards of the world and his own teaching and conduct. The two were in irreconcilable antagonism to one another. Hence the persecution Paul had had to bear. If Timothy were to stand firm, taking Paul's side against the world's, he would undoubtedly have to suffer too.

Continuing in the Word

Paul's mention of the 'evil men and impostors', deceived and deceiving, who would 'go from bad to worse' (verse 13), leads him to his second *su de*, 'But as for you'. This time, rather than just looking back to his past teaching, conduct and sufferings which Timothy had come to know, he also looks to the future: 'But as for you, continue in what you have learned and have become convinced of, because you know those from whom you learned it' (verse 14). These teachers from whom Timothy had learned are probably first his mother and grandmother who had taught him the Old Testament from his infancy (verse 15, *cf.* 1:5) and secondly the apostle, whose 'teaching' (verse 10) Timothy knew and which for us is preserved in the New Testament. Thus Paul contrasts two sets of teachers – on the one hand the impostors and deceivers of verse 13 and on the other Timothy's mother and his mentor (the apostle himself) who had taught him the Scriptures.

We who live at the end of the twentieth century need, ourselves, to heed the same summons. We are not to be like reeds blown by the wind. We are not to bow down before the prevailing trends of society, its covetousness and materialism, its relativism, and rejection of all absolute standards of truth and goodness. Instead, we are to continue faithfully in the Old and New Testament Scriptures. But why? What is Scripture that it should occupy such an important place in our lives? The apostle goes on to stress three fundamental aspects of it.

First, *Scripture is able to instruct us for salvation* (verse 15, RSV). Its primary purpose is practical. It is more a guidebook than a textbook, more a book of salvation than a book of science. This is not to say that the biblical and scientific accounts of the world are in conflict, but rather that they are complementary. Further, God's purpose in Scripture is not to reveal facts which can be discovered by the scientific method of observation and experiment, but rather to reveal truths which are beyond the scope of science, in particular God's way of salvation through Christ.

This is why Jesus Christ is himself the centre of the biblical revelation, since it bears witness to him.[1] As J.-J. von Allmen has expressed it, 'the heart of the Scripture (what sums it up and makes it live) or the head of the Scripture (... what explains it and justifies it) ... is Jesus Christ. To read the Bible without meeting him is to read it badly, and to preach the Bible without proclaiming him is to preach it falsely.'[2] It is because Scripture instructs us for salvation that it instructs us about Christ, by faith in whom salvation is received. Moreover, the reason we love the Bible is that it speaks to us of Christ. It is God's picture, God's portrait, of Christ.

Secondly, *Scripture is God-breathed*. The better-known AV phrase consists of five words, 'given by inspiration of God'. But the NIV is correct to use the one word 'God-breathed' as the precise equivalent of the Greek expression *theopneustos*. This indicates that Scripture is the Word of God, spoken by God, or breathed out of the mouth of God. The implied combination of mouth, breath and word shows that the model of inspiration which is intended is that of human speech. For speech is communication between minds. Often we keep what is 'on our mind' to ourselves. But when we speak, we clothe the thoughts of our minds in the words of our mouth.

We observe also that the text reads 'All Scripture is God-breathed' (verse 16). The NEB, on the other hand, translates the

[1] *Cf.* Jn. 5:39; 20:31.
[2] J.-J. von Allmen, *Preaching and Congregation* (Lutterworth, 1962), p. 24.

clause 'every inspired Scripture is useful ...'. This is almost certainly incorrect. It implies that if every inspired Scripture is useful, there must be other Scriptures which are not inspired and therefore not useful. But, in the first place, the concept of 'uninspired Scripture' is a contradiction in terms; the word 'Scripture' simply means inspired writing. Secondly, the NEB omits, without sufficient warrant, the little word *kai*, meaning 'and' or 'also'. It shows that Paul is not making one statement ('every inspired Scripture is useful') but two ('every Scripture is inspired *and* useful'). Indeed, it is useful to us precisely because it is inspired by God.

Nevertheless, we must not mis-state the truth of inspiration. When God spoke, he did not speak into space. Nor did he write documents and leave them around to be discovered, as Joseph Smith (founder of the Mormon Church) claimed regarding his golden plates. Nor did God dictate Scripture to non-participating secretaries, as Muslims believe Allah dictated the Qur'an to Muhammad in Arabic. No, by the process of inspiration we mean that the human authors, even while God was speaking to and through them, were themselves actively engaged in historical research, theological reflection and literary composition. For much of Scripture is historical narrative, and each author has his own particular theological emphasis and literary style. Divine inspiration did not dispense with human cooperation, or iron out the peculiar contributions of the authors.

So 'God-breathed' is not the only account which Scripture gives of itself, since God's mouth was not the only mouth involved in its production. The same Scripture which says 'the mouth of the LORD has spoken'[1] also says that God spoke 'by the mouth of his holy prophets'.[2] Out of whose mouth did Scripture come, then? God's or man's? The only biblical answer is 'both'. Indeed, God spoke through the human authors in such a way that his words were simultaneously their words, and their words were simultaneously his. This is the double authorship of

[1] *E.g.* Is. 1:20. [2] *E.g.* Acts 3:18, 21 (RSV).

the Bible. Scripture is equally the Word of God and the words of human beings. Better, it is the Word of God through the words of human beings.

It is essential to keep the two authorships together. Some theologians, ancient and modern, Catholic and Protestant, have appealed to the two natures of Christ as an analogy. Although the parallel is not exact, it is illuminating. Just as in the person of Christ (who is both God and human) we must neither affirm his deity in such a way as to deny his humanity, nor affirm his humanity in such a way as to deny his deity, but rather affirm both equally, refusing to allow either to contradict the other, so in our doctrine of Scripture we must neither affirm that it is the Word of God in such a way as to deny that it is the words of human beings (which is fundamentalism), nor affirm that it is the words of human beings in such a way as to deny that it is the Word of God (which is liberalism), but rather affirm both equally, refusing to allow either to contradict the other. Thus on the one hand God spoke,[1] determining what he wanted to say, yet without smothering the personality of the human authors. On the other hand, human beings spoke,[2] using their faculties freely, yet without distorting the truth which God was speaking through them.

We have no liberty to declare that such a combination is impossible. To say so, Dr J. I. Packer has written, would indicate

> a false doctrine of God, here particularly of his providence. . . . For it assumes that God and man stand in such a relationship to each other that they cannot both be free agents in the same action. If man acts freely (*i.e.* voluntarily and spontaneously), God does not, and *vice versa*. The two freedoms are mutually exclusive. But the affinities of this idea are with Deism, not Christian theism. . . . The cure for such fallacious reasoning is to grasp the biblical idea of God's

[1] Heb. 1:1. [2] 2 Pet. 1:21.

> *concursive operation* in, with and through the free working of man's own mind.[1]

The way we understand Scripture will affect the way we read it. In particular, its double authorship demands a double approach. Because Scripture is the Word of God, we should read it as we read no other book – on our knees, humbly, reverently, prayerfully, looking to the Holy Spirit for illumination. But because Scripture is also the words of human beings, we should read it as we read *every* other book, using our minds, thinking, pondering and reflecting, and paying close attention to its literary, historical, cultural and linguistic characteristics. This combination of humble reverence and critical reflection is not only not impossible; it is indispensable.[2]

Thirdly, *Scripture is useful* (verses 16–17). It is able to do more than instruct us for salvation (verse 15); it is also 'useful for teaching, rebuking, correcting and training in righteousness' (verse 16). In other words, it is profitable both for doctrine (teaching truth and correcting error) and for ethics (rebuking sin and training in right living), thus leading us on in Christian belief and behaviour until we become men and women of God, 'thoroughly equipped for every good work' (verse 17). In these ways the Bible has an essential part to play in our growth into maturity in Christ, as we will consider more fully in the next chapter. Over against the errors of the 'evil men and impostors', Timothy was to continue in the Word of God, both the Old Testament Scriptures and the apostle's teaching.

Thank God for the Bible! God has not left us to grope our way in the darkness; he has given us a light to show us the path. He has not abandoned us to flounder in heavy seas; Scripture is a rock on which we may stand. Our resolve should be to study it, believe it and obey it.

[1] J. I. Packer, *'Fundamentalism' and the Word of God* (IVP, 1958), pp. 81–82.
[2] *Cf.* 2 Tim. 2:7.

Preaching the Word

Neither Timothy nor anybody else has the liberty to monopolize Scripture. For Scripture is nobody's private possession; it is public property. Having been given by God, it belongs to all. His Word has been spoken, in order to be passed on. So the apostle, conscious of God's presence and of Christ's future appearing for judgment (4:1), gives Timothy this charge: 'Preach the Word' (verse 2). He must proclaim it like a herald or town crier in the market-place. He must do so boldly, urgently and relevantly, correcting, rebuking and encouraging according to people's state and need, and 'with great patience and careful instruction' (verse 2).

This was all the more necessary, Paul added, because the time was coming when people will 'not put up with sound doctrine'. Instead, suffering from a strange pathological condition called 'itching ears', they will listen to teachers who say what they want to hear, rather than to the truth which God wants to say to them (verses 3–4). Yet the unwillingness of some to listen to the Word of God is no reason why we should give up preaching it! On the contrary, Timothy was to persevere, to keep his head, to endure opposition and to fulfil his ministry faithfully, both as an evangelist and as a teacher (verse 5).

One of the greatest needs of the contemporary church is conscientious biblical exposition from the pulpit (see below, chapter 13). Ignorance of even the rudiments of the faith is widespread. Many Christian people are immature and unstable. And the major reason for this sorry state of affairs is the paucity of responsible, thorough, balanced biblical preachers. The pulpit is not the place to ventilate our own opinions, but to unfold God's Word.

The climax of the apostle's exhortation is reached in verses 6–8. In a previous letter, written about two years earlier, he has described himself as 'an old man'.[1] Now he writes that the time of his departure has come. Indeed, the pouring out of his life

[1] Phm. 9.

like a drink offering has already begun (verse 6). Looking back over his apostolic career, he is able to say that he has fought the good fight, finished the race and kept the faith (verse 7). He has no regrets. He is probably incarcerated in the underground Mamertine Prison in Rome, from which he is not expecting to be released. Already with his mind's eye he sees the flash of the executioner's sword, and beyond it 'the crown of righteousness' which on the last day Jesus, the righteous Judge, will give both him and 'all who have longed for his appearing' (verse 8). It is his sense that his ministry is nearing its end which prompts him to exhort Timothy to stand firm in the Word, continue in it and pass it on.

I hope I shall not be thought too personal if I say that I understand and feel the poignancy of Paul's words, although I do not of course presume to compare myself with him. But as I write these words, I have recently celebrated my seventieth birthday, my statutory 'three score years and ten'.[1] At this age I do not expect to live very much longer. Every new day is a bonus which I receive gratefully from God's hand.

So naturally I ask myself: where are the Timothys of the next generation? Where are the young evangelical men and women, who are determined by God's grace to stand firm in Scripture, refusing to be swept off their feet by the prevailing winds of fashion, who are resolved to continue in it and live by it, relating the Word to the world in order to obey it, and who are committed to passing it on, as they give themselves to the ministry of conscientious exposition?

[1] Ps. 90:10 (AV).

CHAPTER ELEVEN

RESPONDING TO THE WORD

The concept of divine revelation, and of our need to submit to it, is both eminently reasonable and practically wholesome. It is reasonable because it acknowledges that the infinite God is altogether beyond his finite creatures, and that we could never have known him if he had not taken the initiative to make himself known. It is also wholesome because submission to God's self-revelation in Christ and in the full biblical witness to Christ, far from inhibiting the health and growth of the church, is actually indispensable to them. My thesis in this chapter is that God's Word, received and responded to, has a central role in the faith and life of God's people. I give five examples.

Mature discipleship

First, submission to the authority of Scripture is *the way of mature discipleship*. I am not saying that it is impossible to be a disciple of Jesus without a high view of Scripture, for this is manifestly not the case. There are genuine followers of Jesus Christ who are not 'evangelical', whose confidence in Scripture is small, even minimal, and who put more faith in the past traditions and present teaching of the church, or in their own reason or experience. I have no desire to deny the authenticity of their Christian profession. Yet I venture to add that their discipleship is bound to be impoverished on account of their attitude to the Bible. A full, balanced and mature Christian discipleship is impossible whenever disciples do not submit to their Lord's teaching authority as it is mediated through Scripture.

For what is discipleship? It is a many-faceted lifestyle, an amalgam of several ingredients. In particular, it includes worship, faith, obedience and hope. Every Christian is called to worship God, to trust and obey him, and to look with confident hope towards the future. Yet each of these is a response to revelation, and is seriously impaired without a reliable, objective revelation of God.

1. *Worship*. Every Christian is a worshipper. In both public and private, we recognize our duty to worship Almighty God. But how can we worship God unless we know both who he is and what kind of worship pleases him? Without this knowledge, our attempts at worship are almost certain to degenerate into idolatry. At best we would copy that famous altar which Paul found in Athens and which was inscribed 'TO AN UNKNOWN GOD'.[1] But Christians are not agnostic Athenians; we are to love the Lord our God with all our mind[2] and to worship him 'in spirit and in truth'.[3]

What, then, does it mean to worship God? It is to 'glory in his holy name',[4] that is, to revel adoringly in who he is in his revealed character. But before we can glory in God's name, we must know it. Hence the propriety of the reading and preaching of the Word of God in public worship, and of biblical meditation in private devotion. These things are not an intrusion into worship; they form the necessary foundation of it. God must speak to us before we have any liberty to speak to him. He must disclose to us who he is before we can offer him what we are in acceptable worship. The worship of God is always a response to the Word of God. Scripture wonderfully directs and enriches our worship.

2. *Faith*. If every Christian is a worshipper, every Christian is a believer also. Indeed, the Christian life is a life of faith. 'Where is your faith?' Jesus asked the Twelve when they were afraid, and exhorted them, 'Have faith in God.'[5]

But what is faith? It too is a response to the revelation of God. We can no more trust a God we do not know than we can

[1] Acts 17:23. [2] Mk. 12:30. [3] Jn. 4:24. [4] Ps. 105:3.
[5] Lk. 8:25; Mk. 11:22.

worship an unknown God. Consider Psalm 9:10: 'Those who know your name will trust in you, for you, LORD, have never forsaken those who seek you.' If worship is to 'glory' in God for who he is (his 'name'), then faith is to 'trust' him because of who he is. So faith is neither naivety nor gullibility. It is neither illogical nor irrational. On the contrary, faith is a reasoning trust. It rests on knowledge, the knowledge of God's name. Its reasonableness arises from the reliability of the God who is being trusted. It is never unreasonable to trust God, since no more trustworthy person exists.

Faith will grow, therefore, as we reflect on the character of God (who never lies) and on the covenant of God (who has pledged himself to his people). But how can we discover his character and covenant? Only from the Bible, in which these twin truths have been revealed. So the more we meditate on God's self-disclosure in Scripture, the riper our faith will become, whereas without Scripture our faith is bound to be weak and sickly.

3. *Obedience.* Jesus calls his disciples to a life of obedience, as well as of worship and faith.

But how can we obey him, unless we know his will and commandments? Without a knowledge of these, obedience would be impossible. 'If you love me, you will obey what I command,' he said.[1] And again, 'Whoever has my commands (that is, knows them, and treasures them up in his mind and memory) and obeys them, he is the one who loves me.'[2]

Once more, then, the Bible is seen to be indispensable to mature discipleship. For it is there that we learn the commands of Christ and so take the first necessary step towards understanding and doing his will.

4. *Hope.* The Christian hope is a confident expectation regarding the future. No Christian can be a cynic or a pessimist. To be sure, we do not believe that human beings will ever succeed in building Utopia on earth. But, although we have little confidence in human achievement, we have great confidence in

[1] Jn. 14:15. [2] Jn. 14:21.

the purposes and power of God. We are certain that error and evil are not going to be allowed the last word. On the contrary, truth and righteousness will triumph in the end. For Jesus Christ is going to return in strength and splendour, the dead will be raised, death will be abolished, and the universe will be liberated from decay and suffused with glory.

But how can we be so sure of these things? There are no obvious grounds for such confidence. Evil flourishes. The wicked get away with their wickedness. World problems appear intractable. And the mushroom cloud of a nuclear explosion still overshadows the horizon. Is there not more reason for despair than for hope? Yes, there would be – if it were not for the Bible! It is the Bible which arouses, directs and nurtures hope. For Christian hope is quite different from secular optimism. It is a confidence in God, kindled by the promises of God. 'Let us hold unswervingly to the hope we profess,' the author of Hebrews exhorts his readers. Why? 'For he who promised is faithful.'[1] Jesus himself said that he would come again. 'Men will see the Son of Man coming in clouds with great power and glory ... And you will see the Son of Man ... coming on the clouds of heaven.'[2] It is promises like these which stimulate our hope. It is 'in keeping with his promise' that we are looking for a new world, in which righteousness will reign.[3]

Here, then, are four basic ingredients of Christian discipleship – worship, faith, obedience and hope. All four would be irrational without an objective basis in God's revelation, to which they are a response. Worship is a response to the revelation of God's name, faith to the revelation of his character and covenant, obedience to the revelation of his will and commandments, and hope to the revelation of his purpose and promises. And God's name, covenant, commands and promises are all found in Scripture. That is why Scripture is fundamental to Christian growth, and why submission to its authority is the way of mature discipleship.

[1] Heb. 10:23. [2] Mk. 13:26; 14:62. [3] 2 Pet. 3:13.

Intellectual integrity

Secondly, submission to biblical authority is *the way of intellectual integrity.*

Many people would immediately deny this statement and even affirm the contrary. They cannot understand how apparently intelligent Christians at the end of the twentieth century can possibly be so perverse as to believe in biblical inspiration and authority. They regard a commitment to the truth and trustworthiness of Scripture as untenable. They therefore charge those of us who hold it with a lack of intellectual integrity. They accuse us of obscurantism, mental schizophrenia, intellectual suicide and other equally horrid conditions. To these charges, however, we plead 'Not guilty'. We insist that our conviction about Scripture arises from the very integrity which our critics say we lack.

'Integrity' is the quality of an integrated person. In particular, integrated Christians are at peace, not at war, with themselves. Instead of being conscious of a dichotomy between our various beliefs, or between our beliefs and our behaviour, so that we are 'torn apart' inside, there is an inner harmony. We are 'all of a piece', or whole. What is the secret of this integration?

There is no more integrating Christian principle than the affirmation we considered in chapter 5, 'Jesus Christ is Lord'. It is of the essence of integrated discipleship that we both confess his lordship with our lips and enthrone him as Lord in our hearts. We assume the easy yoke of his teaching authority. We seek to 'take captive every thought to make it obedient to Christ'.[1] And when Jesus is Lord of our beliefs, opinions, ambitions, standards, values and lifestyle, then we are integrated Christians, since then 'integrity' marks our life. Only when *he* is Lord do *we* become whole.

But Jesus our Lord himself submitted to the Old Testament Scriptures. In his ethical conduct, in his understanding of his mission, and in his public debates with contemporary religious

[1] 2 Cor. 10:5.

leaders, his primary concern was to be true to Scripture. 'What does the Scripture say?' he would ask. It was always his final court of appeal. Moreover, he indicated his expectation that his disciples would follow his example in this. He also made provision for the Scriptures of the New Testament to be written by choosing, calling, equipping and commissioning his apostles to be the teachers of the church, and he expected the church to submit to them. 'He who listens to you listens to me,' he said.[1] In consequence of this, submission to Scripture by Christian disciples is part and parcel of our submission to Jesus as Lord. For the disciple is not above his teacher. We cannot therefore accommodate ourselves to selective submission. It would be inherently illogical, for example, to agree with Jesus' doctrine of God but disagree with his view of the Word of God. No, selective submission is not authentic submission.

This gives us the clue we need regarding how to deal with the problems in the Bible. For in affirming the inspiration and authority of Scripture, I am not denying that there are problems. There are textual, literary, historical, scientific, philosophical, cultural, theological and moral problems. The observable phenomena of Scripture (which we see inductively) sometimes seem to conflict with our doctrine of Scripture (which we hold deductively, inferring it from the attitude and teaching of Jesus). So what should we do with problems? How can we handle them with integrity?

We need to remember that every Christian doctrine raises problems, not excluding the central doctrines of God (his being, creation, sovereignty, providence and justice), of Jesus Christ (his one person in two natures, his work of atonement, his bodily resurrection, present reign and future return) and of the Holy Spirit (his activity in the church and the world). Or take the love of God. It is a fundamental Christian doctrine. Every Christian without exception believes that God is love (Roman Catholic, Orthodox, Reformed, Lutheran, Episcopal,

[1] Lk. 10:16.

Independent, Pentecostal); if they denied it, they would not be Christians. Yet the problems surrounding this belief are enormous: for example, the origin and spread of evil, the suffering of the innocent, the 'silences' of God and the 'acts' of God, the vastness of the universe, and the apparent insignificance of individual human beings.

Supposing somebody comes to us with a personal problem or dilemma (perhaps the birth of a handicapped child, a natural disaster, or a tragic bereavement) and challenges us: 'Why should this happen to me? How can God be love if he allows this?' How do we react? Do we say that, in order to preserve our intellectual integrity, we must suspend our belief in the love of God until we have solved the problem? I hope not. Nor do we sweep the problem under the carpet and try to forget it. No, instead, in addition to the question how we should respond pastorally to our questioner, we wrestle with the problem in our own mind and heart. We think about it conscientiously, read about it, talk about it and pray about it. And during this process some light is thrown upon the problem. Yet some of the perplexity remains. So what next? The way of intellectual integrity, I suggest, is to determine to retain our conviction about God's love, in spite of the residual difficulties, ultimately for one reason only, namely that Jesus our Lord himself taught it and exhibited it. It was because of Jesus that we came to believe in God's love in the first place; it is for the same reason that we should continue to do so.

It is the same with problems relating to the Bible. We need to learn to face them as we face problems surrounding other Christian doctrines. If somebody comes to us with a biblical problem (a discrepancy, for example, between theology and science, or between two Gospel accounts, or a moral dilemma), what should we do? We should not (from a mistaken integrity) suspend our belief in the truth of Scripture until we have solved the problem. Nor should we place the problem either on a shelf (indefinitely postponing its challenge) or under a carpet (permanently concealing it, even from ourselves). Instead, we should struggle conscientiously with the problem in thought, discussion and prayer. As we do so, some difficulties will be either wholly or partly cleared up. But then, in spite of those which remain, we should retain our belief about Scripture on the ground that Jesus himself taught and exhibited it.

If a critic says to me 'You are an obscurantist to believe the Bible to be the Word of God in defiance of the problems,' I nowadays return the compliment and say, 'OK, if you like, I am. But then you are an obscurantist to believe in the love of God in defiance of the problems.' Actually, however, to believe a Christian doctrine in spite of its problems, because of the acknowledged lordship of Jesus Christ, is not obscurantism (preferring darkness to light) but faith (trusting him who said he was the light of the world). It is more than faith; it is the sober, intellectual integrity of confessing Jesus as Lord.

Ecumenical progress

Thirdly, submission to the authority of Scripture is *the way of ecumenical progress*, that is to say, the means by which to secure an acceptable coming together of churches.

Now I realize that some of my readers may entertain no desire to make any ecumenical progress. You may be (I am guessing) suspicious of the whole ecumenical movement, and of the World Council of Churches to which it has given birth. You see (although it is always misleading to generalize) its tendency to doctrinal indifferentism, its attempted reinterpretation of the Christian mission in terms of socio-political action, and its leaning towards syncretism and universalism in the face of the challenges of other faiths. Indeed, I understand your qualms, for I share them. There is much in contemporary ecumenism to perplex and even distress us. We cannot accept uncritically everything which emanates from Geneva.

Nevertheless, I am also disturbed by the blanket condemnation of ecumenical activity which is expressed by a large section of the evangelical constituency. It is clear to me that we cannot simply dismiss the whole non-evangelical section of Christendom as if it did not exist, or, since it does exist, regard it as non-Christian and resolve to have nothing to do with it. Besides, Jesus our Lord prayed that his people might be one, in order that the world might believe,[1] and his apostle Paul urges us to 'make every effort to keep the unity of the Spirit through the bond of peace'.[2]

There is, of course, room for disagreement among us regarding what shape Christian unity should take. But it should be possible for us to agree that competition between different churches is unseemly, and that the visible unity of the church in some form is a desirable goal. In his reply to a letter from Thomas Cranmer, Archbishop of Canterbury, in 1552, Calvin wrote as follows:

> Doubtless it must be counted among the greatest misfortunes of our century that churches are thus separated from each other . . ., and that the holy communion of the members of Christ, which many confess with their mouth, is only sincerely sought after by few . . . From this it follows that the members being so scattered, the body of the church lies bleeding. This affects me so deeply, that, if anybody could see that I might be of any use, I should not hesitate to cross ten seas for this business, if that were needful . . . Indeed, if learned men were to seek a solid and carefully devised agreement according to the rule of Scripture, an agreement by which the separated churches should unite with each other, I think that for my part I ought not to spare any trouble or dangers.[3]

Calvin's letter to Cranmer is significant, not only because of the end he had in view (the uniting of separated churches), but also because of the means he proposed (agreement according to the rule of Scripture). For the unity Christ himself desires for his church is certainly a unity in truth. His prayer recorded in John 17 clearly links the two, as we shall see in chapter 16. Besides,

[1] Jn. 17:20–23. [2] Eph. 4:3.
[3] *Op. Calv.* XIV, pp. 312–314, quoted in Jean Cadier, *The Man God Mastered* (ET IVF, 1960), pp. 172–173.

since the church is built on the foundation of the apostles and prophets, with Christ himself as the chief cornerstone,[1] it will certainly not grow in size or stability by neglecting, let alone undermining, its foundation. And in its official position the World Council of Churches agrees with this. Its accepted definition of 'the unity we seek' (1961) speaks of 'one fully committed fellowship, holding the one apostolic faith, preaching the one gospel, breaking the one bread' and enjoying a corporate life of prayer, witness and service.[2]

The 'one apostolic faith' has, of course, come down to us in the New Testament, and no union of churches could or should be contemplated which deviates from this rule. In particular, one of the greatest obstacles to unity has been the failure to distinguish between Scripture and tradition. Jesus himself drew a clear distinction between written Scripture and the oral tradition of the elders, subordinated the latter to the former, and even went so far as to reject tradition as 'the words of men' in order that Scripture as the Word of God might have the supremacy.[3] The very same distinction needs to be made today. Yet an example of why some church unity schemes have failed is the tendency of Anglican or Episcopal churches to insist on a particular view of the 'historic episcopate' as non-negotiable. One can understand the historical reasons for this, and I myself would want to defend an episcopal form of government as a pastoral ideal which is consonant with Scripture and conducive to the health of the church. But one cannot insist on it as indispensable, since it belongs to the tradition of the church, and is not required by Scripture.

If only we could agree that Scripture is 'God's Word written' (Anglican Article XX), that it is supreme in its authority over all human traditions however venerable, and that it must be allowed to reform and renew the church, we would take an immediate leap forward in ecumenical relationships. Reformation according to the Word of God is indispensable to reunion.

[1] Eph. 2:20. [2] *The New Delhi Report* (SCM, 1962), p. 116.
[3] *E.g.* Mk. 7:5–13.

Effective evangelism

Fourthly, submission to the authority of Scripture is *the way of faithful and effective evangelism*. My argument so far has been domestic and ecclesiastical, as we have thought about personal discipleship and integrity, and about church relations. All the time the world outside is in great confusion and darkness. Has the church any light for this darkness, any word of hope for the bewildered modern world?

One of the tragedies of the contemporary church is that, just when the world seems to be ready to listen, the church often seems to have little or nothing to say. For the church itself is confused; it shares in the current bewilderment, instead of addressing it. The church is insecure; it is uncertain of its identity, mission and message. It stammers and stutters, when it should be proclaiming the gospel with boldness. Indeed, the major reason for its diminishing influence in the West is its diminishing faith.

A recovery of evangelism is impossible without a recovery of the evangel, the good news. For evangelism according to its simplest definition is 'sharing the evangel'. So biblical evangelism is impossible without the biblical evangel. Many churches throughout the world are regarding the 1990s as a 'decade of evangelism'. It sounds fine. But we shall never agree on what we mean by 'evangelism' if we decline to discuss the content of the 'evangel'. Evangelism really has to be defined in terms of the evangel.

We should be able to agree that Christian witness is essentially witness to Christ, and that the only authentic Christ there is is the Christ of the apostolic witness. For the apostles were the original witnesses, the eyewitnesses; our witness, vital though it is, always remains secondary to theirs. We have no authority to edit their gospel. Our calling is rather to preserve it like stewards, proclaim it like heralds, and argue it like advocates.

In his book on evangelism entitled *Go and Make Disciples*, David Read, who for many years was minister of Madison Avenue Presbyterian Church, New York, wrote: 'Those of us who enjoy visiting other countries are familiar with that solemn moment when at the frontier we encounter a customs official who . . . fixes us with steely eyes and asks "Have you anything to declare?" I have not yet had the nerve to answer "Yes, as a minister of the gospel, it is my duty to declare that Jesus Christ is your Lord and Saviour".' So David Read calls his final chapter 'The Crux: Have you anything to Declare?' It is lack of conviction about the gospel, he writes, which makes 'most of us . . . reluctant evangelists'.[1]

I agree. I think there is no chance of the church taking its evangelistic task seriously unless it first recovers its confidence in the truth, relevance and power of the gospel, and begins to get excited about it again. For this, however, it will have to return to the Bible in which the gospel has been revealed.

Personal humility

Fifthly, submission to the authority of Scripture is *the way of personal Christian humility*. Nothing is more obnoxious in us who claim to follow Jesus Christ than arrogance, and nothing is more appropriate or attractive than humility. And an essential element in Christian humility is the willingness to hear and receive God's Word. Perhaps the greatest of all our needs is to take our place again humbly, quietly and expectantly at the feet of Jesus Christ, in order to listen attentively to his Word, and to believe and obey it. For we have no liberty to disbelieve or disobey him.

The ultimate issue before us and the whole church is whether Jesus Christ is Lord (as we say he is) or not. The question is whether Christ is Lord of the church (to teach and command it) or the church is lord of Christ (to edit and manipulate his teaching). In the contemporary crisis of authority in the world, and loss of authority in the church, my plea is that we return to a humble submission to Scripture as God's Word, and that we do so out of a humble submission to Jesus Christ as Lord, who

[1] David H. C. Read, *Go and Make Disciples* (Abingdon, 1978), pp. 94–95.

himself humbly submitted to Scripture in his own faith, life, mission and teaching.

In so doing, we will find the way of mature discipleship and intellectual integrity, the way to unite churches and evangelize the world, and the way to express a proper humility before our Lord Jesus Christ. That is what I mean by the 'wholesomeness' of submitting to the authority of Scripture.

CHAPTER TWELVE

TRANSPOSING THE WORD

Whenever we pick up the Bible and read it, even in a contemporary version like the Good News Bible, we are conscious of stepping back two millennia or (in the case of the Old Testament) even more. We travel backwards in time, behind the microchip revolution, the electronic revolution, the scientific revolution and the industrial revolution, until we find ourselves in an alien world which long ago ceased to exist. In consequence, the Bible feels odd, sounds archaic, looks obsolete and smells musty. We are tempted to ask impatiently, 'What on earth has that old book got to say to me?'

Our sense of incongruity when we read the Bible, and the consequent difficulty we often experience in receiving a meaningful communication from it, are due primarily neither to the passage of time in itself (from the first century to the twentieth) nor to the mere distance (from the Middle East to the West), but to the cultural differences which remoteness of time and place have caused.

In fact, two distinct but complementary problems confront us. The first is the problem of our own cultural imprisonment, and the second the problem of the cultural conditioning of the biblical authors. That is, both the writers and the readers of Scripture are culture-creatures, the products (and therefore to some degree the prisoners) of the particular cultures in which they were brought up. Consequently, in all our Bible reading there is a collision of cultures between the biblical world and the modern world. Both God's speaking and our listening are culture-conditioned. This fact clearly affects our interpretation of Scripture; in the course of our discusson we will have to ask whether it also affects the authority of Scripture.

The hermeneutical problem

Biblical hermeneutics, that is, the art or science of interpreting Scripture, has become in recent decades a major preoccupation of scholars. Indeed, all Christian people who read the Bible come up against the question of how to understand it rightly.

The problem arises from the extreme cultural particularities of the ancient text and the modern interpreter. Each has a different 'horizon', a limited viewpoint or perspective, and what is needed is what Hans-Georg Gadamer called a 'fusion' of horizons. 'Understanding takes place', writes Dr Tony Thiselton in his classic and comprehensive study *The Two Horizons*,[1] 'when two sets of horizons are brought into relation to each other, namely those of the text and those of the interpreter.'[2]

In this process the interpreter's first task was called by Gadamer 'distancing'. That is, we have to acknowledge 'the pastness of the past', disengage ourselves from the text, and allow it its own historical integrity, without intruding ourselves into it or deciding prematurely how it applies to us. Careful exegesis of the text necessitates studying it in its own cultural and linguistic terms.

But this is only the beginning. If first we stand back from the text, next we seek to enter it. 'There must be present engagement with the text', writes Tony Thiselton, 'as well as critical distancing from it.'[3] Since the interpreter also belongs to a precise and particular context, though different from that of the text, this is not easy. It requires a high degree of imagination, of empathy, if we are to enter that alien world. 'Historical exegesis is essential, but it is not enough. We need *both* distancing *and*

[1] Anthony C. Thiselton, *The Two Horizons: New Testament Hermeneutics and Philosophical Description with Special Reference to Heidegger, Bultmann, Gadamer and Wittgenstein* (Paternoster, 1980). Two shorter essays have brought this debate within reach of ordinary mortals, namely Dr Thiselton's own 'Understanding God's Word Today' in, ed. John Stott *Obeying Christ in a Changing World*, vol. I (Collins, 1977), pp. 90–122, and Dr J. I. Packer's 'Infallible Scripture and the Role of Hermeneutics' in *Scripture and Truth*, ed. D. A. Carson and John D. Woodbridge (Zondervan and IVP, 1983), pp. 323–356.

[2] A. C. Thiselton, *The Two Horizons*, p. 103.

[3] *Obeying Christ in a Changing World*, vol. I, p. 118.

an openness to the text which will yield progress towards the fusion of horizons.'[1]

This leads to an active interaction or dialectic between text and interpreter. However hard we may work at distancing ourselves from the text, we can hardly help bringing to it our presuppositions and our own agenda of problems and questions. The Scripture may respond to these. But, because it has its own agenda, it may not. Instead, it may challenge us to go away and re-shape our questions, even replace them with better ones. We then return with our new agenda, and so the dialogue between us goes on. It is part of what is called 'the hermeneutical circle', although some European and Latin American scholars have preferred the expression 'hermeneutical spiral' because the movement is progressive and upward.[2]

During the sixties some German scholars, especially Ernst Fuchs and Gerhard Ebeling, former students of Bultmann, went further in developing a 'new hermeneutic'. Rejecting objectivity as impossible, on the ground that we cannot jump out of our own particularity into that of a biblical author, they stressed the need to let the text speak. According to their theory of language, its purpose is not so much to convey 'concepts' as to cause an 'event' (a 'language-event'), in which the roles of text and interpreter are reversed and the interpreter listens instead of talking. It seems clear that these post-Bultmannians went too far. Denying that the biblical text has an accessible, objective meaning, they lapsed into an uncontrolled subjectivity. What the text said to them might bear no relation to what it actually meant.

Nevertheless, there is abiding value in what these scholars are feeling for. They take seriously the cultural gulf between the past and the present. They recognize the independent historical particularity of both text and interpreter, and they seek to develop a dialectic between them. The old hermeneutic put into our hands a set of universal rules of interpretation, which we

[1] A. C. Thiselton, *The Two Horizons*, p. 326.
[2] See *e.g. The Willowbank Report: Gospel and Culture* (Lausanne Committee for World Evangelization, 1978), pp. 10–11.

applied to the text; the new hermeneutic is concerned to allow the text to apply its message to us. The old hermeneutic concentrated on the text as *object*; we stood over it, studied it, scrutinized it, applied our rules to it, and almost took control of it. The new hermeneutic, however, concentrates on the text as *subject*; it stands over us, and we sit meekly 'under it', as the Reformers used to put it. It addresses, confronts, challenges and changes us.

Here, then, is the danger of a new polarization between the 'old' and the 'new'. Each is perilously lopsided without the other. For the text is both object and subject. We address it, and it addresses us. But as these two processes develop, we must insist that the object and the subject are the same text and have the same meaning.

We now return to the two cultural problems, and consider each separately.

Our own cultural imprisonment

Every human being who has ever lived has been a creature of culture. Culture is a convenient term with which to denote the complex of beliefs, values, customs and traditions which each generation receives from its predecessor and transmits to its successor, and which binds a society together. We have all drunk in our cultural inheritance with our mother's milk. The way we think, judge, act, talk, dress, eat, work and play are all to a large extent determined by our culture, and we usually do not realize how much our cultural upbringing has enslaved us.

Hence the great value of travel, for then we learn to listen to ourselves through the ears of another culture, and look at ourselves through another culture's eyes. I well remember my first visit to the United States about thirty-five years ago. After the first address I had given on American soil, a lady said to me, 'I do like your English accent.' Accent? Me? She of course had an American accent, but surely I spoke the Queen's English? My speech was the norm; hers was the deviation, the abnorm.

Then, not so long afterwards, I was in Manila, and a little Filipino boy of only about eight years old came up to me, cocked his head, looked into my face and commented cheekily, 'You *do* talk funny!' He was right. I do. But then so do you, and so does everybody.

Our culture includes not only the general views and values, standards and customs, of our society, but also those which apply to our particular sex, age and class. They all affect the way we read the Bible. For example, how can I as a man read Scripture in the same way as a woman who has been hurt by male chauvinism? Or how can I as an old man hear from Scripture what young people hear when they read it? Or again, how can I as a member of an affluent society really listen to what Scripture says about the poor?

Men and women, old and young, black and white, African and Asian, capitalist and socialist, waged and unwaged, middle-class and working-class, all read Scripture differently. Our spectacles have cultural lenses. It is so difficult as to be almost impossible for us to read the Bible with genuine objectivity and openness, and for God to break through our cultural defences and to say to us what he wants to say. Instead, we come to our reading of the Bible with our own agenda, bias, questions, preoccupations, concerns and convictions, and, unless we are extremely careful, we impose these on the biblical text. We may sincerely pray before we read, 'Open my eyes that I may see wonderful things in your law,'[1] but still the same non-communication may persist. For even that introductory prayer, though to be sure it is taken from the Psalter, is suspect because it lays down the kind of message we want to hear.

'Please, Lord, I want to see some "wonderful thing" in your word.'

But he may reply, 'What makes you think I have only "wonderful things" to show you? As a matter of fact, I have some rather "disturbing things" to show you today. Are you prepared to receive them?'

[1] Ps. 119:18.

'Oh no, Lord, please not', we stammer in reply. 'I come to Scripture only to be comforted; I really do not want to be challenged or disturbed.'

In other words, we come to the Bible with our agenda formulated unilaterally, our expectations pre-set, our minds made up, laying down in advance what we want God to say to us. Then, instead of hearing the thunderclap of his voice, all we receive is the soothing echoes of our own cultural prejudice. And God says to us, as he did to his servant through Isaiah: 'Hear, you deaf; look, you blind, and see! Who is blind but my servant, and deaf like the messenger I send?'[1]

Hence the dismal record of the church's unfaithfulness. Seldom in its long history has it been sensitively in tune with God's Word. More often it has been exactly what it has been forbidden to be, namely conformist.[2] It has been influenced more by the world than by the Word. Instead of challenging the *status quo* with the values of the kingdom of God, it has acquiesced in it. Instead of resisting the encroachments of secularism, it has surrendered to them. Instead of rejecting the value system and lifestyle of the world, it has assimilated them. The church has accommodated itself to the prevailing culture, leaped on all the trendiest bandwagons, and hummed all the popular tunes of the day. Whenever the church does this, it reads Scripture through the world's eyes, and rationalizes its own unfaithfulness.

Is this unfair? I do not think so. Consider some examples from the past. For church history is full of the church's cultural blind spots.

How is it, I ask myself, that the Christian conscience not only approved but actually glamorized those terrible medieval Crusades as a Christ-glorifying form of mission, so that European Christian knights in shining armour rode forth to recover the holy places from Islam by force? It was an unholy blunder which Muslims have never forgotten, let alone forgiven, and which continues to obstruct the evangelization of the Muslim world, especially in the Middle East. Or how is it that torture

[1] Is. 42:18–19. [2] Rom. 12:2.

could ever have been employed in the name of Jesus Christ to combat heresy and enforce orthodoxy, so that the thumbscrews were turned on some miserable dissident until he capitulated? One might almost characterize it 'evangelization by torture', and that in the name of the Prince of Peace! Or how is that, although the Franciscans organized missions in the thirteenth century and the Jesuits in the sixteenth, Protestant churches were so inward looking that they had virtually no missions until the time of the Pietists two centuries after the Reformation? Even then, towards the end of the eighteenth century, when William Carey proposed a mission to India, he was greeted with the patronizing retort, 'Sit down, young man; when God wants to convert the heathen, he will do it without your help or mine.' Had his critic never read the Great Commission?

Again, how is it that the cruel degradations of slavery and of the slave trade were not abolished in the so-called Christian West until 1800 years after Christ? Or how is it that racial prejudice and environmental pollution have become widely recognized as the evils they are only since the Second World War?

Such is a catalogue of some of the worst blind spots, which have marred the church's testimony down the ages. None of them can be defended from Scripture, although tortuous attempts have been made to do so. All are due rather to a misreading of Scripture or to an unwillingness to sit under its authority. God's people were blinded by tradition. They had other agendas; they were not in a mind or mood to listen to God.

What, then, about our own contemporary blindness? It is comparatively easy to criticize our forebears for theirs; it is much harder to be aware of ours. What will posterity see as the chief Christian blind spot at the end of the twentieth century? I cannot say with any degree of certainty, because of course I share in the same myopia myself. But I suspect that it will relate to two main areas. First, we Christians who live in the affluence of the North Atlantic still do not seem to have felt sufficiently the injustice of continuing North–South economic inequality, which was forcibly brought to the world's attention by the two Brandt Commission Reports, *North–South* (1980) and *Common Crisis* (1983). Apart from macro-economic questions of trade and development, we do not seem to have allowed the situation to affect our lifestyle. While a thousand million people are destitute, lacking the basic necessities for survival, and while about 10,000 people die of starvation daily, not counting mass starvation in famine conditions, should not the Christian voice of protest be louder and more strident? And should we not continue to simplify our own economic lifestyle, not because we imagine that this will solve the problem, but because it will enable us personally to share more and to express appropriately our sense of compassionate solidarity with the poor?

A second blind spot of at least evangelical Christians seems to me to be our comparative failure to condemn as immoral and indefensible all indiscriminate weaponry – both the use of atomic, biological and chemical weapons as being indiscriminate by nature, and the indiscriminate use of conventional weapons. We should surely be denouncing this as incompatible with the 'just war' theory, let alone with Christian pacifism. It was back in 1965 that the Roman Catholic Church condemned such weapons as 'a crime against God and man himself'. Ecumenical pronouncements followed, declaring indiscriminate warfare 'increasingly offensive to the Christian conscience'. But the evangelical voice, with notable exceptions, has been irresponsibly muted.

The first step towards the recovery of our Christian integrity will be the humble recognition that our culture blinds, deafens and dopes us. We neither see what we ought to see in Scripture, nor hear God's Word as we should, nor feel the anger of God against evil. We need to allow God's Word to confront us, disturbing our security, undermining our complacency, penetrating our protective patterns of thought and behaviour, and overthrowing our resistance.

It is not impossible for God to do this. Once we realize how strong a barrier to his communication with us our culture can be, we will be alert to the problem. Then we will begin to cry to him to open our eyes, unstop our ears, and stab our dull consciences awake, until we see, hear and feel what (through his Word) God has been saying to us all the time.

The Bible's cultural conditioning

It is not only Bible readers who are the products of a particular culture; so were the biblical authors. And God took this into account when he desired to communicate with his people. That is, when he spoke, he neither used his own language (if he has one), nor expressed himself in terms of his own heavenly culture, for such communication would have been unintelligible to human beings on earth. Nor did God shout culture-free maxims out of a clear, blue sky. On the contrary, he humbled himself to speak in the languages of his people (classical Hebrew, Aramaic and common Greek), and within the cultures of the ancient Near East (the Old Testament), Palestinian Judaism (the Gospels) and the hellenized Roman Empire (the rest of the New Testament). No word of God was spoken in a cultural vacuum; every word of God was spoken in a cultural context.

True, the cultural contexts in which the Bible was written are often alien to us. But we must not resent this on the ground that it causes us problems. We should rather rejoice in the divine condescension, that God should have stooped to our level in order to reveal himself in linguistically and culturally appropriate terms. This truth applies both to the incarnation of his Son, who took human flesh, and to the inspiration of his Word, which was spoken in human language.

Nevertheless, we are also faced with this question: How can a divine revelation given in transient cultural terms have permanent validity? How can a revelation addressed to a particular cultural situation have a universal application? Does not the cultural conditioning of Scripture limit its relevance to us, and even its authority over us? Must we not say with David Edwards, 'I admit that a lot in the Bible . . . is culturally conditioned, and therefore out of date'?[1] Is his deduction logical?

My response to David Edwards is to agree that the Bible is a culturally conditioned book (as indeed are all books which have ever been written, including his and mine!), but to disagree that it is on that account necessarily out of date. How then shall we handle the cultural element in Scripture?

The principle, as I see it, can be set forth by an everyday illustration. We have little difficulty in distinguishing between a person and the particular clothing which he or she happens to be wearing. Most of us have several sets of clothes at home. Sometimes we dress up in maximum finery, for a wedding or party perhaps, or in our national costume. At other times we put on more sombre clothing, as when we attend a funeral. Occasionally we dress up in archaic garments, when playing charades or going to a fancy-dress party. We also have our work clothes, our sports clothes and our night clothes. In other words, there is variety in our wardrobe. But the person underneath the clothing remains the same. The clothing changes; the person does not.

Now just as we distinguish between persons and their clothing, so we need to distinguish between the essence of God's revelation (what he is teaching, promising or commanding) and the cultural clothing in which it was originally given. However dated the cultural setting may be, the essential message has permanent and universal validity. The cultural application may change; the revelation does not.

When we are faced with a biblical passage, therefore, whose teaching is obviously clothed in ancient cultural dress (because it relates to social customs which are either obsolete or at least alien to our own culture), how shall we react? We have three options.

The first possibility is *total rejection*. 'Because the culture is out of date,' we could say to ourselves, 'the teaching here is irrelevant. It has nothing to say to me. I may as well take a pair

[1] From a book review in the *Church Times*.

of scissors, cut this passage out of my Bible, and throw it away.' I am not recommending this response!

The second and opposite possibility is *wooden, unimaginative literalism*. The literalist says: 'Because this text is part of God's Word, it must be preserved and followed just as it stands, without modification. Both the substance and its cultural expression have equal authority. To discard either would be to tamper with the Word of God and be guilty of an incipient liberalism.' I do not recommend this response either.

There is a third and more judicious way, which is called *cultural transposition*. The procedure now is to identify the essential revelation in the text (what God is saying here), to separate this from the cultural form in which he chose to give it, and then to re-clothe it in appropriate modern cultural terms. 'Transposition' is a good word for this practice, since we are already familiar with it in musical contexts. To transpose a piece of music is to put it into a different key from that in which it was originally written. To transpose a biblical text is to put it into a different culture from that in which it was originally given. In musical transposition the tune and harmonization remain the same; only the key is different. In biblical transposition the truth of the revelation remains the same; only the cultural expression is different.

Cross-cultural missionaries illustrate the need for cultural transposition, although they have to wrestle with the dialectic between three cultures. Their task is to take the essence of the gospel, which was first revealed in the cultural settings of the Bible, and which they have received in their own cultures, and transpose it into the culture of the people to whom they go, without thereby either falsifying the message or rendering it unintelligible.[1] That, at least, is the theory. In practice, missionaries have often taken with them what Dr René Padilla at the Lausanne Congress in 1974 called a 'culture-Christianity'. In other words, they exported with the gospel their own cultural inheritance.

[1] See *The Willowbank Report: Gospel and Culture*, especially chapter 5.

I remember the shock I felt on my first visit to West Africa and its churches. I saw Gothic spires rising incongruously above the coconut palms, and African bishops sweating profusely in the tropical heat, because they were wearing medieval European ecclesiastical robes. I heard western hymn tunes being sung to the accompaniment of western instruments, and African tongues attempting to get round Jacobean and even Elizabethan English! It is, of course, easy to criticize, and, if we had been in the position of the early missionaries, we would probably have made the same mistake. Nevertheless, this imposition of western cultural forms was a serious blunder. What is needed instead is what Stanley Jones in India called the 'naturalization' of the gospel,[1] which means its transposition into indigenous cultural forms.

Looking again at the three options before us, we might perhaps say that 'total rejection' is to throw out the baby with the bath water; that 'wooden literalism' is to keep both the baby and the bath water; while 'cultural transposition' is to keep the baby and change the bath water.

Examples of cultural transposition

The Bible is concerned about both doctrine and ethics, belief and behaviour, and in both areas cultural transposition is necessary.

Take first the doctrinal or theological teaching of the Bible. It seems obvious that we must learn to distinguish between the truth being affirmed, and the cultural terms in which it is presented; between meaning (the revelation) and medium (its communication). It is in this connection that we have to face the challenge posed by Bultmann's 'demythologization' programme. His argument may without too much distortion be reduced to three points, relating respectively to the biblical authors, their modern readers, and theological communicators. First, the intellectual framework of the biblical writers was

[1] See E. Stanley Jones, *The Christ of the Indian Road* (Hodder and Stoughton, 1926), *e.g.* p. 186.

pre-scientific and therefore 'mythical'. For example, they envisaged heaven above and hell below in a three-decker universe, so that they imagined Jesus literally 'descending to hell' and 'ascending to heaven'. Secondly, if modern scientific men and women are presented today with the gospel (*kerygma*) couched in terms of such an obsolete cosmology, they will reject it as frankly incredible. Thirdly, the task of theologians is therefore to strip away the mythical elements in the Bible, or 'demythologize the *kerygma*', because the purpose of myth is to speak not of historical events but of transcendent reality.

Let us agree at once with the spirit of the second point above. Our priority concern is how to communicate the *kerygma* to modern people in a way that is credible. In order to do so, we have to proclaim biblical *truth*, but not necessarily use biblical *terms*. We may (and must) transpose revealed truth into modern idiom.

With regard to Bultmann's first point, however, I am not myself at all convinced that the biblical authors were the literalists he imagines. To be sure, they used the imagery of the three-decker universe, for it was part of their intellectual framework. But were they actually affirming it? I think not. Take Psalm 75. God is said, when the earth quakes, to 'hold its pillars firm'.[1] So here is the earth (the middle deck) resting on pillars. But in the same psalm God both commands the wicked not to lift up their 'horns' or they will be cut off,[2] and warns that in his hand there is 'a cup full of foaming wine mixed with spices' which he will shortly pour out for the wicked to drink.[3] Now nobody (least of all the psalmist) believed literally that the wicked sprout horns or that God holds a cup of wine in his hand. If, therefore, these are examples of dramatic, poetic imagery, is it not gratuitous to insist that the earth's pillars are meant to be understood literally?

The Old Testament writers affirmed God's sovereign control of the world by saying that he held earth's pillars firm, without committing themselves to a three-decker cosmology. They

[1] Verse 3. [2] Verses 4, 5, 10. [3] Verse 8.

affirmed God's power over evil by referring to his destruction of the primeval monster Leviathan,[1] without committing themselves to the Babylonian creation myth. They also affirmed his general revelation through nature by saying that the sun runs across the sky,[2] without committing themselves to a pre-Copernican universe. These forms of thought and speech, whether we call them 'imagery', 'poetry' or 'myth', were common currency in the ancient Near East. Old Testament writers used them to convey truths about God as Creator and Lord, without affirming the literal truth of the imagery or mythology they were using.

This brings us to Bultmann's third point. We should be able to agree with the need in some degree to 'demythologize', if what is meant is the need to transpose truth from one set of images to another, as we have just seen. But Bultmann goes much further than this, especially in relation to the New Testament. He attempts to reconstruct the *kerygma* (especially the death, resurrection and *parousia* of Jesus) by dissolving these historical events into a 'meaning' which is not historical. Thus, according to Bultmann, when the apostles said that 'Christ died for our sins', they were not referring to any literal sin-bearing sacrifice, but affirming God's love and our own existential experience of being crucified with Christ. When they said that 'he rose', they were not referring to an event but to an experience, namely that he rose in their own revived faith. And when they said that he is coming again to judge, they were not referring to a future event, but to a present challenge to make a responsible decision for Christ today.

The key question, however, is whether the affirmations that Christ died, rose and will return were deliberately mythical ways of referring to something other than historical events, or whether they were real happenings which were themselves part of the *kerygma* being proclaimed. The natural interpretation of the apostolic *kerygma* is that the apostles were intending to

[1] *E.g.* Ps. 74:14; Is. 27:1.
[2] Ps. 19:1–6.

proclaim events in the career of Jesus which were both historically true and theologically significant.

It is, then, legitimate to distinguish between the meaning and the medium, between what is being affirmed and how the affirmation is made, between the revelation of truth and its communication. But it is also essential to ask whether the words and images used are literal or mythical. The defeat of Leviathan is a myth; the death, resurrection and coming of Jesus belong to history. The intention of the author will usually help us to know which is which.

We turn now to three examples of cultural transposition in the ethical field. I will begin with a fairly easy example, so that we may firmly grasp the principle and its application, namely the foot-washing. After Jesus had washed the feet of the Twelve in the upper room and resumed his place, he said: 'Now that I, your Lord and Teacher, have washed your feet, you also should wash one another's feet.'[1] In Jesus' day foot-washing was a common cultural practice. If we had been invited to a meal in a friend's house, we would have walked there barefoot or in sandals through dusty streets, and on arrival a slave would have washed our feet. Today, however, at least in the West, the whole culture has changed. We visit a friend by car or public transport. On arrival, there is certainly no slave to meet us and wash our feet. Instead, our host or hostess will probably ask us, 'Do you want to wash your hands?' How, then, shall we handle a text in which reciprocal foot-washing is commanded? Think of the three options. Shall we go the way of total rejection, on the ground that foot-washing has no place in our culture? No. Shall we obey Jesus' command literally, and go round asking people to take their shoes and socks or tights off, so that we may wash their feet? No. Although the Mennonites, and some African and Asian churches, have a ritual foot-washing as part of their communion service, it seems clear that Jesus' reference was to a social custom, not to a religious ceremony.

[1] Jn. 13:14.

We are left then with the third option of cultural transposition. We ask what Jesus was getting at, what was the essence of his instruction. The answer is not far to seek. He was teaching that if we love one another, we must serve one another, and no service will be too dirty, menial or demeaning for us to perform. If, then, we cannot wash people's feet, we will gladly shine their shoes, or wash the dishes for them, or even clean out the toilets. Nothing will be beneath our dignity. Whatever in our culture is regarded as unpleasant work of low status, *that* will be our privilege out of love to undertake.

A second example of the need for cultural transposition relates to the eating of idol meats.[1] The question was whether it was permissible for the followers of Jesus to eat the meat of animals which, before being put on sale in a butcher's shop, had been offered in an idolatrous sacrifice. New converts, freshly rescued from heathen idolatry, had conscientious qualms about doing so. Would not the eating of idol meats contaminate and compromise them? Paul was clear that it would not. Idols were nothing, he said. There was only one God, the Father, and only one Lord, Jesus Christ.[2] So he saw no reason why he should not eat idol meats. His conscience was 'strong', that is, well educated. But then there were the 'weak' believers to consider. Their 'weakness' was not in their will but in their conscience, which was under-educated and therefore over-scrupulous. If Paul were to eat idol meats in their presence, they might be encouraged to follow his example against their better judgment, in which case their conscience would be defiled. Consequently, out of deference to the weak Christians, Paul refrained.

Reading about this heated controversy in the New Testament sounds very alien to our context, at least in the West. There are no pagan temples in our culture, where animals are sacrificed to idols, nor are there any meat markets in which we could buy food which had been used in idolatrous worship. Yet at least two principles remain, which were laid down by Paul, and which are relevant to Christian people in every culture today.

[1] Paul deals with this issue at some length in both Rom. 14 and 1 Cor. 8.
[2] 1 Cor. 8:4–6.

The first is that conscience is sacred. To be sure, it needs to be educated, but, even when it is weak, it must not be violated. 'Conscientious objection', not only to military service, but in other situations as well, is allowed in those countries which have had a Christian influence. Secondly, love limits liberty. Paul had liberty of conscience to eat, but he denied himself this freedom out of loving concern for those who would be offended if he did. These two principles can be applied in many different cultural contexts today.

My third example is the most controversial. It concerns the position and roles of women. Whole books have been written on this topic; I can hope here only to consider how far cultural transposition may be appropriate and helpful in this area. We are familiar both with Paul's prohibitions, that a woman may not 'teach or . . . have authority over a man',[1] and with his commands, that women are to wear veils and remain silent in public worship.[2] The question which these texts raise is this: Are all these instructions of permanent and universal validity? Or do they contain some cultural elements, which could allow us a little flexibility in interpretation and which may need transposition into our own culture? My response to these questions necessitates first the making of two affirmations, and then the asking of two more questions.

The first affirmation is that the sexes are equal. This is taught in Genesis 1:26–28. Men and women are equal bearers of the divine image, and equal sharers in the earthly dominion. Moreover, if they are equal by creation, they are even more equal (if that is possible) by redemption. For in Jesus Christ 'there is neither . . . male nor female'.[3] That is, we are absolutely equal in worth, dignity and relation to God. The second affirmation is that the sexes are complementary. This is taught in Genesis 2:18–24. Equality does not mean identity. Nor does it necessarily imply a complete interchangeability of roles. Moreover, within this complementarity Paul affirmed the principle of masculine 'headship'. He derived it from the

[1] 1 Tim. 2:12. [2] 1 Cor. 11:4–10; 14:34–35; 1 Tim. 2:11–12. [3] Gal. 3:28.

creation facts of Genesis 2, namely that woman was made after, out of and for man. And he evidently did not see any conflict between this and Galatians 3:28. I do not myself feel at liberty to disagree with the apostle Paul or to dismiss his teaching as rabbinic, cultural or mistaken. On the contrary, he roots it in creation, and what creation has established, no culture is able to destroy.

From the two affirmations I come to the two questions. First, what does 'headship' mean? I do not think we shall find our answer from the etymology of the Greek word *kephalē*, 'head', or from its use in secular Greek, where it may sometimes mean 'source'. The meaning of a word in Scripture is determined less by its origin or its use elsewhere than by its use in the biblical context. This being so, Ephesians 5:21–32 comes to our aid, since there Paul uses 'head' to convey responsibility rather than authority. He argues that the husband's headship (and therefore perhaps masculine headship in general) is to be modelled both on Christ's headship of the church (which led him to give himself up for her) and on our relation to our own body (which leads us to nourish it and care for it). In both cases 'headship' means sacrifice and service. It is the headship of care, not control. Its purpose is not to inhibit, let alone to crush, but to facilitate, to create conditions of love and security in which women are free to be and to develop themselves.

Secondly, how does 'headship' apply? Does it forbid ordination or other forms of ministry? In 1 Corinthians 11 Paul requires women to wear veils in public worship and refers to the veil as a symbol of authority, which in those days it was. It still is in some cultures, but not in the West. Wearing hats in church is a good example of bad transposition, for western ladies' hats tend to symbolize liberation rather than submission! What then about the requirement of silence?

My own belief is that commentators have not sufficiently noticed that Paul draws a double contrast when he writes: 'A woman should learn in quietness and full submission. I do not permit a woman to teach or to have authority over a man; she must be silent.'[1] The first contrast is between authority and submission; it seems to be permanent because creational. The second contrast is between teaching and silence. Is it possible that silence, like the veil, was a first-century cultural symbol of submission to masculine headship, which is not necessarily binding today? Certainly the situation has changed considerably. Women in many cultures today are just as educated as men. And the teaching office today, now that the New Testament canon has been finalized, is much less authoritative. So then, supposing (I ask myself) a woman were to teach men under the authority of Scripture (not claiming an authority of her own), in a meek and humble spirit (not throwing her weight about), and as a member of a pastoral team of which a man were head – might those three conditions enable her to teach men, without exercising an improper authority over them, and without infringing the principle of masculine headship? Would this be a legitimate example of cultural transposition?

My tentative answer to my own questions is, 'Yes, I think so.' I realize that this may seem to some nothing but an irrelevant theory, since in several denominations and in many parts of the world women's ordination is already a reality. But at least I hope it is clear what I have been trying to do. This is to identify and preserve the essence of God's revelation (in this case the creational relation of the sexes), while at the same time seeking to discern appropriate twentieth-century cultural symbols to express it.

I conclude this rather long chapter with two words of reassurance about the practice of cultural transposition.

First, cultural transposition is appropriate only where the biblical text contains two levels of discourse – first, doctrinal or ethical teaching, and, secondly, its cultural or social expression; first (for example) the command to love and serve one another, and secondly the foot-washing. Cultural transposition

[1] 1 Tim. 2:11–12.

is impossible where there is only one level of discourse; it cannot be used to justify the rejection of what Scripture teaches, forbids or commands.

Take as an example the attempt to justify homosexual partnerships by declaring the biblical prohibitions to be culturally conditioned. The argument developed by some liberal thinkers runs like this: 'We grant that some forms of homosexual behaviour were forbidden by Moses in the Old Testament and by Paul in the New. But they were referring to particular cultural practices, in Leviticus to the ritual prostitution which was part of ancient Canaanite fertility religion, and in Paul's letters to promiscuous sexual behaviour, together with the corruption of the young. They were not referring to tender, loving, faithful relationships between two adult men or two adult women. Besides, Moses and Paul had a very limited understanding of human psycho-sexuality; we know much more than they did. So then, because the biblical prohibitions were of culturally specific taboos, they are irrelevant to us, and they cannot be taken to forbid a committed homosexual partnership which is equivalent to a heterosexual marriage.'

But this is a specious argument, which needs to be firmly rejected. The fact is that the reason for the biblical prohibitions of homosexual conduct was not cultural, but creational. They arose from the biblical definition of marriage, which was personally endorsed by Jesus Christ: 'For this reason a man will leave his father and mother and be united to his wife, and they will become one flesh.'[1] In other words, the only kind of marriage or sexual partnership envisaged in Scripture is heterosexual monogamy, which is also the only God-given context for the 'one flesh' experience. So what limits sexual intercourse to heterosexual marriage, and forbids it in all other relationships, is not culture but creation. No attempt at cultural transposition would be legitimate here.

Secondly, cultural transposition is not the thin end of the

[1] Gn. 2:24, quoted by Jesus in Mk. 10:7–9, with the addition, 'Therefore what God has joined together, let man not separate.'

liberal wedge. It is not a conveniently respectable way to dodge awkward passages of Scripture by declaring them to be culturally relative. It is not a sophisticated way of rejecting biblical authority. No. If we go in for total rejection, we certainly cannot obey God's Word. If instead we embrace a position of wooden literalism, our obedience becomes artificial and mechanical. Only if we transpose the teaching of Scripture into modern cultural dress does our obedience become contemporary. Not disobedience, but meaningful obedience, is the purpose of cultural transposition.

CHAPTER THIRTEEN

EXPOUNDING THE WORD

This chapter is about preaching, and as I begin it I am conscious of the need to make three preliminary points. The first is a personal one. There is something fundamentally anomalous about one preacher presuming to preach to other preachers about preaching. I wrote something similar ten years ago in my Introduction to *I Believe in Preaching*. I have not changed my mind in the mean time. For what do I know that you do not know? We have all preached, read and listened to sermons *ad nauseam*. I certainly claim no particular expertise. Often still in the pulpit I am seized with a communication frustration. Seldom if ever do I descend from the pulpit without feeling the need to confess my comparative failure and to pray for grace to do better next time. So I hope this puts us on the level. We are all struggling in this privileged but problematic ministry.

My second point is social. It concerns the widespread disillusion with preaching. Is it not an anachronism, an obsolete medium of communication, a dead art form, 'a sacred relic, a dubious thing of withered skin and dry bones enclosed in a reliquary of fond remembrance, still encrusted with the jewels of past glory'?[1] Who wants to listen to sermons nowadays? People are drugged by television, hostile to authority, weary and wary of words. When the sermon begins, they quickly grow impatient, fidgety and bored. We cannot assume that people want to listen to us; we have to fight for their attention.

Thirdly, and speaking pastorally, in spite of the acknowledged problems, we must persevere. For the health of the

[1] George Target, *Words That Have Moved the World* (Bishopsgate, 1987), p. 13.

church depends on it. If it is true, as Jesus said, endorsing Deuteronomy, that human beings do 'not live on bread alone, but on every word that comes from the mouth of God',[1] it is equally true of churches. Churches live, grow and flourish by the Word of God; they wilt and wither without it. The pew cannot easily rise higher than the pulpit; the pew is usually a reflection of the pulpit. This is the lesson of history. 'Is it not clear', asked Dr Martyn Lloyd-Jones, 'that the decadent periods and eras in the history of the Church have always been those periods when preaching had declined?'[2] I am sure he was right. Indeed, we can see it illustrated in the world today. Although we rejoice in the statistics of church growth, we have to admit with shame that it is often growth without depth. There is much superficiality everywhere. And I am myself convinced from observation that the low level of Christian living is due more than anything else to the low level of Christian preaching. To be sure, it is the Holy Spirit who renews the church, but the Spirit's sword is the Word of God.[3] Nothing, it seems to me, is more important for the life and growth, health and depth of the contemporary church than a recovery of serious biblical preaching.

Let me seek to develop the case for biblical preaching. I begin with a straightforward definition in twenty-four words.

> To preach is to open up the inspired text with such faithfulness and sensitivity that God's voice is heard and God's people obey him.

This definition of preaching contains six implications – two convictions about the biblical text, two obligations in expounding it, and two expectations as a result.

[1] Mt. 4:4; Dt. 8:3.
[2] D. Martyn Lloyd-Jones, *Preaching and Preachers* (Hodder and Stoughton, 1971), p. 24.
[3] Eph. 6:17.

Two convictions

The first conviction about the biblical text is that it is an inspired text. 'To preach is to open up the inspired text.' A high view of the biblical text, as being unlike any other text, unique in its origin, nature and authority, is indispensable to authentic preaching. Nothing undermines preaching more than scepticism about Scripture. Without developing a sustained defence of this statement, I hope I shall carry you with me in reference to three words which belong together in our doctrine of Scripture, namely 'revelation', 'inspiration' and 'providence'.

'Revelation' describes the initiative God took to unveil or disclose himself. It is a humbling word. It presupposes that in his infinite perfections God is altogether beyond the reach of our finite minds. Our mind cannot penetrate his mind. We have no ability to read his thoughts. Indeed, his thoughts are as much higher than our thoughts as the heavens are higher than the earth.[1] Consequently, we would know nothing about God if he had not chosen to make himself known. Without revelation we would not be Christians at all but Athenians, and all the world's altars would be inscribed 'TO AN UNKNOWN GOD'.[2] But we believe God has revealed himself, not only in the glory and order of the created universe, but supremely in Jesus Christ his incarnate Word, and in the written Word which bears a comprehensive and variegated witness to him.

'Inspiration' describes the means God chose by which to reveal himself, namely by speaking to and through the biblical authors. As we have already noted, it was not a dictation process which would have demeaned them into machines, but a dynamic one which treated them as persons in active possession of their faculties. Many of the biblical authors were historians, and much of Scripture is history. For this they engaged in research, and made use of diaries, records and archives. They were also theologians, each with a distinct doctrinal

[1] Is. 55:9. [2] Acts 17:23.

emphasis, and writers, each with his own literary genre, style and vocabulary. These phenomena of historical research, theological concern and literary composition were neither incompatible with, nor smothered by, the process of inspiration. God spoke through them in such a way that the words spoken were simultaneously and equally his and theirs. This is the double authorship of Scripture, on which we reflected in chapter 10.

The third word is 'providence'. This is the loving foresight and provision of God by which he arranged for the words he had spoken first to be written, to form what we call 'Scripture', and then to be preserved across the centuries so as to be available to all people in all places at all times, for their salvation and enrichment.

Scripture then is 'God's word written',[1] his self-disclosure in speech and writing, the product of his revelation, inspiration and providence. This first conviction is indispensable to preachers. If God had not spoken, we would not dare to speak, for we would have nothing to say except our own threadbare speculations. But since God has spoken, we too must speak, communicating to others what he has communicated in Scripture. Indeed, we refuse to be silenced! As Amos put it, 'the Sovereign LORD has spoken – who can but prophesy?',[2] or pass on his Word. Similarly, Paul wrote, quoting Psalm 116, 'I believed; therefore I have spoken.'[3] That is, we speak because we believe what God has spoken.

I pity the preacher who enters the pulpit with no Bible in his hands, or with a Bible which is more rags and tatters than the Word of God. He cannot expound Scripture, because he has no Scripture to expound. He cannot speak, for he has nothing worth saying. But to enter the pulpit with the confidence that God has spoken, that he has caused what he has spoken to be written, and that we have this inspired text in our hands – ah! then our head begins to swim, our heart to beat, our blood to flow, and our eyes to sparkle, with the sheer glory of having God's Word in our hands and on our lips.

[1] Article XX of the Church of England's *Thirty-Nine Articles* (1563). [2] Am. 3:8.
[3] 2 Cor. 4:13; Ps. 116:10.

Our second conviction is that the inspired text is also a partially closed text. If to preach is 'to open up the inspired text', then it must be partially closed or it would not need to be opened up. And at once I think I see your Protestant hackles rising with indignation. 'What do you mean,' you ask me, 'that Scripture is partially closed? Do you not believe with the sixteenth-century Reformers in the "perspicuity" of Scripture (that it has a transparent or "see-through" quality)? Cannot even simple and uneducated people understand it by themselves? Is not the Holy Spirit our God-given teacher?' Yes, indeed; thank you for your questions. I can say a resounding 'Yes' to them. But what you are rightly saying also needs to be qualified.

The Reformers' insistence on the perspicuity of Scripture related to its central message, namely the gospel of salvation through faith in Christ crucified. That is as plain as day in the Bible. But they did not maintain that everything in Scripture is equally plain. How could they when Peter wrote that some things in Paul's letters 'are hard to understand'?[1] If one apostle did not always understand another apostle, it would hardly be modest for us to claim that we see no problems! Consequently, the church needs 'pastors and teachers' to expound or open up the Scriptures, and the ascended Christ still gives these gifts to his church.[2]

The story of the Ethiopian eunuch illustrates well this need for human teachers. While he was sitting in his chariot and reading Isaiah 53, Philip asked him: 'Do you understand what you are reading?' Did the Ethiopian reply, 'Why, of course I do. Don't you believe in the perspicuity of Scripture?'? No, he said: 'How can I (understand) unless someone explains it to me?'[3] Calvin rightly comments on the Ethiopian's humility, and contrasts it with those who, 'swollenheaded' with confidence in their own abilities, are too proud to submit themselves to teaching.

Here, then, is the biblical case for biblical exposition. It

[1] 2 Pet. 3:16. [2] Eph. 4:11. [3] Acts 8:26–39.

consists of two fundamental convictions, namely that God has given us in Scripture a text which is both inspired (having a divine origin and authority) and to some degree closed (difficult to understand). Therefore, in addition to the text, he gives the church teachers to open up the text, explaining it and applying it to people's lives.

Two obligations

My definition of preaching moves on from two convictions about the biblical text to two obligations in expounding it. 'To preach is to open up the inspired text with . . . faithfulness and sensitivity . . .'. The main reason why the biblical text is partially closed and hard to understand is that a wide and deep cultural gulf yawns between the ancient world in which God spoke his Word and the modern world in which we listen to it. It is this cultural chasm, which occupied us in the last chapter, which also determines the task of the biblical expositor and lays down our two major obligations, namely faithfulness to the ancient Word and sensitivity to the modern world.

First comes the call to faithfulness. We have to accept the disciple of exegesis, that is, of thinking ourselves back into the situation of the biblical authors, into their history, geography, culture and language. This task has long been graced with the name 'grammatico-historical exegesis'. To neglect this discipline, or to do it in a half-hearted or slovenly way, is inexcusable; for it expresses contempt for the way God chose to speak. With what painstaking, conscientious and meticulous care should we study ourselves, and open to others, the very words of the living God!

Moreover, the worst blunder that we can commit is to read back our twentieth-century thoughts into the minds of the biblical authors (which is 'eisegesis'), to manipulate what they wrote in order to make it conform to what we want them to say, and then to claim their patronage for our opinions.

Calvin, centuries in advance of his time, understood this principle well. 'It is the first business of an interpreter', he wrote, 'to let his author say what he does say, instead of attributing to him what we think he ought to say.'[1] And some 300 years later, Charles Simeon of Cambridge enunciated the same principle in a letter to his publisher: 'My endeavour is to bring out of Scripture what is there, and not to thrust in what I think might be there.'[2] In our day we urgently need both the integrity and the courage to work by this basic rule, to give the biblical authors the freedom to say what they do say, however unfashionable and unpopular their teaching may be.

Secondly, biblical preaching demands sensitivity to the modern world. Although God spoke to the ancient world in its own languages and cultures, he intends his Word to be for everybody. This means that the expositor is more than an exegete. The exegete explains the original meaning of the text; the expositor goes further and applies it to the contemporary world. We have then to struggle to understand the rapidly changing world in which God has called us to live; to grasp the main movements of thought which have shaped it; to listen to its many discordant voices, its questions, its protests and its cries of pain; and to feel a measure of its disorientation and despair. For all this is part of our Christian sensitivity.

Here, then, are the two obligations which the calling to preach lays upon biblical expositors – faithfulness (to the Word) and sensitivity (to the world). We are neither to falsify the Word, in order to secure a phony relevance, nor to ignore the world in order to secure a phony faithfulness. We are not to fulfil either obligation at the expense of the other. It is the combination of faithfulness and sensitivity which makes the authentic preacher. But, being difficult, it is also rare. The characteristic fault of conservative preachers is to be biblical, but not contemporary. The characteristic fault of liberal preachers is to be contemporary, but not biblical. Very few preachers manage to be both simultaneously.

[1] Quoted by F. W. Farrer in his *History of Interpretation*, the 1885 Bampton Lectures (Macmillan, 1886), p. 347.
[2] Quoted by Hugh Evan Hopkins in *Charles Simeon of Cambridge* (Hodder and Stoughton, 1977), p. 57.

In practice, as we study the text, we need to ask ourselves two distinct questions, and to ask them in the right order. The first is 'What did it mean?' and the second, 'What does it say?' In posing these two questions, our concern begins with the text's original meaning, when it was first spoken or written, and then moves on to its contemporary message, as it addresses people today. We must neither confuse these two questions, nor put them in the wrong order, nor ask either without also asking the other.

The first question, 'What did it mean?', could also be worded 'What *does* it mean?', since a text's actual meaning does not change. It still means today what it meant when it was first written. In his well-known book *Validity in Interpretation*, Dr E. D. Hirsch, formerly Kenan Professor of English at the University of Virginia, reaffirms the 'sensible belief that a text means what its author meant'.[1] He complains of the 'banishment of the author' from legal, biblical and literary texts. The result is pure subjectivism. In legal circles 'the meaning of a law is what present judges say the meaning is'; in Bultmannian biblical exegesis 'the meaning of the Bible is a new revelation to each succeeding generation', and in literary theory a text is 'what it means to us today'.[2] Indeed, in some university literature departments it is nowadays claimed that 'a text is infinitely interpretable', because it 'means' different things to different people. But this is a misleading use of the words 'mean' and 'meaning'. Professor Hirsch insists that it is only the author who determines the meaning of a text, and that to 'banish the original author as the determiner of meaning' is to 'reject the only compelling normative principle that could lend validity to an interpretation'.[3] So then a text's 'meaning' is what its author meant by it, and is therefore permanent, whereas its 'significance' is how it strikes different people and relates to different contexts, and is therefore variable.[4] There is all the difference in the world between Bultmann's 'a text means what it means to

[1] E. D. Hirsch, *Validity in Interpretation* (Yale University Press, 1967), p. 1.
[2] *Ibid*., p. viii. [3] *Ibid*., p. 5.
[4] *Ibid*., pp. 8, 255. *Cf.* also E. D. Hirsch, *The Aims of Interpretation* (University of Chicago Press, 1976), pp. 2–3, 79.

me' and E. D. Hirsch's 'a text means what its author meant'.

So the meaning of a text must be sought and found in the words themselves, the author's words, and not in the reader's thoughts and feelings. As Professor David Wells has put it, endorsing the emphasis of B. B. Warfield: 'Meaning is not to be found above the text, behind it, beyond it, or in the interpreter. Meaning is to be found *in the text*. It is the language of the text which determines what meaning God intends for us to have.' This is because 'words have meanings ... No language allows meaning to float free of the words used ... Unless words and their meaning are rejoined in hermeneutical practice, we can have no access to revelation in anything but a mystical sense'.[1]

The second question we have to ask of the text is, 'What does it say?' That is, having discerned its original meaning (which is fixed by its author), we need next to reflect on its contemporary message (how it applies to people today). This is where spiritual sensitivity comes in. We have to increase our familiarity with the modern world – its presuppositions and preoccupations, its mentality and mood, its volatile culture and falling standards, its values, goals, doubts, fears, pains and hopes, and not least its obsession with self, love and death. Only then shall we be able to discern how the unchanging Word speaks to the changing world. Nothing has helped me to do this more than the reading group of younger professionals who have been meeting with me in London about every six weeks for the last twenty years. We agree at the end of each session which book to read or film to see before our next meeting. We choose, in the main, books and films which express a non-Christian perspective. Then we ask ourselves, (1) What are the main issues which this raises for Christians? and (2) How does the gospel relate to people who think and live like this? In other words, we put our second question to the biblical text, 'What does it say?'

If we grasp the original meaning of a text, without going on to grapple with its contemporary message, we surrender to antiquarianism, unrelated to the present realities of the modern

[1] From Dr David Wells' essay 'Word and World' in *Evangelical Affirmations*, ed. Kenneth S. Kantzer and Carl F. H. Henry (Academie, Zondervan, 1990), pp. 161–162.

world. If, on the other hand, we begin with the text's contemporary message, without first having accepted the discipline of discovering its original meaning, we surrender to existentialism, unrelated to the past realities of revelation. Instead, we must ask both questions, first being faithful in working at the text's meaning and then being sensitive in discerning its message for today. Moreover, there are no short cuts to this. There is only the hard slog of study, seeking to become familiar both with the Scriptures in their fulness and with the modern world in all its variety.

It is, in fact, another case of the discipline of 'double listening', as we listen humbly to Scripture and critically to modernity, in order to relate the one to the other. Such listening is an indispensable preliminary to preaching. On 18 November 1991, the day on which Terry Waite was freed after nearly five years as a hostage in Lebanon, several other former hostages, whose liberation he himself had negotiated, were asked for a comment. One of them was Jean Waddell, who had served as a missionary in Iran. 'He's such a good communicator,' she said; 'he listens.'

Two expectations

After the two convictions about Scripture, and the two obligations in expounding it, come two expectations in consequence. If we do open up the inspired text with faithfulness and sensitivity, what can we expect to happen?

First, we expect God's voice to be heard. This expectation arises from our belief that the God who has spoken in the past also speaks in the present through what he has spoken.

Such an expectation, that through his ancient Word God addresses the modern world, is, however, at a low ebb today. As Dr Langmead Casserley, a scholar of the American Episcopal Church, has said, 'we have devised a way of reading the Word of God, from which no word from God ever comes'. When the time for the sermon arrives, the people clasp their hands and close their eyes with a fine show of piety, and sit back for their customary doze. Moreover, the preacher encourages it by his somnolent voice and manner.

How different it is when both preacher and people are expecting God to speak! The whole situation is transformed and becomes electric. The people bring their Bibles to church, and when they open them, they sit on the edge of their seats, hungrily waiting for what the Lord God may have to say to them. It is a re-enactment of the scene in the house of Cornelius the centurion when the apostle Peter arrived. Cornelius said to him: 'Now we are all here in the presence of God to listen to everything the Lord has commanded you to tell us.'[1] Why may a Christian congregation not experience the same degree of expectation today?

The preacher himself can encourage this attitude. He prepares carefully, in such a way that he is evidently expecting God to give him a message. He prays earnestly before he leaves home for church, and prays again in the pulpit before he preaches, that God will speak to his people. He reads and expounds his text with great seriousness of purpose, feeling deeply what he is talking about. Then, when he has finished, and he prays again, there is a stillness and a solemnity in the presence of the God who has spoken.

Our second expectation is that God's people will obey him. The Word of God always demands a response of obedience. We are not to be forgetful hearers, but obedient doers, of God's Word.[2] Throughout the Old Testament we hear the divine lament, 'Today, oh that you would listen to my voice!'[3] God kept sending his envoys to his people, 'but they mocked God's messengers, despised his words and scoffed at his prophets until the wrath of the LORD was aroused against his people and there was no remedy'.[4]

How then should people respond? What kind of obedience is required? Our answer is that the nature of the response expected is determined by the content of the word expounded. What we *do* in response to God's Word depends on what he *says* to us

[1] Acts 10:33. [2] Jas. 1:22–25. [3] *E.g.* Ps. 95:7–10. [4] 2 Ch. 36:16.

through it. Consider some examples. If, in and through the text expounded, God speaks about himself and his own glorious greatness, we respond by humbling ourselves before him in worship. If instead he speaks about us, our waywardness, fickleness, rebellion and guilt, then we respond in penitence and confession. If he speaks about Jesus Christ, who died to bear our sins and was raised from the dead to prove it, we respond in faith, laying hold of this heaven-sent Saviour. If he speaks about his promises, we determine to inherit them; if about his commands, we determine to keep them. If God speaks to us about the world, and its colossal spiritual and material need, then his compassion rises within us both to preach the gospel and to serve the needy. If, on the other hand, God speaks to us through his Word about the future, the coming of Christ and the glory to follow, then our hope is kindled, and we resolve to be holy and busy until he comes.

The preacher who has penetrated deeply into his text, has isolated and unfolded its dominant theme, and has himself been moved by its message, will hammer it home in his conclusion, and give people a chance to respond to it, often in silent prayer, as each person is brought by the Holy Spirit to an appropriate obedience.

This, then, is the definition of preaching which I venture to offer you. It contains two convictions (that the biblical text is an inspired text which yet needs to be opened up), two obligations (that we must open it up with faithfulness to the text itself and sensitivity to the modern context), and two expectations (that through the exposition and application of the written Word God himself will speak, and that his people will hear his voice and respond to him in obedience).

It is an enormous privilege to be a biblical expositor, that is, to stand in the pulpit with God's Word in our hands and minds, God's Spirit in our hearts, and God's people before our eyes, waiting expectantly for God's voice to be heard and obeyed.

PART FOUR

THE CHURCH

John Wesley was right when he described Christianity as essentially a 'social' religion, and added that to turn it into a 'solitary' religion would be to destroy it. This is not to deny that it offers individual salvation and calls to individual discipleship; it is rather to affirm that the church lies at the centre of God's purpose. Christ gave himself for us, we are told, not only 'to redeem us from all wickedness' but also 'to purify for himself a people that are his very own, eager to do what is good'.[1]

The problem we experience, whenever we think about the church, concerns the tension between the ideal and the reality. The ideal is beautiful. The church is the chosen and beloved people of God, his own special treasure, the covenant community to whom he has committed himself for ever, engaged in continuous worship of God and in compassionate outreach to the world, a haven of love and peace, and a pilgrim people headed for the eternal city. But in reality we who claim to be the church are often a

[1] Tit. 2:14.

motley rabble of rather scruffy individuals, half-educated and half-saved, uninspired in our worship, constantly bickering with each other, concerned more for our maintenance than our mission, struggling and stumbling along the road, needing constant rebuke and exhortation, which are readily available from both Old Testament prophets and New Testament apostles.

In consequence of this distinction between the ideal and the reality, people's opinions of the church vary enormously. On the one hand, P. T. Forsyth could write that 'the church of Christ is the greatest and finest product of human history, . . . the greatest thing in the universe'.[1] On the other, Thomas Arnold wrote: 'The church as it now stands no human power can save . . . When I think of the church, I could sit down and pine and die.'[2]

My purpose in Part IV of this book is to focus on the ideal, on what God intends his church to be, while all the time keeping in view the reality, so that we can more easily grasp the changes which need to be made. The first two chapters are complementary, since in chapter 14 we consider the world's challenge to the church and in chapter 15 the church's mission in the world. In chapter 16 the needed renewal of the church will be seen to include, as Jesus prayed, not one area only (*e.g.* its unity or its spirituality), but every area of

[1] P. T. Forsyth, *The Work of Christ* (Hodder and Stoughton, 1910), p. 5.
[2] J. R. H. Moorman, *A History of the Church of England* (A. and C. Black, 1953), pp. 329, 331.

its life. And to this end those of us who have been ordained to the pastoral ministry of the church need ourselves to be renewed according to God's purpose for us, which is the topic of chapter 17.

CHAPTER FOURTEEN

SECULAR CHALLENGES TO THE CHURCH

One of our greatest needs in today's church is a sensitive awareness of the world around us. If we are true servants of Jesus Christ, we will keep our eyes open (as he did) to human need, and our ears cocked to pick up cries of anguish. And we will respond compassionately and constructively (as again he did) to people's pain.

This does not mean that in every respect we 'let the world set the agenda for the church', as used to be said in the 1960s, or that we trot like a little dog at the world's heels. To behave like that would be to confuse service (which is our calling) with servility (which is not), and to interpret sensitivity (which is a virtue) in terms of conformity (which is a vice). No, first and foremost we have to declare and do what God has sent us to declare and do; we are not to pay obsequious homage to the world.

At the same time, unless we listen attentively to the voices of secular society, struggle to understand them, and feel with people in their frustration, anger, bewilderment and despair, weeping with those who weep, we will lack authenticity as the disciples of Jesus of Nazareth. Instead, we will run the risk (as has often been said) of answering questions nobody is asking, scratching where nobody is itching, supplying goods for which there is no demand – in other words, of being totally irrelevant, which in its long history the church has often been.

I would like to set before you in this chapter the threefold quest of modern, secularized men and women, which is, in fact, the universal, threefold human aspiration, which Jesus Christ himself arouses within people, which he alone can satisfy, and which challenges the church to present him to the world in his fulness.

The quest for transcendence

Until quite recently 'transcendence' was regarded as a rather obscure word, whose use was limited to institutions of theological learning. There students were introduced to the distinction between 'transcendence' (meaning God above and outside the created world) and 'immanence' (meaning God present and active within it). Nowadays, however, nearly everybody has some notion of transcendence, because it has been popularized by the craze for 'transcendental meditation'. The quest for transcendence is, therefore, the search for ultimate reality beyond the material universe. It is a protest against secularization, that is, against the attempt to eliminate God from his own world. It is a recognition that human beings do not 'live on bread alone', for materialism cannot satisfy the human spirit. Consider some examples of the current disillusion with secularism and the persistent search for transcendence.

First, there is *the recent collapse of Euro-Marxism*. I am not now thinking about socialism as a politico-economic ideology, but about classical Marxism as a philosophy which denies the existence of God. Marxism was originally presented as a substitute for outmoded religious faith. But converts were few and far between. As Canon Trevor Beeson wrote about Eastern Europe in the 1970s, 'the basic doctrines of Communism have neither convinced the minds, nor satisfied the emotions, of the intelligentsia or of the proletariat. On the other hand, religious life has displayed remarkable resilience and, far from disappearing, has in many instances found new vitality and power'.[1] Solzhenitsyn said something similar in 1983, specifically about the Soviet Union. He drew attention to something which the Soviet lea'ers had not expected:

[1] Trevor Beeson, *Discretion and Valour* (Collins, 1974), p. 24.

> that in a land where churches have been levelled, where a triumphant atheism has rampaged uncontrolled for two-thirds of a century, where clergy are utterly humiliated and deprived of all independence, where what remains of the church as an institution is tolerated only for the sake of propaganda directed at the west, where even today people are sent to the labour camps for their faith, and where, within the camps themselves, those who gather to pray at Easter are clapped in punishment cells – they (*sc.* the Soviet leaders) could not suppose that beneath this communist steam-roller the Christian tradition could survive in Russia! But there remain many millions of believers; it is only external pressures that keep them from speaking out.[1]

The second sphere in which people are seen to be disillusioned with secularism is *the desert of western materialism.* Secularism is no more satisfying to the human spirit in its capitalistic, than in its communistic, guise. Theodore Roszak is an eloquent American exponent of its emptiness. The significant sub-title of his book *Where the Wasteland Ends* is *Politics and Transcendence in a Post-Industrial Society.*[2] He laments what he calls the 'coca-colonization of the world'.[3] We are suffering, he writes, from 'a psychic claustrophobia within the scientific worldview',[4] in which the human spirit cannot breathe. He castigates science (pseudo-science, I think he means) for its arrogant claim to be able to explain everything, its 'debunking spirit',[5] its 'undoing of the mysteries'. 'For what science can measure is only a portion of what man can know.'[6] This materialistic world of objective science, he goes on, is not nearly 'spacious enough' for us.[7] Without transcendence 'the person shrivels'.[8] His prescription (the recovery of Blake's 'visionary imagination') is woefully inadequate; but his diagnosis is surely

[1] From an address by Solzhenitsyn, when accepting the Templeton Prize in London in May 1983.
[2] Theodore Roszak, *Where the Wasteland Ends* (1972; Anchor, 1973).
[3] *Ibid.*, p. 22. [4] *Ibid.*, p. 66. [5] *Ibid.*, pp. 227–228.
[6] *Ibid.*, p. 67. [7] *Ibid.*, p. 70. [8] *Ibid.*, p. xxi.

right on target. Human beings know instinctively that Reality cannot be confined in a test tube, or smeared on a slide for microscopic examination, or apprehended by cool scientific detachment. For life has another and transcendent dimension, and Reality is 'awesomely vast'.[1]

Thirdly, the quest for transcendence is seen in *the epidemic of drug abuse*. There are, of course, a number of different interpretations of this almost world-wide phenomenon. It is neither a purely innocent experimentation, nor always a self-conscious protest against conventional mores, nor even an attempt to escape from the harsh realities of life. It is also a genuine search for a 'higher consciousness', and even for an objective transcendent reality. As evidence of this we could take Carlos Castaneda, whose books were extremely popular at the end of the 1960s and first half of the 1970s. He claimed that a Yaqui Indian from Mexico named Don Juan had initiated him. He taught him that there are two worlds of equal reality, the 'ordinary' world of living human beings and the 'non-ordinary' world of *diableros* or sorcerers. 'The particular thing to learn is how to get to the crack between the worlds and how to enter the other world . . . There is a place where the two worlds overlap. The crack is there. It opens and closes like a door in the wind.'[2] The person who enters the other world of non-ordinary reality is 'the man of knowledge'; it is essential for him to have an 'ally', that is, 'a power capable of transporting him beyond the boundaries of himself'.[3] And the two main allies are *datura*, also called 'Jimson's weed' or 'devil's weed', which is feminine and gives power, and a mushroom called *humito* or 'little smoke', which is masculine and gives escstasy. The former was drunk or skin-absorbed, the latter smoked. The results were 'divination', bodily flight or bodilessness, adopting alternative bodies, and moving into and through objects.

The fourth example of the quest for transcendence is *the proliferation of religious cults*. Alongside the resurgence of

[1] Theodore Roszak, *The Making of a Counter Culture* (Anchor, 1969), p. 235.
[2] Carlos Castaneda, *The Teachings of Don Juan* (1968; Penguin, 1970), p. 182.
[3] *Ibid.*, pp. 54, 199.

ancient faiths, and the fascination of western youth with eastern mysticism, has gone the emergence of new religions. At least 800 have appeared in Britain since the Second World War,[1] and Alvin Toffler calculates that 1,000 new cults have won a following in the United States from about three million Americans.[2] One of the most alarming was the movement headed by Jim Jones of the People's Temple in San Francisco, nearly one thousand of whose followers died in 'Jonestown', their Guyana jungle colony, in 1978, mostly in a mass suicide by drinking poison. A leading article in *The Economist* warned that 'a groping has begun for new forms of spiritual experience', and added: 'In that search for God, it is all too easy to blunder into the arms of Satan instead.'[3] Peter Berger, the sociologist, has given a similar explanation: 'The current occult wave (including its devil component) is to be understood as resulting from the repression of transcendence in modern consciousness.'[4]

Most striking of all recent religious trends is the rise of the New Age movement. It is a bizarre assortment of diverse beliefs, religion and science, physics and metaphysics, ancient pantheism and evolutionary optimism, astrology, spiritism, reincarnation, ecology and alternative medicine. One of the movement's leaders, David Spangler, writes in his book *Emergence: The Rebirth of the Sacred* that 'from a very early age' he had himself been 'aware of an extra dimension' to the world around him, which as he grew older he came to identify as 'a sacred or transcendental dimension'. 'The rebirth of the sense of the sacred', he adds, 'is at the heart of the new age.'[5]

Here, then, are four contemporary pieces of evidence that

[1] According to Dr Peter Clarke, a lecturer in the history and sociology of religion at King's College, London, as reported in *The Times* on 26 October 1990. He added that those so far documented were only the tip of the iceberg. 'Below the surface there would appear to be a large mass of new religion which has neither been located nor measured with any precision.'

[2] Alvin Toffler, *Third Wave* (Collins, 1980), p. 385.

[3] *The Economist*, 25 November 1978.

[4] Peter L. Berger, *Facing Up to Modernity* (1977; Penguin, 1979), p. 255.

[5] David Spangler, *Emergence: The Rebirth of the Sacred* (Dell Publishing, 1984), pp. 12, 41.

materialism does not satisfy the human spirit, and that in consequence people are looking for another, a transcendent, reality. They seek it everywhere – through yoga, TM and the eastern religions, through sex (which Malcolm Muggeridge used to call 'the mysticism of the materialist'), through music and the other arts, through a drug-induced higher consciousness, through modern cults, New Age speculations, dangerous experiments with the occult and the fantasies of science fiction.

The immediate Christian reaction to this complex phenomenon should be one of sympathy. For we surely understand what is going on, and why. In the words of the apostle Paul before the Athenian philosophers, men and women are 'feeling after God', like blind people in the dark, groping after their Creator who leaves them restless until they find their rest in him.[1] They are expressing the human quest for transcendence. A contemporary example of it has been given by Richard North, environment correspondent of *The Independent*:

> An awful lot of us just need to worship something. But in order to be able to worship, you have to be able to find something outside of yourself – and better than yourself. God is a construct for that. So is nature. We are all falling in love with the environment as an extension to and in lieu of having fallen out of love with God.[2]

This quest for transcendence is a challenge to the quality of the church's public worship. Does it offer what people are craving – the element of mystery, the 'sense of the numinous', in biblical language 'the fear of God', in modern language 'transcendence'? My answer to my own question is 'Not often'. The church is not always conspicuous for the profound reality of its worship. In particular, we who call ourselves 'evangelical' do not know much how to worship. Evangelism is our speciality, not worship. We seem to have little sense of the greatness and

[1] Augustine, *Confessions* (Bk. 1, ch. 1).
[2] Quoted by Jonathon Porritt and David Winner in *The Coming of the Greens* (Collins, 1988), pp. 251–252.

the glory of almighty God. We do not bow down before him in awe and wonder. Our tendency is to be cocky, flippant and proud. We take little trouble to prepare our worship services. Sometimes they are slovenly, mechanical, perfunctory and dull. At other times they are frivolous to the point of irreverence. No wonder those seeking Reality often pass us by!

We need to listen again to the biblical criticism of religion. No book, not even by Marx and his followers, is more scathing of empty religion than the Bible. The prophets of the eighth and seventh centuries BC were outspoken in their denunciation of the formalism and hypocrisy of Israelite worship. Jesus then applied their critique to the Pharisees of his day: 'These people . . . honour me with their lips, but their hearts are far from me.'[1] And this indictment of religion by the Old Testament prophets and by Jesus is uncomfortably applicable to us and our churches today. Too much of our worship is ritual without reality, form without power, fun without fear, religion without God.

What is needed, then? Here are some suggestions. First, we need such a faithful reading and preaching of God's Word that through it his living voice is heard, addressing his people again. Secondly, we need such a reverent and expectant administration of the Lord's Supper that (I choose my words carefully) there is a Real Presence of Jesus Christ, not in the elements but among his people and at his table, Jesus Christ himself objectively and really present, coming to meet us, ready to make himself known to us through the breaking of bread, and anxious to give himself to us, that we may feed on him in our hearts by faith. Thirdly, we need such a sincere offering of praise and prayer, that God's people say with Jacob, 'Surely the LORD is in this place, and I was not aware of it,'[2] and unbelievers present will fall down and worship God, exclaiming, 'God is really among you!'[3]

In sum, it is a great tragedy that modern men and women, who are seeking transcendence, turn to drugs, sex, yoga, cults, mysticism, the New Age and science fiction, instead of to the church, in whose worship services true transcendence should

[1] Is. 29:13; Mk. 7:6. [2] Gn. 28:16. [3] 1 Cor. 14:24–25.

always be experienced, and a close encounter with the living God enjoyed.

The quest for significance

There is much in the modern world which not only smothers our sense of transcendence, but also diminishes (and even destroys) our sense of personal significance, our belief that life has any meaning. Three tendencies may be mentioned.

First, there is the effect of *technology*. Technology can be liberating, of course, in so far as it frees people from domestic or industrial drudgery. But it can also be dreadfully dehumanizing, as men and women feel themselves to be no longer persons but things, 'identified not by a "proper name" but by a serial number punched on a card that has been designed to travel through the entrails of a computer'.[1]

Secondly, there is *scientific reductionism*. Some scientists from different disciplines are arguing that a human being is nothing but an animal (Dr Desmond Morris's 'naked ape', to be more precise), or nothing but a machine, programmed to make automatic responses to external stimuli. It was statements like these which prompted the late Professor Donald MacKay to popularize the expression 'nothing buttery' as an explanation of what is meant by 'reductionism', and to protest against every tendency to reduce human beings to a level lower than the fully personal.

To be sure, our brain is a machine, a highly complex mechanism. And our anatomy and physiology are those of an animal. But that is not a complete account of our humanness. There is more to us than a body and a brain. It is when people affirm that we are 'nothing but' this or that, that they make a serious and dangerous mistake.

Thirdly, *existentialism* has the effect of diminishing people's sense of significance. Radical existentialists may be said to differ from humanists in general by their resolve to take their atheism

[1] Arnold Toynbee, quoted in *The Times* on 5 April 1969. See his *Experiences* (Oxford University Press, 1969).

seriously and face its terrible consequences. Because (in their view) God is dead, everything else has died with him. Because there is no God, there are now no values or ideals either, no moral laws or standards, no purposes or meanings. And although I exist, there is yet nothing that gives me or my existence any significance, except perhaps my decision to seek the courage to be. Meaning is found only in despising my own meaninglessness. There is no other way to authenticate myself.

Bleakly heroic as this philosophy may sound, there must be very few people able to perform the conjuring trick of pretending to have significance when they know they have none. For significance is basic to survival. This is what Viktor Frankl found when as a young man he spent three years in the Auschwitz concentration camp. He noticed that the inmates most likely to survive were those 'who knew that there was a task waiting for them to fulfil'.[1] Later he became Professor of Psychiatry and Neurology in the University of Vienna and founded the so-called 'Third Viennese School of Psychiatry'. He postulated that, in addition to Freud's 'will to pleasure' and Adler's 'will to power', human beings have a 'will to meaning'. Indeed, 'the striving to find a meaning in one's life is the primary motivational force in man'.[2] So he developed what he called 'logotherapy', using *logos* to mean neither 'word' nor 'reason' but 'meaning'. 'The mass neurosis of the present time', he wrote, is 'the existential vacuum',[3] that is, the loss of a sense that life is meaningful. He would sometimes ask his clients, 'Why don't you commit suicide?' (an extraordinary question for a doctor to put to a patient!). They would reply that there was something (perhaps their work or marriage or family) which made life worthwhile for them. Professor Frankl would then build on this.

Meaninglessness leads to boredom, alcoholism, juvenile delinquency and suicide. Commenting on Viktor Frankl's work, Arthur Koestler wrote:

[1] Viktor E. Frankl, *Man's Search for Meaning*, originally published with the title *From Death-Camp to Existentialism* (1959; Washington Square Press, 1963), p. 165.
[2] *Ibid.*, p. 154. [3] *Ibid.*, pp. 167, 204.

> It is an inherent tendency in man to reach out for *meanings* to fulfil and for *values* to actualize . . . Thousands and thousands of young students are exposed to an indoctrination . . . which denies the existence of values. The result is a worldwide phenomenon – more and more patients are crowding our clinics with the complaint of an inner emptiness, the sense of a total and ultimate meaninglessness of life.[1]

According to Emile Durkheim, in his classic study of suicide, the greatest number of suicides are caused by *anomie*, which could be rendered 'normlessness' or 'meaninglessness'. And 'anomic' suicide takes place when somebody either has no goal in life or pursues an unattainable goal, whether power, success or prestige. 'No human being can be happy or even exist unless his needs are sufficiently proportioned to his means.'[2]

If the quest for transcendence was a challenge to the quality of the church's worship, the quest for significance is a challenge to the quality of the church's teaching. Millions of people do not know who they are, nor that they have any significance or worth. Hence the urgent challenge to us to tell them who they are, to enlighten them about their identity, that is, to teach without compromise the full biblical doctrine of our human being – its depravity, yes, but also (and in this context above all) its dignity. See chapter 1.

Christians believe in the intrinsic worth of human beings, because of our doctrines of creation and redemption. As we considered in chapter 1, God made man male and female in his own image and gave them a responsible stewardship of the earth and its creatures. He has endowed us with rational, moral, social, creative and spiritual faculties which make us like him and unlike the animals. Human beings are Godlike beings. As a result of the fall our Godlikeness has indeed been distorted, but it has not been destroyed. Further, 'God so loved the world' that

[1] From the chapter 'Rebellion in a Vacuum', which was Arthur Koestler's contribution to the symposium *Protest and Discontent*, ed. Bernard Crick and William Robson (Penguin, 1970), p. 22.

[2] Emile Durkheim, *Suicide: A Study in Sociology* (1897; ET, 1952; Routledge and Kegan Paul, 1975), p. 246.

he gave his only Son for our redemption. The cross is the chief public evidence of the value which God places on us.

Christian teaching on the dignity and worth of human beings is of the utmost importance today, not only for the sake of our own self-image and self-respect, but even more for the welfare of society.

When human beings are devalued, everything in society turns sour. Women are humiliated and children despised. The sick are regarded as a nuisance, and the elderly as a burden. Ethnic minorities are discriminated against. The poor are oppressed and denied social justice. Capitalism displays its ugliest face. Labour is exploited in the mines and factories. Criminals are brutalized in prison. Opposition opinions are stifled. Belsen is invented by the extreme Right, and Gulag by the extreme Left. Unbelievers are left to live and die in their lostness. There is no freedom, no dignity, no carefree joy. Human life seems not worth living, because it is scarcely human any longer.

But when human beings are valued as persons, because of their intrinsic worth, everything changes. Men, women and children are all honoured. The sick are cared for, and the elderly enabled to live and die with dignity. Dissidents are listened to, prisoners rehabilitated, minorities protected, and the oppressed set free. Workers are given a fair wage, decent working conditions and a measure of participation in both the management and the profit of the enterprise. And the gospel is taken to the ends of the earth. Why? Because people matter. Because every man, woman and child has worth and significance as a human being made in God's image and likeness.

The quest for community

The modern technocratic society, which destroys transcendence and significance, is destructive of community also. We are living in an era of social disintegration. People are finding it increasingly difficult to relate to one another. So we go on seeking the very thing which eludes us – love in a loveless world. I summon as my witnesses three very different people.

The first is Mother Teresa. Born in Yugoslavia, she left for India when she was only seventeen years old. Then, after about twenty years of teaching, she gave up this profession in order to serve the poorest of the poor in Calcutta. The same year (1948) she became an Indian citizen, and two years later founded her own order, the 'Missionaries of Charity'. So India has been her home for over sixty years, and in consequence hers is an authentic Third World vision and voice. This is what she has written about the West:

> People today are hungry for love, for understanding love, which is . . . the only answer to loneliness and great poverty. That is why we (*sc.* the sisters and brothers of her order) are able to go to countries like England and America and Australia, where there is no hunger for bread. But there people are suffering from terrible loneliness, terrible despair, terrible hatred, feeling unwanted, feeling helpless, feeling hopeless. They have forgotten how to smile, they have forgotten the beauty of the human touch. They are forgetting what is human love. They need someone who will understand and respect them.[1]

I remember that, when I first read this assessment of the western world, I was a bit indignant and considered it exaggerated. But I have since changed my mind. I think it is accurate, at least as a generalization.

My second witness is Bertrand Russell, the brilliant mathematician and philosopher, and uncompromising atheist. He wrote with moving candour in the Prologue to his autobiography:

> Three passions, simple but overwhelmingly strong, have governed my life: the longing for love, the search for knowledge,

[1] Desmond Doig, *Mother Teresa, Her People and Her Work* (Collins, 1976), p. 159.

> and unbearable pity for the suffering of mankind. These passions, like great winds, have blown me hither and thither, in a wayward course, over a deep ocean of anguish, reaching to the very verge of despair. I have sought love, first, because it brings ecstasy . . . I have sought it, next, because it relieves loneliness – that terrible loneliness in which one's shivering consciousness looks over the rim of the world into the cold unfathomable lifeless abyss . . .[1]

Woody Allen is my third witness. Most people think of him as a comedian (he was selling jokes to the press while he was still at high school), but 'inside the clown there's a tragedian'.[2] For all his acclaimed brilliance as an author, director and actor, he never seems to have found either himself or anybody else. He describes love-making as 'two psychopaths under one quilt'. In his film *Manhattan* (1979) he quips that he thinks people ought to 'mate for life, like pigeons or Catholics', but he appears unable to follow his own precept. He confesses that all his films 'deal with that greatest of all difficulties – love relationships. Everybody encounters that. People are either in love, about to fall in love, on the way out of love, looking for love, or a way to avoid it.'[3] His biographer ends his portrait of him with these words: 'He is struggling, as *we* are surely struggling, to find the strength to found a life upon a love. As the character says in *Hannah and Her Sisters*, "Maybe the poets are right. Maybe love is the only answer . . .".'[4]

Here are three people of very different backgrounds, beliefs, temperaments and experiences, who nevertheless agree with one another about the paramount importance of love. They speak for the human race. We all know instinctively that love is indispensable to our humanness. Love is what life is all about.

So people are seeking it everywhere. At least since the sixties, some have been breaking away from western individualism and

[1] *The Autobiography of Bertrand Russell* (George Allen and Unwin, 1967), p. 13.
[2] Jack Kroll in *Newsweek*, 24 April 1978.
[3] Graham McCann, *Woody Allen, New Yorker* (Polity Press, 1990), p. 222.
[4] *Ibid*., p. 248.

experimenting with communal styles of living. Others are trying to replace the nuclear family (which is traditional in the West) with the extended family (which for centuries has been traditional in Africa and Asia). Yet others are repudiating the age-long institutions of marriage and the family in an attempt (vain and foolish, Christians believe) to find in this way the freedom and spontaneity of love. Everybody is searching for genuine community and the authentic relationships of love. The lyric from Andrew Lloyd Webber's musical *Aspects of Love* says it all:

> Love, love changes everything:
> hands and faces, earth and sky.
> Love, love changes everything:
> how you live and how you die.
> Love can make the summer fly
> or a night seem like a life-time.
> Yes love, love changes everything;
> now I tremble at your name.
> Nothing in the world will ever be the same.
>
> Love, love changes everything:
> days are longer, words mean more.
> Love, love changes everything:
> pain is deeper than before.
> Love will turn your world around
> and that world will last for ever.
> Yes love, love changes everything,
> brings you glory, brings you shame.
> Nothing in the world will ever be the same.

The world's third challenge, then, concerns the quality of the church's fellowship. We proclaim that God is love, and that Jesus Christ offers true community. We insist that the church is part of the gospel. God's purpose, we say, is not merely to save isolated individuals, and so perpetuate their loneliness, but to build a church, to create a new society, even a new humanity, in which racial, national, social and sexual barriers have been abolished. Moreover, this new community of Jesus dares to present itself as the true alternative society, which eclipses the values and standards of the world.

It is a high-sounding claim. But the tragedy is that the church has consistently failed to live up to its own ideals. Its theological understanding of its calling may be impeccable. But, comparatively speaking, there is little acceptance, little caring and little supportive love among us. People searching for community ought to be pouring into our churches, especially if they offer a small-group experience. Instead, the church is usually the one place they do not even bother to check out, so sure are they that they will not find love there.

Mel White, a Christian writer and film-maker, set out to investigate the causes of the tragic mass suicide at Jonestown in the Guyana jungle in 1978, and published his findings in a book and film entitled *Deceived*. 'How could it happen?' he asked, and 'What can we do to stop it happening again?' In talking to both defectors and survivors, he discovered to his surprise that 'Jones's victims were from our churches' (the title of the book's first chapter), but they did not find love there. Jean Mills, for example, a defector after seven years, said: 'I was so turned off in every church I went to, because nobody cared.'[1] And Grace Stoen, whose lawyer husband Tim became the second most powerful man in the People's Temple in San Francisco, said: 'I went to church until I was eighteen years old . . . and nobody ever befriended me.' In the People's Temple, however, according to Jean Mills, 'everyone seemed so caring and loving. They hugged us and made us welcome . . . and said they . . . wanted us to come back.'[2] It was this discovery which led Mel White in his last chapter, entitled 'It Must Not Happen Again', to list eight resolutions. The first is this: 'I will do my best to help make my church a more loving community to our members, and the strangers in our midst.'[3]

It would be unjust, however, to be entirely negative in our

[1] Mel White, *Deceived* (Spire Books, Revell, 1979), p. 19. [2] *Ibid.*, p. 19.
[3] *Ibid.*, p. 184.

evaluation of the contemporary church. For there are Christian communities all over the world where true, sacrificial, serving, supportive love is to be found. Where such Christian love flourishes, its magnetism is almost irresistible. Bishop Stephen Neill expressed it well:

> Within the fellowship of those who are bound together by personal loyalty to Jesus Christ, the relationship of love reaches an intimacy and intensity unknown elsewhere. Friendship between the friends of Jesus of Nazareth is unlike any other friendship. This ought to be normal experience within the Christian community ... That in existing Christian congregations it is so rare is a measure of the failure of the church as a whole to live up to the purpose of its Founder for it. Where it is experienced, especially across the barriers of race, nationality and language, it is one of the most convincing evidences of the continuing activity of Jesus among men.[1]

Here, then, is a threefold quest on which human beings are engaged. Although they might well not articulate it thus, I think we may say that in looking for transcendence they are trying to find God, in looking for significance they are trying to find themselves, and in looking for community they are trying to find their neighbour. And this is humankind's universal search – for God, our neighbour and ourselves.

Moreover, it is the Christian claim (confident I know, humble I hope) that those who seek will find – in Christ and in his new society. The contemporary secular quest seems to me to constitute one of the greatest challenges – and opportunities – with which the church has ever been presented: people are openly looking for the very things that Jesus Christ is offering!

The only question is whether the church can be so radically renewed, by the Spirit and the Word of God, that it offers an experience of transcendence through its worship, of significance through its teaching, and of community through its fellowship.

[1] Stephen C. Neill, *Christian Faith Today* (Pelican, 1955), p. 174.

For if so, people will turn to it eagerly in their quest, and our proclamation of the good news will have a credibility which otherwise it lacks.

CHAPTER FIFTEEN

EVANGELISM THROUGH THE LOCAL CHURCH[1]

We should be very grateful to the African bishops for proposing, and to the other Anglican bishops for agreeing, that the last ten years of the twentieth century, indeed of the second millennium AD, should be declared 'A Decade of Evangelism'.

This decision of the 1988 Lambeth Conference has brought evangelism to the top of the Anglican church's agenda and challenges us to ask ourselves what we know and believe about evangelism. For the whole Anglican Communion now finds itself obliged to face a responsibility which it has often shirked, namely the call to bear witness to Jesus Christ. Other denominations are also majoring on evangelism in the nineties and setting goals for AD 2000.

According to the definition which the Anglican primates have commended to us, to evangelize is 'to make known by word and deed the love of the crucified and risen Christ in the power of the Holy Spirit, so that people will repent, believe and receive

[1] This chapter was written before Michael Green's mammoth book *Evangelism through the Local Church* (Hodder and Stoughton, 1990) was published and came into my hands. Michael Green is a rare combination of theologian and evangelist, and has had an unusually wide and varied experience of evangelism. With that rollicking, infectious enthusiasm with which he always writes, he divides his theme into four parts: (1) 'Issues for the Church' (the nature, necessity, basis and sphere of evangelism in a multi-faith society), (2) 'The Secular Challenge' (four valuable chapters on apologetics), (3) 'Church-based Evangelism' (evangelistic preaching, personal evangelism, missions and other methods), and (4) 'Practical Appendices' (courses for enquirers, discovery groups for new Christians, the training of teams, the use of drama, leading worship, *etc.*). Here are nearly 600 pages of guidance – theological, personal and practical – from one whose head, heart and hands are together committed to the evangelistic outreach of the local church.

Christ as their Saviour and obediently serve him as their Lord in the fellowship of his church'.

Not that evangelism is foreign to the ethos of Anglicanism. Far from it. The Second Book of Homilies, for example, written mostly by Bishop John Jewel of Salisbury, and published in 1571, contains the following admonition: 'If any man be a dumb Christian, not professing his faith openly, but cloaking and colouring himself for fear of danger in time to come, he giveth men occasion, justly and with good conscience, to doubt lest he have not the grace of the Holy Ghost within him, because he is tongue tied and doth not speak.'

Various forms of evangelism

Evangelism can of course take different forms. Ever since Jesus offered living water to the Samaritan woman at Jacob's well,[1] and Philip sat beside the Ethiopian in his chariot and told him the good news of Jesus,[2] *personal evangelism* has had impeccable biblical precedents. It is still our duty, when the opportunity is given and in a spirit of humility, to share Christ with those of our relatives, friends, neighbours and colleagues who do not yet know him.

Mass evangelism too (the preaching of an evangelist to crowds) has over the centuries been signally blessed by God. The recent disgracing of a few American televangelists does not contradict this fact. Besides, Jesus himself proclaimed the good news of the kingdom to the crowds in Galilee. So did the apostle Paul to the pagans of Lystra[3] and the philosophers of Athens,[4] and Wesley and Whitefield in eighteenth-century Britain and America. Gifted evangelists of many nationalities are still preaching effectively to large crowds today, although they know that their ministry depends on the active cooperation of churches and Christians. And all over the world there are clergy and lay people who take their preaching seriously, and who remember that in their congregation there will often be both

[1] Jn. 4:4–15. [2] Acts 8:26–35. [3] Acts 14:14–18. [4] Acts 17:22–23.

non-Christians and nominal Christians who need to hear the gospel.

Nevertheless, *local church evangelism* can claim to be the most normal, natural and productive method of spreading the gospel today. There are two main reasons for commending it.

First, there is *the argument from Scripture.* According to the apostle Peter, the church is both 'a royal priesthood' to offer spiritual sacrifices to God (which is worship) and 'a holy nation' to spread abroad God's praises (which is witness).[1] Moreover, these responsibilities of the universal church devolve on each local church. Every Christian congregation is called by God to be a worshipping, witnessing community. Indeed, each of these two duties necessarily involves the other. If we truly worship God, acknowledging and adoring his infinite worth, we find ourselves impelled to make him known to others, in order that they may worship him too. Thus worship leads to witness, and witness in its turn to worship, in a perpetual circle.

The Thessalonians set a fine example of local church evangelism. Near the beginning of his first letter to them Paul points out this remarkable sequence: 'Our gospel came to you ... You welcomed the message ... The Lord's message rang out from you.'[2] In this way the local church becomes like a sounding-board which reflects and amplifies the vibrations it receives, or like a communications satellite which first accepts and then transmits a message. Every church which has heard the gospel must pass it on. This is still God's principal method of evangelism. If all churches had been faithful, the world would long ago have been evangelized.

Secondly, there is *the argument from strategy.* Each local church is situated in a particular neighbourhood. Its first mission responsibility must therefore be to the people who live there. The congregation is strategically placed to reach the locality. Any political party would be wildly jealous of the plant and personnel which are at our disposal. The churches in

[1] 1 Pet. 2:5, 9. [2] 1 Thes. 1:5, 6, 8.

many countries have ample resources to disseminate the gospel throughout their land.

Thus biblical theology and practical strategy combine to make the local church the primary agent of evangelism.

But if the local church is to act out its God-appointed role, it must first fulfil four conditions. It must *understand* itself (the theology of the church), *organize* itself (the structures of the church), *express* itself (the message of the church), and *be* itself (the life of the church).

The church must understand itself
The theology of the church

I make no apology for beginning with theology. Many churches are sick because they have a false self-image. They have grasped neither who they are (their identity) nor what they are called to be (their vocation). We all know the importance for mental health of having an accurate self-image. What is true of persons is equally true of churches.

At least two false images of the church are prevalent today.

The first false image is *the religious club* (or *introverted Christianity*). According to this view, the local church somewhat resembles the local golf club, except that the common interest of its members happens to be God rather than golf. They see themselves as religious people who enjoy doing religious things together. They pay their subscription and reckon they are entitled to certain privileges. In fact, they concentrate on the status and advantages of being club members. They have evidently forgotten – or never known – the perceptive dictum attributed to Archbishop William Temple that 'the church is the only co-operative society in the world which exists for the benefit of its non-members'. Instead, they are completely introverted, like an ingrown toenail. To be sure, Temple was guilty of a slight exaggeration, for church members do have a responsibility to each other, as the many 'one another' verses of the New Testament indicate ('love one another', 'encourage one another', 'bear one another's burdens', *etc.*). Nevertheless, our primary responsibilities are our worship of God and our mission in the world.

At the opposite extreme to the religious club is *the secular mission* (or *religionless Christianity*). It was in the 1960s that some Christian thinkers became understandably exasperated by what they saw as the ecclesiastical self-centredness of the church. The church seemed to them so incorrigibly absorbed in its own petty domestic affairs, that they resolved to abandon it and drop out. For the arena of divine service they exchanged the church for the secular city. They were no longer interested in 'worship services', they said, but only in 'worship service'. So they tried to develop a 'religionless Christianity' in which they reinterpreted worship as mission, love for God as love for neighbour, and prayer to God as encounter with people.

How, some thirty years later, should we evaluate this movement? We must surely agree that their distaste for selfish religion was right. Since it is nauseating to God, it ought to sicken us also. But the concept of a 'religionless Christianity' was an unbalanced over-reaction. We have no liberty to confuse worship and mission, even though (as we have seen) each involves the other. There is always an element of mission in worship and of worship in mission, but they are not synonymous.

There is a third way to understand the church, which combines what is true in both false images, and which recognizes that we have a responsibility both to worship God and to serve the world. This is *the double identity of the church* (or *incarnational Christianity*). By its 'double identity' I mean that the church is a people who have been both called out of the world to worship God and sent back into the world to witness and serve. These are, in fact, two of the classical 'marks' of the church. According to the first, the church is 'holy', called out to belong to God and to worship him. According to the second, the church is 'apostolic', sent out into the world on its mission. Alternatively, we may say that the church is summoned by God to be simultaneously 'holy' (distinct from the world) and 'worldly' (not in the sense of assimilating the world's values and standards, but in the sense of renouncing other-worldliness and becoming instead immersed in the life of the world). It was Dr Alec Vidler who admirably captured the church's double identity by referring to its 'holy worldliness'.[1]

Nobody has ever exhibited the meaning of 'holy worldliness' better than our Lord Jesus Christ himself. His incarnation is the perfect embodiment of it. On the one hand, he came to us in our world, and assumed the full reality of our humanness. He made himself one with us in our frailty, and exposed himself to our temptations. He fraternized with the common people, and they flocked round him eagerly. He welcomed everybody and shunned nobody. He identified himself with our sorrows, our sins and our death. On the other hand, in mixing freely with people like us, he never sacrificed, or even for one moment compromised, his own unique identity. His was the perfection of 'holy worldliness'.

And now he sends us into the world as he was sent into the world.[2] We have to penetrate other people's worlds, as he penetrated ours – the world of their thinking (as we struggle to understand their misunderstandings of the gospel), the world of their feeling (as we try to empathize with their pain), and the world of their living (as we sense the humiliation of their social situation, whether poverty, homelessness, unemployment or discrimination). Archbishop Michael Ramsey put it well: 'We state and commend the faith only in so far as we go out and put ourselves with loving sympathy inside the doubts of the doubter, the questions of the questioner, and the loneliness of those who have lost the way.'[3] Yet this costly entry into other people's worlds is not to be undertaken at the expense of our own Christian integrity. We are called to maintain the standards of Jesus Christ untarnished.

Seldom in its long history has the church managed to preserve its God-given double identity of holy worldliness. Instead, it has tended to oscillate between the two extremes. Sometimes (in an

[1] Alec Vidler, *Essays in Liberality* (SCM, 1957), ch. 5. [2] Jn. 17:18; 20:21.
[3] Michael Ramsey, *Images Old and New* (SPCK, 1963), p. 14.

over-emphasis on its holiness) the church has withdrawn from the world and so has neglected its mission. At other times (in an over-emphasis on its worldliness) it has conformed to the world, assimilating its views and values, and so has neglected its holiness. But in order to fulfil its mission, the church must faithfully respond to both its callings and preserve both parts of its identity.

'Mission' arises, then, from the biblical doctrine of the church in the world. If we are not 'the church', the holy and distinct people of God, we have nothing to say because we are compromised. If, on the other hand, we are not 'in the world', deeply involved in its life and suffering, we have no-one to serve because we are insulated. Our calling is to be 'holy' and 'worldly' at the same time. Without this balanced biblical ecclesiology we will never recover or fulfil our mission.

The church must organize itself

The structures of the church

The church must organize itself in such a way as to express its understanding of itself. Its structures must reflect its theology, especially its double identity.

The commonest fault is for the church to be structured for 'holiness' rather than 'worldliness', for worship and fellowship rather than mission. This was the emphasis of the report *The Church for Others* (1968), sub-titled *A Quest for Structures for Missionary Congregations*. One does not have to agree with everything in the book in order to appreciate its thrust that

> the missionary church is not concerned with itself – it is a church for others ... Its centre lies outside itself; it must live 'excentredly' ... The church has to turn itself outwards to the world ... We have to recognize that the churches have developed into 'waiting churches' into which people are expected to come. Its inherited structures stress and embody this static outlook. One may say that we are in danger of

> perpetuating 'come-structures' instead of replacing them by 'go-structures'. One may say that inertia has replaced the dynamism of the gospel and of participation in the mission of God.[1]

Further, our static, inflexible, self-centred structures are 'heretical structures' because they embody a heretical doctrine of the church.

Some zealous churches organize an overfull programme of church-based activities. Something is arranged for every night of the week. On Monday night the committees meet, and on Tuesday night the fellowship groups. On Wednesday night the Bible study takes place, and on Thursday night the prayer meeting. Even on Friday and Saturday evenings other good causes occupy people's time and energy. Such churches give the impression that their main goal is to keep their members out of mischief! Certainly they have neither time nor opportunity to get into mischief since they are busily engaged in the church every single night of the week!

But such a crowded, church-centred programme, admirable as it may look at first sight, has many drawbacks and dangers. To begin with, it is detrimental to Christian family life. Marriages break up and families disintegrate because father and/or mother are seldom at home. It also inhibits church members from getting involved in the local community because they are preoccupied with the local church. It thus contradicts an essential part of the church's identity, namely its 'worldliness'. As Bishop Richard Wilke of the United Methodist Church in the United States has put it, 'our structure has become an end in itself, not a means of saving the world'.[2] In that case it is a heretical structure.

I sometimes wonder (although I exaggerate in order to make my point) if it would not be very healthy for church members to meet only on Sundays (for worship, fellowship and teaching) and not at all midweek. Then we would gather on Sundays and

[1] *The Church for Others* (WCC, Geneva, 1967), pp. 7, 18–19.
[2] Richard Wilke, *And Are We Yet Alive?* (Abingdon, 1986).

scatter for the rest of the week. We would come to Christ for worship and go for Christ in mission. And in that rhythm of Sunday–weekday, gathering–scattering, coming–going and worship–mission the church would express its holy worldliness, and its structure would conform to its double identity.

How, then, should the local church organize itself? Ideally, it seems to me, every five or ten years each church should conduct a survey in order to evaluate itself and especially to discover how far its structures reflect its identity. In fact, it should conduct two surveys, one of the local community and the other of the local church, in order to learn how far the church is penetrating the community for Christ. This idea was recently taken up in Britain by ACUPA (the Archbishop's Commission on Urban Priority Areas), whose influential report was entitled *Faith in the City*. It recommended what it called a 'local church audit', consisting of both 'the church profile' ('to build up an accurate picture of the local church') and 'the parish profile' ('to build up an accurate picture of the parish').[1] Perhaps I could take these in the opposite order:

A local community survey

Each church is set in a particular situation, and needs to become familiar with it in all its particularity. A questionnaire will need to be drawn up. Here are some of the questions which it will probably include:

1. What sort of people live in our parish or locality? What is their ethnic origin, nationality, religion, culture, media preference, and work? What proportions are there of normal families, single-parent families, single people, senior citizens, young people? What are the area's main social needs, relating to housing, employment, poverty, education?

2. Has the locality any centres of education, whether schools, colleges, adult education centres, or playgroups?

[1] *Faith in the City* (Church House, 1985).

3. What places of business are found in it? Factories, farms, offices, shops, or studios? Is there significant unemployment?

4. Where do the people live? Do they occupy houses or flats, and do they own or rent them? Are there any hotels, hostels, student residences, apartment blocks, or homes for senior citizens?

5. Where do people congregate when they are at leisure? Café or restaurant, pub or disco, shopping mall, youth club or other clubs, bingo hall, concert hall, theatre or cinema, sports ground, park or street corner?

6. What public services are situated locally? Police, fire brigade, prison, hospital, public library, other social services?

7. Are there other religious buildings – church or chapel, synagogue, mosque, temple, or Christian Science reading room?

8. Has the community changed in the last ten years, and what changes can be forecast during the next ten?

A local church survey

In this second survey probing questions will need to be asked. Is the church in reality organized only for itself, for its own survival and convenience, and for the preservation of its privileges? Is it organized to serve itself, or to serve God and the community? What are its cherished traditions and conventions which unnecessarily separate it from the community? The questionnaire might include the following areas:

1. *The church building.* Church members tend to be most interested in its *interior* (its beauty, comfort and amenities).

Be we also need to walk round it and look at it through the eyes of an *outsider*: What image does it present? Is it a fortress (dark, forbidding and austere), or is it bright, inviting and welcoming?

As an illustration, let me mention visiting the huge central square of the capital city of a Latin American republic. In the middle was the statue of the national hero, who had rescued the country at the beginning of the last century from the Spanish *conquistadores*. One side of the square was entirely occupied by the Roman Catholic cathedral. I tried to get in, but it was closed. On the steps leading up to its main door, however, were three human beings – a drunk who had vomited copiously, a blind beggar selling matches, and a prostitute who was offering herself to passers-by in broad daylight. A drunk, a beggar and a prostitute, three symbols of human tragedy, and behind them a locked cathedral, which seemed to be saying 'Keep out! We don't want you'. I realize that there may have been good reasons why the cathedral was closed. My concern is with the 'vibes' which were given off by that scene.

A critical look at the inside of the church building will be necessary too, especially through the eyes of non-Christian visitors – its decoration and furniture, lighting and heating, its noticeboards, posters, bookstall and leaflets.

2. *The church services*. As with the first-century Jewish synagogue, so with the twentieth-century Christian church, there are 'Godfearers' on the edge of every congregation, who are attracted but not yet committed to Christ. Are our services exclusively for the committed, designed only for the initiated, and therefore mumbo jumbo to outsiders? Or do we remember the fringe members and non-members who may be present? What about the forms of service, the liturgy and language, the music (words, tunes and instruments), the seating, and the dress of both clergy and congregation? We need to ask ourselves what vibrations all these things give out.

3. *The church membership*. Is our membership mobilized for mission? Or is our church so clericalized (*i.e.* clergy-dominated) as to make this impossible? Has it grasped the New Testament teaching about the 'every-member ministry of the body of Christ'? Or is it less a body than a pyramid, with the clergy at the pinnacle and the lay people in their serried ranks of inferiority at the base? Are the members of the church also members of the community? Or are they either confined to church activities or practising a commuter-Christianity (travelling long distances to church), which makes local involvement difficult, even artificial?

4. *The church programme*. Do we imprison our members in the church? Or do we deliberately release at least some of them (including leaders) from church commitments in order to encourage them to be active for Christ in the community, and then support them with our interest and prayers as they do so? Do we ensure that the biblical truth of the double identity of the church is taught and embodied, and that training is available for those who want to commit themselves to Christian service and witness?

The two surveys (of community and church) will need to be studied by the church leadership (clergy and lay) both separately and in relation to each other. Out of this reflection will grow a strategy for mission. The leadership (preferably with others who may wish to be involved) will set both long-term and short-term goals, and establish a list of priorities. They may decide that the church is suffering from a false self-image and needs above all else some biblical teaching on its holy worldliness and on the implications of this for mission; or that a training programme must be arranged to equip members for evangelism; or that church-based activities should be reduced in order to increase members' involvement in the community. It might be decided to restructure radically the church building, decor, seating or services; or to organize a general visitation of the area, if possible in cooperation with other local churches; or to form specialist groups to penetrate particular, secular segments of the locality. For example, a group of committed young people could adopt a local disco, not in order to make occasional evangelistic raids into it, but between them (in pairs) to visit it regularly over a long period, in order to make friends with the other young people who congregate there. Again, the church may decide to arrange home meetings for neighbours, or a series of apologetic lectures in a local and neutral building, or regular guest services with an evangelistic thrust, to which members would be encouraged to bring their friends. Or the church may determine to take up some special social need in the area, which has surfaced during the surveys, and encourage a group to study it and then recommend action. All such decisions will be designed to help the church to identify with the community, and to develop structures which facilitate an authentically incarnational mission.

The church must express itself
The message of the church

It is not enough for the local church to understand itself and organize itself accordingly; it must also articulate its message. For evangelism, at its simplest and most basic, is sharing the evangel. So in order to define evangelism we must also define the good news.

There can be no doubt that the essence of the gospel is Jesus Christ himself. It would be impossible to preach the Christian good news without talking about Jesus. So we read that Philip, speaking to the Ethiopian, 'told him the good news about Jesus',[1] and that the apostle Paul described himself as 'set apart for the gospel of God . . . regarding his Son . . .'.[2] Moreover, in bearing witness to Jesus we must speak above all of his death and resurrection. To quote Paul again in his famous summary of the apostolic gospel, 'What I received I passed on to you as of first importance: that Christ died for our sins according to the

[1] Acts 8:35. [2] Rom. 1:1, 3.

Scriptures, that he was buried, that he was raised on the third day according to the Scriptures, and that he appeared . . .'.[1] We simply do not share the gospel if we do not declare God's love in the gift of his Son to live our life, to die for our sins and to rise again, together with his offer through Jesus Christ, to all who repent and believe, of a new life of forgiveness and freedom, and of membership in his new society. The Anglican primates' recommended definition includes these essentials.

But how shall we formulate this good news in our world's increasingly pluralistic societies, in such a way that it resonates with them and makes sense? There are two opposite extremes to avoid.

The first extreme I will call *total fixity*. Some Christian people seem to be in bondage to words and formulae, and so become prisoners of a gospel stereotype. They wrap up their message in a nice, neat package; and they tape, label and price-tag it as if it were destined for the supermarket. Then, unless their favourite phraseology is used (whether the kingdom of God, or the blood of Jesus, or human liberation, or being born again, or justification by faith, or the cosmic lordship of Christ), they roundly declare that the gospel has not been preached. What these people seem not to have noticed is the rich diversity of gospel formulation which is found in the New Testament itself. The options I have listed are all biblical, but because all of them contain an element of imagery, and each image is different, it is impossible to fuse them into a single, simple concept. So it is perfectly legitimate to develop one or other of them, according to what seems most appropriate to the occasion.

The opposite extreme is *total fluidity*. Some years ago I heard a British bishop say: 'There's no such thing as the gospel in a vacuum. You don't even know what the gospel is until you enter each particular situation. You have to enter the situation first, and then you discover the gospel when you're there.' Now if he meant that he wanted a gospel in context, not in vacuum, and that we need to relate the gospel sensitively to each person

[1] 1 Cor. 15:3–5.

and situation, I am in full agreement with him; but to say that 'there is no such thing as the gospel in a vacuum' and that 'you discover it' in each situation is surely a serious overstatement. For what the advocates of total fluidity seem not to have noticed is that, alongside the New Testament's rich diversity of gospel formulation, there is also an underlying unity (especially regarding the saving death and resurrection of Jesus) which binds the different formulations together. As Professor A. M. Hunter wrote, 'there is ... a deep unity in the New Testament, which dominates and transcends all the diversities'.[1]

Is there a middle way? Yes, there is. Both the extremes which I have described express important concerns which need to be preserved. The first ('total fixity') rightly emphasizes that the gospel has been revealed by God and received by us. It is both a *paradosis* (a tradition to be preserved) and a *parathēkē* (a deposit to be guarded). We did not invent it, and we have no liberty to edit it or tamper with it. The second ('total fluidity') rightly emphasizes that the gospel must be contextualized, that is to say, related appropriately to each particular person or situation. Otherwise it will be perceived as irrelevant.

Somehow, then, we have to learn to combine these two proper concerns. We have to wrestle with the dialectic between the ancient Word and the modern world, between what has been given and what has been left open, between content and context, Scripture and culture, revelation and contextualization. We need more fidelity to Scripture and more sensitivity to people. Not one without the other, but both.

The church must be itself
The life of the church

The church is supposed to be God's new society, the living embodiment of the gospel, a sign of the kingdom of God, a demonstration of what human community looks like when it comes under his gracious rule.

[1] A. M. Hunter, *The Unity of the New Testament* (SCM, 1943).

In other words, God's purpose is that the good news of Jesus Christ is set forth visually as well as verbally, or in the language of the primates' definition, that it be made known 'by word and deed'. Every educator knows how much easier it is for human beings to learn through what they see and experience than through what they hear. Or rather, word and deed, hearing and seeing, belong essentially together. This is certainly so in evangelism. People have to see with their own eyes that the gospel we preach has transformed us. As John Poulton put it, 'Christians ... need to look like what they are talking about. It is *people* who communicate primarily, not words or ideas ... What communicates now is basically personal authenticity.'[1] Conversely, if our life contradicts our message, our evangelism will lack all credibility. Indeed, the greatest hindrance to evangelism is lack of integrity in the evangelist.

No text has helped me to understand the implications of this for the life of the local church more than 1 John 4:12, 'No-one has ever seen God; but if we love one another, God lives in us and his love is made complete in us.' God is invisible. Nobody has ever seen him. All that human beings have ever seen of him is glimpses of his glory, of the outshining of his being.

Now the invisibility of God is a great problem for faith. It was so for the Jews in the Old Testament. Their heathen neighbours laughed at them for actually worshipping an invisible God. 'You say you believe in God?' they taunted them. 'Where is he? Come to our temples, and we will show you our gods. They have ears and eyes, hands and feet, and mouths and noses too. But where is your God? We can't see him. Ha, ha, ha!' The Jews found this ridicule hard to bear. Hence the complaint of psalmist and prophet: 'Why do the nations say, "Where is their God?"'[2] Of course Israel had its own apologetic. The idols of the heathen were nothing, only the work of human hands. True, they had mouths, but they could not speak, ears but could not hear, noses but could not smell, hands but could not feel, and

[1] John Poulton, *A Today Sort of Evangelism* (Lutterworth, 1972), pp. 60–61, 79.
[2] *E.g.* Ps. 115:2.

feet but could not walk.[1] Yahweh, on the other hand, although (being spirit) he had no mouth, had spoken; although he had no ears, he listened to Israel's prayers; and although he had no hands, he had both created the universe and redeemed his people by his mighty power. At the same time, the people of God longed that he would make himself known to the nations, so that they might see him and believe in him.

The same problem of an unseen God challenges us today, especially young people who have been brought up on the scientific method. They are taught to examine everything by their five senses. Anything which is not amenable to empirical investigation they are told to suspect and even reject. So could it ever be reasonable to believe in an invisible God? 'Let us only see him,' they say, 'and we will believe.'

How, then, has God solved the problem of his own invisibility? First and foremost he has done so by sending his Son into the world. 'No-one has ever seen God; the only Son, who is in the bosom of the Father, he has made him known.'[2] Consequently Jesus could say, 'Anyone who has seen me has seen the Father,'[3] and Paul could describe him as 'the (visible) image of the invisible God'.[4]

To this people tend to reply: 'That is truly wonderful, but it happened nearly 2,000 years ago. Is there no way in which the invisible God makes himself visible *today*?' Yes, there is. 'No-one has ever seen God.'[5] John begins this verse in his first letter with the identical sentence which he has used in the prologue to his Gospel.[6] But now he concludes the sentence differently. In the Gospel he wrote that 'the only Son . . . has made him known'. In the Epistle he writes that 'if we love one another, God lives in us and his love is made complete in us'. Because of John's deliberate repetition of the same statement, this can only mean one thing. The invisible God, who once made himself visible in Christ, now makes himself visible in Christians, *if we love one another*.

[1] *E.g.* Ps. 115:4–7. [2] Jn. 1:18 (RSV). [3] Jn. 14:9. [4] Col. 1:15.
[5] 1 Jn. 4:12. [6] Jn. 1:18.

God is love in his essential being, and has revealed his love in the gift of his Son to live and die for us. Now he calls us to be a community of love, loving each other in the intimacy of his family – especially across the barriers of age and sex, race and rank – and loving the world he loves in its alienation, hunger, poverty and pain. It is through the quality of our loving that God makes himself visible today.

We cannot proclaim the gospel of God's love with any degree of integrity if we do not exhibit it in our love for others. Perhaps nothing is so damaging to the cause of Christ as a church which is either torn apart by jealousy, rivalry, slander and malice, or preoccupied with its own selfish concerns. Such churches urgently need to be radically renewed in love. As one of the group reports of the 1978 Lambeth Conference put it, 'Mission without renewal is hypocrisy.' It is only if we love one another that the world will believe that Jesus is the Christ and that we are his disciples.[1]

Here, then, are the four main prerequisites for evangelism through the local church. First, the church must understand itself (theologically), grasping its double identity. Secondly, it must organize itself (structurally), developing a mission strategy which reflects its double identity. Thirdly, it must express itself (verbally), articulating its gospel in a way which is both faithful to Scripture and relevant to the contemporary world. And fourthly, it must be itself (morally and spiritually), becoming so completely transformed into a community of love that through it the invisible God again makes himself visible to the world.

[1] Jn. 13:35; 17:21.

CHAPTER SIXTEEN

DIMENSIONS OF CHURCH RENEWAL

The twentieth-century church has been characterized by a whole series of renewal movements, each focusing on a particular aspect of ecclesiastical life. At least six may be mentioned.

First, at the beginning of the century the missionary movement received fresh impetus at the World Missionary Conference in Edinburgh in 1910. The church growth movement founded by Dr Donald McGavran, and the Lausanne movement with its congresses on world evangelization (Lausanne 1974 and Manila 1989), have given it considerable further stimulus.

Secondly, there was the biblical theology movement, whose antecedent was the emphasis laid by Karl Barth and Emil Brunner between the wars on the 'otherness' of God and his Word. It flourished between 1945 and 1960 under biblical scholars like Gerhard von Rad (Old Testament) and Oscar Cullmann (New Testament), who stressed the inner unity of Scripture.

Next, the ecumenical movement, though stemming from the 1910 Edinburgh Conference, took shape in the formation of the World Council of Churches in Amsterdam in 1948 and has laid its stress on the need to unite the churches in their witness to the world.

Fourthly, the post-war liturgical movement, specially (though not exclusively) in the Roman Catholic Church, aimed to modernize the eucharistic worship of the congregation. The Second Vatican Council gave it a further boost.

Fifthly, the neo-pentecostal or charismatic movement has

sought to incorporate the distinctive emphases of the pentecostal churches within the mainline denominations, and has been concerned for the restoration of spiritual power and spiritual gifts to the body of Christ.

Sixthly, the social justice movement, ranging from the cluster of liberation theologies to the recovery of the evangelical social conscience, has sought to balance the church's eternal and other-worldly preoccupations with its temporal, this-worldly responsibilities.

Thus mission, theology, unity, worship, power and justice are six legitimate Christian concerns, each of which has gathered round it a devoted clientele of protagonists. Yet the result has been an unhealthily fragmented agenda. What seems to be needed is a holistic or integrated vision of renewal in every dimension of the church's life.

The Roman Catholic word for this, at least since Vatican II (1963–65), has been *aggiornamento*, the process of bringing the church up to date in order to meet the challenges of the modern world. It implies that the world is changing rapidly and that, if the church is to survive, it must keep pace with this change, although without either compromising its own standards or conforming to the world's.

Protestants use a different vocabulary to describe the continuously needed restoring and refreshing of the church. Our two favourite words are 'reform', indicating the kind of reformation of faith and life according to Scripture which took place in the sixteenth century, and 'revival', denoting an altogether supernatural visitation of a church or community by God, bringing conviction, repentance, confession, the conversion of sinners and the recovery of backsliders. 'Reformation' usually stresses the power of the Word of God, and 'revival' the power of the Spirit of God, in his work of restoring the church. Perhaps we should keep the word 'renewal' to describe a movement which combines revival by God's Spirit with reformation by his Word. Since the Word is the Spirit's sword, there is bound to be something lopsided about contemplating either without the other.

For an integrated vision of continuous renewal, we cannot do better than reflect on Jesus' prayer for his people recorded in John 17. It is a mistake to regard this chapter as an exclusively ecumenical text, concentrating on Christian unity. Unity is indeed included, but the concern Jesus expressed in his prayer was considerably wider than this.

John 17, without doubt, is one of the profoundest chapters of the Bible. Whole books have been written to expound it. Thomas Manton, for example, the seventeenth-century British Puritan, who for a while was Oliver Cromwell's chaplain, preached a course of forty-five sermons on John 17.[1] Then the Irish clergyman Marcus Rainsford, who occupied the pulpit of St John's Church, Belgrave Square in London from 1866 to 1897, preached a course of forty-one sermons on the same chapter.[2] Both courses of sermons were published, and both books ran to more than 450 pages; so what can we hope to learn in one brief chapter? There are depths here we will never fathom; all we can do is paddle in the shallows. Here are heights we cannot scale; we can only climb the foothills.

Nevertheless, we must persevere. For if the upper-room discourse (John 13 – 17) is the temple of Scripture, John 17 is its inner sanctuary or holy of holies. Here we are introduced into the presence, mind and heart of God. We are permitted to eavesdrop, as the Son communes with the Father. We need to take off our shoes, since this is holy ground.

Jesus prays first for himself (verses 1–5), as he approaches the cross; secondly for his apostles (verses 6–19), to whom he has revealed the Father, and who are gathered round him as he prays; and thirdly for the whole church present and future (verses 20–26), consisting of all those who will believe in him through the apostles' teaching. We will concentrate on the second and third sections (verses 6–26).

As a matter of fact, Jesus does not begin his prayer for his people until the end of verse 11. Before this, for five and a half

[1] Republished in 1958 by the Sovereign Grace Book Club under the title *An Exposition of John Seventeen.*
[2] Republished in 1950 by Moody Press under the title *Our Lord Prays for His Own.*

verses (verses 6–11a) he describes the people he is going to pray for. It is quite an elaborate description and, although it refers primarily to the apostles, it delineates them rather as ordinary disciples than in their distinctive apostolic ministry. The description has three parts.

First, *they belong to Christ.* Three times Jesus repeats the truth that the Father has 'given' them to him out of the world (verses 6 and 9), so that in consequence they belong to him.

Secondly, *they know the Father.* For if the Father has given them to the Son, the Son has given them a revelation of the Father. This too is repeated. 'I have revealed you (literally, 'your name') to those whom you gave me out of the world' (verse 6). Also, 'I gave them the words you gave me and they accepted them' (verse 8). Of course this revelation of God's name, this gift of God's words, was made in the first instance to the apostles, but from them it has been passed on to all Christ's disciples.

Thirdly, *they live in the world.* 'I will remain in the world no longer,' Jesus says, 'but they are still in the world, and I am coming to you' (verse 11a). Although they have been given to Christ 'out of the world' (verse 6), they nevertheless remain 'in the world' (verse 11a) out of which they have been taken. They are to be spiritually distinct, but not socially segregated. Jesus leaves them behind as his representatives or ambassadors.

Here, then, is Jesus' threefold characterization of his people, beginning with his apostles, but including all later disciples, reaching even to us. First, the Father has given us to the Son. Secondly, the Son has revealed to us the Father. Thirdly, we live in the world. It is this threefold orientation (to the Father, to the Son and to the world) which makes us the 'holy' (that is, distinct) people we are. We live in the world as a people who know God and belong to Christ, and therefore (it is implied) have a unique mission to make him known.

What, then, does Christ pray for his people whom he has so carefully described? The burden of his intercession consists of only two words, which are repeated. 'Holy Father, *protect them* . . . My prayer is . . . that you *protect them* from the evil one' (verses 11b and 15). It is a prayer that the holy Father will keep us the holy people we are, that he will protect and preserve us from any and every evil influence which might spoil the unique position he has given us. It is a prayer that we may be kept true to who we are, to our essential Christian identity, as a people who know God, belong to Christ and live in the world.

More particularly, Jesus prays that his people may have four characteristics, namely truth, holiness, mission and unity.

Truth (verses 11–13)

A literal translation of verse 11b would be 'Keep them in your name', but commentators are not agreed how to translate the preposition 'in'. The NIV renders it 'Protect them by the power of your name'. Yet the context seems to require that God's name is not so much the power by which, as the sphere in which, the disciples are to be kept. I think, then, that the Jerusalem Bible is correct to translate: 'Keep those you have given me true to your name.' The revelation of God's name was 'the enclosing wall, as it were, within which they were to be kept'.[1] For God's name is God himself, who he is, his being and his character. This the Father has revealed to the Son, and the Son in his turn has revealed to the apostles (verse 6). During his earthly ministry Jesus has kept them in it (verse 12, literally). Now, however, he is about to leave the world. So he prays that the Father will keep them loyal to the name he has revealed to them, 'so that they may be one as we are one' (end of verse 11). That is, the major means to their unity will be their loyalty to God's truth revealed in and through Christ.

Truth, then, was the first concern for his church which Jesus expressed in his prayer. He spoke of revelation, of the disclosure by him of God's otherwise hidden name. He made plain his longing that his people would be loyal to this revelation, and that their unity would be based on their common faithfulness to it. Instead, today, I fear that some contemporary church leaders

[1] Charles Ross, *The Inner Sanctuary, An Exposition of John 13–17* (1888; Banner of Truth, 1967), p. 216.

are guilty of serious unfaithfulness. A few are brash enough to deny the fundamentals both of the historic Christian faith and of traditional Christian morality, while others seem as blushingly unsure of themselves and of their beliefs as an adolescent teenager.

There is no possibility of the church being thoroughly renewed until and unless it is renewed in its faith, in its commitment to God's revealed truth in Jesus Christ and in the full biblical testimony to him. Nor is there any chance of the church recovering its unity until it recovers the only authentic basis for unity, which is truth. Jesus prayed first for the truth of the church; we should do the same. For God intends his church to be 'the pillar and foundation of the truth'.[1]

Holiness (verses 14–16)

Jesus prayed that the Father would keep his people not only true to his name, but also 'from the evil one' (verse 15). That is, he desired on the one hand that they would be preserved from error and in truth, and on the other hand from evil and in holiness. The church's final destiny, Paul was later to declare, is to be presented to Christ 'as a radiant church, without stain or wrinkle or any other blemish, but holy and blameless'.[2] But the church's holiness must begin now. So what is meant by 'holiness'?

All down history the church has tended to go to extremes, as we considered in the last chapter. Sometimes, in its proper determination to be holy, it has withdrawn from the world and lost contact with it. At other times, in its equally proper determination not to lose contact, it has conformed to the world and become virtually indistinguishable from it. But Christ's vision for the church's holiness is neither withdrawal nor conformity.

Withdrawal was the way of the Pharisees. Anxious to apply the law to the details of everyday life, they had a false understanding of holiness, imagining that mere contact with evil and

[1] 1 Tim. 3:15. [2] Eph. 5:27.

evil people would bring contamination. And a form of Christian pharisaism or separatism has lingered in the church. It has often been due to a passionate longing for holiness and a zeal to preserve Christian culture from destruction by the wicked world. These motives persuaded the hermits to flee into the desert in the fourth century, and led to the development of medieval monasticism. But, noble as the motives of monks and hermits often were, the kind of monasticism which entailed withdrawal from the world must be pronounced a betrayal of Christ. So is the kind of modern piety which imprisons Christians in a ghetto-like fellowship and effectively cuts them off from non-Christians. For Jesus specifically prayed that, although he wanted his disciples to be protected from the evil one, he did not want them to be taken out of the world (verse 15).

If 'withdrawal' was the way of the Pharisees, and even more of the Essenes who took refuge in their desert communities to pray and wait for the kingdom of God to come, 'conformity' was the way of the Sadducees. Belonging to wealthy, aristocratic families, they collaborated with the Romans and sought to maintain the political status quo. This compromising tradition also persisted in the early church, and still survives today. The motive for it can again be good, namely the resolve to break down barriers between the church and the world, and to be the friends of publicans and sinners, as Jesus was.[1] But he was also 'set apart from sinners'[2] in his values and standards.

In place of these two extreme positions Jesus calls us to live 'in the world' (verse 11), while remaining like himself 'not of the world' (verse 14), that is, neither belonging to it, nor imitating its ways. This is the 'holy worldliness' of the church, about which I wrote in the last chapter, in connection with the church's double identity. We are neither to give in, nor to opt out. Instead, we are to stay in and stand firm, like a rock in a mountain stream, like a rose blooming in mid-winter, like a lily growing in a manure heap.

[1] Mt. 11:19 = Lk. 7:34. [2] Heb. 7:26.

Mission (verses 17–19)

There are fifteen references to 'the world' in Jesus' prayer, which indicates that one of his main concerns was how his people would relate to the world, that is, to non-Christian society or godless secularism. He indicated that they have been given to him out of the world (verse 6), but were not to be taken out of it (verse 15); that they were still living in the world (verse 11), but were not to be of the world (verse 14b); that they would be hated by the world (verse 14a), but were nevertheless sent into the world (verse 18). This is the multi-faceted relationship of the church to the world: living in it, not belonging to it, hated by it and sent into it.

Perhaps the best way to grasp this is that, in place of 'withdrawal' and 'conformity', which are wrong attitudes to the world, the right one is 'mission'. Indeed, the church's mission in the world is possible only if it avoids the two false tracks. If we withdraw from the world, mission is obviously impossible, since we have lost contact. Equally, if we conform to the world, mission is impossible, since we have lost our cutting edge.

It is particularly striking that, although we live 'in' the world (verse 11), we nevertheless need to be sent 'into' it (verse 18). But that is the case. It is all too possible for Christian people to live in the world without having any share in Christ's mission.

Christ's prayer for his people here is that the Father will 'sanctify' us by his word of truth (verse 17), indeed that we may be 'truly sanctified' like Christ who sanctified himself for us (verse 19). What kind of sanctification is in mind, we are obliged to ask, if it is one in which Christ himself participated? How can the sinless Christ be said to have sanctified himself? The answer is surely that sanctification has two complementary aspects, negative and positive. To be sanctified is to be separated *from* evil in all its forms. This is what we usually think about when the word 'sanctification' is used. But to be sanctified is also to be set apart *for* the particular ministry to which God has called us. It is in this sense that Jesus set himself apart for us, namely to come into the world to seek and to save us. We too have been 'sanctified', or set apart for our mission in the world. In fact, we can be described as 'separated from the world to be of service to the world'.[1]

In verse 18 (as in John 20:21) Jesus draws a deliberate parallel between his mission and ours: 'As you sent me into the world, I have sent them into the world.' In what sense, then, did Jesus intend his mission to be the model of ours? There are substantial differences, of course. His being sent into the world entailed both the incarnation and the atonement, whereas we are not God that we could 'become flesh' or die for sinners. Nevertheless, the fact that we are sent into the world like him will shape our understanding of mission. It tells us that mission involves being under the authority of Christ (we are sent, we did not volunteer); renouncing privilege, safety, comfort and aloofness, as we actually enter other people's worlds, as he entered ours; humbling ourselves to become servants, as he did;[2] bearing the pain of being hated by the hostile world into which we are sent (verse 14); and sharing the good news with people where they are. I shall have more to say about Christ as the model of mission in chapter 21, 'The Christology of Mission'.

Unity (verses 20–26)

Jesus' prophetic eyes now peered into the future, into the post-apostolic era. He saw the coming generations of his disciples who would not have seen or heard him in the flesh, as the apostles had done, but who would believe in him through their teaching: 'My prayer is not for them (the apostles) alone. I pray also for those who will believe in me through their message' (verse 20). This means every Christian of every age and place, including us. True, we may have come to believe in Jesus through the witness of our parents, or of a pastor, evangelist, teacher or friend. Yet their witness was a secondary witness, an endorsement from their own experience of the primary witness

[1] Leon Morris, *The Gospel According to John*, in the New London Commentary on the New Testament (Marshall, Morgan and Scott, 1971), p. 730.
[2] Phil. 2:7–8.

of the apostles. The apostles were the eyewitnesses, specially chosen by Jesus to be with him, so that they could bear witness to what they had seen and heard. There is only one authentic Christ, the Christ of the apostolic witness (now preserved in the New Testament), and all believers since the apostolic age have believed in Jesus 'through their message'.

What, then, does Jesus desire for all his believing people throughout the world and the centuries? There can be no doubt about this because he expresses it three times:

verse 21a: 'that all of them may be one'
verse 22b: 'that they may be one'
verse 23b: 'that they may become perfectly one' (RSV)

These are well-known petitions. What is usually not so well known or understood is the nature of the unity for which Christ prayed. He stressed two aspects of it.

First, he prayed that his people would enjoy *unity with the apostles*. Consider carefully what is recorded in verse 20 and at the beginning of verse 21: 'My prayer is not for them alone. I pray also for those who will believe in me through their message, that all of them may be one.' We have already noted that Jesus distinguishes between two groups of people. They are conveniently designated in RSV and NEB 'these' (the little band of apostles gathered round him) and 'those' (the huge company of all subsequent believers), or the teachers and the taught. He then prays that 'all of them', which must mean 'these' and 'those' together, 'may be one'. In other words, Jesus' prayer was first and foremost that there might be a historical continuity between the apostles and the post-apostolic church, that the church's faith might not change with the changing years but remain recognizably the same, and that the church of every generation might merit the epithet 'apostolic' because of its loyalty to the message and mission of the apostles. Christian unity begins, then, as unity with the apostles (through the New Testament which makes their teaching available to us); without this, church unity would not be distinctively Christian.

Secondly, Jesus prayed that his people would enjoy *unity with the Father and the Son*. Although the punctuation of verse 21 is disputed, most English versions regard its second clause as beginning a new sentence. We might render it as follows: 'Father, just as you are in me and I am in you, [I pray that they] may also be in us, that the world may believe . . .' The implications of this petition are staggering. For Jesus prays that the union of his people with God may be comparable to the unity of the Father and the Son with each other in the Godhead. He goes on in verse 23, 'I in them and thou in me, that they may become perfectly one' (RSV).

So then, the Christian unity for which Christ prayed was not primarily unity with each other, but unity with the apostles (a common truth) and unity with the Father and the Son (a common life). The visible, structural unity of the church is a proper goal. Yet it will be pleasing to God only if it is the visible expression of something deeper, namely unity in truth and in life. In our ecumenical concern, therefore, nothing is more important than the quest for more apostolic truth and more divine life through the Holy Spirit. As William Temple put it, 'the way to the union of Christendom does not lie through committee-rooms, though there is a task of formulation to be done there. It lies through personal union with the Lord so deep and real as to be comparable with his union with the Father.'[1]

It is this kind of unity (a shared truth and life) which will bring the world to believe in Jesus (verses 21 and 23). Indeed, the main reason why Jesus prays for the unity of his people is 'in order that' the world may believe in Jesus' divine origin and mission. He prays that all who will in future 'believe' in him (verse 20) may enjoy such unity of truth and life that the world may 'believe' in him too. Thus faith begets faith, and believers multiply.

In the final verses of his prayer (24–26) Jesus looks beyond history to eternity, for it is only in heaven that the unity of his people will be brought to perfection. They will see his glory

[1] William Temple, *Readings in St John's Gospel* (first published in two volumes, 1939 and 1940; Macmillan, 1947), p. 327.

(verse 24), and the end-result of the Son's revelation of the Father will be that they experience in themselves both the very same love which the Father has for the Son and the indwelling of the Son himself (verse 26). This ultimate unity, comprehending the Father, the Son and the church in love, is certainly beyond our imagination, but is not beyond our humble and ardent desire.

Jesus' prayer, then, is much more comprehensive than is commonly realized. It is a prayer for the church's truth ('keep them in your name'), holiness ('keep them from the evil one'), mission ('sanctify them . . . I have sent them into the world') and unity ('that they may be one').

In a notable intervention at the Third Assembly of the World Council of Churches in New Delhi (1961), Archbishop Michael Ramsey said: 'The seventeenth chapter of St. John describes Jesus praying not only that his disciples may be *one*, but also that they may become holy and that they may realize the truth. Unity, holiness, truth go together.'[1] Even then he omitted the fourth topic, mission!

One of the tragedies of the contemporary church is its tendency to atomize this holistic vision of Christ, and to select one or other of his concerns to the exclusion of the rest. But, as Michael Ramsey also said at the New Delhi assembly, 'a movement which concentrates on unity as an isolated concept, can mislead the world and mislead us, as indeed would a movement which had the exclusive label of holiness or the exclusive label of truth'.

The major preoccupation of the twentieth-century church has been the search for structural unity, but often without a comparable quest for the truth and the life which constitute authentic unity and are the means by which it grows.

Others have been preoccupied with truth (doctrinal ortho-

[1] Michael Ramsey made the same point during the epilogue to his address on 'The Church, its Scandal and Glory' during his mission in Oxford University in February 1960. His addresses were published as *Introducing the Christian Faith* (1961; SCM, revised edition, 1970), p. 76.

doxy), sometimes becoming dry, harsh and unloving in the process, forgetting that truth is to be adorned with the beauty of holiness.

Holiness seems of paramount importance to others, that is, the state of the church's interior life. But such people sometimes withdraw into a self-centred piety, forgetting that we have been called out of the world in order to be sent back into it, which is 'mission'.

So mission becomes the obsession of a fourth group, who, however, sometimes forget that the world will come to believe in Jesus only when his people are one in truth, holiness and love.

Truth, holiness, mission and unity belonged together in the prayer of Jesus, and they need to be kept together in our quest for the church's renewal today. I think we may detect them in the earliest Spirit-filled church in Jerusalem, since we are told in Acts 2:42 and 47 that 'they devoted themselves to the apostles' teaching' (truth), 'to the fellowship' (unity), and 'to the breaking of bread and to prayer' (worship expressing their holiness), while 'the Lord added to their number daily those who were being saved' (mission). It seems to me legitimate also to see the same characteristics in the four traditional 'notes' or 'marks' of the church, according to the Nicene Creed, namely that it is 'one, holy, catholic and apostolic'. For 'catholic' includes the concept of embracing all truth, and 'apostolic' includes the vision of being committed to the apostolic mission.

It is important that we do not separate what God has joined. Instead, we must seek the renewal of the church in all four dimensions simultaneously, so that it faithfully guards the revelation which has once for all been entrusted to it, becomes sanctified and unified by this truth which it preserves, and goes out boldly into the world on its God-given mission of witness and service.

CHAPTER SEVENTEEN
THE CHURCH'S PASTORS

It would be difficult to think about the life, mission and renewal of the church without giving thought to its ordained ministers. For it is plain from the New Testament that God has always intended his church to have some form of *episkopē*, that is, pastoral oversight. Moreover the condition of the church in every place depends very largely on the quality of the ministry it receives. As Richard Baxter put it: 'If God would but reform the ministry, and set them on their duties zealously and faithfully, the people would certainly be reformed. All churches either rise or fall as the ministry doth rise or fall, not in riches or worldly grandeur, but in knowledge, zeal and ability for their work.'[1]

Yet there is a great deal of contemporary confusion about the nature and function of ordained clergy. Are they priests, prophets, pastors, preachers or psychotherapists? Are they administrators, facilitators or social workers? Perhaps no more embarrassing exposure of this uncertainty has been made than David Hare's play *Racing Demon*, which won three Olivier Awards in 1990. It portrays four Anglican clergy in a team ministry in South London, together with the diocesan bishop of Southwark (the Rt Rev. Charlie Allen) and his suffragan bishop of Kingston (the Rt Rev. Gilbert Heffernan). Each has a different notion of the purpose of the ordained ministry. To Lionel Espy, the gentle and largely ineffective team rector, 'our job is mainly to learn. From ordinary, working people. We should try to understand and serve them.'[2] 'Mostly, in fact, it's just

[1] Richard Baxter, *The Reformed Pastor* (1656; Epworth, second edition, 1950), p. 24.
[2] David Hare, *Racing Demon* (Faber and Faber, 1990), p. 3.

listening to the anger,' and like a punch-bag absorbing it.[1] In complete contrast, the young charismatic curate, Tony Ferris, is frighteningly self-confident. 'I have this incredible power,' he claims, which enables him to 'spread confidence' around him, but he does it at the expense of other people.[2]

The other characters are more modest in their expectations. The diocesan bishop emphasizes the administration of holy communion. 'Finally, that's what you're there for. As a priest you have only one duty. That's to put on a show.'[3] His suffragan, the episcopal diplomat *par excellence*, sees the heart of his job as 'preventing problems growing into issues'.[4] To Donald Bacon ('Streaky'), who sings tenor, gets drunk and describes himself as 'a happy priest', there are no complications. 'The whole thing's so clear. He's there. In people's happiness.'[5] Harry Henderson, the homosexual clergyman, is a trifle more ambitious. 'There is people as they are. And there is people as they could be. The priest's job is to try and yank the two a little bit closer.'[6] Meanwhile, the sincere, agnostic girl Frances Parnell sees the ordained ministry as the 'waste of a human being . . . always to be dreaming'.[7]

This perplexity about the role of clergy is by no means recent, however. More than a century ago Mark Twain expressed it through his attractive character, Huckleberry Finn. Huck told Joanna that in her uncle Harvey's church in Sheffield there were 'no less than seventeen' clergy, although (he added) 'they don't *all* of 'em preach the same day – only *one* of 'em'.

'Well then,' Joanna responds, 'what does the rest of 'em do?'

'Oh, nothing much,' Huck explains. 'Loll around, pass the plate – and one thing or another. But mainly they don't do nothing.'

'Well, then,' cries Joanna in wide-eyed astonishment, 'what are they *for*?'

[1] *Ibid.*, pp. 34–35. [2] *Ibid.*, pp. 75, 97. [3] *Ibid.*, pp. 3–4.
[4] *Ibid.*, p. 43. [5] *Ibid.*, p. 63. [6] *Ibid.*, p. 71.
[7] *Ibid.*, pp. 66, 69.

'Why, they're for *style*,' Huck replies. 'Don't you know nothing?'[1]

Contrary opinions have, in fact, been held about the importance of the ordained ministry. Some people, seeing clergy marginalized by secular society and the welfare state, and rejoicing in the recovery of Paul's vision of an every-member ministry in the body of Christ, question whether ordained ministers are necessary any longer and suggest that the church would be in a healthier condition without them.

Others react in the opposite way. Whether on theological or pragmatic grounds, they put clergy on a pedestal, or at least acquiesce when they put themselves there. Then, when the reins of ministry are entirely in their hands, the almost inevitable consequences are either clerical breakdown or lay frustration or both.

All down its long history the church has oscillated between these extremes of clericalism (clerical domination of the laity) and anticlericalism (lay disdain for the clergy). Yet the New Testament warns us against both tendencies. To the Corinthians who developed a personality cult of different apostles Paul expostulated: 'What (he deliberately used the neuter) do you think we are, that you pay such exaggerated deference to us? We are only servants, through whom God worked to bring you to faith.'[2] To others, however, who regarded their leaders with contempt, Paul wrote that they must 'respect' them and 'hold them in the highest regard in love because of their work'.[3] Again, 'Here is a trustworthy saying: If anyone sets his heart on being an overseer, he desires a noble task.'[4] Or 'to aspire to leadership is an honourable ambition' (NEB).

We must now return to the basic question what the nature and function of ordained clergy are. In general, the churches have given only two answers, according to whether they have seen the ministry as being directed primarily towards God or towards the church. On the one hand, there is the priestly

[1] Mark Twain, *The Adventures of Huckleberry Finn* (1884; Pan, 1968), p. 343.
[2] 1 Cor. 3:5, paraphrased and expanded.
[3] 1 Thes. 5:12–13. [4] 1 Tim. 3:1.

model, in which the ministry is exercised towards God on behalf of the people. On the other hand, there is the pastoral model, in which the ministry is exercised towards the people on behalf of God.

The priestly model

The Roman Catholic and Orthodox churches see their clergy as priests, especially in relation to their role at the eucharist. Lutheran and Anglican churches have also traditionally called their clergy 'priests', but for a different reason. The Council of Trent affirmed that in the mass a true and propitiatory sacrifice is offered to God, and that the human priest who offers it represents the Christ who offers himself.[1] Moreover, the essence of this teaching was endorsed at the Second Vatican Council. Thus, priests are 'given the power of sacred Order to offer sacrifice . . .'.[2] 'They sacramentally offer the Sacrifice of Christ in a special way when they celebrate mass.'[3] True, they are said to represent the people of God, as well as representing Christ, when they do this. But the heart of their priesthood is still conceived as offering the eucharistic sacrifice.

Protestant Christians, who insist on subordinating all ecclesiastical traditions to the teaching of Scripture, cannot accept this. For the hard fact remains that the New Testament never calls Christian leaders 'priests' and never refers to the eucharist as a sacrifice which they offer. The word *hiereus*, a sacrificing priest, occurs many times in the New Testament. There is one reference to a pagan priest,[4] and there are several to the Jewish priests in the Gospels, the Acts and Hebrews. The word is also applied to the Lord Jesus, our great high priest, who offered himself once for all as a sacrifice for sins.[5] And fourthly it denotes Christian believers who are 'priests of God'.[6] This is 'the priesthood of all believers' on which the Reformers laid much emphasis. Collectively we are a royal and holy

[1] Session 22, 1562. [2] *Decree on the Priestly Ministry and Life*, 1965, I.2.
[3] *Ibid.*, p. I.5. [4] Acts 14:13. [5] *E.g.* Heb. 10:12.
[6] Rev. 1:6; 5:10; 20:6.

'priesthood', who offer 'spiritual sacrifices acceptable to God through Jesus Christ'.[1] If we enquire what these sacrifices are, they will all come under the general rubric of the church's worship. In particular, they include our bodies,[2] our prayer, praise and penitence,[3] our gifts and good deeds,[4] our life laid down in God's service,[5] and our evangelism by which we present our converts as 'an offering acceptable to God'.[6] These eight sacrifices are offered to God by the whole church in its capacity as a holy priesthood. But not once is priestly language or imagery used of a particular group of Christian leaders who might correspond to the priests of the old covenant.

When we remember that the levitical priesthood had for centuries been central to Israel's life and worship, and still was in the Palestinian Judaism of Jesus' day, the fact that Christian leaders are never called or likened to priests must have been deliberate. Charles Hodge, the nineteenth-century Princeton theologian, put the matter forcibly:

> Every title of honour is lavished upon them (*sc.* Christian ministers). They are called the bishops of souls, pastors, teachers, rulers, governors, the servants or ministers of God; stewards of the divine mysteries; watchmen, heralds, but never priests. As the sacred writers were Jews, to whom nothing was more familiar than the word priest, whose ministers of religion were constantly so denominated, the fact that they never once used the word, or any of its cognates, in reference to the ministers of the gospel, ... is little less than miraculous. It is one of those cases in which the silence of Scripture speaks volumes.[7]

This being the case, it may at once be asked why in the sixteenth century some Reformed churches retained the word 'priest' as a designation of their ministers, including the Church

[1] 1 Pet. 2:5, 9. [2] Rom. 12:1. [3] Rev. 5:8; Heb. 13:15; Ps. 51:17.
[4] Phil. 4:18; Heb. 13:16. [5] Phil. 2:17; 2 Tim. 4:6. [6] Rom. 15:16.
[7] C. H. Hodge, *Systematic Theology* (Thomas Nelson and Sons/Charles Scribner and Co., 1875), vol. II, p. 467.

of England. The answer is primarily one of etymology. The English word 'priest' was known to be derived from, and a contraction of, 'presbyter'. It therefore translated *presbyteros* ('elder'), not *hiereus* ('priest'). So 'priest' was kept only because its meaning was theologically unexceptionable and because 'presbyter' was not yet a word of common English currency. At the same time, there is evidence that the Reformers would have preferred the unambiguous word 'presbyter', for 'even in matter of nomenclature', wrote Professor Norman Sykes, 'there was considerable agreement' among them.[1] For instance, Calvin complained in the *Institutes* that the Roman bishops by their ordination created 'not presbyters to lead and feed the people, but priests to perform sacrifices'.[2] In England Richard Hooker, answering the Puritans who criticized the retention of 'priest' in the Prayer Book, expressed a plain preference for 'presbyter', since 'in truth the word *presbyter* doth seem more fit, and in propriety of speech more agreeable than *priest* with the drift of the whole gospel of Jesus Christ'.[3] If this was so at the end of the sixteenth century, it is much more so at the end of the twentieth. For today few people know that 'priest' is a contraction of 'presbyter', and even fewer are able to perform the mental gymnastic of saying 'priest' and thinking 'presbyter'. It would therefore be conducive to both theological clarity and biblical faithfulness to drop the word 'priest' altogether from our vocabulary. We could then follow the wisdom of such united churches as those of South India, North India and Pakistan, and refer to the three orders of ordained ministry as 'bishops, presbyters and deacons'.

Not all Protestant leaders are willing to cut the Gordian knot in this manner, however. Some have made valiant attempts in recent years not only to reinstate the word 'priest', but to defend the priestly character of the ordained ministry. Even though they frankly concede that ministers are never called priests in the New Testament, and were not so called until Tertullian

[1] Norman Sykes, *Old Priest, New Presbyter* (CUP, 1956), p. 43.
[2] Calvin, *Institutes*, IV.v.4.
[3] Richard Hooker, *Laws of Ecclesiastical Polity* (1593–97), Book V.lxxviii.3.

about AD 200, they are still not prepared to renounce either the word or the notion.

The most widely acclaimed attempt is found in *Baptism, Eucharist and Ministry*, often referred to as 'the Lima text', and constituting the fruit of fifty years of ecumenical discussion.[1] It sums up 'the chief responsibility of the ordained ministry' as follows: 'to assemble and build up the body of Christ by proclaiming and teaching the Word of God, by celebrating the sacraments, and by guiding the life of the community in its worship, its mission and its caring ministry'.[2] The commentary adds that these tasks are not performed by the ordained ministry 'in an exclusive way' (since all Christian people can share in them) but 'in a representative way'. Not only is there nothing distinctive about these ministries (which might separate clergy from laity) but, we may add, there is nothing necessarily 'priestly' about them either. Nevertheless, the Lima text later affirms that ordained ministers 'may appropriately be called priests because they fulfil a particular priestly service by strengthening and building up the royal and prophetic priesthood of the faithful through word and sacraments, through their prayers and intercession, and through their pastoral guidance of the community'.[3] The commentary adds that priestly terms 'underline the fact that the ordained ministry is related to the priestly reality of Jesus Christ and the whole community', although the ordained ministry's priesthood 'differs in appropriate ways' from Christ's and the community's.

I confess that these statements baffle me. Why should the strengthening of the community's priesthood be *ipso facto* a 'priestly service'? And in what ways does the claimed priesthood of the ordained ministry differ from Christ's and the community's? The text makes no attempt to answer these questions.

In 1986 the Church of England's 'Faith and Order Advisory Group' produced a document entitled *The Priesthood of the*

[1] *Baptism, Eucharist and Ministry*, Faith and Order Paper no. 111 (WCC, 1982).
[2] *Ibid.*, 'Ministry', II.A.13.
[3] *Ibid.*, 'Ministry', II.C.17.

Ordained Ministry. 'There is no dispute', its authors confess, that *hiereus* is used in the New Testament of the priesthood of Christ and the priesthood of the whole people of God and 'never . . . of an appointed Christian minister'.[1] But they do not follow these admissions to their logical conclusion. Instead, they affirm that 'the common priesthood of the community and the special priesthood of the ordained ministry are both derived from the priesthood of Christ'. Nevertheless the latter differs from the former in that the priestly ministry of the ordained 'is an appointed means through which Christ makes his priesthood present and effective to his people'.[2]

This statement prompts me to ask the same kind of questions as before: why should a ministry which makes the priesthood (and sacrifice) of Christ effective to his people be *ipso facto* a priestly ministry? Again, why must a ministry which helps the people of God 'to realise their priestly character' itself be called priestly?[3]

All this muddle, it seems to me, is due to our failure first to define what (according to Scripture) the essence of 'priesthood' is, and secondly to remember that the Old Testament priests were pastors too. They exercised a dual role. On the one hand, as *priests*, they had a *Godward* ministry: 'Every high priest is selected from among men and is appointed to represent them in matters related to God . . .'[4] In this capacity it was their privilege to approach, or draw near to, God,[5] to offer sacrifices,[6]

[1] *The Priesthood of the Ordained Ministry*, para. 44. [2] *Ibid.*, para. 142.

[3] *Ibid.*, para. 143. Other documents germane to this debate are: R. T. Beckwith, *Priesthood and Sacraments, A Study in the Anglican–Methodist Report* (Marsham Manor Press, 1964), ch. 2; George Carey, 'Reflections upon the Nature of Ministry and Priesthood in the Light of the Lima Report' (*Anvil*, vol. 3, no. 1, 1986), and a response to this by David Wright entitled 'Ministry and Priesthood: Further Reflections' (*Anvil*, vol. 3, no. 3, 1986). In dispute among these authors is the thesis developed by R. C. Moberly in his *Ministerial Priesthood* (John Murray, second edition, 1899). He emphasized that ordained ministers are authorized to represent the whole priestly community, and that they therefore exercise a priestly ministry on their behalf. In particular, Moberly argued that, in offering the eucharistic sacrifice, they are offering on earth the same sacrifice that Christ is offering in heaven. But, we respond, Christ's self-offering was finished on the cross. It is therefore not possible for the church to offer on earth what Christ is not offering in heaven.

[4] Heb. 5:1. [5] *E.g.* Ex. 19:22; Lv. 10:3; 16:2. [6] *E.g.* Ex. 30:20; Heb. 8:3–6.

and to make intercession.[1]

On the other hand, as *pastors*, they had a *people-ward* ministry. In this capacity they cared for the people's welfare; they taught them the law;[2] they blessed the people, that is, sought or pronounced God's blessing upon them;[3] and they acted as judges and made decisions.[4]

In New Testament days, since the cross, no more sacrifices for sin can be offered. And the remaining Godward privileges of the priesthood have through the work of Christ been inherited by the whole people of God. We may all draw near to God,[5] and 'have confidence to enter the Most Holy Place by the blood of Jesus'.[6] We are all invited to offer the 'spiritual sacrifices' of our worship.[7] And we are all to pray for one another. None of these ministries now belongs, as they did in Old Testament days, to a privileged caste, to clergy in distinction from laity. One could argue that intercession is a ministry which belongs peculiarly to clergy. Indeed, it seems to have been in this sense that Archbishop Michael Ramsey thought of the ordained ministry as 'priestly'. 'We are called', he said to a group of men on the eve of their ordination, 'near to Jesus and with Jesus and in Jesus, *to be with God with the people on our heart*. That is what you will be promising when I say to you "Will you be diligent in prayers?" You will be promising to be daily with God with the people on your heart.'[8] Although this ministry of intercession may thus be a special responsibility of clergy, however, it cannot be claimed as a distinctively 'priestly' work which is restricted to them.

Something needs also to be said about the prophets in Old Testament days. The priests and the prophets complemented one another in that both ministries were representative, although in opposite directions. The priests represented the people to God, especially in offering sacrifices; the prophets

[1] *E.g.* Ex. 28:9–14, 29–30; Joel 2:17.
[2] *E.g.* Lv. 10:11; Dt. 17:11; 2 Ch. 15:3; 17:8–9; 35:3; Je. 2:8; Mal. 2:1, 4–9.
[3] *E.g.* Lv. 9:22–23; Nu. 6:22–27; Dt. 21:5. [4] *E.g.* Ex. 28:30; Dt. 21:5.
[5] Eph. 2:18; Jas. 4:8. [6] Heb. 10:19.
[7] *E.g.* 1 Pet. 2:5; Rom. 12:1.
[8] A. M. Ramsey, *The Christian Priest Today* (SPCK, 1972), p. 14.

were spokesmen of God to the people, especially in uttering oracles. Is it not of the essence of the new covenant relationship between God and his people, however, that this double mediatorial ministry is now exercised by Jesus Christ alone? Through him we come to God. Through him God speaks to us. He is the only priest through whom we enjoy access to God, and the only prophet through whom we enjoy the knowledge of God. Human mediators are no longer needed.

It is rather the pastoral ministry of the Old Testament priests, their caring responsibility for the spiritual well-being of the people of God, and in particular their teaching role, which have devolved in New Testament days on clergy. In so far as priests were pastors in the Old Testament, I suppose one could call pastors priests in the New Testament. But pastoral duties do not have anything distinctively priestly about them (except perhaps intercession), and in fact, as we have seen, neither Jesus nor his apostles ever referred to pastoral leaders as priests.

They did indicate, however, that God wants his church to have pastors. True, the pastoral responsibilities of caring and teaching belong in some degree to all the people of God, since we are called to 'teach and admonish one another' and to 'carry one another's burdens'.[1] Nevertheless, the plain New Testament assumption is that each church will have a group of elders or leaders, whose main task will be to pastor God's flock, especially by feeding, *i.e.* teaching, them.[2]

The pastoral model

Since 'pastor' means 'shepherd', and the image comes from a rural context alien to today's burgeoning urban communities, it is sometimes suggested that we need to find a more appropriate term for the church's leaders. City flat-dwellers, perched on the ledges of their perpendicular cliffs of glass and concrete, know little about sheep and shepherds. Yet I doubt if we would be prepared to jettison the self-portrait of Jesus Christ as the 'good

[1] *E.g.* Col. 3:16; Gal. 6:2. [2] *E.g.* Acts 14:23; 20:17, 28; 1 Tim. 3:1–2; Tit. 1:5–9.

shepherd' who came to seek and save lost sheep, and laid down his life for us, or to stop singing the popular hymns which embody this imagery, such as 'The Lord's my shepherd, I'll not want' and 'The King of love my shepherd is'.

We are told that Jesus was moved with compassion when he saw the crowds, 'because they were harassed and helpless, like sheep without a shepherd'.[1] Shepherdless sheep must still arouse his distress and concern. Ultimately, he is himself their shepherd. But he delegates some of his responsibility to under-shepherds;[2] 'pastors and teachers' are still among the gifts with which he enriches his church.[3] In fact, all Christian ministry is derived from Christ. His ministry is the prototype. He is the true servant, who came 'not be served but to serve'.[4] And now calls us to follow him in the path of service, and to be the servants of others for his sake.[5]

Moreover, what is true of the servant, is true of the pastor as well. Jesus called himself 'the good shepherd'.[6] Elsewhere in the New Testament he is named 'the Chief Shepherd', 'that great Shepherd of the sheep' and 'the Shepherd and Overseer of your souls'.[7] If, then, pastors are undershepherds, we will be wise to understudy the good, the great, the chief shepherd. For he both taught and exemplified all the main principles of pastoral ministry. It is right that the Gospel appointed for the Anglican ordination service is John 10:1–16, for here he describes what his ministry is, and what ours should be. The good pastor, who models his ministry on the good shepherd, has at least seven characteristics.

First, the good shepherd *knows* his sheep. He 'calls his own sheep by name . . . I am the good shepherd; I know my sheep and my sheep know me – just as the Father knows me and I know the Father'.[8] Of course the ancient oriental shepherd was different in many ways from modern shepherds in other parts of the world. The main difference is due to whether the sheep are kept for wool or for mutton. Because in the West they are

[1] Mt. 9:36. [2] Acts 20:28. [3] Eph. 4:11.
[4] Mk. 10:45. [5] 2 Cor. 4:5. [6] Jn. 10:11, 14.
[7] 1 Pet. 5:4; Heb. 13:20; 1 Pet. 2:25. [8] Jn. 10:3, 14–15.

mostly reared for mutton, they live only a brief life and no personal relationship with the sheep farmer is possible. In Palestine, however, because the sheep were kept for their wool, and were sheared annually, the shepherd had them in his care for many years and a relationship of trust and intimacy developed between them. The shepherd would even know and call each of them by name.

This was certainly the relationship between Jesus and his disciples. He knew his sheep personally. As in the Old Testament Yahweh called Abraham, Moses, Samuel and others by name, so Jesus knew and called people personally. When he saw Nathanael approaching and said of him, 'Here is a true Israelite, in whom there is nothing false', Nathanael asked in astonishment, 'How do you know me?'[1] Jesus went on to call Zacchaeus by name to come down from the sycamore tree in which he was hiding, and after the ascension called Saul of Tarsus by name on the Damascus road.[2] And although at our own conversion we heard no audible voice, we too can say in truth that he called us personally.

Perhaps the first and most basic characteristic of Christ's undershepherds will be the personal relationship which develops between pastor and people. They are not our clients, constituents, patients or customers. Still less are they names on a register or, worse still, numbers on a computer card. Instead, they are individual persons, whom we know and who know us. Moreover, each of them has a 'proper' name, a symbol of his or her unique identity, and genuine pastors struggle to remember their names. Many years ago I had difficulty in recalling the names of two elderly ladies who came to church every Sunday together. Consequently, when greeting them after services, the best I could do was to hail them as 'you two'. It became a joke between us, not least because at that very time considerable publicity was being given to the shooting down by the Soviet Union of the American surveillance plane 'U2'. So when the ladies in question began to sign their letters 'U2', you can

[1] Jn. 1:47–48. [2] Lk. 19:5; Acts 9:4.

imagine my embarrassment. 'Greet the friends ... by name,' John wrote.[1]

What steps can be taken to overcome a bad memory? I have found two devices helpful. First, it is useless to ask people their name before we can recognize their face, for then we have numerous names floating round our mind with no faces to attach them to. In this situation we resemble the well-known Dr W. A. Spooner (of 'Spoonerism' fame), who is reputed to have accosted someone at a party with the words: 'I know your name so well; I just can't think of your face!' Instead, it is wiser to memorize the face first, and then we are ready to discover the correct name to attach to it.

The second way to remember people's names is to write them down and pray for them. When Paul told the Thessalonians, 'We always thank God for all of you, mentioning you in our prayers,'[2] it sounds as if he had some kind of list. It is, without doubt, the regular mentioning of people's names in prayer which – more surely and quickly than by any other means – fixes them in our mind and memory. To forget somebody's name is, as likely as not, a token of our pastoral prayerlessness.

Jesus also indicated that his relationship with his people would be both reciprocal ('I know my sheep and my sheep know me')[3] and intimate ('just as the Father knows me and I know the Father').[4] There was something transparently open and guileless about Jesus. He had nothing to hide. It was a mark of his true friendship, he said, that he made himself known to his disciples.[5] This does not of course mean that pastors have to disclose all their secrets to the congregation, but at least they should be willing for the costly and humbling step of forgoing some of their privacy and of being known to be frail and vulnerable human beings like everybody else.

At the same time it is possible in some cultures to be too forward, and even presumptuous, in exchanging names with people, because our name symbolizes our personal and private

[1] 3 Jn. 14. [2] 1 Thes. 1:2. [3] Jn. 10:14. [4] Jn. 10:15.
[5] *E.g.* Jn. 14:21; 15:15.

identity. Vincent Donovan discovered this when he was working among the Masai in Tanzania. At first, he has written, 'I quite naturally acted out of my American background, and saw nothing wrong in telling them my name and asking theirs.' He was advised, however, that the Masai regarded this as very rude. In public and with strangers they used titles or designations, not names. One day a Masai man said to him: 'Do not throw my name about. My name is important. My name is me. My name is for my friends.'[1] So, when Vincent Donovan moved to a new area, he adopted the custom of not knowing or disclosing each other's names. Then 'after working among them for a long period of time, and, perhaps as a parting gift to me, one of the elders told me his name, and I told him mine. I was flattered at the exchange. "My name is for my friends".'[2] It would be good in the West too, I think, to cultivate something of this respect for persons and their names. To divulge our name and discover another person's is not to be done lightly; for it is to claim an intimacy of relationship which, however, does belong properly to the family of God.

Secondly, the good shepherd *serves* his sheep. 'I am the good shepherd', Jesus said. 'The good shepherd lays down his life for the sheep.'[3] For he is devoted to their welfare, and his whole life is dominated by their needs. God's chief complaint against Israel's leaders was this: 'Woe to the shepherds of Israel who only take care of themselves! Should not shepherds take care of the flock?'[4] Now sheep are not particularly pleasant animals. We cherish a rather romantic picture of woolly, cuddly lambs. But in their natural state sheep have no concern for their cleanliness, and are afflicted by a variety of nasty pests. Hence the need to plunge them several times a year into powerful chemical solutions. They also have a reputation for being stupid. So there is a good deal of dirty and menial work in shepherding; it

[1] Vincent J. Donovan, *Christianity Rediscovered: An Epistle from the Masai* (1978; SCM, 1982), p. 187.
[2] *Ibid.*, p. 188. [3] Jn. 10:11.
[4] Ezk. 34:2. The New Testament equivalent is Jude 12, which speaks of 'shepherds who feed only themselves'. That is, they use their position to minister to their own ego rather than to the people committed to their care.

includes strengthening the weak ones, healing the sick, binding up the injured and bringing back the strays.[1]

Jesus himself laid down his life for his sheep. He was no hired hand or 'hireling', doing his work for money. He genuinely cared for them, even to the extent of dying for them. His great love was revealed in sacrifice and service, sacrificing himself to serve others. Pastors need this sacrificial, serving love in their ministry today. For like sheep human beings can often be 'perverse and foolish' in straying from the path. Some can also be demanding and unappreciative, and we will find it hard to love them. But then we will remember that they are God's flock, purchased with Christ's blood and entrusted by the Holy Spirit to our care.[2] And if the three persons of the Trinity are committed to their welfare, how can we not be also? We need to hear Christ's words to us as Richard Baxter imagined them: 'Did I die for them, and wilt not thou look after them? Were they worth my blood, and are they not worth thy labour? . . . Have I done and suffered so much for their salvation, and was I willing to make thee a co-worker with me, and wilt thou refuse that little that lieth upon thy hands?'[3]

Thirdly, the good shepherd *leads* his sheep. Here is another difference between oriental and occidental shepherds. In the West shepherds seldom if ever lead their sheep; they drive them from behind with the use of trained sheepdogs. Because of the Palestinian shepherd's close relationship with his sheep, however, he is able to walk in front of them, call them, perhaps whistle or play a pipe, and they will follow him. Chua Wee Hian, former General Secretary of the International Fellowship of Evangelical Students, tells us in his book *Learning to Lead* of an Arab guide who was explaining this tradition to some tourists, who then 'spotted a man in the distance driving a small flock of sheep with a rather menacing stick'. Was the guide mistaken, then? 'He immediately stopped the bus and rushed off across the fields. A few minutes later he returned, his face beaming. He announced, "I have just spoken to the man. Ladies

[1] See Ezk. 34:4. [2] Acts 20:28.
[3] Richard Baxter, *The Reformed Pastor* (1656; Epworth, 1939), pp. 121–122.

and gentlemen, he is not the shepherd. He is in fact the butcher!"'[1]

Israel's relationship to Yahweh, and especially their passage across the wilderness, are likened to the movement of sheep following their shepherd: 'Hear us, O Shepherd of Israel, you who lead Joseph like a flock.'[2] The godly individual Israelite thought of Yahweh in the same way: 'the LORD is my shepherd, I shall not be in want . . . he leads me beside quiet waters . . .'.[3] So Jesus, the good shepherd, took over and developed the same picture: 'The sheep listen to his voice. He calls his own sheep by name and leads them out. When he has brought out all his own, he goes on ahead of them, and his sheep follow him because they know his voice.'[4] The reciprocity is clear. If the good shepherd knows his sheep's names, they in their turn come to know his voice. Christian ears are attuned to the voice of Christ. We develop a certain sensitivity to his mind and will. Gradually we come to know instinctively what would please or displease him. And so we follow where he leads and where he calls.

Something similar is true of Christian pastors. It is our solemn responsibility to lead people in such a way that it is safe for them to follow us. That is, we have to set them a consistent and reliable example. We need to remember that Jesus introduced into the world a new style of leadership, namely leadership by service and example, not by force. The apostle Peter grasped this and echoed it in his teaching: 'Be shepherds of God's flock that is under your care, . . . not lording it over those entrusted to you, but being examples to the flock.'[5] As a matter of fact, for good or evil, whether we like it or not, people will follow us. It is frightening to think how undiscerning many sheep are. That is why it is essential to lead well, to set a good example, with no dichotomy between our preaching and our practice, so that we will not lead them astray.

Fourthly, the good shepherd *feeds* his sheep. 'I am the gate,' Jesus said. 'Whoever enters through me will be saved. He will

[1] Chua Wee Hian, *Learning to Lead* (IVP, 1987), p. 35. [2] Ps. 80:1.
[3] Ps. 23:1–2. [4] Jn. 10:3–4. [5] 1 Pet. 5:2–3.

come in and go out, and find pasture.'[1] The chief concern of shepherds is always that their sheep will have enough to eat. Whether they are being kept for wool or for mutton, their health depends on their having nutritious pasture. So Jesus himself as the good shepherd was preeminently a teacher. He fed his disciples with the good food of his instruction.

Pastors today have the same paramount responsibility. The ordained ministry is essentially a ministry of the Word, with the sacraments understood as 'visible words' (as Augustine called them), dramatizing the promises of the gospel. The pastor is primarily a teacher. This is the reason for two qualifications for the presbyterate which are singled out in the Pastoral Epistles. First, the candidate must be 'able to teach'.[2] Secondly, he must 'hold firmly to the trustworthy message as it has been taught, so that he can encourage others by sound doctrine and refute those who oppose it'.[3] These two qualifications go together. Pastors must both be loyal to the apostolic teaching (the *didachē*) and have a gift for teaching it (*didaktikos*). And whether they are teaching a crowd or congregation, a group or an individual (Jesus himself taught in all three contexts), what distinguishes their pastoral work is that it is always a ministry of the Word.

Nothing is more necessary today, either in the tired churches of the West or in the vibrant churches of many Third World countries, than a faithful and systematic exposition of Scripture from the pulpit. 'Do you love me?' Jesus asked Peter. Then 'Feed my sheep'.[4] Too many congregations are sick and even starving for lack of the 'solid food'[5] of the Word of God. Indeed, the ultimate goal of our pastoral ministry is both 'to present everyone perfect (better, 'mature') in Christ'[6] and 'to prepare God's people for works of service (better, 'for their work of ministry')'.[7] It would be hard to imagine a nobler ambition than through our teaching ministry to lead God's people both into maturity and into ministry.

How, then, do shepherds feed their sheep? Strictly speaking,

[1] Jn. 10:9. [2] 1 Tim. 3:2. [3] Tit. 1:9. [4] Jn. 21:17.
[5] 1 Cor. 3:2; Heb. 5:12. [6] Col. 1:28. [7] Eph. 4:12.

they do not feed them at all. To be sure, if a newborn lamb is sickly, the shepherd may take it into his arms and bottle-feed it. But normally the shepherd's way is to lead his sheep into 'good pasture' or 'good grazing land',[1] where they can browse and so feed themselves. It is not, I think, far-fetched to see in this a parable of sound pastoral education. Spoon-feeding and bottle-feeding are for babes in Christ. Only pasture-feeding will lead them into maturity in Christ. As the preacher opens up the Scriptures, he invites people into them, in order that they may feed themselves in this rich pasturage.

Fifthly, the good shepherd *rules* his sheep, accepting that he has a certain authority over them. I am tempted to omit this dimension, but to do so would lack integrity. Bishop Lesslie Newbigin is right in his book *The Good Shepherd* to complain that 'the figure of the good shepherd has been sentimentalized'.[2] In classical Greek the king was known as the 'shepherd' of his people, and the king-shepherd analogy occurs not infrequently in the Old Testament. For example, the people reminded David how God had said to him: 'You shall shepherd my people Israel, and you shall become their ruler.'[3] Further, the Greek verb *poimainō*, meaning 'to shepherd a flock', came to be used of a harsh rule: 'You will rule them (LXX *poimainō*) with an iron sceptre.'[4] And this verse is applied in the Revelation to Jesus' authority over the nations as their judge.[5] Clearly, we have no liberty either to deduce from this that pastors are to be autocratic or to justify the medieval concept of the prince-bishop. No, regal language ('palaces', 'thrones' and 'reigns') are entirely inappropriate in reference to the biblical presbyter-bishop. Nevertheless, alongside the New Testament's emphasis on the humble service of presbyters, there are also allusions to their leadership role, their being 'over' a local church 'in the Lord',[6] and the need to 'obey' them and 'submit to their authority',[7]

[1] Ezk. 34:14.
[2] Lesslie Newbigin, *The Good Shepherd, Meditations on Christian Ministry in Today's World* (Faith Press, 1977), p. 14.
[3] 2 Sa. 5:2. [4] Ps. 2:9. [5] Rev. 2:27; 12:5; 19:15. [6] 1 Thes. 5:12.
[7] Heb. 13:17.

although their authority is to be exercised through their ministry of the Word and their example.[1] And it is plain from several New Testament passages that, if discipline has to be exercised, it will be done through the local congregation collectively, and not through a single pastor.[2]

Sixthly, the good shepherd *guards* his sheep. The sheep's chief enemy in ancient Palestine was the wolf, fierce and predatory, whether hunting singly or in a pack. Sheep were defenceless against them. If the shepherd was merely a hired hand, he would see the wolf coming, and would abandon the sheep and run away, leaving the wolf to attack and scatter the flock.[3] Only a good shepherd would stay and risk his own life in defending and rescuing his sheep.

There is no difficulty in interpreting Jesus' allegory. 'Watch out for false prophets,' he had said in another place. 'They come to you in sheep's clothing, but inwardly they are ferocious wolves.'[4] If the sheep are God's people and the shepherds are their faithful pastors, then the wolves are false teachers and the hired hands unfaithful pastors who do nothing to protect God's people from error. Alas, there are still wolves in Christ's flock today, deceivers who deny some of the fundamentals of the historic Christian faith. True pastors will not behave like hirelings and run away. They will stand up to the wolves. It will be a costly task. For shepherds cannot shoo wolves away by shouting at them or waving their arms about. They have to get to grips with them, as young David did with both a lion and a bear.[5] Similarly, pastors need to accept the pain and the danger of close combat with false teachers. Vague denunciations will not be enough. Instead, we have to study their literature, listen to their teaching, and wrestle with the issues they are raising, in order to counter their arguments effectively in our teaching.

Yet, if this is a risky ministry, it is also a necessary and compassionate one. We should never relish controversy. It can never be more than a distasteful duty. The only reason we

[1] Heb. 13:7. [2] *E.g.* Mt. 18:15–20; 1 Cor. 5:4–5, 13.
[3] Jn. 10:12–13. [4] Mt. 7:15; *cf.* Acts 20:29–30.
[5] 1 Sa. 17:34–35.

engage in it is out of compassion for the sheep. The hireling takes to his heels because he 'cares nothing for the sheep'.[1] It is only because a good shepherd does care, and care deeply, for the welfare of the people he serves, that he will seek grace and courage to stand up to error in the church. Shepherdless sheep are an easy prey to wolves. Must it be said of God's flock today that 'they were scattered because there was no shepherd, and . . . they became food for all the wild animals'?[2] On the contrary, if we care, we will be vigilant and 'keep watch over our flock', like those shepherds in the fields near Bethlehem. True, it is sometimes said that we must always be positive in our teaching, never negative. But this is not so. Jesus himself opposed false teachers. And the duties of the pastor are not only to teach 'sound doctrine' but also to 'refute those who oppose it'.[3] Feeding the sheep and routing the wolves cannot be separated.

In the seventh place, the good shepherd *seeks* his sheep. 'I have other sheep', Jesus said, 'that are not of this sheep pen. I must bring them also. They too will listen to my voice, and there shall be one flock and one shepherd.'[4] It is clear that by these 'other sheep' Jesus was referring to Gentile outsiders. Yet he could also say 'I have' them and 'I must bring them' in. We need the same kind of assurance in our evangelism. Wherever we live and work, we may be sure that some of Christ's 'other sheep' are there, that they already belong to him in the purpose of God, and that he is determined to, he 'must', bring them in.

This outreach to people who are alienated and lost is an essential part of the pastor's ministry, even if it belongs even more to lay church members who live and work among them. It is true that we customarily distinguish between 'evangelists' who seek lost sheep and 'pastors' who nurture those who have been found. Yet their ministries overlap. If Jesus, the good shepherd, not only feeds the sheep in his fold but also seeks those outside it,[5] his undershepherds who understudy him must do the same. In the Anglican ordination service the candidates are exhorted by the bishop 'to seek for Christ's sheep that are dispersed abroad . . .

[1] Jn. 10:13. [2] Ezk. 34:5. [3] Tit. 1:9. [4] Jn. 10:16.
[5] Lk. 19:10; *cf.* 15:3–7.

that they may be saved by Christ for ever'. If we were to evade this responsibility, God would again complain: 'My sheep . . . were scattered over the whole earth, and no-one searched or looked for them.'[1] And Jesus himself would say to us: 'Did I come down from heaven to earth, to seek and to save that which was lost, and wilt thou not go to the next door or street or village to seek them?'[2] On the other hand, if we do go out in order to bring people in, we shall share in the heavenly rejoicing 'over one sinner who repents'.[3]

Here, then, is the beautiful idea of pastoral ministry which Jesus painted. Wherever there are sheep, whether lost or found, there is a need for pastors to seek and to shepherd them. Following the example of the good shepherd himself, human pastors will endeavour to know and serve, to lead, feed and rule the sheep of Christ's flock, to guard them from marauding wolves and to seek them when they have gone astray. And then, however little they may have been recognized, appreciated or honoured on earth, or have wished to be, they will receive from the Chief Shepherd, when he appears, 'the crown of glory that will never fade away'.[4]

The pastoral ideal exemplified in Jesus the good shepherd, which he wanted leaders to copy, needs to be complemented by two other models which he warned them to avoid. First, he said, there are the secular rulers who 'lord it over' and 'exercise authority over' people. 'Not so with you,' he added emphatically. Leadership in his new community was to be entirely different from leadership in the world. 'Instead, whoever wants to become great among you must be your servant.'[5] As T. W. Manson put it, 'in the kingdom of God service is not a stepping-stone to nobility; it *is* nobility, the only kind of nobility that is recognized'.[6]

Secondly, Jesus urged his disciples not to imitate the Pharisees. They loved both places of honour (at banquets and in the synagogues) and titles of honour, for these were signs of the

[1] Ezk. 34:6.
[2] Richard Baxter, *The Reformed Pastor* (1656; Epworth, 1939), pp. 121–122.
[3] Lk. 15:7. [4] 1 Pet. 5:4. [5] Mk. 10:42–45.
[6] T. W. Manson, *The Church's Ministry* (Hodder and Stoughton, 1948), p. 27.

people's obsequious respect. 'Do not do what they do', Jesus said. Christian leaders are not to be called 'Rabbi' (Teacher), 'Father' or 'Master'. That is, we are not to adopt towards any human being in the church, or allow anybody to adopt towards us, an attitude of helpless dependence, as of a child on his or her father, or of slavish obedience, as of a servant to his or her master, or of uncritical acquiescence, as of a pupil to his or her teacher. To do so, Jesus implied, would be both to usurp the prerogatives of the Holy Trinity (God our Father, Jesus our master, and the Holy Spirit our teacher) and to disrupt the brotherly-sisterly relationships of the Christian family.[1]

Here are two different contemporary models of leadership, one secular (rulers) and the other religious (Pharisees), which nevertheless shared the same basic characteristic: a hunger for power and prestige. Today the most likely model presented to us for imitation is that of business management. It too, despite some acceptable parallels, is often more worldly than Christian. We have to beware lest, as the status of pastors in society declines, we seek to compensate for it by demanding greater power and honour in the church. The essential mark of Christian leadership is humility, not authority; servitude, not lordship; and 'the meekness and gentleness of Christ'.[2]

I will give the last word to Chuck Colson, who before his conversion to Christ had himself tasted the intoxicating wine of power: 'The lure of power can separate the most resolute of Christians from the true nature of Christian leadership, which is service to others. It is difficult to stand on a pedestal and wash the feet of those below.'[3] Again, 'nothing distinguishes the kingdoms of man from the kingdom of God more than their diametrically opposed views of the exercise of power. One seeks to control people, the other to serve people; one promotes self, the other prostrates self; one seeks prestige and position, the other lifts up the lowly and despised.'[4]

[1] Mt. 23:1–12. [2] 2 Cor. 10:1; *cf.* 2 Tim. 2:24.
[3] Charles W. Colson, *Kingdoms in Conflict: An Insider's Challenging View of Politics, Power and the Pulpit* (Morrow-Zondervan, 1987), p. 272.
[4] *Ibid.*, p. 274.

PART FIVE

THE WORLD

In Part IV our concern was with the church; in Part V it will be with the world. 'Church' and 'world' are often bracketed and, more often still, are set in antithesis to one another. In any case, it is hard to think of either without simultaneously remembering the other. For, at least in theory, the world is the old and fallen community, while the church is God's new and redeemed society.

How, then, are these two communities related to each other? Several options have been proposed. Some theologians, anxious to minimize the difference between them, go so far as to identify them by applying to all human beings indiscriminately the epithet 'the people of God'. Others reach almost the same goal by a different route. They allow the world to dictate to the church what its views and values should be, until the church conforms to the world, and the two become virtually indistinguishable. A third group is content for the church and the world to live together in amicable co-existence, with neither invading the other's territory or interfering in the other's affairs.

The fourth possible scenario, however, is what Jesus and his apostles envisaged. It is that the church has a God-given responsibility to infiltrate the world, listening indeed to the world's challenges, but also bringing its own challenge to the world by sharing the good news with it in word and deed. The correct term for this task is 'mission'. 'Mission' is precisely what God sends the church into the world to do. We are going to consider four major aspects of it.

First (in chapter 18), we take up the topic of the uniqueness of Jesus Christ, which is arguably the most important and the most urgent issue before the worldwide church today. Can we still apply to Jesus, and to God's claimed revelation and redemption through him, traditional words like 'unique', 'absolute' and 'final'? Or must we surrender to the pressures of 'pluralism' which insists that Jesus was only one of a number of religious leaders, and that every religion has its own independent validity? If Jesus was and is unique in his person and work, then we are under obligation to make him known. If he is not, then the chief foundation of the Christian mission has been undermined, and we will have to give up our ambition to win the world for Christ.

In the following chapter (chapter 19) we will endeavour to lay down the full biblical basis for the Christian mission. This goes beyond the uniqueness of Christ to the nature of God himself. For mission begins in the heart of God. The living God of the biblical revelation is a missionary God. A rapid survey of the whole of Scripture will demonstrate that each of its five sections has an unavoidably missionary emphasis.

In chapter 20, entitled 'Holistic Mission', we will see that the church's communication of the gospel cannot be in words only, but must also be in works. In the church's mission, as in Christ's, good news and good deeds go together.[1] A multiple argument will be developed that evangelism and social responsibility are in God's purpose married; they must not be divorced.

In the last chapter of Part V (chapter 21) we will return to Christ, since nothing is more important in the Christian mission than a clear and fresh vision of him. Under the title 'The Christology of Mission', we will rehearse the five main events in the saving career of Jesus, in such a way as to note that each has a missionary dimension. From them we will learn the model, costliness, mandate, motivation and urgency of the mission to which we are called.

[1] *Cf.* Mt. 5:16.

CHAPTER EIGHTEEN

THE UNIQUENESS OF JESUS CHRIST

A social worker in Nigeria once visited a youth in one of the back streets of Lagos. On his bedside table he found the following books: the Bible, *The Book of Common Prayer*, the Qur'an, three copies of *Watchtower* (the magazine of the Jehovah's Witnesses), a biography of Karl Marx, a book of yoga exercises, and – what the poor fellow evidently needed most – a popular paperback entitled *How to Stop Worrying.*[1]

On Commonwealth Day (May 24) 1966, the first multi-faith service was held in the church of St Martin-in-the-Fields in London. In it Hindus, Buddhists, Muslims and Christians took part on equal terms, making four affirmations of a supposedly common faith, giving four readings from their respective sacred scriptures (the Buddhist *Tripitaka*, the *Bhagavad Gita*, the Qur'an and the Bible), and pronouncing four blessings, in only one of which the name of Jesus was mentioned for the first and last time. The secular press was enthusiastic, hailing it as 'a significant milestone in religious history'. But the Christian newspapers described it as 'a betrayal of the Christian faith'. It is doubtful if they would write anything similar today, for multi-faith services are regularly held.

These two incidents, the one in Lagos and the other in London, are examples of the spirit of syncretism. Dr W. A. Visser't Hooft, the first General Secretary of the World Council of Churches, has defined syncretism as the view 'that there is no unique revelation in history, that there are many different ways

[1] The story is told by Douglas Webster in *Not Ashamed* (Hodder and Stoughton, 1970), p. 66.

to reach the divine reality, that all formulations of religious truth or experience are by their very nature inadequate expressions of that truth, and that it is necessary to harmonize as much as possible all religious ideas and experiences so as to create one universal religion for mankind'.[1] Dr Visser't Hooft was outspoken in his rejection of this outlook. 'It is high time that Christians should rediscover', he went on, 'that the very heart of their faith is that Jesus Christ did not come to make a contribution to the religious storehouse of mankind, but that in him God reconciled the world unto himself . . .'.[2]

The debate has moved on since the 1960s, however. Today the main challenge to the traditional understanding of the uniqueness of Christ is not 'syncretism', but 'pluralism', not the attempt to fuse the world's religions into a single, universal faith, but the recognition of the integrity of each in all its diverse particularities.

The options before us are now usually summarized as 'exclusivism', 'inclusivism' and 'pluralism'.[3]

'Exclusivism' (an unfortunately negative term, which gives the impression of wanting to exclude people from the kingdom of God) is used to denote the historic Christian view that salvation cannot be found in other religions, but only in Jesus Christ.

'Inclusivism' allows that salvation is possible to adherents of other faiths, but attributes it to the secret and often unrecognized work of Christ. Vatican II embraced this view in its statement

[1] W. A. Visser't Hooft, *No Other Name* (SCM, 1963), p. 11. [2] *Ibid.*, p. 95.

[3] These categories were first employed by Alan Race in *Christians and Religious Pluralism* (Orbis, 1982), were popularized by the Church of England General Synod's Board for Mission and Unity in their report *Towards a Theology for Inter-Faith Dialogue* (Anglican Consultative Council, 1984, second edition, 1986), and were further developed by Paul F. Knitter in *No Other Name?* (SCM, 1985), while the implications of 'pluralism' were explored in *The Myth of Christian Uniqueness*, ed. John Hick and Paul F. Knitter (SCM, 1987). A judicious critique by Dr Christopher Wright of *Towards a Theology for Inter-Faith Dialogue* appeared in *Anvil* (vol. I, no. 3, 1984), and this material has now been incorporated in his booklet *What's so Unique about Jesus?* (MARC, 1990). Then, in 1991 (too late to be considered in this book), there appeared a vigorous riposte to *The Myth of Christian Uniqueness* entitled *Christian Uniqueness Reconsidered: The Myth of a Pluralist Theology of Religions*, ed. Gavin D'Costa (Fowler Wright). It is another symposium, and includes contributions by such leading contemporary theologians as Jürgen Moltmann, Lesslie Newbigin, Wolfhart Pannenberg, Rowan Williams and M. M. Thomas.

that Christ's saving work holds good 'not only for Christians, but for all men of good will in whose hearts grace works in an unseen way'.[1]

'Pluralism' goes further still, for its advocates reject exclusivism as 'presumptuous' and 'arrogant', and inclusivism as 'patronizing' or 'condescending'. Whereas 'plurality' expresses the simple fact that there are many religions, 'pluralism' affirms their independent validity. It renounces every claim that Christianity is 'absolute', 'unique', 'definitive', 'final', 'normative', and 'ultimate' or 'universal'. 'Unlimited growth is cancer, and so would be an ever growing single Christian religion all over the world.'[2] Instead, Christianity must be viewed as only one religion among many, and Jesus as only one saviour among others. This is the so-called 'deeper and larger ecumenism that embraces the whole of humanity', of which the rainbow remains 'a timeless symbol'.[3]

Arguments for pluralism

What is it about 'pluralism' that many find attractive? We shall not be in a position to respond to them until we have listened to them and struggled to understand and feel the appeal of their arguments.

First, there is *the new global consciousness*. Threats to the natural environment, fears of a nuclear conflict and the continuing situation of economic injustice between the North and the South are stimulating people to develop a planetary perspective. The very survival of the human race seems to depend on our learning to live together in harmony and to cooperate for the common good. Whatever divides us, therefore, including our religions, is understandably regarded with increasing disfavour.

In response, Christians should indeed be in the forefront of

[1] *Gaudium et Spes*, para. 22.
[2] This is one possible position described by Raimundo Panikkar in his contribution to *The Myth of Christian Uniqueness*, p. 91.
[3] Stanley J. Samartha in *The Myth of Christian Uniqueness*, pp. 79–80.

those who are seeking global harmony. By God's creation we are one people in the world. We should be committed to international peace-making, participatory democracy, human rights, community relations, environmental responsibility and the search for a new international economic order. Moreover, people of different races and religions can, should and do cooperate in these kinds of social witness and action. In order to do so, however, it is not necessary to renounce our belief in the uniqueness of Jesus Christ. It would be folly to seek unity at the expense of truth, or reconciliation without Christ the mediator. Besides, Christ unavoidably divides people as well as uniting them. He said he had come not 'to bring peace, but a sword'.[1] He envisaged that some conflict would continue, as people ranged themselves for or against him.

Secondly, there is *the new appreciation of other religions*. Modern communications (especially television and travel) have caused the world to shrink. People of strange beliefs and customs, who hitherto have been very remote from us, now live next door to us, and actually enter our homes – on the screen if not in person. This is 'a newly experienced reality for many today'.[2] The sacred books of other faiths, translated into our languages, are now readily available to us. And as we become better acquainted with the world's religions, what Professor John Hick has called their 'immense spiritual riches' have 'tended to erode the plausibility of the old Christian exclusivism'.[3] Further, some ancient faiths are showing signs of resurgence, just when it is being perceived that Christianity, declining in the West, 'has not succeeded in breaking the power of the great historical religions'.[4]

We should welcome today's more thorough knowledge of world faiths, not least through the comparative study of religions in schools. But if we discover 'riches' in other religions, we also discern more clearly the absolute uniqueness of Jesus Christ, as we will see later. 'To make exclusive claims for our

[1] Mt. 10:34. [2] Paul F. Knitter, *No Other Name?* (SCM, 1985), p. 2.
[3] *The Myth of Christian Uniqueness*, p. 17.
[4] Rosemary Radford Ruether in *The Myth of Christian Uniqueness*, p. 139.

particular tradition', writes Stanley Samartha, 'is not the best way to love our neighbours as ourselves.'[1] But on the contrary, it is the very best and highest way to express neighbour-love, if the gospel is true. If it is, we cannot claim to love our neighbours if we leave them in ignorance of Christ. As for the vitality of other religions, and the comparative failure of Christianity, these things should lead us not to the conclusion that the gospel is untrue, but rather to self-examination, repentance, amendment of life, and the adoption of better ways of sharing the good news with others.

Thirdly, there is *the new post-colonial modesty*. For four centuries the West dominated the world in political, military, economic and scientific terms, and took for granted its moral and spiritual superiority as well. Indeed, Christianity's 'attitude to other religions has been shaped by the colonial mentality'.[2] The end of the Second World War, however, heralded the end of the colonial era. As the West underwent a profound cultural shift 'from a position of clear superiority to one of rough parity', a parallel shift took place in theological consciousness. 'This dramatic situation has forced . . . a new understanding of the interrelationships of religions, a new balance of spiritual power, so to speak, on all', Professor Langdon Gilkey has written. It has pushed us all out of 'superiority' into 'parity'.[3] To continue, therefore, to claim Christian universality, it is said, is to lapse into the old imperialist mindset.

It is certainly embarrassing for us in the West to have to acknowledge that during those centuries of colonial expansion, territorial and spiritual conquest, politics and religion, gun and Bible, the flag and the cross, went hand in hand, and that representatives of the imperial power often developed attitudes of proud superiority towards those they ruled. But 'superiority' is a slippery word. It can describe an air of intolerable conceit, and we need to repent of every vestige of this. But the Christian missionary enterprise, in seeking to win to Christ adherents of other religions, is not in itself a mark of arrogance; it indicates

[1] *Ibid.*, p. 76. [2] Tom F. Driver in *The Myth of Christian Uniqueness*, p. 207.
[3] *The Myth of Christian Uniqueness*, pp. 39–40.

rather a profound and humble conviction that the gospel *is* superior to other faiths because it is God's revealed truth.

The attraction of pluralism is more, however, than a concern for global harmony, an appreciation of other religions and a desire for post-colonial modesty. It has even deeper roots, which the twelve contributors to *The Myth of Christian Uniqueness* have examined. These scholars describe themselves as having 'crossed a theological Rubicon', not only from exclusivism to inclusivism, but from inclusivism to pluralism,[1] and they tell us about the three 'bridges' which have led them to make the crossing.

The first they call the *historico-cultural* bridge, or *relativity*. Since people began to apply Einstein's general theory of relativity beyond physics to other spheres (including religion), nothing absolute has seemed to remain. A historical and comparative study of religions, argues Professor Gordon Kaufman, suggests that they are simply 'creations of the human imagination',[2] each from its particular cultural perspective. This being so, Christian theology must give up any claim to absolute or final truth, and understand itself instead as 'a human imaginative response to the necessity to find orientation for life in a particular historical situation'.[3] Professor Tom Driver goes further, declaring that 'even Scripture ... is the creation of us human beings'.[4]

Now of course we also affirm that the Bible is a culturally conditioned book, in the sense that each of its authors belonged to, and spoke within, his own particular culture. But is this emphasis on the human, historical and cultural background of the Bible a complete account of its nature? No. As we considered in chapter 10, there are good reasons for believing in the dual authorship of Scripture, namely that behind the human authors stood the divine author, who spoke his Word through their words, and that his Word transcends both history and culture. It may be that other religions could be described (whatever their claims may be) as 'products of the

[1] *Ibid.*, p. viii. [2] *Ibid.*, p. 8. [3] *Ibid.*, pp. 12–13. [4] *Ibid.*, p. 211.

human imagination'. But the historic Christian belief and claim are that the gospel is the product of divine revelation, although mediated through the minds and mouths of the human authors.

The second 'bridge' across the 'theological Rubicon' is designated *theologico-mystical*, or *mystery*. That is, there is in every religion some sense of the Transcendent or experience of God who, being himself infinite and ineffable, always remains beyond our apprehensions of him. Our theologies are only 'conceptual images of God', and 'like other images, each may be less or more worthy of its Subject', writes Professor Wilfred Cantwell Smith. There is, in principle, he goes on, 'no fundamental difference ... between a doctrine and a statue'. The former is an intellectual image of God, the latter a visual. 'It is wrong for our intellects to absolutize their own handiwork.' For 'both theology and art proffer relative apprehensions of the Absolute'; to absolutize our image of God is idolatry.[1] He goes further: 'For Christians to think that Christianity is true, or final, or salvific, is a form of idolatry. For Christians to imagine that God has constructed Christianity ..., rather than that He/She/It has inspired us to construct it ... that is idolatry.'[2] Or, as Tom Driver sums it up, 'idolatry is the insistence that there is only one way, one norm, one truth'.[3]

In response, we certainly agree that God is the Transcendent Reality beyond all possible human imagination, apprehension or description. Words cannot capture, let alone contain, him. Because he is infinite, we shall never come to the end of him, but spend eternity exploring and worshipping his fathomless being. Nevertheless, to say that he remains a mystery is not incompatible with affirming that he has revealed himself. Moreover, his Word incarnate in Jesus and his Word written in Scripture have a normative position for all Christian believers. It is somewhat extraordinary that the *Myth* contributors regard all Christians of all churches for two millennia, who have believed in the uniqueness of Jesus, as idolaters! If they are referring to

[1] *Ibid.*, pp. 56–57. [2] *Ibid.*, p. 59. [3] *Ibid.*, p. 216.

'Christianity' as a human construct, then perhaps to absolutize it could become an idolatry. To acknowledge the finality and absoluteness of Christ himself, however, is not idolatry but authentic worship.

Thirdly, there is the *ethico-practical* bridge, or *justice*. The four contributors to Part III of *The Myth of Christian Uniqueness* are outraged by the sufferings of the oppressed and united in their commitment to social justice. Borrowing a number of concepts from liberation theology, Professor Paul Knitter writes that 'a preferential option for the poor and the non-person constitutes the necessity and the primary purpose of inter-religious dialogue'. In other words, pluralism is not an end in itself, but a means to the end of liberating the oppressed. For this is too big a task for any one religion to accomplish, which is why 'a worldwide liberation movement needs a worldwide inter-religious dialogue'.[1] The *Myth* contributors also believe that the only possible criterion by which to judge or 'grade' religions must be neither doctrinal nor mystical, but ethical, namely their effectiveness in promoting human well-being.

We must agree that contemporary issues of social justice should be of enormous concern to all Christian people, since we acknowledge the dignity of human beings as persons made in God's image. We should therefore be ashamed that evangelical Christians during this century have tended to be in the rearguard, instead of in the vanguard, of social reformers. We have no quarrel with the proposal to assess religions, including Christianity, according to their social record, since we claim that the gospel is the power of God to transform both individuals and communities. It is because we have both experienced this power in our own lives and seen it at work constructively in human history that we cannot agree with Professor Hick's very negative assessment of the Christian social record as 'a complex mixture of valuable and harmful elements', neither better nor worse than that of other religions.[2]

[1] *Ibid.*, p. 180. [2] *Ibid.*, pp. 23–30.

In sum, our response to the six reasons why some find pluralism attractive is in each case fundamentally the same. They beg the question of truth; we want to press the question of truth. Has God fully and finally revealed himself in Christ, and in the total biblical testimony to Christ, or not?

(1) We agree with the search for global harmony, but not at the expense of truth.

(2) We agree that a greater knowledge of other religions is enriching, but in comparing them we cannot surrender Christ's claim to be the truth.

(3) We agree that colonial attitudes of superiority are arrogant, but still insist that truth is superior to falsehood.

(4) We agree that Scripture is culture-conditioned, but affirm that through it God has spoken his Word of truth.

(5) We agree that the ultimate mystery of God is beyond human apprehension, but affirm that God has truly revealed himself in Christ.

(6) We agree that it is an essential part of our Christian calling to serve the poor, but we are also called to bear witness to the truth.

According to Professor Rosemary Radford Ruether, 'the idea that Christianity, or even the biblical faiths, have a monopoly on religious truth is an outrageous and absurd religious chauvinism'.[1] If by 'monopoly' she means either that other religions possess no truth, or that Christians keep God's revelation to themselves and do not share it, we could perhaps agree with her strident words. But if by 'monopoly' she is referring to the belief that God has revealed himself fully and finally in Christ, then this is neither outrageous nor absurd, but on the contrary humble, wise, sober and considered Christian faith.

It would indeed be arrogant, even 'outrageous', if we were claiming uniqueness or finality for our own fallible opinions and limited experiences. But we are not. As Bishop Lesslie Newbigin put it in his sermon at the fiftieth anniversary of the Tambaram Missionary Conference in 1988:

[1] *Ibid.*, p. 141.

If, in fact, it is true that almighty God, creator and sustainer of all that exists in heaven and on earth, has – at a known time and place in human history – so humbled himself as to become part of our sinful humanity, and to suffer and die a shameful death to take away our sin, and to rise from the dead as the first-fruit of a new creation, if this is a fact, then to affirm it is not arrogance. To remain quiet about it is treason to our fellow human beings. If it is really true, as it is, that 'the Son of God loved me and gave himself up for me', how can I agree that this amazing act of matchless grace should merely become part of a syllabus for the 'comparative study of religions'?[1]

The uniqueness of Jesus Christ

It is essential at the outset to clarify that Christians claim uniqueness and finality only for Christ and not for Christianity in any of its many institutional or cultural forms. I call three witnesses to endorse this statement, who come respectively from Africa, Asia and Europe. First, Professor John Mbiti of Kenya has written: 'The uniqueness of Christianity is in Jesus Christ.'[2] My Asian witness is Sadhu Sundar Singh, the Indian Christian mystic and evangelist. Brought up in a Sikh home, he was converted to Christ as a teenager, and later became a *sadhu*, an itinerant holy man. Visiting a Hindu college one day, he was asked by an agnostic professor of comparative religion what he had found in Christianity which he had not found in his old religion. 'I have Christ,' he replied. 'Yes, I know,' said the professor a little impatiently. 'But what particular principle or doctrine have you found that you did not have before?' 'The particular thing I have found', he replied, 'is Christ.'[3]

The European witness I call is that widely travelled Anglican scholar, the late Bishop Stephen Neill. He strongly emphasized

[1] The full text of his sermon appears in the *International Review of Mission*, July 1988, pp. 325–331.
[2] John Mbiti, *African Religions and Philosophy* (Heinemann, 1969), p. 277.
[3] Stanley Jones, *The Christ of the Indian Road* (1925; Hodder and Stoughton, 1926), p. 64.

the centrality of Christ in the debate with pluralism. In his fine book *Christian Faith and Other Faiths*,[1] which was replaced by *Crises of Belief*, he wrote: 'The old saying "Christianity is Christ" is almost exactly true. The historical figure of Jesus of Nazareth is the criterion by which every Christian affirmation has to be judged, and in the light of which it stands or falls.'[2] Then, as he approached the end of his wide-ranging, sensitive response to Judaism, Islam, Hinduism, Buddhism, primal religion and secularism, in which he faced the critics of Christianity honestly, he asked:

> Have our interlocutors ever really looked at Jesus Christ and tried to see him as he is? For, if we take the Gospels seriously . . ., Jesus is not in the least like anyone else who has ever lived. The things that he says about God are not the same as the sayings of any other religious teacher. The claims that he makes for himself are not the same as those that have been made on behalf of any other religious teacher. His criticisms of human life and society are far more devastating than those that any other man has ever made. The demands he made on his followers are more searching than those put forward by any other religious teacher.[3]

Our claim, then, is not just that Jesus was one of the great spiritual leaders of the world. It would be hopelessly incongruous to refer to him as 'Jesus the Great', comparable to Alexander the Great, Charles the Great or Napoleon the Great. Jesus is not 'the Great'; he is the only.[4] He has no peers, no rivals and no successors.

So how did the early Christians think of him? They gave him many names and titles. Often he is plain 'Jesus' or 'Christ', or, when his human name and messianic title are combined, 'Jesus (the) Christ'. Often again 'the Lord' is added, whether 'the Lord

[1] (OUP, 1961).
[2] Stephen C. Neill, *Crises of Belief* (Hodder and Stoughton, 1984), published in the States as *Christian Faith and Other Faiths* (IVP USA, 1984), p. 23.
[3] *Ibid.*, p. 286.
[4] See P. Carnegie Simpson, *The Fact of Christ* (1930; James Clarke, 1952), pp. 19–22.

Jesus' or 'the Lord Christ' or 'the Lord Jesus Christ'. But when his title is spelled out in full, he is 'our Lord and Saviour Jesus Christ'. It comes, for example, at the conclusion of Peter's second Letter: 'But grow in the grace and knowledge of our Lord and Saviour Jesus Christ.'[1]

Within this complete designation three distinct affirmations are implied, namely that Jesus is Lord, Jesus is Saviour, and Jesus is ours. All three declare him to be unique.

Jesus is Lord

We have already considered in chapter 5 that *Kyrios Jēsous* ('Lord Jesus') was the earliest of all Christian creeds. It is assuredly a witness to the incarnation, since it is an affirmation of the identity of the human Jesus and the divine Lord. The word *kyrios* was used with a wide variety of meanings. On the one hand, it could be used simply as a courtesy title ('Sir') or to designate the owner of any kind of property. On the other hand, it was used throughout the classical Greek period in reference to the gods, who were thereby acknowledged as having authority over nature and history. It then came to be used of human rulers, especially the emperor (*Kyrios Kaisar*), and it was the regular paraphrase used for Yahweh by the scholars who put the Hebrew Bible into Greek. That it came to be used in the New Testament of the risen Christ,[2] with the implication that his followers were his slaves committed to worship and obey him, is a clear indication that they acknowledged his deity. It is all the more remarkable that his first Jewish disciples used this epithet, because they were as fiercely monotheistic as any Muslim is today. They recited the *Shema* daily, confessing that 'the LORD our God, the LORD is one'.[3] Yet in spite of this, they boldly called Jesus Lord, and worshipped him as God.

There is nothing like this in any other religion. The Jews still reject the deity of Jesus, of course. So do Muslims. Misunderstanding the incarnation in grossly physical terms, Muhammad

[1] 2 Pet. 3:18. [2] *E.g.* Acts 2:36; Rom. 10:9; *cf.* Mt. 28:18. [3] Dt. 6:4.

wrote in the Qur'an: 'Allah forbid that he himself should beget a son.'[1]

Early or classical Buddhism had no god and no worship. Divine status and honour were not accorded to the Buddha until some 500 years after his death. We cannot therefore accept the parallel Professor Hick makes when he writes: 'Buddhology and Christology developed in comparable ways.'[2] That is, each 'came to be thought of' as an incarnation, as a result of the religious devotion of his followers. The comparison is inept, however, for Jesus' own contemporaries called him 'Lord', while half a millennium passed before the Buddha was worshipped as God.

Hinduism, it is true, claims a number of *avatars* or divine 'descents', in which the god Vishnu is said to have appeared in Rama, Krishna and others. In the *Bhagavad Gita* Krishna tells Arjuna that he frequently takes human form: 'I have been born many times, Arjuna . . . Although I am unborn, everlasting, and I am the Lord of all, I come to my realm of nature and through my wondrous power I am born.'[3] Perhaps even more striking was the claim of Ramakrishna, the nineteenth-century Hindu reformer, who spoke of himself as 'the same soul that had been born before as Rama, as Krishna, as Jesus, or as Buddha, born again as Ramakrishna'.[4]

But 'incarnation' is not an apt or accurate rendering of the Sanskrit word *avatar*; it tends to conceal the two fundamental differences between the Hindu and the Christian claims. First, there is the question of *historicity*. Vishnu's *avatars* belong to Hindu mythology. Hinduism is a philosophical, mystical and ethical religion, and it is of no importance to Hindus whether the *avatars* actually happened or not. Christianity, however, is essentially a historical religion, based on the claim that the incarnation of God in Jesus Christ was an event of history which took place in Palestine when Augustus was emperor of

[1] Chapter on Mary, in *The Koran*, translated by N. J. Dawood (Penguin, 1968), p. 34.
[2] John Hick (ed.), *The Myth of God Incarnate* (SCM, 1977), p. 169.
[3] Translated by Juan Mascaro, *Bhagavad Gita* (Penguin, 1962), pp. 61–62.
[4] Quoted by W. A. Visser't Hooft, *No Other Name* (SCM, 1963), pp. 36–37.

Rome. If its historicity could be disproved, Christianity would be destroyed.

The second difference lies in the *plurality* of the *avatars*. Krishna spoke of his multiple, even 'frequent', rebirths. But 'incarnation' and 'reincarnation' are two fundamentally different concepts. The *avatars* were temporary manifestations or embodiments of Vishnu in human beings. But none involved the actual assumption of humanity by divinity or is in any way central to Hinduism. The Christian claim, by contrast, is that in Jesus of Nazareth God took human nature to himself once and for all and for ever; that his incarnation in Jesus was decisive, permanent and unrepeatable, the turning-point of human history and the beginning of the new age; and that reigning at God's right hand today is precisely 'the man Christ Jesus', still human as well as divine, although now his humanity has been glorified. Having assumed our nature, he has never discarded it, and he never will.

So the first aspect of the uniqueness of Jesus is that he is Lord. He is God's eternal, personal 'Word' or 'Son' who became a human being. Consequently, 'in Christ all the fulness of the Deity lives in bodily form'.[1] He is the sovereign ruler of the universe and of the church. It is true that he exercises his rule through humble love, for the Lord became the servant and washed his disciples' feet. Yet our place is on our faces at *his* feet.

Jesus is Saviour

The second affirmation contained within the full title of Jesus is that he is Saviour. Indeed, the divine Lord is the divine Saviour. And, although the vocabulary of salvation is distasteful to many people today, we cannot possibly give it up. For Christianity is in essence a rescue religion; it announces good news of salvation. As the churches have recited for centuries in the Nicene Creed, 'for us men (human beings) and for our salvation he came down from heaven . . .'.

Now 'salvation' is a comprehensive word, embracing the

[1] Col. 2:9.

totality of God's redeeming purpose for his alienated creatures. In a word, as we saw in chapter 2, salvation is freedom, with corresponding negative and positive aspects. It includes freedom from the just judgment of God on our sins, from our guilt and our guilty conscience, into a new relationship with him in which we become his reconciled, forgiven children and we know him as our Father. It is freedom from the bitter bondage of meaninglessness into a new sense of purpose in God's new society of love, in which the last are first, the poor rich and the meek heirs. It is freedom from the dark prison of our own self-centredness into a new life of self-fulfilment through self-forgetful service. And one day it will include freedom from the futility of pain, decay, death and dissolution into a new world of immortality, beauty and unimaginable joy. All this – and more! – is 'salvation'.

It was to secure these great blessings that Jesus Christ came into the world, died on the cross, and rose again. It is he not we who took the initiative: 'the Son of Man came to seek and to save what was lost.'[1] He likened himself to a shepherd who left the rest of his sheep on their own in order to go after the one which was lost. Far from abandoning it, in the hope that it might bleat and stumble its way home, he risked his own life to search it out.[2] In fact, 'the good shepherd' did lay down his life for his sheep.[3] Deliberately and voluntarily Jesus went to the cross, in order to identify himself with us. God in Christ took our place, bore our sins, assumed our guilt, paid our penalty, died our death, in order that we might be forgiven and re-created. And then he was raised from death in a supernatural event, in order to reverse the human verdict upon him and to vindicate his divine-human person and saving work.

This too is unique. It is not only in his incarnation, but also in his atoning death and historical resurrection, that his uniqueness is to be seen. The whole concept of a gracious God, who refused either to condone our sins or to visit them upon us, who instead took the initiative to rescue us, who gave himself to

[1] Lk. 19:10. [2] Lk. 15:1–7. [3] Jn. 10:11, 15.

the shame and pain of death on the cross, and who broke the power of death in his resurrection, has no parallel in other faiths. 'If any other religion has anything in the least like the doctrines of incarnation and atonement . . .', wrote Bishop Stephen Neill, 'I have yet to find it.'[1] But it cannot be found. Emil Brunner was right to refer to 'the self-confident optimism of all non-Christian religion', teaching various forms of self-salvation, whereas in the gospel the whole emphasis is on the gracious 'self-movement' of God towards sinners and on self-despair as 'the ante-chamber of faith'.[2]

Buddhism sees the human predicament in suffering rather than sin, and in the 'desire' which it sees as the root of suffering. Deliverance comes only through the abolition of desire by self-effort. There is no God and no Saviour. 'Strive without ceasing' were the Buddha's last words to his disciples before he died.

Philosophical Hinduism locates our problem in *maya*, usually understood as the 'illusion' of our space-time experience. Popular Hinduism, on the other hand, teaches the inflexible doctrine of *karma*, retribution through reincarnation. Each person must eat the fruit of his own wrong-doings, in future lives if not in this one. From this endless cycle (*samsara*) of rebirths or reincarnations there is no escape by forgiveness, but only by that final release called Nirvana, involving the extinction of individual being and absorption into impersonal divine reality (Brahman).

Judaism continues, of course, to teach the possibility of forgiveness to the penitent, which the Old Testament promised, but denies both that Jesus is the Messiah and that his sin-bearing death is the only ground on which God can forgive. That painstaking and honest Jewish scholar, C. G. Montefiore, saw the 'greatness and originality' of Jesus in his new attitude to sinners. Instead of avoiding them, he actively sought them out. The rabbis had said that God receives sinners who return

[1] From an article in the *Church of England Newspaper* on 28 May 1976.
[2] Emil Brunner, *The Mediator* (1927; ET Westminster, 1947), pp. 291–299.

to him; they had not spoken of a divine love which makes the first move to seek and to save them:

> This direct search for, and appeal to, the sinner, are new and moving notes of high import and significance. The good shepherd who searches for the lost sheep, and reclaims it and rejoices over it, is a new figure . . .[1]

Islam clearly proclaims the mercy of God. Each of the 114 *suras* (chapters) of the Qur'an is introduced by the words 'In the Name of Allah, the Compassionate, the Merciful'. But it discloses no costly historical display of his mercy. And when we probe into its exercise, we find that Allah is merciful to the meritorious, to those who pray, and give alms, and fast in Ramadan. There is no message for sinners who deserve judgment, except that they will receive the judgment they deserve.

> Moreover, that which we ask the Muslim to look for in Jesus is in itself a cause of grave offence to Muslim pride. We suggest – we cannot do otherwise – that he find a Saviour. The Muslim affirms that he has no need of any such thing.[2]

There can be no doubt that the chief difference between Christianity and the world's religions, and the chief stumbling-block which they find in it, is the cross. It humbles all pride and dashes all hopes of self-salvation. It also speaks of the uncalculating generosity of the love of God in providing this way of salvation. It was here that Toyohiko Kagawa (died 1960), the Japanese Christian leader, found Christianity's uniqueness:

> I am grateful for Shinto, for Buddhism, and for Confucianism. I owe much to these faiths . . . Yet these three faiths utterly failed to minister to my heart's deepest needs. I was a

[1] C. G. Montefiore, *The Synoptic Gospels* (Macmillan, second edition, 1927), vol. I, pp. cxviii, 55; vol. II, pp. 520–521.
[2] S. C. Neill, *Crises of Belief/Christian Faith and Other Faiths*, p. 87.

pilgrim journeying upon a long road that had no turning. I was weary. I was footsore. I wandered through a dark and dismal world where tragedies were thick ... Buddhism teaches great compassion . . ., but since the beginning of time, who has declared, 'this is my blood of the covenant which is poured out for many unto remission of sins'?[1]

Jesus is ours

Jesus Christ's full title is not 'the Lord and Saviour' but '*our* Lord and Saviour'. We must not miss this personal possessive adjective. It is a small word, but a highly significant one. It indicates that there is a third affirmation hidden in his title, namely *Jesus is ours*.

Already in the Old Testament the possessive adjective 'my' regularly expressed the personal relationship which God's covenant people enjoyed with him, especially when they addressed him in prayer, as in the Psalms. For example, 'O LORD, my Rock and my Redeemer,' 'The LORD is my shepherd,' 'The LORD is my light and my salvation, ... the stronghold of my life,' 'He alone is my rock and my salvation; he is my fortress,' and 'O God, you are my God, earnestly I seek you.'[2]

In the New Testament what is claimed is a comparable personal relationship with Jesus Christ. Both Paul and Peter give us notable examples. Here is Paul: 'I consider everything a loss compared to the surpassing greatness of knowing Christ Jesus my Lord.'[3] As for Peter, he claims this intimate relationship not for himself alone, but for his readers too: 'Though you have not seen him (*sc.* Christ), you love him; and even though you do not see him now, you believe in him and are filled with an inexpressible and glorious joy.'[4]

Here are assertions that Christ is our contemporary. The Jesus who was born into our world, and who lived and died in

[1] T. Kagawa, *Christ and Japan* (SCM, 1934), pp. 108, 113.
[2] Pss. 19:14; 23:1; 27:1; 62:2; 63:1.
[3] Phil. 3:8. [4] 1 Pet. 1:8.

first-century Palestine, also rose from the dead, is now alive for ever, and is available and accessible to his people. Jesus Christ is not to be relegated, like other religious leaders, to history and the history books. He is not dead and gone, finished or fossilized. He is alive and active. He calls us to follow him, and he offers himself to us as our indwelling and transforming Saviour.

Often this is explained in the New Testament as meaning that his availability to us is through the Holy Spirit, who is his Spirit.[1] Paul indicates this when he prays for the Ephesians, that 'he (*sc.* the Father) may strengthen you with power through his Spirit in your inner being, so that Christ may dwell in your hearts through faith'.[2] Indeed, the Christian faith is essentially trinitarian. We come to the Father through the Son and by the Spirit,[3] and the Father comes to us through the Son by the Spirit.[4]

Once again this is unique. There is nothing comparable to it in the other religions. The Buddhist does not claim to know the Buddha, nor the Confucianist Confucius, nor the Muslim Muhammad, nor the Marxist Karl Marx. Each reveres the founder of his religion or ideology as a teacher of the past. To Christians too Jesus is a teacher, but even more he is our living Lord and Saviour. Phrases claiming this 'recur on page after page of the New Testament, and make clear that it is this intimate and personal relationship of trust, devotion and communion, which is the very heart of the Christian faith'.[5]

Lord Coggan, when Archbishop of Canterbury, drew attention to this when referring to the 164 occurrences of Paul's favourite formula, 'in Christ':

> It is a strange phrase. We can scarcely find a parallel use to it in ordinary life. If, let us say, an intimate friend of Churchill who had spent many years with him and then had given a decade to the writing of his life were talking to us about that great man, he might sum up his relationship to him in a wide

[1] *E.g.* Jn. 14:16–18, 21; Rom. 8:9–10. [2] Eph. 3:16–17. [3] Eph. 2:18.
[4] Jn. 14:16–23.
[5] Stephen C. Neill, *Christian Faith Today* (Penguin, 1955), pp. 17–18.

variety of ways. He might say that he feared him, or admired him, or revered him, or even loved him. But he never would say, 'I am a man in Churchill'. It would never occur to him to use such a phrase. But Paul was, above everything else, 'a man in Christ'.[1]

Although it is right to emphasize in this way the believer's personal, individual relationship to Christ, indicated by the singular possessive 'my', yet his full title actually includes the *plural* possessive 'our'. For God is calling out a people for himself, and the focus of his people's unity is Jesus Christ. It is he who comes and stands among us when we meet to worship. 'I am with you,' he says, even when only two or three assemble in his name.[2] And he repeats his promise to us when we go out to make disciples of the nations: 'I am with you always, to the very end of the age.'[3]

Here, then, are three major aspects of the uniqueness of Jesus Christ. He is Lord. He is Saviour. He is ours. For he is 'our Lord and Saviour, Jesus Christ'. Historically speaking, these are allusions to his birth, death and resurrection. Theologically speaking, they refer to the incarnation, the atonement and the risen Lord's gift of the Spirit.

Indeed, because in no other person but the historic Jesus of Nazareth has God become human, lived on earth, died for our sins, conquered death, been exalted to heaven, and sent the Holy Spirit, therefore there is no other Saviour. For there is no other person who possesses these qualifications, on account of which he is competent to save.

Hendrik Kraemer, the Dutch theologian who dominated the Tambaram Missionary Conference in 1938, laid great stress on the uniqueness of the Christ events. Fifty years later Bishop Lesslie Newbigin said:

[1] Donald Coggan, *Paul – Portrait of a Revolutionary* (Hodder and Stoughton, 1984), p. 75.
[2] *Cf.* Mt. 18:20. [3] Mt. 28:20.

> Kraemer did not claim uniqueness for Christianity, which is a changing, variegated and ambiguous human phenomenon; he claimed uniqueness for the events that form the substance of the gospel. In Kraemer's favourite phrase, these events are *sui generis*. There may be ideas, stories, myths, legends that reflect the same motifs, but if we are talking about history, . . . there is nothing to be put alongside this story. The gospel is, strictly, *sui generis*, unique.[1]

It is not enough, therefore, to declare that Jesus is unique in the sense that every human being is unique, as indeed every snowflake is unique, and every blade of grass. Nor can we follow Professor Paul Knitter in his attempt to interpret the 'one and only' phraseology of the New Testament in relation to Christ. It is the language of testimony, not theology, he says; of love, not science; of enthusiastic faith, not analytical philosophy. It is, he goes on, 'much like the language a husband would use of his wife . . .: "you are the most beautiful woman in the world . . . you are the only woman for me"'.[2] It is poetry, hyperbole, not literal truth. Later, Professor Knitter argues that it is 'action language', whose *primary* purpose was neither to define doctrine nor to exclude others, but rather to urge action for Christ in 'total commitment to his vision and way'.[3]

But no. This appeal to different uses of language, although ingenious, is surely special pleading. A careful study of the 'one and only' texts, in their context, should convince us that they are not purely poetic expressions of faith and love, meant to be taken with a pinch of salt. On the contrary, they are solemn affirmations of truth, which have eternal consequences in relation to salvation. Moreover, all of them, implicitly if not explicitly, draw their negative conclusion ('no other') from their positive statement (he alone). Thus, it is because only he knows the Father that only he can make him known,[4] and it is because he is 'the way and the truth and the life' that nobody can come

[1] *International Review of Mission*, July, 1988, p. 327.
[2] P. F. Knitter, *No Other Name?*, p. 185.
[3] *The Myth of Christian Uniqueness*, p. 196. [4] Mt. 11:25–27.

to the Father except through him.[1] Similarly, it is because the name of Jesus Christ, whom God has raised from the dead, is mighty to save, that there is no other saving name.[2] So too (even in the thoroughgoing syncretism of the Graeco-Roman world) 'there is but one God, the Father, . . . and there is but one Lord, Jesus Christ . . .';[3] there is one high priest who offered one sacrifice (of himself) as a sin offering once for all;[4] and in consequence of his death as a ransom for all, 'there is one God and one mediator between God and men, the man Christ Jesus'.[5]

Only one way, only one name, only one God, only one Lord, only one Mediator. The claim is exclusive, and the implication inescapable. What is genuinely unique has universal significance and must be universally made known, whereas, to quote Visser't Hooft again, 'there is no universality if there is no unique event'.[6] Thus uniqueness and universality belong together. It is because God has super-exalted Jesus, and given him the unique name of 'Lord', towering above every other name, that every knee must bow to him. It is because Jesus Christ is the only Saviour, that we are under obligation to proclaim him everywhere. The 'inclusivism' of the mission is precisely due to the 'exclusivism' of the Mediator. In addition, universal authority over the nations has been given to him; that is why he commissions us to go and disciple the nations.[7]

In conclusion, I would like to try to answer two questions which may well be in the reader's mind, as they are certainly in mine. Both concern our relationships with adherents of other faiths.

Your first question might be this: 'Are you suggesting a total discontinuity between Christianity and other religions, so that all truth is contained in it and no truth in them?' No. Christians do certainly believe that God has revealed himself in Jesus Christ, as witnessed to in Scripture, in a unique and final way,

[1] Jn. 14:6. [2] Acts 4:10–12. [3] 1 Cor. 8:5–6. [4] Heb. 10:12–14.
[5] 1 Tim. 2:5–6.
[6] W. A. Visser't Hooft, *No Other Name*, p. 102. [7] Mt. 28:18–29.

so that, in this life, he has nothing more to reveal than he has revealed, although of course we have much more to learn. But we are not suggesting that outside the church we consider God inactive and truth absent. Not at all. God sustains all his creatures, and therefore 'is not far from any of them'. By creation they are his 'offspring', who 'live and move and have (their) being' in him.[1] Also Jesus Christ, as the *logos* of God and the light of men,[2] is himself ceaselessly active in the world. Because he is described as 'the true light that gives light to every man',[3] we dare to claim that all beauty, truth and goodness, wherever they are found among human beings, derive from him, whether people know it or not. This is an aspect of God's so-called 'common grace', his love shown to all humankind; it is not, however, his 'saving grace', which he extends to those who humbly cry to him for mercy.

Your second question may well follow on from the first: 'Is there no hope of salvation, then, for those who belong to other religions, and who may never even have heard of Jesus?' In seeking to respond to this extremely poignant question, I shall try to do so biblically. That is to say, we need to combine confidence and agnosticism, what we know (because Scripture plainly teaches it) and what we do not know (because Scripture is either unclear or even silent about it).

What we know from Scripture is that there is no possibility of self-salvation. For all human beings, on account of God's general revelation, have some knowledge of God and of goodness; all have failed to live up to their knowledge; and all are therefore guilty before God, and are in the state of 'perishing' (unless God intervenes). This is the argument of Romans 1 – 3. Nobody can achieve salvation by his or her religion, sincerity or philanthropy. Those who claim to be Christians cannot, and nor can anyone else. Moreover, Cornelius the centurion is not an exception to this rule, as has sometimes been suggested. His story teaches that salvation is available to Gentiles as well as to Jews, and on the same terms; it does not teach that he attained it

[1] Acts 17:27–28. [2] Jn. 1:1–5. [3] Jn. 1:9.

by his own righteousness, piety or generosity. On the contrary, he needed to hear the gospel and respond to it in order to receive salvation, life, cleansing and the Holy Spirit.[1] So self-salvation is impossible. We also know that Jesus Christ is the only Saviour (because he alone has the necessary qualifications, as we have seen), and that salvation is by God's grace alone, on the ground of Christ's cross alone, by faith alone.

What we do not know, however, is exactly how much knowledge and understanding of the gospel people need before they can cry to God for mercy and be saved. In the Old Testament, people were certainly 'justified by grace through faith', even though they had little knowledge or expectation of Christ. Perhaps there are others today in a somewhat similar position. They know they are sinful and guilty before God, and that they cannot do anything to win his favour, so in self-despair they call upon the God they dimly perceive to save them. If God does save such, as many evangelical Christians tentatively believe, their salvation is still only by grace, only through Christ, only by faith.

Something else we know is that the final number of God's redeemed people will be actually countless,[2] in final fulfilment of God's promise to Abraham that his posterity (spiritual as well as physical) will be 'as numerous as the stars in the sky and as the sand on the seashore'.[3] In the same vein we seem to be assured by Paul that many more people will be saved than lost, because Christ's work in causing salvation will be more successful than Adam's in causing ruin, and because God's grace in bringing life will overflow 'much more' than Adam's trespass in bringing death.[4]

Although we have solid biblical grounds for cherishing this expectation, we are not told how God will achieve it. But while we remain agnostic about this, we can have no uncertainty about our duty. We are commissioned, by him who has authority to do so, to preach the gospel and make disciples. It is hard for people to call on one they have not believed in, or to

[1] Acts 11:14, 18; 15:9. [2] Rev. 7:9. [3] Gn. 22:17. [4] Rom. 5:15–21.

believe in one of whom they have not heard, or to hear if no-one preaches to them.[1] It is much easier for people to believe once they have heard the good news of Christ crucified. It is when they learn from the cross about God's mercy to sinners that they cry, 'God be merciful to *me*, a sinner!' As Paul put it, 'faith comes from hearing the message, and the message is heard through the word of Christ'.[2]

So then, to deny the uniqueness of Christ is to cut the nerve of mission and make it superfluous. To affirm his uniqueness, on the other hand, is to acknowledge the urgency of making him universally known.

[1] Rom. 10:14. [2] Rom. 10:17.

CHAPTER NINETEEN

OUR GOD IS A MISSIONARY GOD

The whole concept of 'mission' is out of favour in today's world, and hostility to it is growing. Evangelism, missionary zeal, attempts to convert other people, are all rejected as 'incompatible with the spirit of tolerance', 'a gross infringement of individual liberties', and 'a most distasteful form of arrogance'. Even in the church some members are completely indifferent to the church's mission, while others are actively resistant to it. 'How can one religion claim a monopoly of truth?' people ask. 'Are there not many different ways to God?' 'What right have we to interfere in other people's privacy, or attempt to impose our views on them? Let's rather mind our own business, and devoutly hope that other people will mind theirs.'

Half hidden in this negative rhetoric lie three main objections to the Christian mission, namely that it is guilty of intolerance, arrogance and violence. How should we respond to these criticisms?

Tolerance is perhaps the most prized virtue in western culture today. But people do not always define what they mean by it. It contributes to clarity if we distinguish between three different kinds of tolerance. The first may be called *legal* tolerance; it seeks to ensure that every minority's religious rights (usually summarized as the freedom to 'profess, practise and propagate' religion) are adequately protected in law. Christians should be in the forefront of those demanding this. Another kind is *social* tolerance, which encourages respect for all persons, whatever views they may hold, seeks to understand and appreciate their position, and promotes good neighbourliness. This too is a virtue which Christians wish to cultivate; it arises naturally from our recognition that all human beings are God's creation and bear his image, and that he wants us to live together in amity. But what about *intellectual* tolerance, which is the third kind? To cultivate a mind so broad that it can accommodate every opinion, however false or evil, without ever detecting anything to reject, is not a virtue; it is the vice of the feeble-minded and amoral. It ends up in an unprincipled confusion of truth with error and goodness with evil. Christians who believe that truth and goodness have been revealed in Christ cannot possibly come to terms with it. We are resolved to bear witness to Christ, who is the embodiment of both. It was this conviction which led William Temple, when Archbishop of Canterbury, to decline invitations to become associated with the World Congress of Faiths and to write that 'Christianity is, I am persuaded, a profoundly intolerant religion'.[1]

If mission is not in the wrong sense intolerant, is it arrogant? I think we should begin by agreeing that some Christian attitudes and evangelistic methods could justly be described as 'proud' and 'patronizing'. We need to be sensitive to these Christian failings, which other people see in us, and repent. Evangelists should never be imperialists, ambitious for the growth of their personal empire or for the prestige of their church or organization, but only for the kingdom of God. The crusading spirit, the triumphalist mindset and the swashbuckling style are all inappropriate in Christ's ambassadors. Humility is the preeminent Christian virtue and should characterize all our thoughts, words and deeds.

The Willowbank Report, which summarized the findings of an international consultation on 'Gospel and Culture', held in January 1978, included a whole section entitled 'Wanted: Humble Messengers of the Gospel!' Half of it is 'an analysis of missionary humility'; it focuses on the need for cultural humility. Some western missionaries have made the mistake of

[1] From a letter to Lord Samuel, dated 26 November 1942, published in *Some Lambeth Letters*, ed. F. S. Temple (OUP, 1963), pp. 40–41.

confusing Christ with culture. They have then become 'guilty of a cultural imperialism which both undermines the local culture unnecessarily and seeks to impose an alien culture instead'.[1] The report continues:

> We know we should never condemn or despise another culture, but rather respect it. We advocate neither the arrogance which imposes our culture on others, nor the syncretism which mixes the gospel with cultural elements incompatible with it, but rather a humble sharing of the good news – made possible by the mutual respect of a genuine friendship.[2]

Granted the need to repent of both personal and cultural arrogance, is the very concept of mission inherently arrogant? Bishop Kenneth Cragg, the acknowledged Christian expert in Islam, argues that the opposite is the case:

> The description of mission as religious egoism may have some validity in relation to some of its disloyalties. But it is finally the abeyance of mission which would be the supremely damnable egoism, for it would argue a proprietary right in that which is too big to belong to a few and too inclusive to be arrogated to some alone . . . To believe in Christ at all is to acknowledge him a universal Christ. Because he is requisite for all, he is perquisite to none. The Christian mission is simply an active recognition of the dimensions of the love of God.[3]

The third objection to the Christian mission is that it is a violent assault on people. Evangelism seems to them both aggressive and intrusive, involving an unwelcome invasion of private territory. Again we have to acknowledge that this is sometimes true. But the Great Commission gives us no warrant

[1] *The Willowbank Report: Gospel and Culture* (Lausanne Committee for World Evangelization, 1978), p. 14.
[2] *Ibid.*, p. 16.
[3] Kenneth Cragg, *The Call of the Minaret* (OUP, 1956), pp. 182–183.

to encroach on other people's personal space or crash the barriers with which they seek to protect themselves. Personally speaking, I wish we could agree to purge our evangelistic vocabulary of all violent metaphors. 'Crusades' are too reminiscent of medieval military expeditions to the Holy Land, 'campaigns' of army operations, and even 'missions' of bombing-raids in wartime, while talk of 'targeting' communities is more suggestive of bombs and bullets than of the gospel of peace. How can we evangelize with integrity if we do not display the 'meekness and gentleness' of the Christ we proclaim?[1]

When people talk disparagingly of 'proselytism', they generally seem to have in mind some kind of conversion by force. This being so, it must be sharply distinguished from true evangelism. Indeed, there is a broad measure of agreement among churches that 'proselytism' is a synonym for 'unworthy witness'.[2] Moreover, the 'unworthiness' of a proselytizing witness may refer to our motives (concern for our own glory, instead of the glory of Christ), or to our methods (trust in psychological pressure techniques or in the offer of benefits on condition of conversion, instead of in the power of the Holy Spirit), or to our message (focusing on the alleged falsehood and failures of others, instead of on the truth and perfection of Jesus Christ). Besides, there is no need to resort to any kind of 'unworthy witness'. For truth is going to prevail in the end. As Paul put it, 'we cannot do anything against the truth, but only for the truth'.[3] Those who use improper pressures are thereby admitting the weakness of their own case.

Authentic Christian mission, then, is fully compatible with a true tolerance, a genuine humility and a Christlike gentleness. It is also integral to historic Christianity. Christianity without mission is Christianity no longer. This is partly, as we saw in the last chapter, because Christianity affirms both the finality of Christ (he has no successors) and the uniqueness of Christ (he

[1] 2 Cor. 10:1.
[2] See, for example, the joint Roman Catholic and World Council study document entitled *Common Witness and Proselytism* (1970).
[3] 2 Cor. 13:8.

has no peers or rivals). His uniqueness gives him universal significance; he must be made known throughout the world.

More than that. Christian mission is rooted in the nature of God himself. The Bible reveals him as a missionary God (Father, Son and Holy Spirit), who creates a missionary people, and is working towards a missionary consummation. If this chapter were a sermon, I would have to announce my text as being the whole Bible! It would not be possible to select a shorter one, if we are to lay an adequate biblical foundation for the Christian mission. I propose, therefore, to make a rapid survey or overview of the Bible, dividing it into its five main sections. We shall look first at the Old Testament and at God the Father, the Creator of the world, the covenant God of Israel; secondly at the Gospels, and at our Lord Jesus Christ, the Saviour of sinners; thirdly at the Acts, and at the Holy Spirit at work in and through the apostles; fourthly at the Letters, and at the church they depict, living and witnessing responsibly in the world; and fifthly at the Revelation, and at the climax of history, when the redeemed people of God will be gathered from all nations. Each successive stage is a fresh missionary disclosure.

The God of the Old Testament is a missionary God

The idea that the Old Testament is a missionary book, and that its God is a missionary God, comes as a surprise to many people. For they have always thought of the God of the Old Testament as having been exclusively the God of Israel. They remember how he called Abraham and made a covenant with him and his descendants; how he renewed his covenant with Isaac and Jacob, and then with the twelve tribes whom he rescued from their Egyptian slavery and brought to Mount Sinai, where he promised to be their God and to make them his people; how he settled them in the promised land and blessed them with kings, priests and prophets, preparing them for the coming of the Messiah.

And all this is true. But it is only a part of the truth. For the

Old Testament begins not with Abraham but with Adam, not with the covenant but with the creation, not with the chosen race but with the human race. It declares emphatically that Yahweh, the God of Israel, was no petty tribal godling like Chemosh, the god of the Moabites, or Milcom, the god of the Ammonites, but the Creator of heaven and earth, the Lord of the nations, and 'the God of the spirits of all flesh'.[1] That is its perspective throughout.

Further, the call of Abraham did not contradict this world view; it established it. Yahweh had told Abraham to leave his country, people and household for another land he would be shown. Now God said to him:

> 'I will make you into a great nation
> and I will bless you;
> I will make your name great,
> and you will be a blessing.
> I will bless those who bless you,
> and whoever curses you I will curse;
> and all peoples on earth
> will be blessed through you.'[2]

Thus Abraham was to leave his own country and be shown another, to leave his own people and be made into another. God promised not only to bless him, but to make him a blessing; not only to give him a posterity, but through it to bless 'all peoples on earth'.

It is no exaggeration to say that Genesis 12:1–4 is the most unifying text of the whole Bible. For God's saving purpose is encapsulated in it, namely to bless the whole world through Christ, who was Abraham's seed. The rest of the Bible is an unfolding of it, and subsequent history has been a fulfilment of it. For God first prepared Israel for Christ's coming, and then through his coming has been blessing the world ever since. We ourselves would not be followers of Jesus today if it were not

[1] Nu. 16:22; 27:16 (RSV). [2] Gn. 12:1–4.

for this text: we are beneficiaries of the promise God made to Abraham about four thousand years ago. 'If you belong to Christ,' Paul wrote, 'then you are Abraham's seed, and heirs according to the promise.'[1] Again, if we share his faith, 'he is the father of us all'.[2] For God's promise was an advance announcement to Abraham of the gospel, namely that he was going to 'justify the Gentiles by faith'.[3]

The tragedy of the Old Testament is that Israel kept forgetting the universal scope of God's promise. They overlooked the fact that God had chosen one family in order to bless all families. They became preoccupied with themselves and with their own history. They even perverted the truth of divine election into the error of divine favouritism, which led them to boast of their privileged status and to assume that they were immune to the judgment of God.

So the prophets had to keep trying to broaden their outlook, and to remind them that God's purpose through Abraham's descendants was to bless the nations. For example, God would make the *nations* the Messiah's 'inheritance' and 'possession';[4] *all nations* would serve him;[5] he would be a light for the Gentile *nations*,[6] and in that day *all nations* would stream to the mountain of the Lord's temple.[7]

The Christ of the Gospels is a missionary Christ

In 1850 David Livingstone, the intrepid pioneer missionary in Africa, wrote to his sister Agnes:

> Forbid it that we should ever consider the holding of a commission from the King of kings a sacrifice, so long as other men esteem the service of an earthly government an honour ... I am a missionary heart and soul. God had an only son, and he was a missionary and a physician. A poor,

[1] Gal. 3:29. [2] Rom. 4:16–17. [3] Gal. 3:8.
[4] Ps. 2:8. [5] Ps. 72:11. [6] Is. 49:6.
[7] Is. 2:2.

> poor imitation of him I am . . . In this service I hope to live; in it I wish to die.[1]

A few years later Robert Speer, travelling secretary of the Student Volunteer Movement in the United States, wrote in his journal: 'If you want to follow Jesus Christ, you must follow him to the ends of the earth, for that is where he is going . . . We cannot think of God without thinking of him as a missionary God.'

It is true that twice Jesus is recorded by Matthew as having restricted his mission to 'the lost sheep of Israel'. He told the Twelve not to evangelize Gentile or Samaritan areas, but to 'go rather' to Israel's lost sheep;[2] and later he told a Canaanite woman, who had appealed to him on behalf of her demonized daughter, that he 'was sent only' to Israel's lost sheep.[3] This sounds disturbing, even shocking, until we remember that it was merely a temporary, historical limitation, relating only to Jesus' earthly ministry. He added that through his death, resurrection and gift of the Spirit, salvation would be offered to all the nations, to whom he therefore later instructed his followers to take the good news.

Even the Gospel of Matthew, which is the most Jewish of the four, and is the only Gospel to include the two references to Israel's lost sheep, makes this global horizon clear. It begins with the genealogy of Jesus, which is traced to Abraham, surely to indicate that the promise is at last to be fulfilled.[4] Next, after the birth of Jesus, it describes the visit of those mysterious Magi, who perhaps were Zoroastrian astrologers from Persia, who brought their treasures to 'the king of the Jews', and whom Matthew sees as forerunners of the Gentile multitudes who would later do homage to Jesus.[5] Matthew also records Jesus' remarkable prediction that 'many will come from the east and the west, and will take their places at the feast with Abraham, Isaac and Jacob in the kingdom of heaven'.[6] And Matthew's

[1] W. G. Blaikie, *David Livingstone* (1908).
[2] Mt. 10:6. [3] Mt. 15:24. [4] Mt. 1:2.
[5] Mt. 2:1–12. [6] Mt. 8:11.

Gospel ends with the fullest version we are given of the so-called 'Great' or 'Universal' Commission. The mission of the Twelve during Jesus' public ministry may have been restricted to 'the lost sheep of Israel', but the mission of the church has no such limitation. The followers of Jesus are to 'go and make disciples of all nations', welcoming them by baptism into the Christian community, and teaching them to obey all their Master's instructions.[1] This commission to the nations has never been rescinded; it is still binding on the people of God. It was issued by the risen Christ who was able to claim that 'all authority in heaven and on earth' had been conferred on him. A link between the 'all authority' he claimed and the 'all nations' he commissioned his followers to disciple is clearly intended. The universal mission of the church springs from the universal authority of Jesus.

The Holy Spirit of the Acts is a missionary Spirit

Roland Allen, that remarkable High Church Anglican missionary in northern China from 1895 to 1903, burned with a passionate longing that the church would recover those three indigenous principles (self-governing, self-supporting, self-propagating) which characterized the missionary policy of the apostle Paul. His best-known books are *Missionary Methods, St Paul's or Ours?* (1912) and *The Spontaneous Expansion of the Church* (1927). Less well known is his little study of the Acts, *Pentecost and the World*, sub-titled *The Revelation of the Holy Spirit in the Acts of the Apostles.* In it he writes: 'The book of the "Acts" is strictly a missionary book ... The conclusion is irresistible that the Spirit given was ... in fact a missionary Spirit.'[2] This, he continues, is 'the great, fundamental, unmistakeable teaching of the book ... It is in the revelation of the Holy Spirit as a missionary Spirit that the "Acts" stands alone in the New Testament'.[3]

Roland Allen was right. The Holy Spirit is the chief actor in

[1] Mt. 28:19–20. [2] Roland Allen, *Pentecost and the World* (OUP, 1917), p. 36.
[3] *Ibid.*, p. 40.

the Acts. The book begins with the 120 disciples waiting. In the upper room during his last evening with the Twelve, Jesus had promised the coming of the Spirit and had described the Spirit's future ministry of convincing, teaching and witnessing. During the forty days which elapsed between the resurrection and the ascension, the repeated message was that the Spirit would give them 'power' for witness[1] and that they must wait for him to come.[2]

So Pentecost was a missionary event. It was the fulfilment of God's promise through the prophet Joel to pour out his Spirit 'on all people',[3] irrespective of their race, sex, age or social standing. And the foreign languages which the disciples spoke (which seems clearly to have been what the 'tongues' were, at least on the Day of Pentecost) were a dramatic sign of the international nature of the Messiah's kingdom which the Holy Spirit had come to establish.

The rest of the Acts is a logical unfolding of that beginning. We watch enthralled as the missionary Spirit creates a missionary people and thrusts them out on their missionary task. They began to witness to their fellow Jews in and around Jerusalem, the Jewish headquarters. Then Philip took the bold initiative to witness to Samaritans, who were a half-way house between the Jews and the Gentiles.[4] Next came the conversion of the centurion Cornelius, one of those Gentile 'Godfearers', who accepted the monotheism and ethical standards of the Jews, but remained a Gentile, on the fringe of the synagogue without accepting full conversion. The Holy Spirit gave the clearest possible evidence that Cornelius was now a fully accredited member of the church.[5] Soon afterwards, some unknown believers took the plunge and 'began to speak to Greeks also, telling them the good news about the Lord Jesus'.[6] The three missionary journeys of Paul the apostle to the Gentiles followed, in which he evangelized the provinces of Galatia, Asia, Macedonia and Achaia, the Holy Spirit both restraining and leading him.[7] The

[1] *E.g.* Lk. 24:49; Acts 1:8. [2] Acts 1:4. [3] Joel 2:28; Acts 2:17.
[4] Acts 8:5–8. [5] Acts 10 and 11. [6] Acts 11:20.
[7] Acts 16:6–10.

book ends with Paul in Rome, the capital of the world and the city of his dreams, not as a free man but as a prisoner, yet still an indefatigable evangelist, preaching Jesus and the kingdom to all who visited him, 'boldly and without hindrance'.[1]

Throughout the Acts Luke makes it plain that the impetus for mission came from the Holy Spirit. This is Harry R. Boer's theme in his book *Pentecost and Missions*. The Acts, he writes,

> is governed by one dominant, overriding and all-controlling motif. This motif is the expansion of the faith through missionary witness in the power of the Spirit ... Restlessly the Holy Spirit drives the church to witness, and continually churches rise out of the witness.[2]

Harry Boer makes the further important point that the momentum for this evangelism came from the Holy Spirit, not from the Great Commission, which, in fact, is not mentioned again after Acts 1. He writes:

> We must cease preaching the Great Commission as a command to be obeyed, but must present it *as a law that expresses the nature, and that governs the life, of the church* ... The outpouring of the Spirit is in and by reason of its (? his) very nature the effectuation of the Great Commission in the life of the church.[3]

The church of the Letters is a missionary church

The members of the local church (whether in imagination or in reality) are often seen sitting in a circle facing each other. This picture is not wrong, inasmuch as we belong to each other and need each other's support. Indeed, we are frequently urged in the New Testament to love one another, encourage, comfort and exhort one another, and bear one another's burdens. And

[1] Acts 28:31.
[2] Harry R. Boer, *Pentecost and Missions* (Lutterworth, 1961), pp. 161–162.
[3] *Ibid.*, p. 217.

this 'one anotherness' of the Christian fellowship can be enjoyed and developed only when we face one another. Although legitimate, however, 'meeting in a circle' is also dangerous. For whenever we turn inwards towards one another, we have turned our backs on the world. In order to enjoy mutual fellowship, we have also extricated ourselves from the world. It is permissible – but only if it is temporary. We come apart from the world for worship and fellowship, in order to return to it strengthened to live as Christ's witnesses and servants.

Now the twenty-one Letters of the New Testament, even those addressed to individuals, are all intended in their different ways to build up the church and to secure its growth in both maturity and extent. True, the Letters address the domestic affairs of the church, its doctrine, worship, ministry, unity and holiness. But they also assume throughout that the church lives in the world and is responsible to reach out in compassion towards it.

To begin with, Paul assumes that the churches will share in his own apostolic ministry by their support, their gifts and above all their prayers. He thanks God for the Philippians' 'partnership in the gospel'.[1] He asks the Thessalonians to pray that through him 'the message of the Lord may spread rapidly and be honoured';[2] the Colossians that God will 'open a door for our message';[3] and the Ephesians that he may be given utterance, clarity and boldness in his preaching.[4]

The apostles also assume that the church will itself be involved in spreading the faith. Paul calls it 'the pillar and foundation of the truth',[5] which suggests that it must hold the truth high (as pillars thrust a building aloft) and hold it firm (acting like a structure's foundation). Peter calls the church 'a chosen people, a royal priesthood, a holy nation, a people belonging to God', in order that its members may 'declare the praises' or 'proclaim the triumphs' (NEB) of the Saviour who has called them 'out of darkness into his wonderful light'.[6]

[1] Phil. 1:5. [2] 2 Thes. 3:1. [3] Col. 4:3. [4] Eph. 6:19–20. [5] 1 Tim. 3:15.
[6] 1 Pet. 2:9.

And each local church is to exhibit the missionary character of the whole church. The Philippians, who lived 'in a crooked and depraved generation', were told both to 'shine like stars in the universe' and to 'hold out the word of life', displaying it as a merchant does his goods, or as a waiter does the dishes at a feast.[1] The Thessalonians are described as having not only 'welcomed' the Lord's message but as having made it ring out in the neighbouring regions.[2]

Individual church members are also to be involved in Christian witness. The apostles urge them to be conscious of the 'outsiders' who are watching them. Here is an example: 'Be wise in the way you act towards outsiders; make the most of every opportunity. Let your conversation be always full of grace, seasoned with salt, so that you may know how to answer everyone.'[3] It is a very practical instruction. We are to be sensible in our relationships with outsiders, to seize every chance to witness, to combine grace with salt (perhaps wholesomeness or even wit) in our conversation, and to be ready to answer whatever questions are put to us. This last point reminds us of Peter's similar direction: 'Always be prepared to give an answer to everyone who asks you to give the reason for the hope that you have.'[4]

So the church of the Letters is a missionary church, whether we are thinking of the universal church or the local church or individual church members. As we saw in chapter 15, mission is an essential part of the church's identity. In Bishop Lesslie Newbigin's forthright words, 'the commission to disciple all the nations stands at the centre of the church's mandate, and a church that forgets this, or marginalizes it, forfeits the right to the titles "catholic" and "apostolic"'.[5]

[1] Phil. 2:15–16. [2] 1 Thes. 1:6, 8. [3] Col. 4:5–6. [4] 1 Pet. 3:15.

[5] From his address, 'The Enduring Validity of Cross-Cultural Mission', given at the opening of the Overseas Ministries Study Centre's new premises in New Haven, Connecticut, on 5 October 1987, and published in the *International Bulletin of Missionary Research*, April 1988.

The climax of the Revelation is a missionary climax

When John was permitted a peep through the 'door standing open in heaven',[1] he saw a great crowd of people standing before God's throne. They were wearing white robes (the symbol of righteousness) and holding palm branches (the symbol of victory), and they were joining in a mighty chorus of worship, attributing their salvation to God and to the Lamb. John also describes this great multitude as coming 'from every nation, tribe, people and language'.[2] So the mission of the church will not be fruitless. On the contrary, it will result in a huge ingathering of people, a multi-racial and multi-national throng, whose different languages and cultures will not prevent, but rather enrich, their ceaseless celebration of the grace of God.

The redeemed multitude will also be countless. Only then will God's ancient promise to Abraham be completely fulfilled. In order to emphasize the limitless numbers of Abraham's posterity, both physical (the Jews) and spiritual (believers, whether Jews or Gentiles), God promised that they would be as numerous as the dust of the earth,[3] the stars in the sky,[4] and the sand on the seashore.[5] Each metaphor symbolizes numberlessness. 'I will make your offspring like the dust of earth, so that *if anyone could count the dust*, then your offspring could be counted.'[6] 'Look up at the heavens and count the stars – *if indeed you can count them*.'[7] With our twentieth-century understanding of the universe, it seems that the myriads on myriads of stars in the billions of galaxies do perhaps number as many as all the grains of sand and specks of dust throughout the world. Although we must be content to remain agnostic about how God will achieve this end, we can meanwhile rejoice that the missionary labours of the church will come to such a glorious and God-honouring climax.

From this rapid overview of Scripture we have seen that the God of the Old Testament is a missionary God (he called one

[1] Rev. 4:1. [2] Rev. 7:9–10. [3] Gn. 13:16. [4] Gn. 15:5. [5] Gn. 22:17.
[6] Gn. 13:16. [7] Gn. 15:5.

family in order to bless all the earth's families); that the Christ of the Gospels is a missionary Christ (he commissioned the church to go and make disciples of the nations); that the Holy Spirit of the Acts is a missionary Spirit (he drove the church out to witness); that the church of the Letters is a missionary church (a world-wide community with a world-wide vocation); and that the climax of the Revelation will be a missionary climax (a countless, international crowd).

So the religion of the Bible is a missionary religion. The evidence is overwhelming, irrefutable. Mission cannot be regarded as a regrettable deviation from religious toleration, or as the hobby of a few eccentric enthusiasts. On the contrary, it arises from the heart of God himself, and is communicated from his heart to ours. Mission is the global outreach of the global people of a global God.

If, then, we have resisted the missionary dimension of the church's life, or dismissed it as if it were dispensable, or patronized it reluctantly with a few perfunctory prayers and grudging coins, or become preoccupied with our own narrow-minded, parochial concerns, we need to repent, that is, change our mind and attitude. Do we profess to believe in God? He's a missionary God. Do we say we are committed to Christ? He's a missionary Christ. Do we claim to be filled with the Spirit? He's a missionary Spirit. Do we delight in belonging to the church? It's a missionary society. Do we hope to go to heaven when we die? It's a heaven filled with the fruits of the missionary enterprise. It is not possible to avoid these things.

If some of us need to repent, all of us need to take action. The authentic Christianity of the Bible is not a safe, smug, cosy, selfish, escapist little religion. On the contrary, it is deeply disturbing to our sheltered security. It is an explosive, centrifugal force, which pulls us out from our narrow self-centredness and flings us into God's world to witness and to serve. So we must find practical ways, individually and through our local church, of expressing this commitment.

In 1885 General William Booth, 'his eyes twinkling, challenged a mass rally of London Salvationists: "How wide is the girth of the world?" From the serried ranks came the full-throated response: "Twenty-five thousand miles". "Then", roared Booth, arms outspread, "we must grow till our arms get right round about it".'[1]

[1] Richard Collier, *The General Next to God* (Collins, 1965), p. 146.

CHAPTER TWENTY

HOLISTIC MISSION

'Holistic' (from 'holism', the philosophical notion that 'the whole is greater than the sum of its parts') is perhaps not a very satisfactory epithet to apply to the Christian mission. Yet it is intended to emphasize that authentic mission is a comprehensive activity which embraces evangelism and social action, and refuses to let them be divorced.

During at least the last thirty years, beginning in the ecumenical community, but more recently in the evangelical constituency as well, there has been considerable disagreement about these two responsibilities. It has been stated in different ways: as the tension 'between God's action in and through the church and everything God is doing in the world apparently independently of the Christian community';[1] 'between the vertical interpretation of the gospel as essentially concerned with God's saving action in the life of individuals, and the horizontal interpretation of it as mainly concerned with human relationships in the world';[2] between God seeking the justification of sinners and God seeking justice in and among nations; between redemption and providence, the salvation of the soul and the improvement of society.

At times the difference between these viewpoints has not been a tension only, but a sterile polarization, usually along the lines of the evangelical–liberal divide, each overreacting to the other's position. The former have tended to focus exclusively on evangelism to the neglect of social need, whether food for the

[1] See R. K. Orchard (ed.), *Witness in Six Continents* (Edinburgh House Press, 1964), p. 157.
[2] W. A. Visser't Hooft in Norman Goodall (ed.), *The Uppsala 1968 Report* (WCC, 1968).

hungry or freedom and justice for the oppressed. The latter have gone to the opposite extreme and have tended to neglect evangelism, or have tried to reinterpret it in terms of socio-political action such as the humanization of communities or the liberation of the downtrodden. Thus, the evangelical stereotype has been to spiritualize the gospel, and deny its social implications; while the ecumenical stereotype has been to politicize it, and deny its offer of salvation to sinners. This polarization has been a disaster.

Most (though not all) Christians are agreed that our responsibilities are both evangelistic and social. For example, in his opening remarks to the World Congress on Evangelism in Berlin in 1966, Dr Carl Henry stressed

> that evangelical Christians have a message doubly relevant to the present social crisis . . . For they know *the God of justice and of justification* . . . Whenever Christianity has been strong in the life of a nation, it has had an interest in both law and gospel, in the state as well as the church, in jurisprudence and in evangelism.[1]

Or, using more striking imagery, Dr Raymond Bakke has written that 'we Christians are the only people on this earth who have the integrated world view of matter and spirit that enables us to tackle sewer system development and the salvation of souls with equal gusto'.[2] Although we may be agreed in such 'both–and' statements as these, however, we have problems first in defining the *relationship* between evangelism and social responsibility, and secondly in what *vocabulary* we should use to express this relationship.

[1] Carl F. H. Henry, *Evangelicals at the Brink of Crisis* (Word Books, 1967), pp. 71–72.
[2] Raymond Bakke, *Urban Mission*, September 1986, p. 7.

The relationship between evangelism and social responsibility

A broad welcome was given to the Lausanne Covenant (1974) which contained outspoken statements on 'The Nature of Evangelism' and 'Christian Social Responsibility'.[1] The latter also included the affirmation 'that evangelism and socio-political activity are both part of our Christian duty'. Again, however, it is only a 'both–and' statement. The paragraphs on evangelism and social responsibility stand side by side without any attempt to relate them to one another. Or rather, more accurately, the only mention of a relation between them is the statement in paragraph 6 that 'in the church's mission of sacrificial service evangelism is primary'.

The Lausanne movement has remained true to this assertion of the primacy of evangelism, and its 'Consultation on the Relationship between Evangelism and Social Responsibility', held in Grand Rapids in 1982, endorsed and explained this primacy in two ways. First, evangelism has a certain logical priority: "The very fact of Christian social responsibility presupposes socially responsible Christians, and it can only be by evangelism and discipling that they have become such.' Secondly,

> evangelism relates to people's eternal destiny, and in bringing them good news of salvation, Christians are doing what nobody else can do. Seldom if ever should we have to choose between . . . healing bodies and saving souls . . . Nevertheless, if we must choose, then we have to say that the supreme and ultimate need of all humankind is the saving grace of Jesus Christ, and that therefore a person's eternal, spiritual salvation is of greater importance than his or her temporal and material well-being.[2]

[1] The Lausanne Covenant, paras. 4 and 5.

[2] *Evangelism and Social Responsibility: An Evangelical Commitment*, The Grand Rapids Report (Paternoster, 1982), pp. 24–25.

The Manila Manifesto (1989) made a similar statement: 'Evangelism is primary because our chief concern is with the gospel, that all people may have the opportunity to accept Jesus Christ as their Lord and Saviour.'[1]

To reaffirm the primacy of evangelism does not solve the problem, however. It leaves the relationships between evangelism and social responsibility still undefined.

It was to tease out these relationships that the Grand Rapids Consultation was called in 1982. Its members clarified three of them. First, 'social activity is a *consequence* of evangelism'. For evangelism brings people to faith, 'faith works through love', and love issues in service.[2] Indeed, 'social responsibility is more than a consequence of evangelism; it is also one of its principal aims', since we are saved 'unto good works'.[3] Secondly, 'social activity can be a *bridge* to evangelism'. In spite of the danger of making 'rice Christians', who profess conversion only because of the material benefits they are offered, it remains true that love in action 'can break down prejudice and suspicion, open closed doors, and gain a hearing for the gospel'. Thirdly, 'social activity not only follows evangelism as its consequence and aim, and precedes it as its bridge, but also accompanies it as its *partner*. They are like the two blades of a pair of scissors or the two wings of a bird', as they were in the public ministry of Jesus. 'The partnership is, in reality, a marriage.'[4]

This partnership applies both to the individual Christian and to the local church. Of course different Christians receive different specialist gifts and callings (see chapter 8), qualifying them to concentrate on specialist ministries, just as the Twelve were called to a pastoral, and the Seven to a social, ministry.[5] Of course also, different Christians find themselves in different emergency situations, which demand specialized responses. We do not blame either the good Samaritan for tending the traveller's wounds and not enquiring into his spiritual state, or

[1] *The Manila Manifesto: An Elaboration of the Lausanne Covenant 15 Years Later* (Lausanne Committee for World Evangelization, 1989), para. 4, p. 15.
[2] *Cf.* Gal. 5:6, 13. [3] *Cf.* Eph. 2:10; Tit. 2:14.
[4] *Evangelism and Social Responsibility*, pp. 21–24. [5] Acts 6:1–7.

Philip for sharing the gospel with the Ethiopian and not enquiring into his social needs. Nevertheless, these are particular callings and situations. Generally speaking, all followers of Jesus Christ have the responsibility, according to the opportunities which are given them, both to witness and to serve.

It is similar with each local church. The needs of its local community will be many and varied. But everybody cannot do everything. Consequently, in a church of any size, its members should be encouraged to form themselves into 'study and action groups', according to their gifts, callings and interests, each taking up a particular evangelistic, pastoral or social need in the neighbourhood. In this way it will be possible to respond to a number of different challenges. Nevertheless, it will be important for the local church to recognize its specialist groups, to support them with encouragement, advice, prayer and finance, as necessary, and to give them the opportunity from time to time to report on their progress. Thus 'owning' the groups, the church will be able through them to reach out in compassion to the community and serve a number of its diverse needs.

So far we have been thinking about the *relationships* between evangelism and social responsibility. The second problem we have concerns the *vocabulary* we should use to express the partnership between them. According to the report of the first National Evangelical Anglican Congress, held at Keele University in 1967, 'evangelism and compassionate service belong together in the mission of God'.[1] I myself tried to elaborate this later by writing: '"Mission" describes . . . everything the church is sent into the world to do', namely 'Christian service in the world comprising both evangelism and social action'.[2]

Some evangelical leaders have criticized this definition of 'mission'. They believe it is potentially damaging to the Christian mission, because it will deflect missionaries from their priority tasks of evangelizing, discipling and church planting.

[1] *Keele '67*, the National Evangelical Anglican Congress Statement, ed. Philip Crowe (Falcon, 1967), para. 2.20, p. 23.

[2] John Stott, *Christian Mission in the Modern World* (Falcon, 1975; Kingsway, 1986), pp. 30, 34.

They therefore urge that we retain the traditional understanding of 'mission' and 'missionary' to refer only to these evangelistic activities, although they concede that all Christians have social and political responsibilities as well. Certainly, the last thing of which I would desire to be guilty is hindering the mission of the church! It is also true that 'mission' itself is not a biblical word, any more than 'Trinity' and 'sacrament' are. Yet it is a useful piece of shorthand for a biblical concept, namely what Christ sends his people into the world to do. I still insist that this cannot be limited to proclamation evangelism, even though I have already said that this has primacy in the church. The issue is not merely one of semantics (What does the word 'mission' mean?), but of substance (Why are we sent into the world?). Even if I were to concede that the word 'mission' cannot bear the weight I have put upon it, it would make no difference to the argument that we are sent into the world both to witness and to serve. Nor do I feel able to withdraw the conviction that our mission is to be modelled on Christ's. Just as his love for us is like the Father's love for him,[1] so his sending us into the world is like his Father's sending him into the world.[2] If words and works went together in his ministry, they should also in ours.

The main fear of my critics seems to be that missionaries will be sidetracked. The best way to avoid this, in my view, is not to deny that 'mission' is broader than evangelism, but rather to insist that each 'missionary' must be true to his or her particular calling. I have already suggested that in the local church, although some members are called to this ministry and some to that, yet the church itself will be lopsided if it does not include a variety of ministries. Similarly, although some missionaries are called to primary evangelism, discipling, church-planting, and Bible-translating, and others to specialist medical, educational, or developmental ministries, yet the national church (and the mission agencies cooperating with it) would be lopsided if together they did not include such a wide variety

[1] Jn. 15:9. [2] Jn. 17:18; 20:21.

of ministries. Indeed, there is much to be said for multi-national, multi-functional mission teams, composed of nationals and expatriates, men and women, evangelists and social workers, specialists in church-planting and experts in development, pastors and teachers.

The biblical basis for this partnership

Evangelical Christians are nothing if not biblical Christians. At least our overriding desire (whether we are successful in doing it or not) is to live 'under' or 'according to' Scripture. Is there, then, good biblical warrant for holding evangelism and social action together? There is. It has been variously stated, but I will content myself with three fundamental arguments.

First, there is *the character of God.* The God of the biblical revelation, being both Creator and Redeemer, is a God who cares about the total well-being (spiritual and material) of all the human beings he has made. Having created them in his own image, he longs that they will discover their true humanness in their relationships to him and to each other. On the one hand, God yearns after his creatures in their lostness. He takes no pleasure in the death of the wicked, and is not willing that any should perish. So he begs them to listen to his word, to return to him in penitence, and to receive his forgiveness. On the other hand, God cares for the poor and the hungry, the alien, the widow and the orphan. He denounces oppression and tyranny, and calls for justice. He tells his people to be the voice of the voiceless and the defender of the powerless, and so to express their love for them. It is neither an accident nor a surprise, therefore, that God's two great commandments are that we love him with all our being and our neighbour as ourselves.

The outworking of these commandments is made clear in the law. For example, God's people were to 'fear', 'love' and 'serve' him. How? Partly by 'walking in his ways' and 'obeying his commands', because he is 'God of gods and Lord of lords', who is on that account to be worshipped; and partly by following his example who 'defends the cause of the fatherless and the widow, and loves the alien, giving him food and clothing'.[1] Thus worship and obedience on the one hand, philanthropy and justice on the other, belong together as the double duty of the people of God.

Then came the prophets, who kept reminding the people of the law and urging each of them to obey it. 'He has showed you, O man, what is good. And what does the LORD require of you? To act justly and to love mercy and to walk humbly with your God.'[2] Again, justice and mercy to the neighbour and humility before God are united.

Alongside this prophetic witness to God's law went bold denunciations of those who flouted it. Elijah was an outstanding example. Living in a time of national apostasy, his ministry was encapsulated in his two major confrontations, first at Mount Carmel when he challenged the people to choose between Yahweh and Baal,[3] and then at Jezreel when he accused King Ahab of murdering Naboth and confiscating his property, and warned him of God's judgment.[4] It is striking to find the same prophet acting as the champion of both religious loyalty and social justice.

Then 150 years later we find the two great exilic prophets, Jeremiah and Ezekiel, continuing the same tradition of protest. Why was disaster to fall upon Jerusalem? According to Jeremiah, because the people had 'forsaken' Yahweh in favour of 'foreign gods' and had filled Jerusalem with 'the blood of the innocent'.[5] According to Ezekiel, the city would bring down judgment upon itself 'by shedding blood in her midst and . . . by making idols'.[6] In both cases the acme of Israel's sin was the combination of 'idols' and 'blood' – idolatry being the worst sin against God and murder the worst against the neighbour.

The law and the prophets thus reflect the character of God. What he is, his people must be also, sharing and reflecting his concerns. In particular, there is no dualism in the thinking of God.

[1] Dt. 10:12–20. [2] Mi. 6:8. [3] 1 Ki. 18. [4] 1 Ki. 21. [5] Je. 19:4.
[6] Ezk. 22:3–4; *cf.* 36:18–19.

> We tend to set over against one another in an unhealthy way soul and body, the individual and society, redemption and creation, grace and nature, heaven and earth, justification and justice, faith and works. The Bible certainly distinguishes between these, but it also relates them to each other, and it instructs us to hold each pair in a dynamic and creative tension.[1]

The second ground for keeping evangelism and social concern together is *the ministry and teaching of Jesus*. There can be no question that words and works went together in his public ministry. True, he was a preacher. He announced the coming of the kingdom of God. But he also demonstrated its arrival by his works of compassion and power. Thus we read both that 'he went about among the villages teaching . . .'[2] and that 'he went about doing good and healing'.[3] The similarity between these statements is the fact that 'he went about'; he had an itinerant ministry, and criss-crossed the Palestinian countryside. The dissimilarity concerns what he 'went about' for. According to Mark it was 'teaching', according to Luke 'doing good and healing'. There was in his ministry an indissoluble bond between evangelism and compassionate service. He exhibited in action the love of God he was proclaiming. 'He was concerned', Chuck Colson has written, 'not only with saving man from hell in the next world, but with delivering him from the hellishness of this one.'[4]

So then his words explained his works, and his works dramatized his words. Hearing and seeing, voice and vision, were joined. Each supported the other. For words remain abstract until they are made concrete in deeds of love, while works remain ambiguous until they are interpreted by the proclamation of the gospel. Words without works lack credibility; works without words lack clarity. So Jesus' works made his words visible; his words made his works intelligible.

[1] *Evangelism and Social Responsibility*, p. 20. [2] Mk. 6:6 (RSV).
[3] Acts 10:38 (RSV).
[4] Charles Colson, *Loving God* (Zondervan, 1983), p. 145.

What Jesus exhibited in his life and ministry he also included in his teaching. Let me share with you a reflection on two of his best-known, best-loved parables, namely those of the prodigal son[1] (which highlights conversion) and the good Samaritan[2] (which highlights social action). There are obvious similarities between them. Both, for example, are recorded by Dr Luke alone, who was concerned to portray Jesus (and so God) as the lover of the outsider and the underdog, in the one case the self-willed boy and in the other the victim of thugs. Again, both depict tragic situations which, it is implied, are displeasing to God. God does not want human beings made in his image either to become demoralized and lost in a far country or to be assaulted and abandoned half-dead in the gutter. His desire is that both the lost and the battered be brought home.

More important for my purpose now, however, are the dissimilarities between the two parables. If we hold them together, they enforce the necessary nexus between evangelism and social action. First, in both there is a victim, a man who finds himself in a desperate plight. In the parable of the prodigal son he is the victim of his own sin; in the parable of the good Samaritan he is the victim of other people's sins, that is, he is 'the sinned against' (to borrow an expression popularized by Raymond Fung at the 1980 Melbourne Consultation). Moreover, in the first parable it is personal sin which is described, in the second social sin, namely the evil of public disorder. Both should arouse our compassion. We are concerned both for the sinning and for the sinned against.

Secondly, in both parables there is a rescue – from alienation in a distant land and from violent assault on the road. In the first parable the sinner repents, comes back and is forgiven (it is salvation by faith); in the second the victim can do nothing; he owes his rescue to the charity of the Samaritan (it is a rescue by good works). Thirdly, in both there is a display of love. In the parable of the prodigal son we see the love of God, as the father welcomes the boy home; in the parable of the good Samaritan

[1] Lk. 15:11–32. [2] Lk. 10:30–37.

we see the love of neighbour for neighbour, as the Samaritan binds up the victim's wounds. Moreover, in both cases love triumphs over prejudice. The prodigal is forgiven *although* he deserves no such treatment; the Samaritan takes pity on the robbers' victim, *although* he is an unknown Jew who has no claim on him.

Fourthly, in both parables there is a sub-plot, which dramatizes the alternative to what is being commended. In the parable of the lost son, his elder brother refuses to rejoice in his repentance and return. In the parable of the Samaritan, the priest and Levite refuse to get involved in the battered man's plight. We might even say that those who resist the call to evangelism, and leave people alone in their sins, resemble the elder brother, while those who resist the call to social action, and leave people alone in their sufferings, resemble the priest and Levite who 'passed by on the other side'.

Thus each parable emphasizes a vital aspect of Christian discipleship – its beginning when like the prodigal son we come home for salvation, and its continuing when like the good Samaritan we go out in mission. Each of us resembles the prodigal; each of us *should* resemble the Samaritan. First we face our own sins, and then we face the world's sufferings. First we come in and receive mercy, and then we go out and show mercy. Mercy cannot be shown until it has been received; but once it has been received it must be shown to others. Let us not divorce what Christ has married. We have all been prodigals; God wants us all to be Samaritans too.

In addition to the example and teaching of Jesus Christ, I would like to mention his emotions. In chapter 7 we considered how, face to face with the 'last enemy', death, which he had come to destroy, Jesus both 'snorted' with anger against this evil and then 'wept' with compassion for its victims. I went on to suggest that the same two emotions should motivate us, whenever we find ourselves confronting evil – whether the evil of human lostness or the social evils of our day.

I have only recently read General William Booth's book *In Darkest England and the Way Out*. Published in 1890, its title was deliberately parallel to H. M. Stanley's *In Darkest Africa*, which had appeared earlier the same year. Part I is called 'The Darkness' and Part II 'Deliverance'. Booth wrote with deep feeling about the miseries caused by poverty, unemployment, homelessness, hunger, exploited labour, drunkenness, disease, slums, white slavery and prostitution. 'The blood boils with impotent rage at the sight of these enormities,' he confessed, 'callously afflicted, and silently borne by these miserable victims.'[1] Of course he longed for their conversion, and maintained that he always put salvation first. But 'what is the use of preaching the gospel', he asked, 'to people whose whole attention is concentrated upon a mad, desperate struggle to keep themselves alive?'[2] 'In providing for the relief of temporary misery,' he added, 'I reckon that I am only making it easy where it is now difficult, and possible where it is now all but impossible, for men and women to find their way to the cross of our Lord Jesus Christ.'[3] In pursuit of this policy, the second part of his book contains an amazing array of proposals – for a farm colony, an overseas colony, a travelling hospital, 'the prison gate brigade', rescue homes for prostitutes and 'preventive homes for unfallen girls in danger', an 'enquiry office for lost people', 'refuges for the children of the streets', 'industrial schools', 'model suburban villages', 'the poor man's bank', a legal aid scheme for the poor, *etc.* And as this remarkable combination of social and spiritual concerns became known, 'inevitably public fancy endowed the Army with a slogan which has stuck ever since: "soup, soap and salvation"!'[4]

The third biblical argument for the partnership of evangelism and social action concerns *the communication of the gospel.* How is it to be made known? To begin with, it must be verbalized. Since God himself chose to speak, that is, to communicate with human beings in words, Christians should not despise them nor share in the current disenchantment with speech as a medium of communication. There is a precision in

[1] William Booth, *In Darkest England and the Way Out* (Salvation Army, 1890), p. 14.
[2] *Ibid.*, p. 45. [3] *Ibid.*, Preface, p. 4. *Cf.* p. 257.
[4] Richard Collier, *The General Next to God* (Collins, 1965), p. 199.

verbal communication, whether the words are spoken or written, which is absent from all other media. At the same time, the personal Word of God 'became flesh', in consequence of which people 'have seen his glory'.[1] If God's Word became visible, our words must too. We cannot announce God's love with credibility unless we also exhibit it in action. So we cannot stand aloof from those to whom we speak the gospel, or ignore their situation, their context. We have to enter into their social reality and share in their sufferings and their struggles. At that point, says J. H. Bavinck, our actions 'become preaching'.[2]

This brings us back to the ministry of Jesus.

> We are called today (says the Manila Manifesto) to a similar integration of words and deeds. In a spirit of humility we are to preach and teach, minister to the sick, feed the hungry, care for prisoners, help the disadvantaged and handicapped, and deliver the oppressed. While we acknowledge the diversity of spiritual gifts, callings and contexts, we also affirm that good news and good works are inseparable.[3]

Five objections considered

Although the biblical basis for the partnership between evangelism and social responsibility appears to be well laid, a number of objections to it are raised.

First, *shouldn't Christians steer clear of politics?* This objection often continues with the comment that, although all Christians agree with social service (*i.e.* philanthropy), we are not so sure about social action (*i.e.* political involvement).

Our answer to this first objection will largely depend on the connotation we give to the word 'politics'. If we take the narrow definition (referring to policies and programmes for legislative change, developed by political parties), then Christians

[1] Jn. 1:14.
[2] J. Herman Bavinck, *An Introduction to the Science of Missions* (1954; ET Presbyterian and Reformed, 1960), p. 113.
[3] *The Manila Manifesto*, para. 4: 'The Gospel and Social Responsibility', p. 15.

should not get involved unless they are prepared to do their homework. Politics is for the politicians, who have gained the necessary expertise. There is little more embarrassing than the sight of Christians pontificating on political issues from positions of ignorance.

The broader definition of 'politics', however, refers to the life of the *polis*, the city, and to the art of living together in community. In this sense all of us are involved in politics, since Jesus calls us to live in the secular world.

We must also agree that social service is not enough. Working – even agitating – for legislative change is an essential expression of neighbour-love. For example, we have to go beyond healing individuals to building hospitals where different medical specialities are concentrated; beyond feeding the hungry to the establishment of a new international economic order in which hunger is abolished; beyond binding up people's wounds like the good Samaritan to the task of ridding the Jericho road of brigands; and beyond the fair treatment of slaves to the abolition of the institution of slavery itself. There may be no explicit biblical warrant for these things, and certainly Jesus never called for the emancipation of slaves. But are we not profoundly thankful that his followers did centuries later? Political action (which could be defined as love seeking justice for the oppressed) is a legitimate extrapolation from the biblical emphasis on the practical priorities of love.

Secondly, *isn't this going back to the old 'social gospel'?* No, it is not. We must distinguish between the social gospel of theological liberalism, developed by Walter Rauschenbusch and his friends at the beginning of this century, and the social implications of the biblical gospel.

The 'social gospel' attempted to identify the kingdom of God with socialized society, and then spoke of socio-political action in terms of 'building the kingdom of God on earth'. The vision was proud, self-confident and Utopian. The social implications of the biblical gospel are different, however. Once we have become new people in Christ, and are members of his new society, we must accept the responsibility he gives us to permeate the old society as its salt and light.

Thirdly, *isn't this social concern the same as 'liberation theology'?* No, again it is not. Our main evangelical critique of liberation theology is that it attempts to equate the social, political and economic liberation of human beings with the 'salvation' which Christ came, died and rose to win. It has also tended to endorse Marxist theories (especially its social analysis) and to espouse violence. Having said that, the total liberation of human beings from everything which oppresses, demeans or dehumanizes them is surely pleasing to God their Creator. I wish evangelical Christians had got in first with a truly *biblical* theology of liberation. But to equate material 'liberation' with 'salvation' is to misunderstand and misrepresent Scripture.

Fourthly, *isn't it impossible to expect social change unless people are converted?* Once more, no it isn't. Of course we long for people to be converted. But Jesus Christ through his people has had an enormous influence for good on society as a whole. Think, for example, of the rising standards of health and hygiene, the wider availability of education, the growing respect for women and children, the concern for human rights and civil liberties, better conditions in factory, mine and prison, and the abolition of slavery and the slave trade.

Legislation can secure social improvement, even though it does not convert people or make them good. Even fallen human beings retain sufficient vestiges of the divine image to prefer justice to injustice, freedom to oppression, and peace to violence. Martin Luther King was right when he said:

> Morality cannot be legislated, but behaviour can be regulated. Judicial decrees may not change the heart, but they can restrict the heartless ... The law cannot make an employer love me, but it can keep him from refusing to hire me because of the colour of my skin.[1]

[1] Martin Luther King, in *Strength to Love* (Collins, 1963), p. 34, and in *Stride Toward Freedom: The Montgomery Story* (Harper and Row, 1958), p. 198.

Fifthly, *won't commitment to social action distract us from evangelism?* Yes, it might, but no, it need not. Certainly we should take warning of this possibility. We should be grateful for evangelical watchdogs who bark loud and long if they see any signs in us of a diminished commitment to evangelism. But if we live in the light of Jesus' death, resurrection and ascension, our incentives to evangelism will be continuously renewed at that perennial spring. In particular, his exaltation to the supreme place of honour will inspire us to desire that he be given the glory due to his name. Then social action, far from diverting us from evangelism, will make it more effective by rendering the gospel more visible and more credible.

Some examples of the partnership

'Social action in mission', wrote the American missiologist Dr R. Pierce Beaver, 'can be traced from the time of the apostles.' Moreover, 'concern was never limited to relief'; it included what today we call 'development', enabling communities to become self-reliant, whether by introducing improved plants and livestock, eliminating diseases, digging deeper wells for pure and constant water, or establishing industrial schools. In addition, the missionaries stood for social justice. They were

> constantly the protectors of native peoples against exploitation and injustice by government and commercial companies ... They played a very important part in the abolishing of forced labour in the Congo. They resisted black-birding in the South Pacific. They fought fiercely for human rights in combating opium, foot-binding, and exposure of girl babies in China. They waged war against widow-burning, infanticide and temple prostitution in India, and above all broke the social and economic slavery of the caste system for the low and outcaste peoples ...[1]

[1] From his introduction to *Christian Mission and Social Justice* by Samuel Escobar and John Driver (Herald, 1978), pp. 7–9.

The main difference between those days and today is that the responsibility for social witness has now in many places passed from the missionaries to the national church. Expatriates should engage in it only if invited by church leaders to do so.

There was, in fact, a certain inevitability about these concerns. It was literally impossible for the early missionaries to proclaim the message of God's love in Christ for the salvation of sinners and at the same time ignore the people's social conditions. The gospel itself, whose messengers they were, obliged them to oppose whatever was incompatible with it, whether slavery in Africa, untouchability and other evils in India, or the exploitation of tribespeople and the degrading poverty of the masses in Latin America. Similarly, it is impossible to evangelize in the West and simply turn a blind eye to the plight of the unemployed and the homeless, or of alienated youth and single-parent families in decayed and deprived inner-city areas. Has the gospel nothing to say about these things? Is our God interested only in bringing people to heaven, and not in ameliorating their circumstances on earth? No, to ignore the dehumanizing evils of society, while preaching the humanizing influence of salvation, is to be guilty of an inner contradiction which misrepresents God and distorts the gospel. Compassionate involvement in other people's felt needs is part and parcel of incarnational mission, and is demanded by the gospel of Christ.

Dr David Howard, General Secretary of the World Evangelical Fellowship from 1982 to 1992, has written about the ministry of his friend Gregorio Landero. Describing him as 'one of the most gifted evangelists I have ever known', he goes on:

> As he travelled around in evangelistic outreach to many parts of northern Colombia, he became heavily burdened because the people to whom he was ministering concerning their souls were suffering for lack of nutrition. He agonized about how he could preach a gospel of salvation when they were starving and suffering diseases which could be avoided with more adequate help. He began to study the possibilities of a more full-orbed outreach of the gospel. The result, over several

> years of hard work, was the development of United Action, a programme of total outreach for the needs of people. Gregorio is the leader of United Action and has given the vision and impetus to the entire development of the programme. Today, along with his evangelistic preaching, he and his colleagues are helping people to improve agricultural methods, developing family poultry projects that will put more protein into their diet, teaching home hygiene, carrying on dental work, literacy work and other things which will develop the family and community life of the people. There have also been efforts to help conserve the natural resources which are a part of the total creation.[1]

Festo Kivengere from Uganda had a similar holistic vision and commitment. He was first and foremost an evangelist. And when he became bishop of the diocese of Kigezi, he continued his extraordinarily effective world-wide evangelistic ministry, in which many were won to Christ. But he also concerned himself with development in his diocese, and especially with improved education, health and agriculture. His message centred on love and reconciliation through Christ, but he also pleaded for justice. Although not a political bishop, in the sense that he took no part in the work of the legislative, judicial or executive functions of the state, he nevertheless played a major role in the overthrow of Idi Amin. Several times he risked his life by confronting Amin in private and protesting against his reign of terror. 'Festo was so courageous,' his colleagues recalled. 'As the arrests continued, he kept going back to Amin to face him with the enormity of what he was doing.'[2]

Bishop Festo saw no inconsistency between these different aspects of his ministry. In a seminar he led at a 1987 convention in Amsterdam, he spoke of 'the tragic divide between what, according to the Old Testament and the New Testament, are the two sides of the same coin – *the salvation of the lost souls of*

[1] David Howard, *The Great Commission for Today* (IVP USA, 1976), pp. 84–85.
[2] Anne Coomes, *Festo Kivengere: The Authorized Biography* (Monarch, 1990), p. 318.

men ... and *the concern for their social needs*'.[1] And Bishop Shannon Mallory from California, who chaired the 'Partners in Mission' Consultation in Uganda in 1985, said of him:

> Our dear Festo was a fiery prophet in the midst of that debate (*sc.* about human rights violations being perpetrated at the time), calling passionately on the one hand for the spiritual renewal and reconciliation of the Church of Uganda, and at the same time boldly standing up (almost alone, it seemed) to speak out and condemn the political and military tyranny that was still going on in the country.[2]

Thus evangelistic witness and political protest, far from being incompatible, were and are natural twins. Although few Christian people may be called to engage in them simultaneously, since different people are called to different ministries, nevertheless the church as a whole must engage in both, since both belong to its God-given mission in the world.

[1] *Ibid.*, p. 455. [2] *Ibid.*, p. 434.

CHAPTER TWENTY-ONE

THE CHRISTOLOGY OF MISSION

'Missiology' is a recognized discipline with increasingly broad parameters. It includes the history of Christian missions; the comparative study of religions, the theology of religions and the uniqueness of Christ; the biblical basis for mission; mission strategies and church growth; missionary motives and methods; questions of culture, contextualization and church formation; the relations between evangelism and social responsibility; and the renewal of the church. Yet sometimes missing from this list is what might be called the 'Christology' of mission, which acknowledges Christ as the source and way, the heart and soul, the ground and goal, of all mission. Nothing is more important for the recovery of the church's mission (where it has been lost), or its development (where it is weak), than a fresh, clear and comprehensive vision of Jesus Christ. When he is demeaned, and specially when he is denied, in the fulness of his unique person and work, the church lacks motivation and direction, our morale crumbles and our mission disintegrates. But when we see Jesus, it is enough. We have all the inspiration, incentive, authority and power we need.

I propose in this chapter, then, that we take a fresh look at our Lord and Saviour, that we rehearse the six major events in his saving career (his incarnation, cross, resurrection, exaltation, Spirit-gift and parousia), and that we note the inescapable (though often neglected) missionary dimension of each.

The incarnation of Christ
The model for mission

According to the Willowbank Report on *Gospel and Culture* (1978), already mentioned several times, the incarnation was 'the most spectacular instance of cultural identification in the history of mankind'.[1] For the Son of God did not stay in the safe immunity of his heaven, remote from human sin and tragedy. He actually entered our world. He emptied himself of his glory and humbled himself to serve. He took our nature, lived our life, endured our temptations, experienced our sorrows, felt our hurts, bore our sins and died our death. He penetrated deeply into our humanness. He never stayed aloof from the people he might have been expected to avoid. He made friends with the dropouts of society. He even touched untouchables. He could not have become more one with us than he did. It was the total identification of love.

Reflecting on the meaning of mission, I have sometimes compared and contrasted in my mind Christ's mission to the earth with the Apollo mission to the moon. The analogy is shallow, no doubt, but it is also instructive, for there are both similarities and dissimilarities between them. They are similar, one might say, in that each is described as a 'mission', and consisted of a sensational, cross-cultural journey, in the case of Christ from heaven to earth, and of the astronauts from earth to moon. They are different, however, in the degree and depth of the identification involved. The Apollo astronauts never identified with the moon; if they had attempted to do so, they would have been dead in a moment. Instead, they took with them the accoutrements of the earth – earth's oxygen, equipment, clothing and food. But when Jesus came from heaven to earth, he left heaven behind him and brought nothing but himself. His was no superficial touchdown. He became a human being like us and so made himself vulnerable like us.

Yet, as we noted in chapter 15, when Christ identified with

[1] Page 28.

us, he did not surrender or in any way alter his own identity. For in becoming one of us, he yet remained himself. He became human, but without ceasing to be God.

Now he sends us into the world, as the Father sent him into the world.[1] In other words, our mission is to be modelled on his. Indeed, all authentic mission is incarnational mission. It demands identification without loss of identity. It means entering other people's worlds, as he entered ours, though without compromising our Christian convictions, values or standards.

I take the apostle Paul as an example. You could argue, and some people have argued, that Paul did *not* enter personally into the lives of the people he sought to evangelize; that he was essentially a preacher to anonymous faces, in the synagogue or in the open air; and that he kept his distance from the people he addressed. But no, that is not how he himself saw his ministry. On the contrary, although he was free, he made himself everybody's slave. 'To the Jews I became like a Jew, to win the Jews ... To those not having the law I became like one not having the law ..., so as to win those not having the law. To the weak I became weak, to win the weak. I have become all things to all men so that by all possible means I might save some.'[2] That is the principle of the incarnation. It is identification with people where they are.

In the history of missions there have been many dramatic examples of Christians trying to apply this principle. I mention three, taken from the last three centuries. In 1732 Count Zinzendorf, the Moravian leader, sent two of his missionaries to the West Indian sugar plantations. They found that the only way to reach the African slaves was to join their chain gangs and share their huts. In 1882 Major Frederick Tucker launched the Salvation Army in India. General Booth's last words to him were, 'Get into their skins, Tucker.' He did. Deeply concerned for the outcastes, he decided that he and his soldiers must live their life. So they donned saffron robes, adopted Indian names, walked barefoot, cleaned their teeth with charcoal, and ate their

[1] Jn. 17:18; 20:21. [2] 1 Cor. 9:19–22.

curry and water sitting cross-legged on the floor.[1]

Then in 1950 a young Italian Roman Catholic priest, Mario Borelli, horrified by the loveless, homeless plight of the *scugnizzi*, Naples' street children, decided that the only way to reach them was to become one of them. He took on 'their dress, their speech, their habits'. He may well have gone too far.[2] And missionaries are not always wise to 'go native', 'principally because a foreigner's attempt to do this may not be seen as authentic but as play-acting'.[3] Nevertheless, one cannot but admire these daring attempts to follow the example of Christ's incarnation.

For most of us, however, the incarnational model will involve a more mundane struggle. First, there is the need to enter into other people's *thought* world. In this connection I have always liked the title of Jim Sire's book *The Universe Next Door.*[4] He sub-titles it *A Basic World View Catalogue* and sketches the meaning of deism, naturalism, nihilism, existentialism, eastern pantheistic monism, *etc.* His point is that such people live in another universe of thought; it will therefore take a kind of incarnation to reach them.

Similarly, at the ecumenical missionary conference in Melbourne in May 1980, John V. Taylor, then Bishop of Winchester, emphasized that we will never be able to commend the gospel to modern sceptics 'so long as we remain inside our own cultural stockades. Genuine outsiders', he continues, 'can only be reached outside ... If we do not naturally belong to the world of the particular "outsiders" we want to reach, some of us must take the trouble to cross over and learn to be at home in that alien territory . . .'.[5]

We should, I believe, be praying and working for a whole new generation of Christian thinkers and apologists who will dedicate their God-given minds to Christ, enter sympathetically

[1] Richard Collier, *The General Next to God* (Collins, 1965), pp. 91–98.

[2] Morris West, *Children of the Sun* (1957; Pan, 1958), especially pp. 82–104.

[3] *The Willowbank Report: Gospel and Culture* (Lausanne Committee for World Evangelization, 1978), para. 6(b), p. 18.

[4] James Sire, *The Universe Next Door* (IVP, 1976; second edition, 1990).

[5] *Your Kingdom Come* (WCC, 1980), p. 143.

into their contemporaries' dilemmas, unmask false ideologies, and present the gospel of Jesus Christ in such a way that he is seen to offer what other religious systems cannot, because he and he alone can fulfil our deepest human aspirations. At least in the West, where the Enlightenment has run out of steam, the time is now ripe, urges Bishop Lesslie Newbigin, for 'a genuinely missionary encounter with post-Enlightenment culture'.[1]

Secondly, we need to enter other people's *heart* world, the world of their *Angst* and their alienation, and to weep with those who weep.[2] In every non-Christian (and many Christians too), even in the jolliest extraverts, there are hidden depths of pain. We can reach them only if we are willing to enter into their suffering. It will also include entering into people's social reality, as we saw in the last chapter, for it is impossible to share the gospel with people in a social vacuum, isolating them from their actual context and ignoring their suffering.

The cross of Christ
The cost of mission

One of the most neglected aspects of biblical mission today is the indispensable place in it of suffering, even of death. Yet it is plain in Scripture. Let me give you three examples.

First, we see it clearly in *Isaiah's suffering servant*. Before the servant can be a light to the nations and bring salvation to the ends of the earth,[3] he offers his back to those who beat him, his cheeks to those who pull out his beard, and his face to mockery and spitting.[4] Before he can 'sprinkle many nations',[5] he is 'despised and rejected by men, a man of sorrows, and familiar with suffering'.[6] More than that, he bears our sins and dies for us as a guilt offering.[7] Douglas Webster laid a proper emphasis on this. He wrote:

[1] Lesslie Newbigin, *The Other Side of 1984* (WCC, 1983), especially pp. 22 and 31. See also his *Foolishness to the Greeks* (SPCK, 1986), in which he appeals to us to challenge both 'the scientific worldview' and 'atheistic materialism'.
[2] Rom. 12:15 (RSV). [3] Is. 49:6; *cf.* 42:1–4. [4] Is. 50:6–7. [5] Is. 52:15.
[6] Is. 53:3. [7] Is. 53:4–12.

> Mission sooner or later leads into passion. In biblical categories . . . the servant must suffer . . .; it is that which makes mission effective . . . Every form of mission leads to some form of cross. The very shape of mission is cruciform. We can understand mission only in terms of the Cross . . .'.[1]

Secondly, *the Lord Jesus himself* taught and exhibited this principle, and extended it to his followers. When those Greeks wanted to see him, he said: 'The hour has come for the Son of Man to be glorified (*sc.* on the cross). I tell you the truth, unless a grain of wheat falls to the ground and dies, it remains only a single seed. But if it dies, it produces many seeds.'[2] In other words, only through his death would the gospel be extended to the Gentile world. So death is more than the way to life; it is the condition of fruitfulness. Unless it dies, the seed remains alone. But if it dies, it multiplies. It was so for the Messiah; it is the same for the messianic community. For 'whoever serves me must follow me', Jesus said.[3]

Thirdly, *the apostle Paul* applied the same principle to himself. Consider these extraordinary texts:

> I ask you, therefore, not to be discouraged because of my sufferings for you, which are your glory.[4]

> Therefore I endure everything for the sake of the elect, that they too may obtain the salvation that is in Christ Jesus, with eternal glory.[5]

> So then, death is at work in us, but life is at work in you.[6]

These three verses contain some truly startling statements. Paul dares to claim that through his sufferings others will enter into glory, that through his endurance others will be saved, and that through his death others will live. Is the apostle out of his mind? No! Does he really mean it? Yes! It is not, of course, that

[1] Douglas Webster, *Yes to Mission* (SCM, 1966), pp. 101–102. [2] Jn. 12:23–24. [3] Jn. 12:26. [4] Eph. 3:13. [5] 2 Tim. 2:10. [6] 2 Cor. 4:12.

he attributes any atoning efficacy to his own sufferings and death, as he does to the sufferings and death of Jesus Christ. It is rather this. People can receive salvation, life and glory only when the gospel is preached to them, and those who preach the gospel with faithfulness invariably suffer for it. Paul knew what he was talking about. The reason why he became a prisoner, and was chained, is that he had been faithful to the 'heavenly vision' that Gentiles would be received into the Christian community on precisely the same terms as Jews. It was this aspect of the gospel which aroused almost fanatical opposition to him. And the Gentiles owed their salvation to his willingness to suffer for his proclamation of this good news.

There have been many examples since Paul of suffering for the gospel. It is not an accident that the Greek word for 'witness' is *martys*. The pages of church history are replete with stories of persecution. Sometimes it has been *physical*. In 1880, soon after the Salvation Army had been founded in Britain,

> 'publicans and brothel-keepers were launching a savage all-out counter-attack ... The Army learned the bleak truth of the Spanish proverb: "He who would be a Christian must expect crucifixion" ... In one year – 1882 – 669 Salvation Army officers were knocked down or brutally assaulted.' When Salvationists dedicated their children in the 1880s, they confessed their willingness that their children should be 'despised, hated, cursed, beaten, kicked, imprisoned or killed for Christ's sake'.[1]

At other times the suffering was more *mental* than physical. The Maréchale, for example, as the eldest daughter of General Booth was always known, wrote an article in 1883 for the *War Cry* from her prison cell in Neuchâtel, Switzerland, in which she reflected on inward crucifixion.

[1] Richard Collier, *The General Next to God* (Collins, 1965), pp. 104–109.

> Jesus was crucified ... Ever since that day, men have tried to find an easier way, but the easier ways fail. If you would win thousands who are without God, you must be ready to be crucified: your plans, your ideas, your likes and your inclinations. Things have changed, you say, there is liberty now. Is there? Go and live Christ's life, speak as he spoke, teach what he taught, denounce sin wherever you find it, and see if the enemy will not turn on you with all the fury of hell ... Christ wasn't crucified in the drawing-room. His was no easy-chair business ... Do you shrink from being bated, misrepresented and spoken evil of? It is time you were crucified ...[1]

Yet a third kind of suffering is *social.* Vincent Donovan, an American Roman Catholic priest who laboured for seventeen years among the Masai in Tanzania, once asked himself what the distinguishing mark of a missionary was. This is the answer he gave himself:

> A missionary is essentially a *social martyr*, cut off from his roots, his stock, his blood, his land, his background, his culture ... He must be stripped as naked as a human being can be, down to the very texture of his being ... (he must) divest himself of his very culture, so that he can be a naked instrument of the gospel to the cultures of the world.[2]

This call to suffering and death, as the condition for mission fruitfulness, sounds very alien, however, in our contemporary western ears. The respectable middle-class captivity of the church is not exactly an arena for persecution. Where is the willingness to suffer for Christ today? In the evangelical tendency to triumphalism there seems little place for tribulation. And the false 'prosperity gospel', promising unlimited health and wealth, blinds people to the biblical warnings of adversity.

[1] Carolyn Scott, *The Heavenly Witch: The Story of the Maréchale* (Hamish Hamilton, 1981), p. 113.
[2] Vincent Donovan, *Christianity Rediscovered: An Epistle from the Masai* (1978; SCM, 1982), pp. 193–194.

Yet the fact remains that if we compromised less we would assuredly suffer more.

There are three main reasons for opposition; they belong to the spheres of doctrine, ethics and discipline. As for doctrine, the gospel of Christ crucified remains folly to the intellectually proud and a stumbling-block to the self-righteous; both groups find it humiliating. As for ethics, Christ's call is to self-denial and self-control; the self-indulgent find its challenge unacceptable. As for discipline, both baptism and the Lord's Supper presuppose repentance and faith in those who wish to receive them; to deny these gospel sacraments to anybody, even to those who openly admit that they neither repent nor believe, nevertheless provokes them to outrage. Thus those who seek to be faithful in doctrine, ethics and discipline are sure to arouse persecution, in the church as well as in the world.

Are we ready, then, to bear the pain of being ridiculed, the loneliness of being ostracized, the hurt of being spoken against and slandered? Indeed, are we willing if necessary to die with Christ to popularity and promotion, to comfort and success, to our ingrained sense of personal and cultural superiority, to our selfish ambition to be rich, famous or powerful?

It is the seed that dies, which multiplies.

A brother from Orissa, India, once told me that, when he was eight years old, his evangelist father had been martyred, killed by hired assasssins. At the time of his father's death, he added, there were only twelve churches in the region; when he spoke to me, there were one hundred and fifty.

The resurrection of Christ
The mandate for mission

It is of the greatest importance to remember that the resurrection preceded the Great Commission. It was the risen Lord who issued his commission to his followers to go and make disciples of all nations. He could not have issued it earlier, before he had been raised from death and invested with authority. 'All authority in heaven and on earth has been given to me,' he could now say. 'Therefore go and make disciples . . .'[1]

This is a major theme of a book by Johannes Blauw, a former secretary of the Netherlands Missionary Council. It was called *The Missionary Nature of the Church*, and sub-titled *A Survey of the Biblical Theology of Mission.* His thesis is that the Old Testament perspective was one of 'universalism' (God promising that all the nations he had made would come and worship him),[2] but not of 'mission' (Israel going out to win the nations). The prophetic vision of the last days was of a 'pilgrimage of the nations' to Jerusalem. Mount Zion would be exalted as chief among the mountains, and 'all nations will stream to it'.[3] In the New Testament, however, this 'centripetal missionary consciousness' is replaced by a 'centrifugal missionary activity'.[4] That is, instead of the nations streaming to the church, the church now goes out to the nations. And what was the moment of change? 'The Great Turning-Point',[5] argues Johannes Blauw, was the resurrection. It preceded the Great Commission to go, all authority having now been given to Christ in fulfilment of Daniel 7:13–14. 'With Easter a new age has begun, the enthronement of a new ruler of the world, and the proclamation of this new ruler among the nations. *Mission is the summons of the Lordship of Christ.*'[6]

'If the mission of the New Testament', Johannes Blauw elaborates later, 'seems at first glance centrifugal, it is to enable it to be centripetal. We go out into the world to gather it together; we cast the net to draw it in; we sow to reap.'[7] Moreover, 'in Paul's own person the centripetal and centrifugal aspects of the preaching are brought together'.[8] That is, while going out to preach the gospel, he is gathering both Gentiles and Israel, and bringing them home.

The resurrection, however, is the key to both movements. It is the risen Lord who sends us out into the world, and it is the

[1] Mt. 28:18–19. [2] *E.g.* Ps. 86:9. [3] *E.g.* Is. 2:1–3.
[4] Johannes Blauw, *The Missionary Nature of the Church* (1962; Eerdmans, 1974), pp. 34, 54, 66. See also Joachim Jeremias, *Jesus' Promise to the Nations* (1956; ET SCM, 1958), especially pp. 58–67 which emphasize the centripetal pilgrimage.
[5] *Ibid.*, p. 83. [6] *Ibid.*, p. 84. [7] *Ibid.*, p. 166. [8] *Ibid.*, p. 101.

same risen Lord who gathers people in to his church. The universal mission of the church derives its legitimacy from the universal lordship of Christ. In this way the resurrection supplies the mandate for mission.

The exaltation of Christ
The incentive for mission

Motivation is a very important aspect of every human enterprise. We need to know not only *what* we should be doing, but *why* we should be doing it. When our motives are sound and strong, we can persist in any task almost indefinitely. But when our motivation is faulty, we immediately begin to flag. This is undoubtedly true of the Christian mission. To seek to win people for Christ is hard work, widely unappreciated and unpopular, and, as we have just seen, it often provokes active opposition. The church will need powerful incentives, therefore, if it is to persevere. My argument in this section is that the exaltation of Jesus Christ to the Father's right hand, that is, to the position of supreme honour, provides the strongest of all missionary incentives.

It is better in this context to refer to Christ's 'exaltation' than to his 'ascension', for, although it is true that 'he ascended into heaven', yet to say that 'he was exalted' indicates that it was God the Father who thus vindicated, promoted, enthroned and invested his Son. Moreover, the apostolic statements of Jesus' exaltation are at pains to emphasize that he was elevated above all possible rivals, indeed '*far above* all rule and authority, power and dominion, and every title that can be given, not only in the present age but also in the one to come'.[1] This is 'the highest place' to which God has exalted Jesus[2] and the 'supremacy' which he wants him to enjoy.[3]

This throws light on the use of the word 'superiority', which is viewed with distaste by those who are forsaking the old exclusivism and inclusivism in favour of the new pluralism (see

[1] Eph. 1:21. [2] Phil. 2:9. [3] Col. 1:18.

chapter 18). Certainly, to adopt an 'air of superiority' towards the adherents of other faiths is a horrid form of discourtesy and arrogance. Certainly too, as Professor Hick points out, 'in the eighteenth and nineteenth centuries the conviction of the decisive superiority of Christianity' gave a powerful impetus to the imperial expansion of the West.[1] But it is not 'Christianity' as an empirical institution or system for which Christians should claim superiority. It is Christ, and only Christ. We should affirm without any sense of embarrassment or shame that he is 'superior' to all other religious leaders, precisely because he alone humbled himself in love even to the cross and therefore God has raised him 'above' every other person, rank or title.

Consequent upon his elevation or exaltation to the highest place, God desires 'every knee' to bow to him and 'every tongue' to confess his lordship.[2] The repeated 'every' is absolute; it admits of no exceptions. If God has given this supreme honour to Jesus, and desires everybody else to honour him, then the people of God should share his desire. This is sometimes spoken of in Scripture in terms of 'zeal', and even 'jealousy'. The prophet Elijah, for example, deeply distressed by the apostasy of Israel, in particular their worship of the Canaanite Baals, said: 'I have been very zealous for the LORD, the God of hosts.'[3] The apostle Paul spoke of himself as 'jealous ... with a godly jealousy' for the Corinthians, because he had betrothed them to Christ as their one husband, but was afraid that they might now be led astray from their 'sincere and pure devotion to Christ'.[4] Similarly, Henry Martyn, that brilliant and faithful Christian missionary in Muslim Iran towards the beginning of the nineteenth century, once said: 'I could not endure existence if Jesus were not glorified; it would be hell to me if he were to be always thus dishonoured.'[5]

This same sense of pain whenever Jesus Christ is dishonoured, and this same sense of jealousy that he should be

[1] John Hick and Paul F. Knitter (eds.), *The Myth of Christian Uniqueness* (SCM, 1987), p. 20.
[2] Phil. 2:9–11. [3] 1 Ki. 19:10 (RV). [4] 2 Cor. 11:2–3.
[5] Constance E. Padwick, *Henry Martyn: Confessor of the Faith* (1922; IVP, 1953), p. 146.

given the honour due to him, should stir within us at the end of the twentieth century, in whatever particular culture we live. The primary motive for mission is neither obedience to the Great Commission, nor even love for those who are oppressed, lonely, lost and perishing, important as both those incentives are, but rather zeal or 'jealousy' for the glory of Christ. It was 'for his name's sake',[1] in order that it might receive the honour which it deserved, that the first missionaries went out. The same passionate longing should motivate us.

This, surely, is our answer to those who tell us that we should no longer evangelize or seek conversions. Professor Gregory Baum of the University of Toronto, for example, has said that 'after Auschwitz the Christian churches no longer wish to convert the Jews', for 'the churches have come to recognize Judaism as an authentic religion before God, with independent value and meaning, not as a stage on the way to Christianity'.[2] Similarly a Greek Catholic bishop, on his resignation, wrote to his friends: 'As a bishop, a preacher of the gospel, I never tried to convert a Jew or Arab Moslem to Christianity; rather to convert them to be a better Jew, a better Moslem.'[3] Have these men, then, no jealousy for the honour of Jesus Christ? Do they not care when he is despised and rejected? Do they not long, as God does, that all human beings, whatever their culture or religion, will bow their knee to Jesus, and submit to him as their Lord?

It is this zeal for Christ which integrates the worship and witness of the church. How can we worship Christ and not mind that others do not? It is our worship of Christ which impels us to witness to Christ, in order that others may come and worship him too.

[1] Rom. 1:5; *cf.* 3 Jn. 7.

[2] Quoted in Gerald H. Anderson and Thomas F. Stransky (ed.), *Christ's Lordship and Religious Pluralism* (Orbis, 1981), pp. 115–117. See also *A Theological Understanding of the Relationship between Christians and Jews*, a paper commended for study by the General Assembly of the Presbyterian Church, USA, in 1987.

[3] Quoted by Cormac Murphy-O'Connor, Bishop of Arundel and Brighton, in *The Family of the Church* (DLT, 1984), p. 41.

The Spirit-gift of Christ
The power for mission

The World Missionary Conference held in Edinburgh in 1910 was described by John R. Mott, its leading figure, as 'the most significant gathering ever held in the interest of the world's evangelization'.[1] After surveying the opportunities, the problems and the encouragements, in relation to world evangelization, John Mott listed four 'requirements of the present situation'. He began with (1) an adequate plan, (2) an adequate home base, and (3) an efficient church on the mission field. Then the fourth requirement he called 'the super-human factor'. He went on to say that, although missionaries, nationals and mission leaders differ substantially regarding plans, means and methods, they

> are absolutely united in the conviction that the world's evangelization is a divine enterprise, that the Spirit of God is the great Missioner, and that only as he dominates the work and workers can we hope for success in the undertaking to carry the knowledge of Christ to all people. They believe that he gave the missionary impulse to the early church, and that today all true mission work must be inaugurated, directed and sustained by him.[2]

Already during his public ministry Jesus had drawn attention to the missionary nature and purpose of the Holy Spirit. He had likened him to 'streams of living water' irrigating the desert, and had promised that they would flow out from within every believer.[3] 'No one can ... be indwelt by the Spirit of God', comments William Temple, 'and keep that Spirit to himself. Where the Spirit is, he flows forth; if there is no flowing forth, he is not there.'[4] And so it proved to be in the early church from

[1] From his Preface to *The Decisive Hour of Christian Missions* (Church Missionary Society, 1910).
[2] *Ibid.*, p. 193. [3] Jn. 7:37–39.
[4] William Temple, *Readings in St. John's Gospel* (1945; Macmillan, 1955), p. 130.

the Day of Pentecost onwards, as we saw in chapter 19.

There are, of course, differences between and within the churches regarding the charismatic or neo-pentecostal movement, the so-called 'baptism of the Spirit', the diversity of spiritual gifts, and the place of 'signs and wonders' in evangelism and church growth. But all of us should be able to affirm together that evangelism is impossible without the Holy Spirit, without God the Evangelist, as Professor David Wells calls him in a book of that title.[1] To summarize the Spirit's indispensable ministry, I do not think I could do better than quote from the Manila Manifesto (1989):

> The Scriptures declare that God himself is the chief evangelist. For the Spirit of God is the Spirit of truth, love, holiness and power, and evangelism is impossible without him. It is he who anoints the messenger, confirms the word, prepares the hearer, convicts the sinful, enlightens the blind, gives life to the dead, enables us to repent and believe, unites us to the Body of Christ, assures us that we are God's children, leads us into Christlike character and service, and sends us out in our turn to be Christ's witnesses. In all this the Holy Spirit's main preoccupation is to glorify Jesus Christ by showing him to us and forming him in us.
>
> All evangelism involves spiritual warfare with the principalities and powers of evil, in which only spiritual weapons can prevail, especially the Word and the Spirit, with prayer. We therefore call on all Christian people to be diligent in their prayers both for the renewal of the church and for the evangelization of the world.
>
> Every true conversion involves a power encounter, in which the superior authority of Jesus Christ is demonstrated. There is no greater miracle than this, in which the believer is set free from the bondage of Satan and sin, fear and futility, darkness and death.
>
> Although the miracles of Jesus were special, being signs of

[1] David Wells, *God the Evangelist* (Eerdmans and Paternoster, 1987).

his Messiahship and anticipations of his perfect kingdom when all nature will be subject to him, we have no liberty to place limits on the power of the living Creator today. We reject both the scepticism which denies miracles and the presumption which demands them, both the timidity which shrinks from the fulness of the Spirit and the triumphalism which shrinks from the weakness in which Christ's power is made perfect.

We repent of all self-confident attempts either to evangelize in our own strength or to dictate to the Holy Spirit. We determine in future not to 'grieve' or 'quench' the Spirit, but rather to seek to spread the good news 'with power, with the Holy Spirit and with deep conviction'.[1]

There is an urgent need for us to humble ourselves before the sovereign Holy Spirit today. Sociological knowledge and communications expertise are important. Indeed, they are gifts of God to be used in evangelism. But we have to beware lest they diminish our reliance on the power of the Holy Spirit. Only the Holy Spirit of God can take words spoken in human weakness and carry them home with power to the mind, conscience and will of the hearers.[2] Only he can open the eyes of the blind to see the truth as it is in Jesus, unstop the ears of the deaf to hear his voice, and loosen the tongues of the dumb to confess that he is Lord. The Holy Spirit is the chief witness; 'without *his* witness, *ours* is futile'.[3]

The parousia of Christ
The urgency of mission

There was something fundamentally anomalous about the attitude of the Twelve immediately after the ascension. They had been commissioned to go 'to the ends of *the earth*', but they

[1] *The Manila Manifesto: An Elaboration of the Lausanne Covenant 15 Years Later* (Lausanne Committee for World Evangelization, 1989), para. B.5.
[2] See 1 Cor. 2:1–5; 1 Thes. 1:5. [3] The Lausanne Covenant, para. 14.

were standing on the Mount of Olives 'looking into *the sky*'![1] They were then promised that the Jesus who had just disappeared would in due time reappear. For this event they must wait; no amount of sky-watching would hasten it. Meanwhile, once they had been clothed with the Spirit's power, they must get on with their task. Earth, not sky, was to be their preoccupation. Thus the four stages of the divine programme were plain. First, Jesus returned to the Father (ascension). Secondly, the Spirit came (Pentecost). Thirdly, the church goes out to make disciples (mission). Fourthly, Jesus will return (parousia). Between the first and the fourth events, the ascension and the parousia, the disappearance and the reappearance of Jesus, there was to be an unspecified 'inter-adventual' period. During it no further saving event would take place. The gap was to be filled with the world-wide witness of the church. So the implied message of the angels after the ascension was this: 'You have seen him go. You will see him come. But between that going and coming there must be another. The Spirit must come, and you must go – into the world for Christ.'[2]

It is in this way that the parousia of Jesus is linked with the mission of the church. The parousia will terminate the mission-period which began with Pentecost. We have only a limited time in which to complete our God-given responsibility. We need, then, to recover the eager eschatological expectation of the first Christians, together with the sense of urgency which it gave them. Jesus had promised that the end would not come until the gospel of the kingdom had been preached throughout the world to all nations.[3] But we have no liberty to presume that we have plenty of time, and so drag our feet or slacken our pace in mission. On the contrary, the church is 'on the move – hastening to the ends of the earth to beseech all men to be reconciled to God, and hastening to the end of time to meet its Lord who will gather all into one'.[4] The two ends will coincide.

Another important link between the church's mission and the

[1] Acts 1:8, 11. [2] See John Stott, *The Message of Acts* (IVP, 1990), p. 51.
[3] Mt. 24:14; *cf.* Mk. 13:10.
[4] Lesslie Newbigin, *The Household of God* (SCM, 1953), p. 25.

Lord's return has to do with judgment. 'We must all appear before the judgment seat of Christ,' Paul wrote, 'that each one may receive what is due to him . . .'[1] This is evidently not the universal judgment relating to our eternal destinies, but a particular judgment of God's people relating to our Christian life and ministry. It concerns the promise of recognition and recompense of some kind, or their opposite. The next verse reads: 'Since, then, we know what it is to fear the Lord, we try to persuade men.'[2] That is, the reason why we seek to persuade people of the truth of the gospel is that we stand in awe of the Lord Jesus and his tribunal, before which we will one day have to give an account. I am reminded of those solemn passages in the prophecy of Ezekiel,[3] in which God appoints him 'a watchman for the house of Israel' and makes him responsible to warn them of the coming judgment. If he fails to give a wicked person adequate warning, and does not speak out to dissuade him from his evil ways, God says, 'I will hold you accountable for his blood.'[4]

In a similar way the apostle grounded his charge to Timothy to 'preach the Word' with urgency not only on 'the presence of God and of Christ Jesus', but also 'in view of his appearing and his kingdom', who 'will judge the living and the dead'.[5] To live, work and witness in conscious anticipation of Christ's parousia and judgment is a wholesome stimulus to faithfulness. Scripture bids us remember that, from God's perspective, the time is short, the need is great, and the task is urgent.

Let me recapitulate what Christ's saving career says to us about mission. The *model* for mission is his incarnation (identification without loss of identity), its *cost* is his cross (the seed which dies multiplies), its *mandate* is his resurrection (all authority is now his), its *motivation* is his exaltation (the honour of his name), its *power* is his gift of the Spirit (who is the paramount witness), and its *urgency* is his parousia (we will have to give him an account when he comes).

[1] 2 Cor. 5:10. [2] 2 Cor. 5:11. [3] Ezk. 3 and 33. [4] Ezk. 33:8.
[5] 2 Tim. 4:1–2.

It seems to me that the church needs to keep returning, for its inspiration and direction, to this christological basis of mission. The challenge before us is to see Jesus Christ as adequate for our task. We have to repent of our pessimism (especially in the West), our low expectations, our cynical unbelief that, although the church may grow elsewhere, it cannot grow among us. Fiddlesticks! If only we could gain a fresh and compelling vision of Jesus Christ, incarnate and crucified, risen and reigning, bestowing the Spirit and coming again! Then we would have the clarity of purpose and strength of motive, the courage, the authority, the power and the passion for world evangelization in our time.

In an early anniversary sermon of the Church Missionary Society (I believe in 1805), John Venn, the Rector of Clapham, described a missionary in the following terms. His eloquent portrait is equally applicable to every kind of Christian witness:

> With the world under his feet, with heaven in his eye, with the gospel in his hand and Christ in his heart, he pleads as an ambassador for God, knowing nothing but Jesus Christ, enjoying nothing but the conversion of sinners, hoping for nothing but the promotion of the kingdom of Christ, and glorying in nothing but in the cross of Christ Jesus, by which he is crucified to the world, and the world to him.[1]

[1] Michael Hennell, *John Venn and the Clapham Sect* (Lutterworth, 1958), p. 245.

CONCLUSION

THE NOW AND THE NOT YET

I began in the Introduction with the tension between the 'then' (past) and the 'now' (present); I end with another tension, between the 'now' (present) and the 'not yet' (future). The first concerns the connection between the historical and the contemporary; the second between the contemporary and the eschatological. Yet the two tensions belong together. For in and through Jesus Christ, the then, the now and the not yet, the past, the present and the future are brought into a creative relationship. Christians live in the present, but do so in thankfulness for the past and in anticipation of the future.

This final chapter is an essay in what I like to call 'BBC'. In this context these letters stand neither for the British Broadcasting Corporation, nor for Beautiful British Columbia, nor for the Bankok Bible College, but for Balanced Biblical Christianity. Balance is a rare commodity these days in almost every sphere, not least among us who profess to follow Christ.

I do not claim any close personal acquaintance with the devil: it is even possible that some of my readers know him better than I! But what I do know is that he is a fanatic, and the enemy of all common sense, moderation and balance. One of his favourite pastimes is to upset our equilibrium, and tip Christians (especially evangelical Christians) off balance. If he cannot induce us to deny Christ, he will get us to distort Christ instead. In consequence lopsided Christianity is widespread, in which we over-emphasize one aspect of a truth, while under-emphasizing another. Thank God, however, that he has given us two ears, so that we may engage in double listening, and may pay careful attention to both sides of every question; two eyes, so that we may see straight and not squint; two hands, so that we may grasp both extremes of every biblical antinomy; and two feet, so that we may walk steadily and not limp our way through life.

A balanced grasp of the now–not yet tension would be very conducive to Christian unity, and especially to a greater harmony among evangelical believers. I confess to being deeply disturbed by the barriers which separate us who share the same fundamental biblical faith. I am not now thinking either of the divide between Rome and the churches of the Reformation, or of the gulf between conservative and liberal Christians, that is to say, between those who believe in the givenness of revealed truth and those whose chief authority is what they call 'the climate of modern opinion'. I am referring rather to disunity within the evangelical movement itself. It goes without saying that we believe the Apostles' and the Nicene Creeds, and the substance of the major Reformation confessions as well. More than that, we have recently found a useful theological rallying-point in the Lausanne Covenant (1974) and its elaboration in the Manila Manifesto (1989). So we are agreed on the doctrinal and ethical fundamentals of the faith. Yet we seem to be constitutionally prone to quarrelling and dividing, or simply to going our own way and building our own empire. We appear to suffer from a pathological inability to get on with each other or to cooperate in the cause of the kingdom of God. We ought not to make light of this grievous situation.

Do you know Saki's marvellous short story *The Secret Sin of Septimus Brope*?[1] In it Mrs Troyle expresses dismay at the thought of losing her maid, Florinda. 'I am sure I don't know what I should do without Florinda . . . She understands my hair. I've long ago given up trying to do anything with it myself. I regard one's hair as I regard husbands; as long as one is seen together in public, one's private divergences don't matter!' But we have no liberty to regard each other as Mrs Troyle regarded her hair and her husband. Both our public and our private divergences do matter. For they are undoubtedly displeasing to

[1] Saki (H. H. Munro), *The Chronicles of Clovis* (1911).

God and damaging to our mission in the world.

One example concerns the extraordinary world-wide development of the Pentecostal churches and the charismatic movement. They are growing faster than any other Christian group. Yet some Christians take up towards them such a completely negative stance that they seem to be in danger of quenching the Spirit, while some charismatics are so triumphalistic that they find it hard to listen to those who have serious theological questions about their distinctive Pentecostal beliefs and practices. Is it possible, then, for charismatic and non-charismatic evangelicals to respect and accept each other sufficiently to permit genuine fellowship and active collaboration? I think it *is* possible, even if problematic, and that an insight into the tension between the 'already' and the 'not yet' should contribute considerably to mutual understanding.

Kingdom come and coming

Fundamental to New Testament Christianity is the perspective that we are living 'in between times' – between the past and the future, between the first and the second comings of Christ, between what has been done and what remains to be done, between present reality and future destiny, between kingdom come and kingdom coming, between the 'now already' in relation to the inauguration of the kingdom and the 'not yet' in relation to its consummation. Physically speaking, it is of course impossible to face in opposite directions simultaneously; but spiritually speaking, it is essential to do so, looking back to the incarnation and all that it involved, and looking forward to the parousia and all that it will bring. A sample text, if I may elaborate it a little, would be this: 'Dear friends, now already we are God's children, but not yet has it been revealed what we will be.'[1]

The theological basis for this tension is to be found in Jesus' own teaching about the kingdom of God. It is universally

[1] 1 Jn. 3:2, my paraphrase.

agreed both that the kingdom featured prominently in his teaching and that he announced its coming. Where scholars have disagreed, however, is over the time of its arrival. Has the kingdom already come, because Jesus brought it with him? Or is its coming still future, so that we await it expectantly? Or does the truth lie between these positions, and combine them?

Albert Schweitzer, the amazingly versatile German musician, doctor, theologian and missionary (who died in 1965), argued in his famous book *The Quest of the Historical Jesus* (1906) that, according to Jesus, the kingdom lay entirely in the future. He was an apocalyptic prophet, who taught (mistakenly) that at any moment God was about to intervene supernaturally and establish his kingdom. The radical demands Jesus made on his disciples (*e.g.* to sell their goods, to turn the other cheek, and not to resist evil) were an 'interim ethic' in the light of the imminent arrival of the kingdom. Schweitzer's position has been called either 'thoroughgoing' or 'consistent' eschatology, because he developed his single thesis with thoroughness and consistency.

At the opposite extreme was C. H. Dodd (who died in 1973). In his book *The Parables of the Kingdom* (1934) he elaborated his 'realized eschatology', namely that the coming of the kingdom is wholly past. Although God's rule is eternal, yet it irrupted into space and time in the person of Jesus. Dodd laid a heavy emphasis on two verses whose verbs are in the perfect tense, namely 'The kingdom of God has arrived'[1] and 'The kingdom of God has come upon you'.[2] Further, according to Dodd, there is no future coming of the kingdom. Verses which speak of one must be understood as concessions to a popular, primitive Christian eschatology; they were not part of Jesus' own teaching.

In place of these extreme polarities (Schweitzer declaring the kingdom's coming to be wholly future, and Dodd wholly past), most scholars have taken a median position, that Jesus spoke of the kingdom as both a present reality and a future expectation.

[1] Mk. 1:15, as he translated *ēngiken*. [2] Mt. 12:28, *ephthasen*.

On the one hand he had himself inaugurated it, and on the other he would at his parousia consummate it. Joachim Jeremias, for example, wrote in his book *The Parables of Jesus* (1947) of 'eschatology in process of realization'. A. M. Hunter, in his *Interpreting the Parables* (1960) preferred the term 'inaugurated eschatology'. A similar stance was adopted by the Dutch theologian Herman Ridderbos in *The Coming of the Kingdom* (1950) and by the American George Eldon Ladd both in his *The Gospel of the Kingdom* (1959) and in his mature treatment of the subject, *The Presence of the Future* (1974). Ladd's central thesis was that the kingdom of God, meaning God's redemptive and dynamic rule,

> which will appear as an apocalyptic act at the end of the age, has already come into human history in the person and mission of Jesus to overcome evil, to deliver men from its power, and to bring them into the blessings of God's reign.[1]

So the kingdom did come with Jesus. 'But it did not come without remainder: the consummation still lay in the indeterminate future.'[2]

That Jesus regarded and described the kingdom as a present phenomenon is indubitable. He taught that the time of fulfilment had arrived;[3] that 'the strong man' was now bound and disarmed, facilitating the plundering of his goods, as was evident from his exorcisms;[4] that the kingdom was already either 'within' or 'among' people;[5] that it could now be 'entered' or 'received';[6] and that, since the time of John the Baptist his forerunner, who had announced its imminent arrival, 'forceful men' had in fact been 'laying hold' of it or 'forcing their way' into it.[7]

Yet in Jesus' perspective the kingdom was a future expectation as well. It would not be perfected until the last day. So he

[1] G. E. Ladd, *The Presence of the Future* (1974; SPCK, 1980), p. 218. [2] *Ibid.*, p. 323.
[3] *E.g.* Mk. 1:14; Mt. 13:16–17.
[4] Mt. 12:28–29; *cf.* Lk. 10:17–18. [5] Lk. 17:20–21. [6] *E.g.* Mk. 10:15.
[7] Mt. 11:12; Lk. 16:16.

looked forward to the end, and taught his disciples to do so also. They were to pray 'Your kingdom come'[1] and to 'seek' it first,[2] giving priority to its expansion. At times he also referred to the final state of his followers in terms of 'entering' the kingdom[3] or 'receiving' it.[4]

In particular, his agricultural parables (*e.g.* those of the seed growing secretly, the mustard seed, and the wheat and the tares)[5] bring together the processes of planting, growth and harvest. Like seed the kingdom had already been planted in the world; now it would grow by invisible divine activity until the end. This seems to be what Jesus meant by 'the mystery (or secret) of the kingdom'.[6] Its presence was unobtrusive, yet also revolutionary, as the power of God would cause it to grow until finally it would become manifest to all.

Another way in which Scripture expresses the tension between the 'now' and the 'not yet', the present and the future, is by the terminology of the two 'ages'. From the perspective of the Old Testament, history is divided into 'this age' and 'that age',[7] between 'this present age' (which is evil) and 'the age to come' or 'the last days', namely the kingdom of righteousness to be introduced by the Messiah.[8] Sometimes this age is likened to a long, dark night, to be followed by the dawn of a new day. This simple structure of two consecutive ages was decisively changed, however, by the coming of Jesus. For he brought in the new age, and died for us in order to deliver us 'from the present evil age'.[9] In consequence, through Jesus the Father has already 'rescued us from the dominion of darkness and brought us into the kingdom of the Son he loves'.[10] We have even been raised from death and seated with Christ in the heavenly realm.[11]

At the same time, the old age persists. So the two ages overlap. 'The darkness is passing and the true light is already shining.'[12] 'Side by side ... with the continuation of this older

[1] Mt. 6:10. [2] Mt. 6:33. [3] Mk. 9:47; *cf.* Mt. 8:11. [4] Mt. 25:34.
[5] Mk. 4:26–29; Mt. 13:31–32, 24–29, 36–42.
[6] Mk. 4:11. [7] Lk. 20:34–35. [8] *E.g.* Is. 2:2; Mt. 12:32; Mk. 10:30.
[9] Gal. 1:4. [10] Col. 1:13; *cf.* Acts 26:18; 1 Pet. 2:9.
[11] Eph. 2:6; Col. 3:1. [12] 1 Jn. 2:8.

scheme (*sc.* the new age succeeding the old), the emergence of a new one, involving a co-existence of the two worlds or states, can be observed.'[1] One day the old age will be terminated (which will be 'the end of the age'),[2] and the new age, which was inaugurated by Christ's first coming, will be consummated at his second. Meanwhile, while the two ages continue, and we feel ourselves caught in the tension between them, we are summoned not to 'conform any longer to the pattern of this world', but rather to 'be transformed' according to God's will, in fact to live consistently as children of the light.[3]

Nevertheless, the tension remains. Indeed, it finds expression in almost every metaphor which the New Testament uses for the blessing of belonging to Christ. Thus, already we have been saved, yet also we shall be saved one day.[4] Already we 'have redemption', yet the day of redemption is still future.[5] Already we are God's adopted children, yet we also are waiting for our adoption.[6] Already we have 'crossed over from death to life', yet eternal life is also a future gift.[7] Already we are a new creation, although not yet has God made everything new.[8] We are already 'filled', but not yet up to the fulness of God.[9] Already Christ is reigning, although his enemies have not yet become his footstool.[10]

Caught between the present and the future, the characteristic stance of Christians is variously described as hoping,[11] waiting,[12] longing,[13] and groaning.[14] For we are still suffering grievous trials and tribulations.[15] Indeed, 'we must see the reality of

[1] Geerhardus Vos, *The Pauline Eschatology* (1930; Baker, 1979), p. 37; *cf.* Oscar Cullmann, *Christ and Time* (1946; ET SCM, 1951) and Stephen H. Travis, *I Believe in the Second Coming of Jesus* (Hodder, 1982).
[2] *E.g.* Mt. 13:39; 28:20.
[3] Rom. 12:2; 13:11–14; 1 Thes. 5:4–8.
[4] Rom. 8:24; 5:9–10; 13:11.
[5] Col. 1:14; Eph. 4:30. [6] Rom. 8:15, 23.
[7] Jn. 5:24; 11:25–26; Rom. 8:10–11.
[8] 2 Cor. 5:17; Rev. 21:5. [9] Col. 2:10; Eph. 5:18; 3:19.
[10] Ps. 110:1; Eph. 1:22; Heb. 2:8.
[11] Rom. 8:24. [12] Phil. 3:20–21; 1 Thes. 1:9–10.
[13] Rom. 8:19. [14] Rom. 8:22–23, 26; 2 Cor. 5:2, 4.
[15] Mk. 10:30; Acts 14:22; Rom. 8:17; 1 Pet. 4:12.

this suffering as a concrete manifestation of the "not yet"'.[1] Meanwhile we must wait both 'eagerly'[2] and also 'patiently'.[3] As John Murray has written:

> Attempts to claim for the present life elements which belong to consummated perfection, . . . are but symptoms of that impatience which would disrupt divine order. Expectancy and hope must not cross the bounds of history; they must wait for *the end*, 'the liberty of the glory of the children of God'.[4]

The essence of the interim period between the 'now' and the 'not yet', between kingdom come and kingdom coming, is the presence of the Holy Spirit in the people of God. On the one hand, the gift of the Spirit is the distinctive blessing of the kingdom of God, and so the principal sign that the new age has dawned.[5] On the other, because his indwelling is only the beginning of our kingdom inheritance, it is also the guarantee that the rest will one day be ours. The New Testament uses three metaphors to illustrate this. The Holy Spirit is the 'firstfruits', pledging that the full harvest will follow,[6] the 'deposit' or first instalment, pledging that the full payment will be made,[7] and the foretaste, pledging that the full feast will one day be enjoyed.[8] In this way the Holy Spirit is 'both a fulfilment of the promise and the promise of fulfilment: he is the guarantee that the new world of God has already begun, as well as a sign that this new world is still to come'.[9]

It is time now to develop some examples of the tension between the 'now' and the 'not yet'.

[1] G. C. Berkouwer, *The Return of Christ* (1961 and 1963; Eerdmans, 1972), p. 116.
[2] Rom. 8:23; 1 Cor. 1:7. [3] Rom. 8:25.
[4] John M. Murray, *The Epistle to the Romans, the New International Commentary on the New Testament* (Eerdmans, 1959 and 1965), vol. I, p. 310.
[5] *E.g.* Is. 32:15; 44:3; Ezk. 39:29; Joel 2:28; Mk. 1:8; Heb. 6:4–5.
[6] Rom. 8:23. [7] 2 Cor. 5:5; Eph. 1:14. [8] Heb. 6:4–5.
[9] Johannes Blauw, *The Missionary Nature of the Church* (1962; Eerdmans, 1974), p. 89.

Revelation, holiness and healing

The first example is in *the intellectual sphere*, or the question of *revelation*.

Already, we affirm with joyful confidence, God has revealed himself to human beings, not only in the created universe, in our reason and our conscience, but supremely in his Son Jesus Christ, and in the total biblical witness to him. 'In the past God spoke to our forefathers through the prophets at many times and in various ways, but in these last days he has spoken to us by his Son.'[1] Already, therefore, we dare to say that we know God, because he has made himself known to us. He has himself taken the initiative to draw aside the curtain which would otherwise hide him from us. We rejoice greatly in the glories of God's self-disclosure. Truly, his Word throws light on our path.[2]

Not yet, however, do we know God as he knows us. Our knowledge is partial because his revelation has been partial. This must be what is meant by the proverb that 'it is the glory of God to conceal a matter . . .'.[3] He has revealed everything which he wills to reveal, and which he considers to be for our good, but not everything which there is to reveal. There are many mysteries left, into which we should not try to penetrate because God has kept them from us. 'We live by faith, not by sight.'[4]

In particular, to borrow the striking imagery Luther used when addressing his fellow Augustinian monks at Heidelberg in 1518, all we can see so far is 'the visible back of God as disclosed in suffering and the cross', not his face. As Dr Alister McGrath has put it, 'the God who addresses us in the cross is – to use Luther's breathtakingly daring phrase – "the crucified and hidden God"'.[5]

We should take warning from Eunomius, who was bishop of Cyzicus in Mysia in the fourth century. He was one of the leaders of a heretical group called the 'Anomoeans', extreme

[1] Heb. 1:1–2. [2] Ps. 119:105. [3] Pr. 25:2. [4] 2 Cor. 5:7.
[5] Alister McGrath, *The Enigma of the Cross* (Hodder and Stoughton, 1987), pp. 103–105.

Arians who taught that the Son was 'unlike' (*anomoios*) the Father, and indeed had been created by the Father. Eunomius was once brash enough to claim, 'I know God as well as he knows himself.' A modern (but more humorous) equivalent might be the old-fashioned revival preacher from the American Deep South who once said: 'Today I'm going to explain to you the unexplainable. I'm going to define the indefinable. I'm going to ponder the imponderable. I'm going to unscrew the inscrutable.'[1]

We would be much wiser to take our stand alongside those biblical authors who, although they knew themselves to be vehicles of divine revelation, nevertheless confessed humbly that their knowledge remained limited. Moses, 'whom the LORD knew face to face', acknowledged: 'O Sovereign LORD, you have only (RSV) begun to show to your servant your greatness and your strong hand.'[2] Then the apostle Paul, to whom the church is permanently indebted for his profound teaching, yet called his knowledge partial and imperfect, and likened it both to the immature thoughts of a child and to the distorted reflections of a mirror.[3] And the apostle John, who had penetrated deeply into the mind of Christ, admitted that 'what we will be has not yet been made known'.[4]

So then, although it is right to glory in the givenness and finality of God's revelation, it is also right to confess our ignorance of many things. We know and we don't know. 'The secret things belong to the LORD our God, but the things revealed belong to us and to our children for ever, that we may follow all the words of this law.'[5] It is very important to maintain this distinction between the revealed things and the secret things, for then we shall be confident, even dogmatic, about the former, which belong to us, while remaining agnostic about the latter, which belong to God. Then too we will be free to explore the revealed things, and firm in not trespassing into God's secrets. Conversely, while holding ourselves in check

[1] Quoted by Bruce Larson in *Wind and Fire: Living Out the Book of Acts* (Word, 1984), p. 11. [2] Dt. 34:10; *cf.* Nu. 12:8; Dt. 3:24.
[3] 1 Cor. 13:9–12. [4] 1 Jn. 3:2. [5] Dt. 29:29.

before the secret things, we must not be diffident in believing, expounding and defending what God has disclosed. I would like to see among us more boldness in proclaiming what has been revealed, and more reticence before what has been kept secret. Agreement in plainly revealed truth will be necessary for unity, even while we give each other liberty in the area of the *adiaphora*, the 'matters indifferent'. The criterion for discerning these will be when Christians who are equally anxious to be submissive to Scripture nevertheless reach different conclusions about them. I am thinking, for example, about controversies over baptism, church government, liturgy and ceremonial, charismatic claims and the fulfilment of prophecy.

The second tension is in *the moral sphere*, or the question of *holiness*.

Already God has put his Holy Spirit within us, in order to make us holy.[1] Already the Spirit is actively at work within us, subduing our fallen, selfish human nature and causing his ninefold fruit to ripen in our character.[2] Already, we can affirm, he is transforming us by degrees into the image of Christ.[3]

Not yet, however, has our fallen nature been eradicated, for still 'the sinful nature desires what is contrary to the Spirit',[4] so that 'if we claim to be without sin, we deceive ourselves'.[5] Not yet have we become completely conformed to God's perfect will, for not yet do we love God with all our being, or our neighbour as ourselves. These things await the coming of Christ. As Paul put it, we have 'not ... already been made perfect', but we 'press on towards the goal', confident that 'he who began a good work in (us) will carry it on to completion until the day of Christ Jesus'.[6]

So then, we are caught in a painful dialectic between the 'now' and the 'not yet', between defeat and victory, between dismay over our continuing failures and the promise of ultimate freedom, between the cry of longing, 'Who will rescue me from this body of death?' and the cry of assurance, 'Thanks be to

[1] 1 Thes. 4:7–8. [2] Gal. 5:16–26. [3] 2 Cor. 3:18. [4] Gal. 5:17. [5] 1 Jn. 1:8. [6] Phil. 3:12–14; 1:6.

God – through Jesus Christ our Lord!'[1] On the one hand, we must take with the utmost seriousness God's command, 'Be holy because I . . . am holy',[2] Jesus' instruction, 'Go, and do not sin again',[3] and John's statements that he is writing so that his readers 'will not sin', and that 'no-one who is born of God will continue to sin'.[4] On the other hand, we have to acknowledge the reality of indwelling sin alongside the reality of the indwelling Spirit.[5] The sinless perfection we long for continues to elude us, although, in rejecting perfectionism, we refuse to embrace reductionism, that is, to acquiesce in low standards of attainment.

Bishop Handley Moule summed up this tension in the first chapter of his book *Thoughts on Christian Sanctity* (1888), entitled 'Aims, Limits, Possibilities'. Under 'Aims' he wrote: 'We aim at nothing less than to walk with God all day long; to abide every hour in Christ . . .; to love God with all the heart and our neighbour as ourselves . . .; to "yield ourselves to God" . . .; to break with all evil, and follow all good.'[6] He continued: 'We are absolutely bound to put quite aside all secret purposes of moral compromise, all tolerance of besetting sin . . . We cannot possibly rest short of a daily, hourly, continuous walk with God, in Christ, by the grace of the Holy Ghost.'[7] But then under 'Limits' (not in our aims but in our attainment) he added: 'I hold with absolute conviction, alike from the experience of the Church and from the infallible Word, that, in the mystery of things, there will be limits to the last, and very humbling limits, very real fallings short. To the last it will be a *sinner* that walks with God.'[8] Similarly, according to Bishop J. C. Ryle, 'Old John Newton', the converted slave-trader, said: 'I am not what I ought to be, I am not what I want to be, I am not what I hope to be in another world, but still I am not what I once used to be, and by the grace of God I am what I am.'[9]

[1] Rom. 7:24–25. [2] *E.g.* Lv. 19:2. [3] Jn. 8:11 (RSV). [4] 1 Jn. 2:1; 3:9.
[5] *E.g.* Rom. 7:17, 20; 8:9, 11.
[6] H. C. G. Moule, *Thoughts on Christian Sanctity* (Seeley, 1888), p. 13.
[7] *Ibid.*, p. 15. [8] *Ibid.*, p. 16.
[9] J. C. Ryle, *Home Truths* (Charles Thynne, ninth edition, undated), pp. 94–95.

The third tension between the 'already' and the 'not yet' is to be found in *the physical sphere* or the question of *healing*.

Already, we affirm, the long promised kingdom of God has been inaugurated, since it broke into history with Jesus Christ. Moreover, Jesus was not content merely to proclaim the kingdom; he went on to demonstrate its arrival by his mighty works in the physical realm. He walked on water, and he changed water into wine. He rebuked the wind, stilled a storm and multiplied loaves and fishes. Nature was subservient to him. His power was specially evident in the human body as he healed the sick, expelled demons and raised the dead.

He also gave authority to both the Twelve and the Seventy to extend his messianic mission in Israel, and to perform miracles. How much wider he intended his authority to go is a matter of dispute. Generally speaking, miracles were 'the signs of a true apostle'.[1] Nevertheless, it would be ludicrous to attempt to limit or domesticate almighty God. The God who created the universe, and who through Jesus brought in the kingdom, cannot possibly be put in a strait-jacket by us. We must allow him his freedom and his sovereignty, and be entirely open to the possibility of physical miracles today.

Not yet, however, has God's kingdom come in its fulness. For 'the kingdom of the world' has not yet 'become the kingdom of our Lord and of his Christ' when 'he will reign for ever and ever'.[2] He is still waiting for that day. In particular, our bodies have not yet been redeemed. Nor has nature yet been entirely subjugated to Christ's rule. Instead, 'the whole creation has been groaning as in the pains of childbirth right up to the present time', waiting for the new world to be born. 'Not only so, but we ourselves . . . groan inwardly as we wait eagerly for our adoption as sons, the redemption of our bodies.'[3]

So then, we have to recognize the 'already'–'not yet' tension in this sphere too. To be sure, we have 'tasted . . . the powers of the coming age',[4] but so far it has been only a taste. Again, it is part of our Christian experience that the resurrection life of

[1] 2 Cor. 12:12 (RSV). [2] Rev. 11:15. [3] Rom. 8:22–23. [4] Heb. 6:5.

Jesus is 'revealed in our mortal body',[1] his life in the midst of our death, his strength in our weakness, giving us a certain physical vigour and vitality which we would not otherwise know. At the same time, our bodies remain frail and mortal, and to claim perfect health now is to anticipate our resurrection. The bodily resurrection of Jesus was the pledge, and indeed the beginning, of God's new creation. Not yet, however, has God risen from his throne to utter the decisive word, 'I am making everything new!'[2] To sum up, those dismissive of the very possibility of miracles today forget the 'already' of the kingdom, while those who expect them as what has been called 'the normal Christian life' forget the kingdom's 'not yet'.

Church and society

Fourthly, the same tension is experienced in *the ecclesiastical sphere*, or the question of *church discipline*.

Already, we rightly affirm, Jesus the Messiah is gathering round him a people of his own. And already the messianic community is characterized by the truth, love and holiness to which he has called it. The church is 'the pillar and foundation of the truth',[3] that is, its foundation to hold it firm and its pillar to thrust it high. As for love, Christ has by his cross 'destroyed . . . the dividing wall of hostility' between people of different races, nations, tribes and classes, in order 'to create in himself one new man'.[4] As for holiness, his new society is variously called a holy nation, a holy priesthood and a holy people.[5] So truth, love and holiness are already essential marks of the new society of Jesus Christ.

Not yet, however, has Christ presented his bride to himself 'as a radiant church, without stain or wrinkle or any other blemish, but holy and blameless'.[6] On the contrary, her present life and witness are marred by many blemishes, by error, discord and sin. Church history is the story of God's

[1] 2 Cor. 4:10–11. [2] Rev. 21:5. [3] 1 Tim. 3:15. [4] Eph. 2:14–15.
[5] *E.g.* 1 Pet. 2:5, 9. [6] Eph. 5:27; *cf.* Rev. 21:2.

incredible patience with his wayward people.

So then, whenever we think about the church, we have to hold together the ideal and the reality. The church is both committed to truth and prone to error, both united and divided, both pure and impure. Not that we are to acquiesce in its failures. 'The undeniable "not yet" can never serve as an alibi for our defeats.'[1] We are to cherish the vision of both the purity and the unity of the church, namely its doctrinal and ethical purity and its visible unity. Since these things are God's will, they must be our goal. In consequence, we are called to 'fight the good fight of the faith'.[2] We are also to 'make every effort to keep the unity of the Spirit through the bond of peace'.[3] And in pursuit of these things there is a place for discipline in cases of serious heresy or sin.

And yet error and evil are not going to be completely eradicated from the church in this world. They will continue to coexist with truth and goodness. 'Let both grow together until the harvest,' Jesus said in the parable of the wheat and the tares.[4] Some people argue that, because in this parable 'the field is the world',[5] the coexistence Jesus is referring to is in the world, not the church. But the enemy sows weeds 'among the wheat',[6] and it is 'out of his kingdom'[7] that the Son of Man will ultimately root out evil. Neither Scripture nor church history justifies the use of severe disciplinary measures in an attempt to secure a perfectly pure church in this world.

The fifth area of tension between the 'now' and the 'then', the 'already' and the 'not yet', is *the social sphere*, or the question of *progress*.

Already, we affirm, God is at work in human society. This is partly in his 'common grace', as he gives the world the blessings of family and government, by which evil is restrained and relationships are controlled. But it is also through the members of his redeemed community, who maintain without compromise the values of his kingdom. They must penetrate society,

[1] G. C. Berkouwer, *op cit.*, p. 138.
[2] 1 Tim. 6:12. [3] Eph. 4:3. [4] Mt. 13:30.
[5] Mt. 13:38. [6] Mt. 13:25. [7] Mt. 13:41.

Jesus taught, like salt and light. It is legitimate to deduce from these models that Jesus intended his followers to influence the world for good. For both are effective commodities. They make a difference in the environment in which they are placed, salt hindering decay and light dispelling darkness. In consequence there has been over the centuries, alongside social decay, measurable social progress – the greater availability of health care, the spread of literacy and education, the defence of human rights, improved working conditions, the abolition of slavery and the slave trade, and the protection of the weak and the vulnerable.

Not yet, however, has God created the promised 'new heaven and . . . new earth, the home of righteousness'.[1] Not yet has the justice of the kingdom ousted all oppression, and the peace of the kingdom all violence. There are still 'wars and rumours of wars'.[2] Not yet have swords been beaten into ploughshares and spears into pruning hooks.[3] The nations have not yet renounced war as a method of settling their disputes. Selfishness, cruelty and fear continue.

So then, although it is right to campaign for social justice and to expect to improve society further, in order to make it more pleasing to God, we know that we shall never perfect it. Christians are not utopians. Although we know the transforming power of the gospel and the wholesome effects of Christian salt and light, we also know that evil is ingrained in human nature and human society. We harbour no illusions. Only Christ at his second coming will eradicate evil and enthrone righteousness for ever. For that day we wait with eagerness.

Here, then, are five areas (intellectual, moral, physical, ecclesiastical and social) in which it is vital to preserve the tension between the 'already' and the 'not yet'. One might even say that there are three distinct types of Christian according to the degree to which they manage to maintain this biblical balance.

First, there are *the 'already' Christians*. These are the sunny

[1] 2 Pet. 3:13; Rev. 21:1. [2] Mk. 13:7. [3] Is. 2:4.

optimists. They rightly emphasize what God has already done for us through Christ and bestowed on us in Christ. But they give the impression that, in consequence, there are now no mysteries left, no sins which cannot be overcome, no diseases which cannot be healed, and no evils which cannot be eradicated from the church, or even from the world. In short, they seem to believe that perfection is attainable now. They remind me of those Corinthian believers to whom Paul wrote: 'Already you have all you want! Already you have become rich! You have become kings – and that without us!'[1]

The motive of the 'already' Christians is blameless. They want to glorify Christ. So they refuse to set limits to what he is able to do. They consider it derogatory to him not to claim the possibility of perfection now. But their optimism can easily degenerate into presumption and end up in disillusion. They forget the 'not yet' of the New Testament, and that perfection awaits the parousia.

Secondly, there are *the 'not yet' Christians*. These one might not unfairly style the gloomy pessimists. They rightly emphasize the incompleteness for the time being of the work of Christ, and they rightly look forward to the parousia when Christ will complete what he has begun. But they give the impression of being extremely negative in their attitudes. They seem to be preoccupied with our human ignorance and failure, the pervasive reign of disease and death, and the impossibility of securing either a pure church or a perfect society. They pour cold water on every claim that Christ may be victoriously active in any of these areas.

Their motive is excellent too. If the 'already' Christians want to glorify Christ, the 'not yet' Christians want to humble sinners. They are determined to be true to Scripture in their emphasis on our human depravity. But their pessimism can easily degenerate into complacency; it can also lead to an acquiescence in the status quo and to apathy in the face of evil. They forget the 'already' of what Christ has done by his death,

[1] 1 Cor. 4:8.

resurrection and Spirit-gift, and of what he can do in our lives, and in church and society, as a result.

Thirdly, there are *the 'already–not yet' Christians*. These are the biblical realists. For they want to give equal weight to the two comings of Jesus, to what he has done and what he is going to do. They rejoice in the former and wait eagerly for the latter. They want simultaneously to glorify Christ and to humble sinners. On the one hand, they have great confidence in the 'already', in what God has said and done through Christ, and great determination to explore and experience to the fullest possible extent the riches of Christ's person and work. On the other hand, they exhibit a genuine humility before the 'not yet', humility to confess that much ignorance and sinfulness, much physical frailty, ecclesiastical unfaithfulness and social decay remain – and will remain as symptoms of a fallen, half-saved world until Christ perfects at his second coming what he began at his first.

It is this combination of the 'already' and the 'not yet', of kingdom inaugurated and kingdom consummated, of Christian confidence and Christian humility, which characterizes authentic biblical evangelicalism, and which exemplifies that 'BBC' which is so urgently needed today.

The three great acclamations about Christ sum up our position as 'contemporary Christians':

Christ has died!
Christ is risen!
Christ will come again!

His death and resurrection belong to the 'already' of the past, his glorious parousia to the 'not yet' of the future. His ultimate triumph is nonetheless certain. Indeed, 'the hope of the final victory', wrote Professor Oscar Cullmann, 'is so much the more vivid because of the unshakeably firm conviction that the battle that decides the victory has already taken place'.[1]

[1] Oscar Cullmann, *Christ and Time* (1946; ET SCM, 1951), p. 87.

Index of names

Index of subjects

THE CONTEMPORARY CHRISTIAN
STUDY GUIDE

The aim of this study guide is to help you get to the heart of what John Stott has written and to challenge you to apply what you learn to your own life. The questions have been designed for use both by individuals and also by small groups of Christians meeting, perhaps for an hour or two each week, to study, discuss and pray together.

The guide provides material for the Introduction, Conclusion, and each of the twenty-one chapters of the book. When used by a group with limited time, the leader should decide beforehand which questions are most appropriate for the group to discuss during the meeting. The rest should perhaps be left for group members to work through by themselves or in smaller groups during the week.

In order to be able to contribute fully and learn from the group meetings, each member of the group needs to read through the chapter or chapters under discussion.

It is important not to let these studies become merely academic exercises. Guard against this by making time to think through and discuss how what you discover works out in practice for you. Make sure you begin and end each study with a time of focusing on God in praise and prayer. Ask the Holy Spirit to speak to you through your discussion together.

INTRODUCTION
The then and the now

Christianity both historical and contemporary

1 Why does Christianity have 'an even stronger claim to be historical' than other religions (p. 15)? Why is this important?

2 'The younger generation tell us they are not interested in history' (p. 16). Why do you think this is? What can be done about it?

3 'Throughout the whole history of the church Jesus Christ has suffered a process of repeated crucifixion' (Thielicke, quoted on p. 19). In what ways has this happened?

Attempts to modernize Jesus

4 List the twelve attempts to 'modernize Jesus' which the author discusses (pp. 19–23). What is wrong with them? Why?

The challenge before us is to present Jesus to our generation in a way that is . . . new in the sense of 'fresh', not new in the sense of being a novelty (p. 24).

---

5 Why do we tend to 'betray' the authentic Jesus (p. 24)? To what extent do you and your church do this? What is the solution?

The call for double listening

6 What does the author mean by his key phrase 'double listening' (pp. 27–29)? Why is it 'indispensable to Christian discipleship and Christian mission' (p. 29)?

PART I: THE GOSPEL

CHAPTER ONE *The human paradox*

1 Why is the question 'What is man?' so important (pp. 33–34)?

2 In their view of humankind, in what ways do modern thinkers tend to be 'either too naive in their optimism or too negative in their pessimism' (p. 34)? Why?

Our human dignity

3 What does it mean for human beings to bear the divine 'image' (pp. 35–40)? What five features does the author draw out? Explain their biblical basis.

Our human depravity

4 Read Mark 7:14–21. What does Jesus teach about human evil (pp. 40–42)?

5 'All those who have caught even a momentary glimpse of the holiness of God have been unable to bear the sight . . .' (p. 42). Why? What examples can you think of? Has anything similar happened to you?

The resulting paradox

6 What features of your own experience may illustrate the paradox of human dignity and depravity (pp. 42–43)?

7 'So our most urgent need is . . .' what (p. 44)? Is this how you see it? Why?

8 What implication for social progress is there in the fact that we 'retain vestiges of the divine image' (p. 45)? How does this affect your view of society and the value of working to change things for the better?

CHAPTER TWO
Authentic freedom

1 'One of the best ways of sharing the gospel with modern men and women is to present it in terms of freedom' (p. 46). What is your experience of this? How does the author support this statement?

The negative: freedom *from*

2 What are the forces 'which tyrannize us and so inhibit our freedom' (pp. 48–51)?

3 Why is it wrong to claim that all guilt is false guilt (p. 48)?

4 What does the Bible mean by 'sin' (pp. 49–50)? How does this differ from what people tend to think?

5 Which fears overshadow the lives of some of the men and women you know (pp. 50–51)?

The positive: freedom *for*

6 Why is it 'a serious error' to define freedom in entirely negative terms (p. 52)?

True freedom is freedom to be our true selves, as God made us and meant us to be (p. 53).

---

7 Why is true freedom 'the exact opposite of what many people think' (p. 55)?

CHAPTER THREE

Christ and his cross

Begin by reading 1 Corinthians 2:1–5.

The Word of God

1 Where must all true evangelism begin (p. 58)? Why?

2 How do we know that Paul was renouncing 'neither doctrinal substance, nor rational argument' (p. 58)? How important are these things to you?

The cross of Christ

The gospel is not preached if the saving power is proclaimed and the saving events omitted, especially the cross (p. 57).

---

3 How would you reply to someone who suggested that all we need for effective evangelism is the Holy Spirit?

4 What is wrong with the view that 'Paul repented of the distorted gospel he had preached in Athens and resolved in Corinth to limit his message to the cross' (p. 60)?

5 Why is the message of the cross 'deeply despised' (p. 62)? How have you faced the choice between faithfulness and popularity on this issue?

6 Why is the message of the cross incompatible with 'a truce in inter-religious competition' (p. 64)?

7 'Still today nothing keeps people out of the kingdom of God more than . . .' what (p. 65)? How does the message of the cross emphasize this?

8 John Stott mentions two further objections to the message of

Christ and the cross (pp. 65–67). What are these? In what ways are they relevant today?

The power of the Spirit

9 'Paul was not afraid to admit that he was afraid' (p. 68). Why not? What can you learn from his perspective?

CHAPTER FOUR

The relevance of the resurrection

What does the resurrection mean?

1 Resurrection 'does not mean the mere survival of an influence' (p. 72). Why not?

2 The risen Lord 'is not a resuscitated corpse' (p. 73). Explain the difference between resurrection and resuscitation.

The grand affirmation of the New Testament is not 'he lives', but 'he is risen'. The resurrection becomes an experience for us only because it was first an event which actually inaugurated a new order of reality (p. 73).

---

3 What is Bultmann's 'demythologized reconstruction' (p. 74)? Why is it mistaken?

4 Why is it wrong to say that 'the risen Lord is just an expanded personality' or 'resurrection is a living experience of the Spirit' (p. 75)?

5 What then are we to understand by the resurrection of Jesus (pp. 77–78)?

Did the resurrection really happen?

6 What explanations are there for the disappearance of Jesus' body from the tomb? Why is his resurrection the only satisfactory explanation (pp. 78–79)?

7 What explanations are there for the reported appearances of Jesus on and after the first Easter Day? Why is his resurrection the only satisfactory explanation (pp. 79–80)?

8 How is the resurrection connected with the history of the church's beginnings (p. 80)?

Why is the resurrection important?

9 How would you answer someone who said that 'the resurrection happened too long ago to be of any great importance for us today' (pp. 81–85)?

10 In the light of the author's discussion, what areas of your life and thinking need to be reshaped by the truth of the resurrection?

CHAPTER FIVE

Jesus Christ is Lord

Theological conviction

1 Read Philippians 2:9–11. What are the three things this passage shows about how the early Christians thought of Jesus (pp. 87–90)?

2 Why do the New Testament writers *assume* rather than *argue* the divine lordship of Jesus (p. 89)?

3 Why is it wrong to 'distinguish sharply between Jesus the Saviour and Jesus the Lord' (p. 90)? What truth is this separation intended to safeguard?

Radical commitment

4 Do you think of yourself as a 'slave of Jesus Christ' (p. 90)? How does this make you feel?

John Stott goes on to explore what personal ownership by Jesus means in practice.

5 'Disciples have no liberty to disagree with their divine teacher' (p. 91). In what areas do you do this?

6 What is the place of God's law in the Christian life? Are we free to disobey it (pp. 92–93)? Are there areas where you are using a wrong view of law to justify disobedience?

7 What does 'ministry' mean (p. 93)? To what extent are you a minister?

8 In view of the state of the world today, how can we possibly claim that Jesus is Lord of society (pp. 94–97)?

9 What conflicts do you face between Christ and the modern equivalent of 'Caesar' (pp. 96–97)? At what point does discipleship call for disobedience to the state?

10 What are the implications of saying that Jesus has *universal* lordship (p. 97)?

Mission is . . . an unavoidable deduction from the universal lordship of Jesus Christ (p. 98).

PART II: THE DISCIPLE

CHAPTER SIX

The listening ear

Involuntary deafness is a grievous handicap; deliberate deafness is both a sin and a folly (p. 102).

Listening to God

1 Does God speak to you (pp. 103–106)? How?

2 In what ways do you 'separate the Word from the Spirit or the Spirit from the Word' (p. 105)? Why is it wrong to do this?

3 What does the author identify as 'the main cause of the spiritual stagnation we sometimes experience' (p. 105)? How does this apply to you? What can you do about it?

Listening to one another

4 In your own experience of the different relationships John Stott discusses, what scope is there for improved communication (pp. 106–108)?

5 Why does the discipline of listening sometimes 'cause acute mental pain' (p. 109)? What situations can you think of where this is important for you?

Listening to the world

6 What does 'contextualization' mean (p. 110)? What examples does the author give?

God has given us two ears, but only one mouth, so that he evidently intends us to listen twice as much as we talk (quoted on p. 112).

CHAPTER SEVEN
Mind and emotions

The mind

1 'A responsible use of our minds glorifies our Creator' (p. 115). How? Does yours?

2 How would you respond to someone who claimed that 'faith and reason are incompatible' (p. 116)?

3 'They expect God to flash on to their inner screen answers to their questions and solutions to their problems, in such a way as to bypass their minds' (p. 117). What is wrong with this kind of expectation?

4 'Our evangelistic appeal should never ask people to close or suspend their minds' (p. 117). Have you experienced appeals like this? Why is it wrong?

Being the Spirit of truth, the Holy Spirit brings people to faith in Christ because of the evidence, and not in spite of it (p. 118).

5 What are 'elitism' and 'intellectualism' (pp. 118–119)? Why do we need to guard against these things? How can we do so?

The emotions

6 'From all this evidence it is plain that our emotions are not to be suppressed' (p. 121). What evidence?

7 When were you last conscious of 'an inexpressible and glorious joy' (p. 121)? Is this sort of experience important? Where does it come from?

8 Explain the place of emotion in the preaching of the gospel (pp. 122–123).

9 What moved Jesus to (a) anger and (b) compassion? Why? Do similar things move you in the same way?

Mind and emotions

10 How are our mind and our emotions to be related to one another (pp. 125–127)? Can you think of examples in your own life where this relationship is not as it should be?

Beware equally of an undevotional theology (i.e. *mind without heart) and of an untheological devotion* (i.e. *heart without mind) (Handley Moule, quoted on p. 127).*

CHAPTER EIGHT

Guidance, vocation and ministry

Guidance

1 Explain the distinction between God's 'general' will and his 'particular' will (p. 129). Why is this important?

2 What is God's general will for us (p. 129)? How do we know?

3 What place does the Bible have in helping us to discover God's will for our lives (p. 129)?

4 The author suggests five steps to discovering God's

particular will (pp. 130–131). What are they? Why is each important?

Vocation

5 What is the difference between the modern, popular meaning of 'vocation' and its meaning in the Bible (pp. 131–132)?

6 To what does God call each of us (pp. 132–134)? What does this involve?

7 Do you see the situation you were in when you first became a Christian as something to which God has called you (pp. 135–140)?

8 In their thinking about vocation, against what in particular were the Reformers reacting (pp. 136–139)? How much does the false distinction between the sacred and the secular distort your thinking about yourself?

9 'The God many of us worship is altogether too religious' (p. 139). Is this true of you?

Ministry

10 How can the author be so 'dogmatic' in affirming that 'all Christians without exception are called to ministry' (pp. 140–141)?

11 Why is it 'essential to note that both distributing food and teaching the word were referred to as ministry' (p. 141)? Is this how you see it? How is what *you* do 'ministry'?

There is a crying need for Christian men and women who see their daily work as their primary Christian ministry and who determine to penetrate their secular environment for Christ (p. 142).

---

12 How can you be 'stretched' in the service of Christ and of people, so that nothing he has given you is wasted, and everything he has given you is used (p. 144)?

13 Do you fear God's will for your life, or that you will never discover it? Why do you not need to (pp. 144–145)?

CHAPTER NINE

The first fruit of the Spirit

Love, joy and peace

1 What sort of things do people identify as the chief distinguishing mark of a Christian (pp. 147–148)? Why? Why is love preeminent?

2 'Those who pursue happiness never find it' (p. 149). Why not? Where then does happiness come from?

3 How would you answer someone who said that 'in order to love other people we need to learn to love ourselves' (pp. 150–151)?

Love in action

4 What 'positive attitudes and concrete actions' does love lead to (p. 151)? What do these things mean in practice for you?

5 Why does John Stott suggest that 'love is "balanced" by self-control' (p. 152)? What qualities does he refer to?

Love is the fruit of the Spirit

6 What exactly does Paul mean by the 'flesh' and the 'Spirit' (pp. 152–153)? In what ways are these words sometimes misunderstood?

7 What three truths does Paul bring out about the conflict

between the flesh and the Spirit (pp. 153–155)? Which of the two is winning in your life? Why?

Our new nature will gain the victory over the old only in so far as we feed the new and starve the old (pp. 155–156).

---

8 What is your overriding ambition (p. 157)?

PART III: THE BIBLE

CHAPTER TEN
Continuing in the Word

Begin by reading 2 Timothy 3:1 – 4:8.

Standing in the Word

1 Explain what Paul means by 'the last days' (pp. 163–165). What will resisting and standing firm against the trends of our day lead to?

Continuing in the Word

2 Paul goes on to stress the importance of the teaching (a) of the Old Testament and (b) of himself as an apostle (p. 166). Why? What is so special about these things?

3 What is Scripture for (p. 167, 170)? Is this how you use it?

4 In what ways do people 'mis-state the truth of inspiration' (p. 168)? How is the idea best understood?

Preaching the Word

5 'One of the greatest needs of the contemporary church is

conscientious biblical exposition from the pulpit' (p. 171). Why? How much of a priority is this in your life and that of your church?

CHAPTER ELEVEN

Responding to the Word

Mature discipleship

1 What four areas does the author mention in which our discipleship depends on being able to respond to God's revelation (pp. 174–176)? How would a better biblical diet help you in these areas?

Intellectual integrity

2 How can 'apparently intelligent Christians at the end of the twentieth century . . . possibly be so perverse as to believe in biblical inspiration and authority' (p. 177)?

3 How do you handle problems in the Bible (pp. 178–180)? How does what the author says here help?

Ecumenical progress

4 What is your attitude to ecumenical progress (pp. 180–182)? According to John Stott, what should it be? Where does the Bible fit in?

Effective evangelism

5 Why is there 'no chance of the church taking its evangelistic task seriously' (pp. 183–184) unless we return to the Bible?

Personal humility

6 'Perhaps the greatest of all our needs is . . .' what? Why?

CHAPTER TWELVE

Transposing the Word

The hermeneutical problem

1 What does 'biblical hermeneutics' mean (pp. 187–189)? Why is there a 'hermeneutical problem'? What is the difference between the 'old' and the 'new' hermeneutic? Why do we need both?

Our own cultural imprisonment

2 When reading the Bible, to what extent is cultural imprisonment inevitable (pp. 190–191)? What does it lead to?

3 'What will posterity see as the chief Christian blind spot[s] at the end of the twentieth century?' (p. 192) What do you think?

4 Can anything be done to lower our cultural barrier to God's communication through the Bible (pp. 193–194)?

The Bible's cultural conditioning

5 How would you respond to someone who said that 'since the Bible is a culturally conditioned book, it is therefore out of date' (pp. 194–195)?

6 What does the author mean by 'cultural transposition' (p. 196)? Why is it important?

Examples of cultural transposition

7 What is the 'challenge posed by Bultmann's "demythologization" programme' (p. 197)? Where does he go too far?

8 How would you culturally transpose Jesus' command to wash each other's feet (pp. 200–201)? Give examples.

9 What modern equivalents of eating meat which had previously been sacrificed to idols can you think of (pp. 201–202)? What principles does the Bible give to apply in such a situation?

10 How does John Stott apply the technique of cultural transposition to the position and roles of women (pp. 202–204)? Do you agree with his method and conclusion? Why or why not?

11 What is wrong with using cultural transposition to justify homosexual partnerships (p. 205)?

CHAPTER THIRTEEN
Expounding the Word

1 Is preaching important to you (pp. 207–208)? Why?

Nothing . . . is more important for the life and growth, health and depth of the contemporary church than a recovery of serious biblical preaching (p. 208).

Two convictions

2 Why does 'authentic preaching' need 'a high view of the biblical text' (p. 209)?

3 What do 'revelation', 'inspiration' and 'providence' mean (pp. 209–210)? Why are they important when thinking about the Bible and preaching (p. 210)?

4 To what extent is the Bible a 'partially closed' text for you (pp. 211–212)? In the light of this, what is the role of preaching?

Two obligations

5 Why is giving 'the biblical authors the freedom to say what they do say' (p. 213) so important?

6 What steps can we take to ensure that we remain 'sensitive to the world' (p. 213)?

7 What are the two questions which it is essential that we ask if we are to expound the Bible properly (pp. 213–216)?

Two expectations

8 What two expectations should we have of preaching (pp. 216–218)? How strongly do you hold these expectations?

PART IV: THE CHURCH

CHAPTER FOURTEEN
Secular challenges to the church

The quest for transcendence

1 Describe the 'quest for transcendence' (p. 223)? Do you think it is more widespread than it used to be? Why?

2 What evidence of the quest for transcendence do you have from your own experience or that of others? What examples does John Stott give (pp. 223–227)?

3 What aspect of the church's life does this quest challenge (pp. 227–228)? How well does the church to which you belong meet this? What steps can *you* take to improve things?

The quest for significance

When human beings are devalued, everything in society turns sour (p. 232).

4 What features of our modern world tend to undermine our sense of significance (pp. 229–231)? What effects does this have on society?

5 What makes you think you are significant?

6 What aspect of the church's life does this quest for significance challenge (pp. 231–232)? How well does your church meet this challenge? What steps can *you* take to improve things?

The quest for community

7 How much of a priority are loving relationships in your life? Why?

8 What aspect of the church's life does this quest for community challenge (pp. 235–237)? How well does your church meet this challenge? What steps can *you* take to improve things?

The contemporary secular quest seems to me to constitute one of the greatest challenges – and opportunities – with which the church has ever been presented: people are openly looking for the very things that Jesus Christ is offering! (p. 237).

CHAPTER FIFTEEN

Evangelism through the local church

Various forms of evangelism

1 Which forms of evangelism does the author mention (pp. 240–241)? Which of them helped you to faith?

2 How can local church evangelism 'claim to be the most normal, natural and productive method of spreading the gospel today' (p. 241)?

The church must understand itself (The theology of the church)

3 What false images of the church does the author mention (pp. 242–243)? Which do you tend to slip into?

4 How then should we view the nature of the church (pp. 243–245)? Why is this so important?

The church must organize itself (The structures of the church)

5 Are the structures of your church in any way 'heretical' (p. 246)? Why? What needs to be done to correct this?

The church must express itself (The message of the church)

6 How would you define the basic message of the gospel (pp. 251–252)?

7 How would you answer someone who insists on a particular stereotyped presentation of the gospel (p. 252)?

8 How would you answer someone who suggests that 'you can only discover what the gospel is once you're in the situation' (p. 252)?

The church must be itself (The life of the church)

9 What is 'the greatest hindrance to evangelism' (p. 254)?

10 How much of a difficulty for you is the invisibility of God (pp. 254–256)? How has God solved this problem?

11 What stops God being more visible through you and your church?

CHAPTER SIXTEEN

Dimensions of church renewal

1 John Stott mentions six renewal movements in the life of the twentieth-century church (pp. 257–258). Which of them has influenced your church?

2 What do the words 'reform', 'revival' and 'renewal' mean (p. 258)?

3 Read John 17. Explain the significance of 'Jesus' threefold characterization of his people' (p. 260).

Truth (verses 11–13)

4 'There is no possibility of the church being thoroughly renewed until and unless . . .' what (p. 262)? Why? Where does your church stand?

Holiness (verses 14–16)

5 What is 'holiness' (pp. 262–263)?

6 Are you more like a Pharisee or a Sadducee (pp. 262–263)? In what ways?

Mission (verses 17–19)

7 How should the church relate to godless society (p. 264)? What happens when it does as it should?

8 What does it mean to be 'truly sanctified' (p. 264)?

9 How does 'the fact that we are sent into the world like [Jesus] . . . shape our understanding of mission' (p. 265)?

Unity (verses 20–26)

10 What is 'the nature of the unity for which Christ prayed' (pp. 266–267)? How does this affect your approach to ecumenical relations?

The visible, structural unity of the church is a proper goal. Yet it will be pleasing to God only if it is the visible expression of something deeper, namely unity in truth and in life (p. 267).

---

11 Spend some time praying for the church in the light of what you have discovered about the priorities for renewal expressed by Jesus in John 17.

CHAPTER SEVENTEEN

The church's pastors

1 How would you describe the purpose of the ordained ministry (pp. 270–273)?

2 Can you define and say what is wrong with (a) clericalism and (b) anticlericalism (p. 272)?

The priestly model

3 Why do the Roman Catholic and Orthodox churches see

their clergy as priests (p. 273)? What is wrong with this?

4 What justification is there then for Reformed churches to retain the word 'priest' as a designation of their ministers (pp. 274–278)?

The pastoral model

5 What does 'pastor' mean (pp. 279–280)? Why is it such an appropriate way of describing the church's leaders?

6 The author lists seven characteristics of the pastor (pp. 280–290). Identify each one and set out what it has to teach about Christian leadership. How does your experience (of leading and being led) match up to these qualities?

7 Jesus warned his disciples to avoid two particular models of leadership (pp. 290–291). Which two? Why?

PART V: THE WORLD

CHAPTER EIGHTEEN
The uniqueness of Jesus Christ

1 What are 'syncretism', 'pluralism', 'exclusivism' and 'inclusivism' (pp. 296–298)?

Arguments for pluralism

2 What is it about pluralism that people find attractive (pp. 298–304)?

The uniqueness of Jesus Christ

3 Why is it 'essential at the outset to clarify that Christians claim uniqueness and finality only for Christ and not for

Christianity' (p. 305)? To what extent does your own experience of evangelism reflect this distinction?

Jesus is Lord

4 How is the uniqueness of Jesus supported by the affirmation that he is Lord (pp. 307–309)?

5 What crucial differences are there between Hinduism and Christianity on the idea that God has assumed human form (pp. 308–309)?

Jesus is Saviour

6 What does 'salvation' mean (pp. 309–310)?

7 How is the uniqueness of Jesus supported by Christian claims about salvation (pp. 310–313)?

Jesus is ours

8 What is the significance of the Christian's claim that 'Jesus is *my* Lord and Saviour' (pp. 313–315)?

9 Is there, then, *no* truth in religions other than Christianity (pp. 317–318)?

10 Can those who belong to other religions, and who may never even have heard of Jesus, be saved (pp. 318–320)? How do you know?

To deny the uniqueness of Christ is to cut the nerve of mission and make it superfluous. To affirm his uniqueness, on the other hand, is to acknowledge the urgency of making him universally known (p. 320).

CHAPTER NINETEEN

Our God is a missionary God

1 What three main objections to Christian mission does John Stott identify (pp. 321–324)? How do you respond to them?

2 'Christianity without mission is Christianity no longer' (p. 324). Why?

The God of the Old Testament is a missionary God

3 Why is Genesis 12:1–4 'the most unifying text of the whole Bible' (p. 326)?

4 'The tragedy of the Old Testament is that Israel kept forgetting the universal scope of God's promises' (p. 327). To what extent is this your tragedy too?

The Christ of the Gospels is a missionary Christ

5 What evidence is there for the 'global horizon' of Jesus' missionary concern (pp. 328–329)?

The Holy Spirit of the Acts is a missionary Spirit

6 What is the 'dominant, overriding and all-controlling motif' of the Acts (p. 331)?

7 'We must cease preaching the Great Commission as a command to be obeyed' (p. 331). Why?

The church of the Letters is a missionary church

8 What evidence is there that the first Christians were members of 'missionary' churches (pp. 332–333)?

The climax of the Revelation is a missionary climax

9 What perspectives on mission does Revelation add (p. 334)?

Mission cannot be regarded as a regrettable deviation from religious toleration, or as the hobby of a few eccentric enthusiasts. On the contrary, it arises from the heart of God himself, and is communicated from his heart to ours (p. 335).

10 In the light of this chapter, what action do you need to take?

CHAPTER TWENTY

Holistic mission

1 What is the expression 'holistic mission' intended to convey (p. 337)?

2 Which do you see as more important: the salvation of a soul or the improvement of society (p. 337)? Why?

The relationship between evangelism and social responsibility

3 What do you see as the relationship between evangelism and social responsibility (pp. 339–341)? How can the church respond to the need to hold these two things together?

4 Why are some people uncomfortable with the statement that '"Mission" describes . . . everything the church is sent into the world to do' (p. 341)? How may their objections be answered?

The biblical basis for this partnership

5 Is there 'good biblical warrant for holding evangelism and social action together' (p. 343)? What three aspects does John Stott deal with?

[Jesus] was concerned not only with saving man from hell in the next world, but with delivering him from the hellishness of this one (Charles Colson, quoted on p. 345).

6 How do the parables of the prodigal son and the good Samaritan help us to sort out the relationship between evangelism and social action (pp. 346–347)?

Five objections considered

7 How would you answer someone who said that 'Christians should steer clear of politics' (pp. 349–350)?

8 How would you respond to the view that 'it is impossible to expect social change unless people are converted' (p. 351)?

9 How can we guard against the danger that 'social action will distract us from evangelism' (p. 352)?

Some examples of the partnership

10 What examples could you add to those given by John Stott (pp. 352–355)?

CHAPTER TWENTY-ONE

The Christology of mission

1 'Nothing is more important for the recovery of the church's mission (where it has been lost), or its development (where it is weak), than . . .' what (p. 356)? Why?

The incarnation of Christ (The model for mission)

2 What does the incarnation tell us about mission (pp. 357–360)? How does this principle apply to you?

STUDY GUIDE

The cross of Christ (The cost of mission)

3 Why is suffering an 'indispensable' aspect of biblical mission (pp. 360–364)? What 'form of cross' does mission lead you to?

4 Why is mission so opposed (p. 364)?

The resurrection of Christ (The mandate for mission)

5 'It is of the greatest importance to remember that the resurrection preceded the Great Commission' (p. 364). Why?

The exaltation of Christ (The incentive for mission)

6 How does the exaltation of Christ provide 'the strongest of all missionary incentives' (p. 366)? Does it do so for you?

I could not endure existence if Jesus were not glorified; it would be hell to me if he were to be always thus dishonoured (Henry Martyn, quoted on p. 367).

The Spirit-gift of Christ (The power for mission)

7 Why is evangelism 'impossible without the Holy Spirit' (p. 370)?

8 What otherwise good gifts of God tend to diminish your reliance on the Holy Spirit (p. 371)?

The parousia of Christ (The urgency of mission)

9 How is the return of Jesus linked with the mission of the church (pp. 371–373)?

CONCLUSION

The now and the not yet

1 'A balanced grasp of the now–not yet tension would be very conducive to Christian unity' (p. 376). How?

Kingdom come and coming

2 Describe 'consistent eschatology', 'realized eschatology' and 'inaugurated eschatology' (pp. 378–379).

3 What evidence is there that Jesus regarded the kingdom of God as both a present phenomenon and a future expectation (pp. 379–380)? What happens when either of these views is held to the exclusion of the other?

Revelation, holiness and healing

4 In what way is revelation an area where we see the 'now–not yet' tension (pp. 383–385)?

5 How does the 'now–not yet' tension help us to approach issues where Christians disagree (pp. 384–385)?

6 Why does 'the sinless perfection we long for' continue to elude us (p. 386)? What should be our attitude to holiness?

7 How would you answer someone who suggested either (a) that 'we should never expect to see miracles of healing today' or (b) that 'miraculous healing should be our normal experience' (pp. 387–388)?

Church and society

8 'Whenever we think about the church, we have to hold together the ideal and the reality' (p. 389). What ideal and what reality? Do you hold the two together?

STUDY GUIDE

9 How can the 'now–not yet' tension help us to work out a biblical attitude to society (pp. 389–390)?

10 In this area of the 'now' and the 'not yet' John Stott suggests that Christians fall into one of three groups (pp. 390–392). Which one are you in, and how do you need to change?